New Children of Israel

New Children of Israel

Emerging Jewish Communities in an Era of Globalization

Nathan P. Devir

The University of Utah Press | Salt Lake City

The Defiance House Man colophon is a registered trademark of the
University of Utah Press. It is based on a four-foot-tall Ancient Puebloan
pictograph (late PIII) near Glen Canyon, Utah.

Library of Congress Cataloging-in-Publication Data

Names: Devir, Natan, author.
Title: New children of Israel : emerging Jewish communities in an era of
    globalization/Nathan P. Devir.
Description: Salt Lake City : The University of Utah Press, [2017] | Includes
    bibliographical references and index. |
Identifiers: LCCN 2017021790 (print) | LCCN 2017025736 (ebook) |
    ISBN 9781607815853 () | ISBN 9781607815846 (pbk.)
Subjects: LCSH: Jews—Identity. | Jews—Cultural assimilation—Ghana. | Jews—
    Cultural assimilation—Cameroon. | Jews—Cultural assimilation—India.
Classification: LCC DS143 (ebook) | LCC DS143 .D47 2017 (print) |
    DDC 305.6/96091724—dc23
LC record available at https://lccn.loc.gov/2017021790

Portions of chapter 3, "Online Spiritual Volition: The 'Internet Jews' of Cameroon,"
were printed in *The Shadow of Moses: New Jewish Movements in Africa*, edited by
Daniel Lis, William F. S. Miles, and Tudor Parfitt (Los Angeles: African Academic
Press/Marymount Institute Press/Tsehai Publishers, 2016), 113–30.

All photographs by author unless otherwise noted.

Printed and bound in the United States of America.

CONTENTS

ILLUSTRATIONS

ACKNOWLEDGMENTS

And furthermore, my son, be admonished: of making many books
there is no end; and much study is a weariness of the flesh.

—Ecclesiastes 12:12

ACKNOWLEDGMENTS ARE A tricky genre. They almost always suggest a clear value hierarchy of those to whom one is indebted. To circumvent such a potentially misleading categorization, I have listed below, in alphabetical order, the organizations and individuals whose assistance has been instrumental in the completion of this book. I humbly ask for forgiveness from any person or entity whose name I may have forgotten to mention here.

This book was written in sixteen different countries over a period of five years. As one might imagine, the expenditures accrued in conducting the research were significant. I therefore gratefully acknowledge the financial support of the Council of American Overseas Research Centers, the Earhart Foundation, the Lucius N. Littauer Foundation, the Maurice Amado Program in Sephardic Studies at the University of California–Los Angeles, the National Endowment for the Humanities, the Posen Foundation, the Simon-Dubnow-Institut für jüdische Geschichte und Kultur at the University of Leipzig, and several different administrative bodies at my home institution, the University of Utah, including the College of Humanities Career Development Committee, the Council of Dee Fellows, the Tanner Humanities Center, and the University Research Committee.

Organizations whose members and staff assisted me in innumerable practical and intellectual ways include those at the American Institute of Indian Studies, Be'chol Lashon, the Ben Zvi Institute, the David Sassoon Library, the Israel Folktale Archives at the University of Haifa, Kulanu, the National Archives of Ghana, the National Library of Israel, Osmania University, the West African Research Association, and the Younes and Soraya Nazarian Library at the University of Haifa.

Individuals whose encouragement and feedback have helped to shape, enrich, and challenge the ideas presented in this book include: Viany Alain Abia, David Ahenkorah, John Alley, Raherimasoandro Andriamamonjy, Ashrey Dayves Andrianarisoa, Alex Armah, Jocelyn Bailey, Thomas Beebee, Ziad Bentahar, Harriet Bograd, Marla Brettschneider, Vincent Cheng, Suhi Choi, Benjamin Cohen, Caroline Eckhardt, Yulia Egorova, Serge Etele, Caren Frost, Sharon Galsulkar, Katharina Gerstenberger, Erin Greb, Jane Hacking, Baruch Halpern, Mampionona Hugues, Kathryn Hume, Ralphy Jhirad, Nathan Katz, Yehudah Kimani, Admiel Kosman, Ramesh Kumar, Dierk Lange, Afotey Laryea, Nii Tackie Adama Latse II, Janice Levi, Daniel Lis, Tessie Lombe Lusale, Colleen McDannell, Nii Abekar Mensah, Nuumo Adwaa Mensah III, William F. S. Miles, Frédérick Ndawo, Ranen Omer-Sherman, Tudor Parfitt, Shahid Perwez, Ndriana Rabarioelina, Lucien Razanadrakoto, Fernando Rubio, Muriel Schmid, Julie Schoelles, Maeera Shreiber, Jeff Spiegel, Bonita Sussman, Vera Tembo-Chiluba, Peter Terry, Diane Tobin, Colby Townsend, Daniel Walden (z"l), Dan Yacobi, Shmuel Yacobi, Yacob Yacobi, Yehoshua Yacobi, Abraham Yago, and Cornet Alexandre Zokou. I also wish to acknowledge the time and insight of many friends and contacts who, for various reasons, must remain unnamed. You know who you are.

One individual, Deberniere Torrey, has undoubtedly done more than any other to help bring this manuscript to completion. She therefore merits a special place at the top of a hierarchy that I have otherwise explicitly strived to steer clear of. My favorite colleague as well as my wife, she has been my most kind and unwavering supporter, not to mention a formidable intellectual interlocutor. An adventurer herself, she never doubted the inherent value of the project, even when dicey conditions and innumerable complications would have surely made others throw up their hands in dismay.

Finally, I would like to extend an expression of heartfelt thanks to all of the people who advised me against taking on such a potentially unwieldy scholarly venture. From the very beginning of the project, part of my motivation to persevere lay in the desire to put the naysayers in their place. To them, and to everyone else whose advice I have ever ignored, do I gratefully dedicate this book.

IN NOVEMBER 2012, I spent a month in Ghana studying a rural community of ethnic Sefwi who consider themselves descendants of the ancient Hebrews. The fieldwork on this subgroup of the indigenous Akan people was part of a larger scholarly project, some of which is included in this book, on so-called "neo-Jewish," "Judaizing," or "self-defining" Jewish communities from the developing world.[1] Whether through an identification with a Hebraic or Israelite ancestry, or simply out of a newfound spiritual volition to follow Mosaic Law, these emerging groups with heretofore unknown or hotly disputed ties to established Jewish communities elsewhere are increasingly seeking to become part of what is called in Hebrew *klal yisrael*: the worldwide Jewish community. Part of my research in Ghana involved interviewing non-Jews about their perceptions of the self-defining Sefwi Jews, who had embraced a religion with essentially no known history in this Sub-Saharan West African country.

"Edward" (not his real name) was one of my non-Jewish interviewees.[2] Edward had invited me to his home, where the interview was to take place. After some casual conversation in the main greeting room, he excused himself and asked me to wait while he retrieved from the bedroom "something to show me." I expected Edward to come back with news clippings, a book, or some other relevant piece of information about his supposedly Jewish neighbors. Instead, he returned with a shotgun in one hand, a box of ammunition in the other. Strangely, I did not feel the least bit nervous, despite the fact that we had met only briefly, a number of days earlier. Something in his demeanor put me at ease. Then again, perhaps part of my calm was due to the effects of the ginseng hooch we had been drinking. It was a specialty in this backwater province.

"Please show me how to use this," Edward said, pointing to the shotgun. "I saw something similar in an American action movie, and then went to have a rip-off copy made at the local gun shop." He smiled sheepishly. I hesitated, remembering that I would be traveling to Accra, Ghana's capital, via the regional airport in Kumasi the next day. I doubted that the security team at the tiny airstrip had the necessary equipment to detect any gunpowder residue on my fingers, but the prospect of spending the rest of my first university research leave in a West African bush prison made me think twice.

"You must know how to use one, right?" Edward asked, sensing my indecision. "Don't all Americans hunt?" Recalling a dialogue from an episode of the short-lived Jackie Mason sitcom *Chicken Soup*, I thought of telling him that I usually "bought mine at the store," but didn't have the heart. Instead, I nodded, grateful that a wild childhood in Montana and my stint as an officer in the Israel Defense Forces had apparently been good for something. "I can show you how to use this," I said, "but I'd rather not actually fire the gun. You never know if they'll be able to detect the residue on my hands at the airport tomorrow."

"You are very cautious!" Edward said. "Okay, no problem. But please, show me how it works." He listened carefully to my instructions about how to safely load and fire the weapon. I expected that, when he was ready to shoot, we would exit the house and proceed, in the same cautious manner, to an area near the perimeter of the forest outside of his home. Instead, Edward led me into the kitchen, where he loaded the shotgun, took aim through the open window at a palm tree about twenty feet away, and fired. A large branch of the tree crashed to the ground.

Edward's children and an elderly uncle ran into the kitchen to see what was going on. "That's great!" he exclaimed, slapping me on the shoulder. "Thank you so much!" The children held their hands over their ears and asked Edward in Sefwi, the local language, what the *obruni* (white guy) was doing in their house. Edward shooed them away and invited his uncle to squeeze off a few rounds. Before long, the poor tree had gotten a permanent face-lift from the buckshot of my new friend's weapon.

I had met Edward one Saturday morning as I attempted to find my way to the synagogue in New Adiembra, a small village located near the town of Sefwi Wiawso, the birthplace of the Ghanaian Jewish community. Edward noticed me walking in circles around the area of his mother's compound, and asked if I might help him unload some crates from a parked vehicle. We spoke about my research, and he was intrigued. He agreed to drive me to my destination. When he dropped me off at the synagogue—an unfinished concrete structure painted blue and white, the colors of the Israeli flag, with tin panels for a roof—we exchanged cell-phone numbers and agreed to meet at a later occasion. Before we parted ways, he asked: "By the way, how do you say, 'I like you' in Jew?" I gave him the correct Hebrew usage. He repeated it back to me and we parted with a handshake.

The members of the Ghanaian Jewish community, whom Edward knew well, had begun practicing a kind of impromptu Old Testamentism in the late 1970s.[3] The founders of the community, all members of a nascent Bible study group, noticed some curious parallels between pre-colonial Sefwi practices and those of the ancient Hebrews. The recognition of such cultural parallels had previously escaped them, due in part to the tendency of mission schools and local churches to focus on teachings from the New Testament. Both groups had in common rites such as circumcision, menstrual seclusion, Saturday Sabbath observance, taboos related to food and burial practices, a spring yam festival reminiscent of the biblical Passover, and a kind of monotheism. Some members of the study group, galvanized by these connections, insisted that the Sefwi must be descended from one of the Ten Lost Tribes, which were scattered from the Northern Kingdom of Israel in the eighth century BCE after the invasion of the Assyrian Empire. Others maintained that they had journeyed through Africa from the Holy Land at a much later stage. Conflicting information from oral heritage narratives could be used to corroborate both suppositions, so they acknowledged that it would be impossible to establish the exact point of origin and method of arrival in Ghana. There was one thing, however, that they all agreed on: they were of Hebrew stock. They decided to call their movement the "House of Israel."

Curious to see if there were any other lost Hebrews in the world, they sent a delegation to make an official inquiry at the Ministry of the Interior in Accra. Unsure of what to do, officials from the ministry sent them to the Israeli embassy in Abidjan, the commercial capital of the Ivory Coast, which borders Ghana to the west. The letter the group wrote there to their long-lost brethren, which detailed their location and the desire to make contact, was entrusted to the baffled Israeli staff. Somehow, the letter made its way to a synagogue in Des Moines, Iowa. And thus began the extraordinary journey of a community of pastoralists and cocoa farmers toward modern-day Jewish observance.

According to the Sefwi Jews, all ethnic Sefwi are Hebrew by origin. Some of them just don't know it yet. Even Edward, who practiced animist ancestor worship and spoke affectionately of his favorite fetish priest, was full of praise for the practicing Jews in New Adiembra. "They are helping to restore what the colonialists stole from us," he told me during our conversation. "The British raped, pillaged, and destroyed our native culture. I am not part of these Jews' religious community, and I will continue my own religion in my own way. But I believe in what they are doing."

For Edward, the great heroes of the Jewish tradition—Moses, Joshua, David, Samson, and Judah Maccabee—had proven to the world that resistance to the forces of oppression was laudable. Echoing the sentiments expressed by many formerly colonized peoples whose encounters with Christianity may have been advantageous in the realms of health and literacy, but devastating in the loss of many central aspects of their indigenous cultures, Edward insisted that "turning the other cheek" entailed the inevitable loss of "pride, autonomy, and self-respect."

Such statements of support for those returning to their ancient roots are not confined to this Ghanaian Jewish community. In the developing world, particularly in areas where European missionaries helped to foster awareness of certain biblical characters, practices, and narratives, or where popular nineteenth-century ideas about "historic races" took hold among colonial administrators, many such self-defining Jewish groups are emerging with surprising frequency. They exist in, among other places, Brazil, Cameroon, Equatorial Guinea, Ethiopia, Gabon, Ghana, India, Ivory Coast, Kenya, Madagascar, Malawi, Mozambique, Myanmar (Burma), Nigeria, Peru, Rwanda, South Africa, Uganda, Zambia, and Zimbabwe. While it is difficult to say exactly how many individuals belong to such groups, the numbers are likely in the millions.[4]

Most are formerly Christianized peoples who have come to Judaism through religious communities whose focus is primarily on the Old Testament, such as those from Sabbatarian, Seventh-day Adventist, Messianic, or Prophetic movements.

Interestingly, most people from these groups have little knowledge of, or regard for, notions of secular Jewishness. I initially found this disparity quite striking, since the Jewish relationship with modernity in the West has been inextricably linked with secularism. Indeed, from the period of the *Haskalah*, or the movement toward "Jewish Enlightenment" that began around the end of the eighteenth century, much of the discourse surrounding Jewishness has involved notions of emancipation and assimilation, as well as the shift from legalistic religiosity to a relatively murky form of secularized identity politics. Among emerging Jewish communities, however, professing one's Jewishness by way of ethnocultural affiliation, à la Woody Allen, without adhering to formal Jewish religious praxis, is almost unheard of. In retrospect, this now seems logical. For the most part, traditional cultures still value propriety and piety, and regard religious observance as somewhat of a logical sequitur for an existence in which, according to John S. Mbiti, there is "no formal distinction between the sacred and the secular, between the religious and the non-religious, [or] between the spiritual and material areas of life."[5] In Charles Liebman's view, such a worldview "consumes the life of the individual" because it "imposes attitudes and behaviors" that distinguish it from secular lifestyle options in the West. These secular options, Liebman posits, are part and parcel of "the culture of personalism and voluntarism" that pervades most facets of secular Western society.[6]

In this digital era of globalized interconnectedness, emerging Jewish communities from developing nations are redefining what it means to be Jewish vis-à-vis their coreligionists elsewhere in the world. The relationship may not be entirely reciprocal, but it has a firm basis in shared ideas. And ideas are like a contagion: one can never know who will get the bug. Seeing cellular modems used to access proper Sabbath liturgy from a mud hut in the savanna has convinced me of this. The prophecy of Isaiah 11:12, according to which God will "assemble the dispersed of Israel, and gather together the scattered of Judah from the four corners of the earth," is a prediction taken seriously by many more people than some of us in the West might ever imagine.

In the modern period, world Jewry has experienced transformations on the cultural, geopolitical, and demographic levels. Jewish emancipation and national aspirations have reached their zenith; and yet, the Jewish people has also come close to total annihilation. Two of the twentieth century's most tumultuous, watershed events for the Jews—the Holocaust and the birth of the modern-day state of Israel—brought about changes that were far-reaching for Jewish communities all over the globe. An unprecedented wave of self-defining Jews from the developing world, who will complicate, enrich, reenvision, and stretch the traditional parameters of God's covenant with Israel, will be modern Jewry's next watershed event. The changes in the character of Jewishness brought about by the influence of these "new Children of Israel," as they have often been referred to, will happen with or without the acknowledgment or support of officially recognized Jews from the outside world. Indeed, we should make no mistake: these changes are already taking place.

New Children of Israel

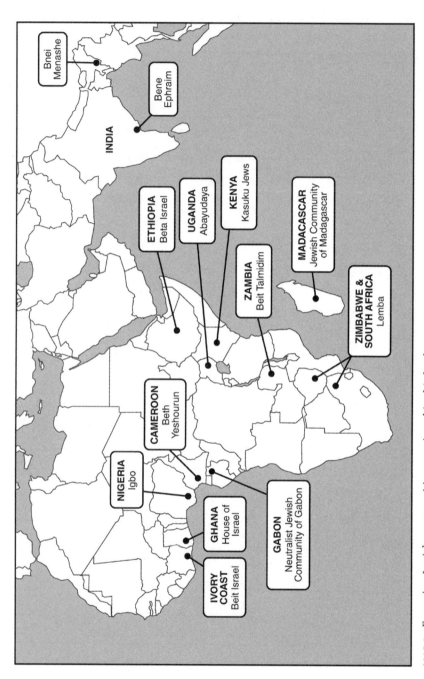

MAP 1. Emerging Jewish communities mentioned in this book

Introduction **1**

This book presents and analyzes field-based case studies of three different Judaizing movements from the developing world. These contextually driven, in-depth analyses are based on extensive fieldwork and sociohistorical research on the genesis of those movements. Two are located in former British colonies; one is in a former French colony. They are the House of Israel of Ghana (chapter 2); the *Beth Yeshourun* (House of the Righteous) of Cameroon (chapter 3); and the *Bene Ephraim* (Children of Ephraim) of India (chapter 4). Necessary background information and explanations of other relevant components of the study—methodological, theoretical, epistemological, and conceptual—are given throughout this introductory chapter. The conclusion (chapter 5) offers a recapitulation of the typologies and themes explored in each case study, as well as relevant information about several new groups not covered in the preceding chapters.

Among the questions that this study attempts to address are the following: What is the symbolic or ideological impetus behind each organized Judaizing movement? What, if anything, do their oral histories and heritage narratives have in common? How does each community define "Jewishness" for the purposes of its own identity, as well as vis-à-vis its overseas coreligionists? What are the possible points of contention between the former and the latter? To what extent does exposure to Christianity or Islam influence the development of such communities? What are the differences between indigenous Christian movements that simply favor the Old Testament over the New, and movements whose adherents categorically reject Christianity, choosing instead to adopt an exclusively Jewish identity? Do claims of shared genealogical heritage help communities to secure new adherents by referencing Judaism as a kind of privileged hereditary signifier, or might the attraction to belong be explained by relating to Judaism as a faith like any other? How does the draw of Judaism as a pre- or anticolonial phenomenon grow or ebb in different political contexts? What role does the discursive matrix of globalized media and culture play in the acquisition of Jewish knowledge by these groups? And, finally, what are the political implications of millions of self-defining Jews for the future of the state of Israel, which offers immediate naturalization and a generous benefits package to Jewish immigrants from developing countries?[1]

Preliminary answers given in this book to some of these questions have been greatly informed by previously published scholarship in this domain, as have other working hypotheses on related topics; I acknowledge those specific sources wherever applicable. Varying forms of evidence, exposure, and experience particular to my own engagement with this subject have led me to grapple with the aforementioned questions in ways that differ from approaches taken by colleagues who have written before me. For instance, while much of the book's thematic content and objects of inquiry bear similarities with, and owe a great deal to, the work of those scholars mentioned in the acknowledgments, almost none of the factual information on the Ghanaian or Cameroonian communities has been previously analyzed in any academic publication.[2] Similarly, many details made available on these communities in popular fora have been, for the first time here, scrutinized and subjected to rigorous scholarly examination in relation to existing oral narratives and/or the written historical record. The chapter on the Indian community presents several exciting new perspectives on and developments in a movement previously studied in depth by Yulia Egorova and Shahid Perwez, and focuses on highlighting key discursive aspects of that movement that were outside the purview of those authors' illuminating publications.[3] It also provides a control group outside of the African context, the situational criteria of which may be assumed to include causal factors for the formations of Jewishness evidenced in the two previous examples.

On the subject of similarly themed studies, one particular intellectual debt that I should acknowledge at the outset is to the groundbreaking theoretical work done on the psychological interplay between the colonizer and the colonized, first disseminated widely by the Afro-Caribbean psychiatrist Frantz Fanon.[4] As the earliest scholar to convincingly demonstrate the ways in which subjugated peoples have a propensity to undermine their own cultural continuity by linking their evolution with the narrative histories of their conquerors, Fanon set the stage for other scholars to psychologize that trauma through a hermeneutics of the colonial legacy. Some of those scholars whose work has been particularly influential for me include Aijaz Ahmad, Homi Bhabha, Albert Memmi, Ella Shohat, and Gayatri Spivak.[5] This book draws on their work in its appraisals of the raisons d'être of the Judaizing movements profiled herein, inasmuch as many of these movements see Judaism as a redemptive antidote to the evils of colonialism. In that sense, Jewishness as a phenomenological trope is not necessarily confined to peoples historically associated with the chronological development of the Judeo-Christian tradition. To phrase it in a somewhat more vulgar fashion, this may explain why the popular Jewish version of the commiserative "Shit happens" adage—"Why does shit always happen to us?"—should be intrinsically appealing to certain populations that have no documented historical relations with other Jewish groups.

In a related vein, this book relies heavily on the pioneering scholarship on Judaizing movements undertaken by Tudor Parfitt, the world's foremost scholar on that topic. The work done by Parfitt on the reasons for which Jewish identities were "constructed almost everywhere in the colonial situation and were subsequently internalized by a surprising variety of peoples" was not only what initially inspired me to pursue this line of research; it was also key to laying the groundwork for my own specific contributions.[6] In that regard, Parfitt's supposition according to which colonized groups tend to adopt for themselves exclusive Jewish lineages in order to "turn the Bible back on their colonial masters" has been particularly insightful.[7] Similarly, Edith Bruder's estimation that Judaism has "a rooted historicity that people with little or no recorded history may find compelling" has proven to be very true in my dealings

with the communities discussed here, as have many of her other observations on related themes.[8]

The reader will notice that nowhere above is there any professed
intent to investigate or establish whether or not these communities are
"really" Jewish. Following the commendable positions taken by Parfitt
and Bruder in their scholarly work on emerging Jewish communities,
I have refrained from trying to "prove" which of the groups discussed
in this study are "authentically" Jewish. Put differently, the approach is
epistemic rather than empirical, as verisimilitude is not a concern of
this research. Even if such a categorical judgment regarding Jewishness
were possible—taking into account, of course, the varying components
of the conceptual frameworks through which Jewishness is constructed,
not to mention the conflicting religious, national, socioethnic, or genetic
perspectives on the matter—it is not my place to do so. On that point,
Parfitt's comment that "what a group thinks about itself is at least as
important as what outsiders think about it" has been my guiding logic
all throughout this study.[9] Such an approach also mirrors the stance
taken by, among other scholarly associations, the Pew Research Center
in its forum on Religion and Public Life. For instance, its 2011 report on
Global Christianity stipulates that the descriptions of that religious phenomenon are "sociological rather than theological" and include views
that "may be viewed as unorthodox or heretical" by some coreligionists.[10]

In other words, I am not concerned with evidence-based data that
might corroborate claims of either Hebraic or Israelite ancestry. Nor do I
wish to engage in what Valentin Y. Mudimbe calls "epistemological eth-
nocentricism" by attempting to classify people according to externally
imposed notions of categorization.[11] Granted, familiarity with the long-
standing debate about how to best authenticate Jewishness is important
for any discussion in which claims of belonging are under scrutiny.
To that end, an overview of the debate is given later on in this chapter.
But this is for familiarity's sake only.

What I have been interested in investigating are the practical and
symbolic ways in which these communities construct their ideas about
what Jewishness means to them. In the same spirit of the protocol used
by John L. Jackson in his innovative work on autoethnography, I focus on,
in his terms, "some of the ways in which common assumptions about

Jewishness get reimagined" in a number of specific contexts.[12] I set out
to understand how people perceive and articulate their own notions of
what it means to be Jewish, how these perceptions and articulations are
informed by particular social and historical circumstances, and what
kinds of intercultural exchanges result from these encounters. Therefore, the principal phenomena of inquiry are the self-conscious articulations, performances, and drives to substantiate claims of Jewishness
as they are understood by their claimants—as well as the metalevels
of such discourses—but not the claims themselves. Historical and/or
analogical postulations, limited necessarily to periods relevant to the
subject at hand, are given simply in order to contextualize the assertions
of the populations under study. The reader is encouraged to consult
more wide-ranging historical surveys for further information, some of
which I have included in the notes at the ends of some chapters.

The significance of this project lies in its examination of the
heretofore-neglected links between cultural variables and attitudes
toward Jewishness, especially within the framework of current scholarship accorded to the pressing question of what precisely constitutes
the definition of "Jewish." In that sense, the theoretical assumptions
of this work rest on the recognized ethnographic deduction according
to which the generalizing banner of "the Jewish people," as Caryn Aviv
and David Shneer astutely point out, "does not describe how Jewish
identities and communities operate."[13] According to Aviv and Shneer,
such broad terminology is "often mobilized to create a semblance of
collective solidarity in response to historical persecution or in order to
make Jews feel responsible for people with whom they may have very
little in common."[14]

As case studies, the narratives of each community profiled here
demonstrate how subcultural particularities among divergent Jewish
groups illustrate the ways in which the interpretation of Jewish meta-
narratives is codetermined. Namely, this codetermination takes place via
the conceptual and geopolitical frameworks through which Jews from
differing backgrounds reference or reenvision religious themes or ideas
about proper praxis from Judaism's discursive reservoir and textual tradition. My working hypothesis in this project is that the ways in which
these groups relate to Jewish issues and ideologies are highly dependent

on contextual factors, including (but not exclusively limited to) proximity to missionary activity; familiarity with notions of Hebraic or Israelite ancestry based on legends regarding the Ten Lost Tribes; similar precolonial customs and life-cycle events; relations with philo-Judaic religious movements; and the incorporation of local lore into standard biblical stories that have, until now, only been described in generalities.

As a scholar of Jewish cultures interested in the intersections of narrative, praxis, and ethnicity, I am naturally concerned with subcultural constructions of Jewish identity inasmuch as they challenge other subcultural constructions. And, since a time-honored way of understanding a cultural phenomenon is to examine its margins, the fruits of this research on little-known communities that self-identify as Jewish are certain to be regarded as viable contributions to existing Jewish Studies scholarship, both in academia and for educators in the private sector. In particular, this research, which documents a myriad of largely unexplored experiences and traditions, complements and is in dialogue with recent work done on emerging Jewish communities and divergent Jewish identities. Comparing and contrasting these notions surrounding Jewishness also contributes to the growing body of knowledge on the subject of internal Jewish diversity. Finally, it adds to the corpus of scholarship on globalized religious movements outside of the Jewish realm, which, in Paul Hopper's words, are part of an era "marked not only by the greater intensity and extensity of cultural flows, but also by the greater velocity with which they travel from place to place."[15]

NOTES ON THE METHODOLOGY

For better or worse, I am a practitioner of the interdisciplinary. And just as this book is the product of research conducted in many different national, ethnocultural, and religious settings, the methods employed in gathering and processing information related to the research themes integrate manifold approaches, both practically and conceptually. These approaches include sociohistorical criticism, discourse analysis, and especially, quotidian ethnography. I offer below a brief explanation of the ways in which each method has been used to examine the relevant data.

Except in the case of Cameroon, where very little exists in the way of genealogical claims to Jewish heritage, every Judaizing community profiled in this book is part of a larger cultural template of supposed ethnic or national links to a distinctly Jewish legacy. Showcasing the dominant discourse surrounding such links, while providing a survey and analysis of each area's sociohistorical record, provides the reader with knowledge about the situational contexts and zones of contact from which these Judaizing groups arise. Trying to make sense of the phenomena in this way by no means negates or minimizes the relevance of others' concurrent efforts to understand them by using dissimilar means.

Sources that elucidate such circumstances include travel narratives, popular journalism, indigenous oral histories, pre- and postindependence archival materials, missionary testimonies, and of course, scholarly literature in public and private library collections. This approach to source criticism, contextualist and exploratory in nature, ensures that the local environment is properly examined when discussing these new ethnoreligious movements.[16] As Robert W. Wyllie advises, this approach can also provide a means by which to probe "the strains, tensions, or incongruities which result from the meeting of cultures or their representatives."[17]

Discourse analysis, which involves the study of communicative-based practices of interaction, concerns itself with the content of messages transmitted by semantic or semiotic means. It looks at elements of discursive patterns such as code, register, trope, symbolism, and rhetoric, overt or covert, conscious or unconscious, which are employed during cultural interaction. These may appear in everyday conversation, or in communication using web-based materials (blogs, social media, videos, etc.), which are increasingly becoming as common as, or more frequent than, face-to-face communicative interaction. They may also take the form of structured ceremonies or correspondence. Discourse analysis of the interactions between members of Judaizing communities, or of the interactions between those community members and other outside individuals (Jewish or not), helps to establish the common denominator of the larger metalevels of discourse that reverberate on topics relevant to this discussion. In many cases, the questions asked during these interactions are more significant than the answers given.

As noted, quotidian ethnography has been the predominant method of data collection for this study, since the aims are largely synchronic rather than diachronic.[18] Although my formal academic training did not include coursework in the discipline of ethnography, I do possess certification in ethnographic research methods.[19] Similarly, I am sufficiently familiar with the standard scholarly approaches to writing about interactions with human subjects that doing so in this project has not posed much of a challenge. Among such approaches, I should note that I have been particularly impressed with, and influenced by, the captivating case studies of ethnographic fieldwork published in the University of Pennsylvania Press series on the Ethnography of Political Violence.[20]

The ethnographic research techniques used to gather data for this book include the customary methods that one might expect to find in studies of cultural anthropology. Participant observation, unobtrusive direct observation, overt observation, informal interaction, theme-based and free-flowing discussions with individuals and groups, naturalistic observation of public behavior, and structured, semi-structured, or unstructured interviewing, both impromptu and planned, are included here. In principle, I have relied more on a qualitative approach based on observation and reflection than on the so-called "hard" approaches to data collection as are often found in the social sciences.

In that regard, my impression has been that allowing the interviewee(s) to dictate the flow and, to some extent, the content of the conversations, rather than requesting their adherence to a set script, allows for more open interaction and trust between the parties involved. Participants' remarks in these conversations have either been recorded, transcribed simultaneously, or written down to the best of my memory afterwards in the form of field notes. All information showcased has been gathered from natural settings, save for interaction via telephone, e-mail, or Skype. Observations of religious rituals are included in the field notes but have not been highlighted as a dominant motif due to the relative ease of communities in accessing "proper" ritual procedure online and then carbon-copying it in their own settings. There have been no controlled experiments.

The participant populations under study consist of those individuals involved with the specific self-defining Jewish communities in Ghana,

Cameroon, and India. Other interested parties (neighbors, friends, family members, passersby, etc.) who expressed a desire to converse about these communities have also been included. Expatriate communities in these countries made up of Jews from Western nations or from Israel, or Jewish settlers of non-African origin, do not form part of the participant populations. Languages of communication have included French, English, and sometimes Hebrew, all of which I speak fluently. While I acknowledge that communicating with people in a language other than their mother tongue can be a symbolically charged act—especially if those languages were imposed upon them by a colonial regime—there was, unfortunately, no feasible alternative. In several instances, when informants did not speak any of the above-stated languages, I enlisted the assistance of a local translator. In transcriptions of these verbal interactions, I give only the English translation. For written or e-mail correspondence, I include the original language of the citation, followed by a translation. Occasionally I have paraphrased certain communications due to considerations of space.

Pursuant to the procedures outlined by the University of Utah's Institutional Review Board, each person quoted in this book supplied the provision of oral consent before being interviewed. Even so, I have given many key informants pseudonyms or referred to them indirectly, in the unlikely event that the opinions expressed here may be damaging to them. At times, I have altered details of a person's background or the place in which we met in order to ensure discretion. Confidentiality of the data has been maintained via study codes and elimination of identifiable facts. Access to these codes has been restricted solely to the author. Individuals who have high-profile community roles or who have been repeatedly identified in open-source materials in the public domain are acknowledged by name. No bibliographic citations are given for those whose interaction with me was verbal.[21] Precise dates are given for e-mail correspondence and interaction via Skype only if the sender has not requested anonymity. Comments originating from popular social media sites such as Facebook are not dated, in order to eliminate identifiable data.

What were the selection criteria for the study participants? None, save the provision that minors' opinions and responses were not within the scope of the project. On the whole, anyone who wished to discuss these Judaizing communities in any way was welcome to join in the conversation. Contact with the interviewees was usually initiated by me, whether by telephone, e-mail, or snail mail correspondence, and often with the aid of referrals from colleagues or mutual acquaintances. Sometimes I was approached by people who knew about my interest in Judaizing communities. Due to my limited time on the ground and the innumerable ways in which people join and break from religious movements, the study is necessarily selective rather than exhaustive. Nonetheless, this selective profile of ontological experience is, I think, sufficiently representative to provide a balanced overview of the phenomena in question and the relevant issues surrounding them.

In many cases, I have been able to locate potential informants by searching social media sites for specific keywords. As wild as it may sound, I found a number of communities heretofore unknown to outsiders by combining the word "Jews" with an unlikely selection of country names in the Google search engine. Lo and behold, there were indeed organized, self-defining Jewish communities where no one had yet thought to look! Profiles of several such communities found in this manner did not make it into this book but are the subjects of forthcoming publications. The selection of mostly African communities reflects the fact that the majority of Judaizing communities come from that continent.

I recognize that certain shortcomings inevitably arise from the aforementioned methods. To begin with, a well-known problem with qualitative study procedures is the inclusion of the researcher's bias. Although I have endeavored to present sober assessments, I do not claim to be an entirely impartial spectator. In fact, I happen to share the perspective of the celebrated anthropologist Ruth Landes, who dismisses the notion that such a thing as a "neutral" observer even exists.[22] I also concur with Bruce Lincoln's similar assessment, according to which discourses of scholarship are, to a certain extent, always "conditioned by the interests of their authors."[23]

A correlated issue on which I see eye to eye with Marla Brettschneider has to do with the interactions between American Jewish researchers and self-declared Jews from emerging communities. In Brettschneider's view, these interactions may inadvertently put "into play a power differential not dissimilar from other race and gender dynamics."[24] I have taken to heart her advice to remain cognizant of the fact that publications resulting from such encounters have "direct policy implications" for the communities in question.[25] I have also kept in mind the concerns expressed by Diane Tobin, director of the Institute for Jewish and Community Research, who writes that "characterizations that either insult or trivialize" the genuineness of emerging Jews who "are legitimately fighting for recognition" are ethically problematic.[26]

On the topic of researcher bias, several additional clarifications are in order. The first has to do with the notion of alleged boosterism. People with whom I discuss my work often ask me: Are you a scholar, or an activist? The answer is, I am a scholar with a deep affection and concern for the people who have allowed me into their lives, their homes, and their worldviews. Indeed, it is difficult to describe the intense emotional effect of traveling ten thousand miles to a strange country and being greeted with embraces and cries of "Brother!" by people whom one has never previously laid eyes upon. I do not take such gestures lightly. Such meetings create deep bonds that, ostensibly, seem to violate materialistic assumptions about how the world works. As a result, many of the informants in this book have become close friends with whom I maintain regular contact, and for whom I wish all the best that life has to offer. In some cases, after completion of the research, I have been consulted as an informal, unpaid advisor on Jewish topics, and have been delighted to be an address for information resources for those contacts.

Conversely, a small number of the people featured in this book were downright hostile to me in their behavior, and I have preserved no further contact with them. One even threatened to slice and dice me with a machete in the same manner (according to him) in which Samuel disposed of Agag, king of the Amalekites (1 Sam. 15:33). Luckily, that scenario did not come to pass. Either way, I have not engaged in hyperbole or fabrication in order to make any persons look better than I found them to be in real life; and no single unpleasant encounter has been twisted so as to cast a negative light on the claims of any particular movement in general. Nothing genuine ever comes from exoticising or fetishizing, and the mere concept of "dirty laundry" leaves little room for critical apparatus. I do believe that one can maintain an analytical distance from the phenomenological lens of others without resorting to objectivism. That has been my goal.

A popular joke about two overzealously pro-Israel American Jewish tourists in Tel-Aviv helps to illustrate this point. One evening, the two young men are wandering around Israel's largest city, and happen to come upon a comedy club. They go inside. On stage is an Israeli comedian performing a stand-up routine in Hebrew. One of the American Jewish tourists begins to laugh uncontrollably. The other, puzzled, looks at him and exclaims, "I didn't realize that you understood Hebrew!" The first manages to say, between guffaws, "Oh, I don't." And then, calming himself, he adds, with the utmost seriousness: "But I trust the Israelis."

The second point of clarification regarding the boosterism charge involves the questions that I am always asked about the "authenticity" of these new communities. As noted, my concern is not to measure the extent of anyone's Jewishness, be it on the biological, spiritual, or historical levels. These are all nonsensical categories, in my opinion. My purpose has been to examine the ways in which the said communities articulate their own senses of what constitutes Jewishness—their typologies, taxonomies, and plain gut feelings about it—and what that means to them in their daily lives. Terminology that may suggest lines of demarcation between authentic and inauthentic, such as "neo-Jewish" or "Judaizing," as opposed to merely "Jewish," has been included only in order to establish for the reader a clear delineation between those groups whose Jewishness is conventionally accepted and those whose Jewishness is not. With these differences in terminology I imply no value judgment whatsoever.

I emphasize this point again in order to dispel any mistaken impression that, because I care about these people, I would embellish their Jewishness so that recognition of their communities might be more forthcoming. Such an impression would be inherently unsound, because my research concerns do not involve establishing validity. In fact, the most I can do is offer a picture that is contextualized and explanatory. Granted, some of the people under study may have exaggerated their claims because of the presence of a foreign Jewish researcher (me), but performativity and telephone-game miscommunications, conscious or unconscious, are present in every facet of life, not just in ethnographic research. Moreover, on the practical plane, there was no economic incentive for embellishment, since interviewees were not paid for their time, and I gave no guarantee that I would report "favorably" on their practices. If people asked me what I thought about their genealogical or spiritual claims, I told them. If they did not ask, I did not say. I sought neither to corroborate nor to refute. I listened.

I suspect that many involved in Jewish policymaking who read this book will be impressed at the level of each community's manifested dedication to Judaism. I also suspect that many may be aghast at what they see as the appropriation of Judaism by millions of opportunistic fortune-seekers. It is a safe bet that most of the former will come from the liberal streams of Judaism, and the latter, from the more conservative denominations. This is of course a gross generalization. Whether or not readers ultimately support these groups' eventual integration into the larger Jewish world is a matter that will most likely be determined by their own preconceived notions of what constitutes Jewishness in the first place. This study is unlikely to win any converts (pun intended), but I hope it will help to clarify the parameters of the debate, which is going on whether or not anyone—Jew or Gentile, from the "First" World or the "Third"—decides to read the book.

Other limitations of the methodology that should be explained revolve around conflicting cross-cultural notions of what precisely constitutes research. As has been pointed out by many a scholar before me, people in developing countries who are unfamiliar with academic methodologies often consider interviews on research topics to be akin to simple conversations—something like back-and-forth banter or a friendly exchange. This happens often despite repeated explanations given by the researcher about the investigative protocol, provisions of consent, or the intent to use elements of the conversation in future publications. I have done my best to minimize any miscommunications arising from differing ideas about the end-goals of our interaction.

With regard to the treatment of heritage narratives or oral history, there is no supposition on my part that such texts should be interpreted literally. Rather, the interest in presenting elements from these narratives is to provide a window into, in Jan Vanina's terms, "the subjectivity of the encoder of the message."[27] By the same token, I am in full accord with Robert W. Harms, who reminds us that such histories are "living documents" that change given the settings in which they are recounted. In Harms's view, they should be considered as "stories told by specific people in specific places under specific conditions."[28] For the purposes of this book, the messages taken from those stories have been analyzed more with the aim of elucidating the present than with amplifying the past.

An additional limitation of the interaction detailed here is tied to the value attributed to each contact's lived experience and individualized components of personhood. Obviously, there are always specific variations among people. Individuals remain conceptually organized in their own identities, even if those identities are often juxtaposed with those of the group. The intent in speaking about the perceptions of "communities" is neither to homogenize individuals nor to reduce any one person's cognitive or motivational biases to mere groupthink. Rather, it is to reveal the interpretive frameworks in which dispositional agency and situational factors intermingle, and from which many notions of Jewishness among neophytes might stem. The links between the individual and the collective are particularly poignant with respect to ethnographic and discourse analyses of new religious movements, since such approaches focus on what Robert Jay Lifton calls the "interface of individual and collective identities."[29] Concerns over social hierarchy, conflicting genres of information, expectations regarding freedom of expression, and memory distortion are duly noted in the analyses where such factors constitute apparent limitations to obtaining the full picture as a result of these human encounters.

With regard to such human encounters, I should note that my healthy sense of humor—something which, many might argue, is an emphatically Jewish trait—should not be mistaken in any way for mockery or disrespect of the people, ceremonies, or situations described in this book. If humor comes through, it is only because I am reacting in a way that betrays my own culturally specific attitudes and convictions, which I neither defend unconditionally nor uphold as sacrosanct. For example, when a person in Kothareddypalem, India, told me that he could obtain pictures for me of "women practicing menstrual seclusion" in order to substantiate his community's claim of properly upholding Jewish ritual practice, I had to laugh out loud; and I would expect any reader with a background similar to my own to do the same. When I was told by a prominent theologian in Cameroon who self-defined as a Jew that the damned souls in Hell, which he had seen in a vision, included "fornicators, adulterers, and homosexuals," and, for reasons I can only guess—a certain contemporary American pop star whose deviant sexual excesses are legendary—controlling my reaction was simply not possible. As I have seen with my students, these entertaining anecdotes often give way to fantastic teaching moments. I know that many of my newfound friends agree about this, because they have told me that they, too, have found many aspects of my behavior—about which, by the way, they have not hesitated to laugh with their friends and families—as curious and amusing as I do theirs. Humor is often but one component of a very serious story. And, as the saying goes, it's all in the family.

A final word about the participant composition is in order. The overwhelming majority of participants profiled in this study are men. I acknowledge that this lack of gender balance constitutes a major shortcoming in the project. For the most part, only generalities about women's roles (communicated mainly by men, or by a small number of women in the presence of men) have informed my understanding of gender-based differences in Jewish worldviews among the members of these groups. Local custom is partly responsible for this gap, as convention has almost always dictated that I not be alone with women to conduct interviews; and I did not want to insult or offend those in my host communities. As of this writing, I have secured the permission of the *Beit Israel* (House of Israel) Judaizing community in the Ivory Coast to interview women-only participant groups, and I hope that this forthcoming work on gender paradigms in one particular Judaizing community will present a useful case study for exploring notions of gender agency among other such communities.[30] For now, I concede that women are woefully absent from this study, but look forward to establishing a greater gender equilibrium in future publications.

FROM LOST TO FOUND?

The communities profiled in this book differ in several fundamental ways from mainstream Jewish groups whose Jewishness has not been put into question. All of the members of these groups self-identify as Jews, despite the fact that they have not, until quite recently, been branded as such by their neighbors. Prior to several decades ago, none of them had any documented contact with other Jewish communities around the world, nor the knowledge of Hebrew; the absence of these standard discursive connections therefore marks them as different from almost every other conventionally accepted Jewish community since the Destruction of the Second Temple in 70 CE. None have written community histories, save for recent compilations of supposed heritage narratives. Nor, for that matter, do they have any history of mass literacy, which has been part and parcel of Jewish existence since at least the rabbinic period. Perhaps most important, all except the Cameroonian group emphasize what I call the "genealogical trope" as the most important element in their claims to Jewishness. That is to say, they assert some kind of ancestral descent linked directly to the ancient Hebrews or Israelites, often through a specific progenitor, which is a rather precise hereditary assertion not usually highlighted as a defining factor in the identity formation of conventional Jewish communities. In most cases, the development of the genealogical trope occurs in tandem with historical associations tied to the legend of the Ten Lost Tribes of Israel. To provide context on this important factor, which is present in two out of the three heritage narratives presented in this book, a brief overview of the story is given below.

Aside from the enigma surrounding the eventual resting place of the lost Ark of the Covenant, perhaps no other biblical mystery has endured with such persistence as the uncertain fate of the Ten Lost Tribes. In the Judeo-Christian tradition, their eventual ingathering to the Land of Israel is a precursor to the arrival—or the return, depending on your theological disposition—of the Messiah. Consequently, many consider the attempt to locate the Lost Tribes as a potentially redemptive, rather than merely symbolic, act. In Zvi Ben-Dor Benite's estimation, part of the reason for which religious groups from an ecumenically diverse constituency have, since the twentieth century, combined and organized their efforts toward this goal in a heretofore unprecedented fashion stems from the perceived theological implications of the establishment of the state of Israel in 1948. In that vein, Ben-Dor Benite calls Israel "the first and sole institution in history vested with the political power" to identify, legitimize, and relocate communities believed to descend from lost Israelites.[31]

How did the Israelite tribes come to be lost? According to the account given in the Bible, the ten tribes that made up the Northern Kingdom of Israel—Reuben, Ephraim, Manasseh, Issachar, Gad, Asher, Simeon, Zebulun, Dan, and Naphtali—were exiled to Assyria after the invasion by that empire into Israel in 722 BCE. God allowed the tribes to be carried away to servitude in "Halah, and in Habor, on the river of Gozan, and in the cities of the Medes" (2 Kings 17:6) because of Israel's iniquities.[32] The Southern Kingdom of Judah, made up of the tribes of Judah and Benjamin, as well as members of the Levite priestly class and a small number of those from Simeon, maintained its loyalty to God's decrees and were thus spared the fate of their brethren to the north. Although the compilers of the Bible are silent about where the tribes eventually settled, the prophets insisted that they were alive and well and that their return would one day come to pass.[33]

As Parfitt has noted, the rabbis of the Talmud are conspicuously at odds about the destiny of the Lost Tribes, betraying what he labels their "purely theoretical" interest in the topic.[34] Rabbi Akivah, for example, was of the opinion that the tribes would never return, while Rabbi Eliezer insisted that one day "it would become light for them"—i.e., that they would return from darkness (*Sanhedrin* 110b). In this postexilic phase of Jewish existence, much attention was paid to a mythical river called the "Sambation," which, according to the story, stopped flowing on the Jewish Sabbath, and beyond which the Lost Tribes were said to dwell. Titus Flavius Josephus (37–c. 100 CE), the famed author of *The Jewish War*, mentions the river, as do Pliny the Elder and the compilers of the Targum Pseudo-Jonathan. In the medieval period, the celebrated mystic Abraham Abulafia (1240–1291) set out on what would be an ultimately unsuccessful mission to find the river, whose waters were rumored to be protected by an impenetrable barrier of flames.

Several centuries before Abulafia's doomed quest, legends about the Sambation and the Lost Tribes had been cemented into the popular imagination by the famed adventurer Eldad the Danite, who himself claimed provenance from the tribe of Dan.[35] Speaking a strange

Hebrew and recounting tall tales about lost Jews in Persia and from a land beyond Ethiopia, Eldad, who was probably a Jewish seafarer from Yemen, entertained audiences all along the Mediterranean with stories about Israel's lost remnant. Eldad's account was most likely the basis for the famous letters of Prester John, the supposed descendant of the Magi who lived either in India or Ethiopia, depending on the particular version of the story told.[36] That patriarch warned the leaders of medieval Christendom that the Lost Tribes, alongside whom he claimed to dwell, were ready at any moment to make war on the Christians.[37] John, who also wrote of unicorns and dragons, described the Sambation as "a river full of precious stones [that] descends so swiftly that nobody can cross it except on Saturday when it stands still; and whatever it encounters, it carries into the Sandy Sea."[38]

Because the myth of the Ten Lost Tribes deals with a people scattered beyond its borders, it has become a fitting allegorical device for depicting the dispersed nation of Israel as a whole after the Destruction of the Second Temple. On this point, Allen H. Godbey has incisively posited about the tribes that "it is not a race that has survived, but a peculiar cultus with many sects."[39] Throughout history, many individuals belonging to these "sects," in Godbey's terminology, have tended to view almost any previously unencountered peoples as lost Israelites. Such exotic groups whose provenance has been ascribed to the tribes include the Native Americans, Gengis Khan's Mongol warriors, and the inhabitants of the Indian subcontinent. Stuart Kirsch remarks that this model, which formed an integral part of the *tabula rasa* of "colonial powers and missionaries," almost invariably assigned "the histories of indigenous peoples" to this foundational myth.[40] In that sense, a major figurative element of the biblical library was transposed into the colonial one.

To date, the only group to be officially recognized by the majority of world Jewry as descended from one of the Ten Lost Tribes—and the community that has served as the most common point of reference against which most discussions of neo-Jewish movements have been oriented—is the *Beta Israel* ("House of Israel" in Amharic), the Jews of Ethiopia. Often called "Falashas," an out-of-vogue derogatory term that refers to foreigners, immigrants, or those who could not own land; this group captured the imagination of the world when approximately seven thousand of them were airlifted to Israel in "Operation Moses" in 1984–1985, and approximately fourteen thousand again in "Operation Solomon" in 1991. William Safire's assertion that "for the first time in history, thousands of black people are being brought to a country not in chains but in dignity, not as slaves but as citizens," accurately encapsulates Western public sentiment about their plight at the time of the first airlift.[41] Symbolically, it also reinforces the Jewish continuity of the Exodus motif evidenced in the title of the first operation.

Several different heritage narratives attesting to the Beta Israel's Jewish connections have been propagated. One metastory connected to the legend popularized by Eldad the Danite, and later reinforced in a ruling by Rabbi David ben Abi Zimra (1479–1573), traces their lineage to the tribe of Dan. This was the narrative preferred and referenced by Ovadia Yosef, chief Sephardic rabbi of Israel from 1973 to 1984. Rabbi Yosef confirmed the Beta Israel's status as lost Jews during the first year of his appointment to that position, much to the chagrin of many in the Israeli government, including Shlomo Goren, the chief Ashkenazi rabbi of Israel at the time, who took two years to reflect before he decided to agree with his colleague. (Israel has two chief rabbis: one from the Sephardic community, who represents those Jews who hail from North Africa and the Middle East; and one from the Ashkenazi community, who represents those hailing from Europe.) At the time of Rabbi Yosef's ruling, then prime minister Golda Meir is reported to have said about the Ethiopians' claims: "Don't we have enough problems? What do we need these blacks for?"[42] A more popular metanarrative among the Beta Israel, which attests to the descent of all of Ethiopia's inhabitants from the legendary Menelik, son of King Solomon and the Queen of Sheba, was considered too wide-ranging to be viable for the purposes of targeted immigration to Israel. Consequently, it was largely ignored by the rabbinical authorities.

Interestingly, the awareness of the Beta Israel took a long time to percolate among Jews elsewhere in the world. Many in the West had been aware of the Ethiopian Jews' existence since Jacques Faitlovitch, the Polish-born Jewish Orientalist, first published his *Notes d'un voyage chez les Falachas* (*Notes from a Journey among the Falashas*) in 1905.[43] But Faitlovitch failed to generate much enthusiasm for the Ethiopians' cause. Instead, it was a combination of later geopolitical factors, rather than insular interest in recovering the Lost Tribes, which brought their case to the forefront of contemporary Jewish concerns.

Tudor Parfitt was in the Sudan in 1984 at the refugee camps to which Ethiopian Jews had flocked, many on foot, after fleeing political repression and the most severe drought on record. Parfitt notes wryly that, prior to their highly publicized existential crisis and the pressure put on the American and Israeli governments to intervene, "There was not exactly a stampede on the part of Western Jews to go and greet their long-lost black brethren in Ethiopia."[44] Indeed, this was precisely the case. As the first eyewitness to publish an account of how these lost Jews sought refuge from Marxist Ethiopia's tyrannical regime, Parfitt provides an insightful look into the reasons why, this time, the world— in particular, the Jews of North America—took special notice of the Jews of Ethiopia:

> The plight of Ethiopia's Jews attracted an enormous amount of sympathy and expressions of solidarity from all over the Jewish world, particularly North America. Indeed, there have been few Jewish issues in recent times which have generated as much feeling or have developed so potent a mystique. This is partly because North American Jews, even more than French or British Jews and certainly more than Israeli Jews, inhabit a world very largely dominated by the memory of the Holocaust and consequently feel acutely protective of any Jewish community which appears to be at risk. And it is partly because the Ethiopian Jews are black. The Falashas' cause has thus represented an opportunity for American Jews to express liberal views which were sometimes more difficult to express in an American context, especially since American blacks had started counting the Jews (and Israel) among their political enemies. The Falashas—black, suffering Jews, persecuted in a distant (Marxist) land—moved the hearts of a broad cross-section of American Jewry in a particularly acute way.[45]

As this judgment of the situation demonstrates, the events surrounding Operation Moses intertwined forevermore the destiny of the Beta Israel with that of Western Jewry. At least part of the reason for this appears to be reactive and connected to that particular moment in time, especially with regard to the systematic disenfranchisement of the Beta Israel by the totalitarian regime of Mengistu Haile Mariam, which ruled Ethiopia between 1974 and 1987.

And what of the credibility of the Ethiopians' claims? Just because the chief rabbis of Israel declare a community to be descended from a Lost Tribe does not mean that American or Israeli Jews—whose stances on issues of Jewish law have long been at odds with those favored by the conservative rabbinical establishment—would automatically take the rabbis' opinions on the matter to be factually correct. The key formula for the majority of world Jewry to accept the Ethiopian narrative, it seems, was one that favored, and ensured, their integration into normative (i.e., rabbinic) Judaism. A categorical approval of the community's origin story and the acceptance of some of their highly divergent customs were not likely to be granted without the stipulation that, eventually, the Ethiopians would adopt the lifestyle choices of Jews from the West. Their acculturation in Israel was therefore seen as some kind of a guarantee that such a change would indeed take place.

The least contentious peculiarities of such customs centered around what Parfitt calls the Ethiopians' "Old Testament, pre-exilic Judaism, based on a literal obedience of the Pentateuch."[46] Because the Ethiopian Jews were presumably not in contact with other Jews (read: Israelites) since the time of the Assyrian exile, it was logical that they would have no familiarity with the postexilic festivals, such as Purim and Hanukkah. Similarly, they would not have had exposure to any rabbinic texts. But what of their knowledge of Hebrew? Somewhere along the line, this, too, had been lost. Instead, their sacred writings were composed in Geez, the liturgical language of the Ethiopian Orthodox Church. Although these factors were seen as somewhat of a curiosity by some, they did not really pose a problem for the Ethiopians' eventual integration into the normative Jewish community. The more contentious pieces of the puzzle included customs such as the adherence to an Oral Law different from that of the Talmud; clitoral excision; confession; and celibacy.[47]

Much historical scholarship on the question of the Beta Israel has attempted to explain how such divergent customs came about.

In contrast to the opinions of Rabbis Goren and Yosef, many scholars have posited that the Beta Israel are merely an outgrowth of an Old Testament–centered indigenous form of Ethiopian Christianity, which was able to develop organically for many centuries without exterior ecclesiastical influence. Edward Ullendorff, for instance, has posited that the Jewish practices of the Beta Israel are "merely the reflection of those Hebraic and Judaic practices and beliefs which were implanted on parts of south-west Arabia in the first post-Christian centuries and subsequently brought into Abyssinia."[48] A further point that Ullendorff brings to our attention is that many other non-Christian ethnic groups in Ethiopia, such as the Gafat and the Kemant, have also been associated with legends of lost Jews.[49] These groups, however, have not been the focus of many Lost Tribe seekers. More recently, the meticulous scholarship of Steven Kaplan has demonstrated that the evolution of the religious canon of the Beta Israel is closely tied to that of the Ethiopian monastic tradition.[50] According to Kaplan, their appearance as a distinct movement centered on the Old Testament is no more than around five centuries old.[51]

What are the implications of the differences in opinion between the academic and rabbinical authorities? At stake is the possibility that research such as that published by Ullendorff and Kaplan may, as Daniel Orenstein warns, "weaken the standing of the Ethiopian Jewish community in its various political battles in Israel."[52] Because the Ethiopians who have immigrated to Israel are at the bottom of the socioeconomic ladder in the Jewish demographic and, generally speaking, remain poorly assimilated, they continue to face discrimination and major obstacles to further integration into Israeli society, despite some notable successes. In Moran Peled's no-nonsense assessment, they are seen by many in Israel as "poor, diseased, swarthy, retarded, and bankrupt."[53] This is in spite of the fact that almost all of the new immigrants have adopted a modern Orthodox lifestyle, serve in the army, and, at least in relation to other Jewish Israeli citizens, are quite patriotic.

Does research that questions the historical-religious origins of the Ethiopian Jews harm their standing in the eyes of Jewish Israelis? In my opinion, it does not. Most Israelis who were or are against the naturalization of the Beta Israel have voiced their opposition in mainly economic terms. That rationale will not be bolstered by academic scholarship, written mainly in English, which is out of the range of interests of those Israelis. Conversely, religious Israelis or those from the nationalistic camps, who wish to bring as many Jews to Israel as possible in order to strengthen the Jewish demographic or to hasten the arrival of the Messiah, are not dissuaded by the expenditures involved in such massive immigration projects. And, in any event, there are not many members of the Beta Israel left in Ethiopia to bring (back) to Israel.[54]

An incident from my time as an education officer in the Israeli military illustrates common fears over such economic liabilities. For a time during my service, I was in charge of an academic reserve program for high school students of Ethiopian origin who were approaching the age of the compulsory draft. One official from a government educational body, with whom I worked on this same program, told me in a moment of candid frustration: "Those Negros cost the state way too much money! We should never have brought them here." In my experience, such views are pervasive among Israelis who are squeezed by an ever-tightening monetary noose. Thus, preconceived notions about the strain on the disappearing welfare state, which is exacerbated by the needs of poor immigrants, discourage many from keeping an open mind about facilitating the further immigration of individuals of questionable Jewish origin from similarly impoverished countries, given that Israel offers immediate naturalization and a generous social welfare package for Jews seeking political refuge.

Outside of the fiscal domain, another perspective that works against the Ethiopian immigrants in Israel is the feeling among a vocal minority of religious Jews that the ruling by Goren and Yosef was flawed. Such people are resentful for what they see as liberal American Jewish pressure that forced Israel to absorb people with a dubious Jewish background. For instance, it has been reported that headmasters of some parochial schools refuse the admittance of Ethiopian pupils because they do not acknowledge the Ethiopians as authentically Jewish; and that certain well-known rabbis will not perform marriage ceremonies between Ethiopians, even if one of them is a native-born Israeli citizen whose parents are Ethiopian.[55] Some religious rites of the Ethiopian Jewish community still have a strong stigma attached to them, despite the widespread acceptance of rites from other non-mainstream communal denominations now present in Israel.[56]

One reason for these rebuffs is that certain powerful figures in the religious establishment claim that, according to the prophecy of Jeremiah (3:18), the Ten Lost Tribes are to be found only to the northeast, and not to the south, of Israel.[57] The Ethiopians who claim to be descended from Dan may have had contact with a remnant of that tribe, the dissenters reason, but this remnant could not have lingered long enough to foster an unequivocal connection. Therefore, for a number of Ethiopian Jews, the only route to full acceptance in Israel is to undergo an Orthodox conversion to Judaism. Many consider this drawn-out ritual process even more of an insult to their integrity than the *giyyur lekhumrah* (precautionary conversion) ceremony forced upon their parents or grandparents before their immigration to the Promised Land. This touchy situation may improve if the Rabbinate has a change of heart. But, even if it does, academic scholarship on the topic published in English is unlikely to count among the criteria according to which the religious authorities will decide on such a change.

To date, the only other group to be recognized as a Lost Tribe by Israel is the *Bnei Menashe* (Children of Manasseh) movement from the Mizoram and Manipur regions of northeastern India. Since their initial recognition as part of the tribe of Manasseh in 2005 by then chief Sephardic rabbi Shlomo Amar, this group has made headlines around the world due to the much-publicized immigration of thousands of their members to the state of Israel. Tracing their origins to the aforementioned Lost Tribe, these former Christians of ethnic Kuki, Mizo, and Chin stock indicate that, according to their oral heritage narratives, they reached their present location in India after sojourning through Afghanistan and China. Like the Ethiopian Jews, they have neither knowledge of Hebrew nor any discursive relations with established Jewish groups around the world. They do, however, have certain customs and beliefs that resemble those of the ancient Israelites, many of which have been documented in Hillel Halkin's best-selling book on their movement, *Across the Sabbath River: In Search of a Lost Tribe of Israel.*[58]

The public perception surrounding the claims of the Bnei Menashe is quite different from that of the Ethiopian Jews for several reasons.

First, unlike the Beta Israel, the Bnei Menashe are being brought to Israel primarily (as of this writing) by a privately run, nonprofit organization called *Shavei Israel* (Hebrew: "the Returnees of Israel"). Second, although underprivileged, this Indian community seems to be in no clear existential danger in its current location. As of this writing, the fate of the Bnei Menashe who remain in India is unclear, but all signs point to a continuation of the efforts undertaken thus far to bring them to Israel and to help them, per their wishes, convert to Orthodox Judaism.[59]

Understandably, there are those who posit that, aside from economic or religious factors, the reluctance to embrace unconventional Jewish groups from developing countries stems from an intrinsic racism against people of color. According to such long-held attitudes, as Jonas Zianga posits, "only whites can be true Jews, whereas the Jewishness of black or other non-Caucasian people is questionable."[60] Because Zianga's point deserves due attention regarding the historical and socioreligious perspectives surrounding Jewish "color" in the approximately four-thousand-year continuum of Judaism, some space is devoted below to exploring the issue.

At various points in the Bible, Canaan, Cush (Ethiopia), and Egypt are all referred to as countries with black-skinned inhabitants, as are the peoples of Midian, Kedar, Elam, and Hattusa. Among the most notable biblical characters considered by modern standards to be black are Zipporah, Melchizedek, Ephron the Hittite, Hagar the Egyptian, Rahab the harlot, and Ebedmelech the Ethiopian. In antiquity, the Queen of Sheba, who was likely of southwestern Arabian origin, was not always considered as black; those depictions come quite later, and mostly from the influence of Christian theological circles.[61]

As a continent, Africa vacillates in the biblical imagination between a locus of revelation and a site of pestilence. On the one hand, Moses receives his divine calling in Africa, and Joseph takes an African wife (Asenath). On the other, the peoples of Africa were considered for centuries, by both Jews and Christians (and later by Muslims), to be descended from Ham, the son of Noah. Ham had been cursed because he "saw the nakedness of his father" (Gen. 9:22) when Noah was in a drunken stupor. According to the biblical account, when Noah awoke from the stupor and realized what had happened, he cursed Canaan, Ham's son, and ordained that "a servant of servants shall he be unto his brethren" (Gen. 9:25). This curse was often invoked to justify the enslavement of dark-skinned peoples, mainly in Africa but also in parts of Asia, who had supposedly been "blackened" by this transgression. As Edith R. Sanders remarks, such perspectives bolstered by the so-called "Hamitic hypothesis" permitted "exploitation of the Negro for economic gain," without those involved in enslavement being confronted by any "doubts as to the moral issues involved."[62]

Postbiblical Jewish texts are for the most part similarly negative in their depictions of dark-skinned peoples. The Talmud goes further than the biblical account in its depiction of Ham's sin, maintaining that Ham was "punished in his skin" (*Sanhedrin* 108b) for copulating while in the ark. One *midrash* (an exegetical or hermeneutic interpretation of a biblical text) from Genesis *Rabbah* (36:7) foretells that Canaan's children will be "ugly and black." In his *Guide for the Perplexed*, the great medieval Jewish philosopher Moses Maimonides (1135–1204) calls the Cushites "irrational beings" who are "below mankind, but above monkeys, since they have the form and shape of man, and a mental faculty above that of the monkey."[63] Such attitudes were the mainstay until the arrival on the scene of the Ethiopian Jews in the nineteenth and twentieth centuries. Their entry into the worldwide Jewish consciousness represents the first public encounter in the modern period between large numbers of Jews of color and Jews from established Ashkenazi and Sephardic communities.

And what of other groups of self-declared chosen peoples who diverge religiously, culturally, and historically from the normative streams of Judaism, but who are not dark-skinned or do not hail from impoverished countries where accusations of economic opportunism related to their newfound Jewish identities are rife? It seems prudent to end this section on the subject of potential exclusion from the main body of normative Jewry with a brief discussion of two groups that testify to the possibility of diversity in the realm of Jewish praxis, as well as to the potential inclusion of conflicting views in the Jewish theological matrix. These groups, neither of which includes Jews of color or those geographically distanced from the Land of Israel, are the Karaites and the Samaritans.

The Karaites, whose Hebrew appellation *Bnei mikra* signifies "Followers of the Bible" or, more figuratively, "Scripturalists," are thought to have originated as an organized substratum of Judaism either in Egypt or Iraq between the seventh and ninth centuries CE.[64] Despite proper evidence that would testify to such a connection, many casually conjecture that the Karaites may have been responsible for Judaism's expansion in the North African Berber and, later, Arabized areas. According to the classification of Daniel Frank and Leon Nemoy, the Karaites are a "Jewish sect" that acknowledges "only the Hebrew Scriptures as the source of divinely inspired legislation, and denies the authority of the post-biblical Jewish tradition (the Oral Law) as recorded in the Talmud and in later rabbinic literature."[65] There are an estimated fifty thousand Karaites in the world today, most of them in Israel.[66] Despite their uniform rejection of rabbinic Judaism, they are recognized as Jewish by the overwhelming majority of normative Jewish religious bodies.

In addition to their refutation of all postbiblical Jewish textual practice, Karaites differ from Jews who follow normative Judaism in several significant ways. Like the ancient Hebrews and Israelites, they follow patrilineal rather than matrilineal descent; have codes regarding corporeal purity that are stricter than those mandated in the Talmud; and, in the tradition of the Sadducees of the Second Temple Period, believe that each person studying the Torah (the Jewish Written Law) should rely upon one's own interpretation and instincts for illumination, rather than following the explanations of earlier generations. A source frequently cited to buttress this argument is Deuteronomy 4:2, which states, "Ye shall not add unto the word which I command you, neither shall ye diminish from it, that ye may keep the commandments of the LORD your God which I command you."

The Samaritans, who trace their lineage to the tribes of Ephraim and Manasseh, as well as to the priestly Levites, are an acknowledged branch of world Jewry who follow an Abrahamic faith based on the Samaritan Pentateuch. Called *Shomronim* in Hebrew, "Keepers of (the Law)," Samaritans consider themselves the followers of the true Israelite religion that existed before the period of the Babylonian exile.[67] Divided between the Israeli city of Holon and the West Bank settlement of Kiryat Luza, in the vicinity of Mount Gerizim (the site they believe to be the true intended location for the Holy Temple), the Samaritans today number around eight hundred people, almost all of whom hail from four distinct families.[68]

Samaritans trace the beginning of their schism with the Israelites to the return of that group from Babylon, when the scribe and priest Ezra introduced a supposedly corrupted version of the Torah into the land. Like the Karaites, they insist on maintaining the purity of the Israelite faith by rebuffing any postbiblical textual addenda. Major ways in which Samaritan practice differs from rabbinic practice include the following: the continuation of animal sacrifice, maintenance of a high priesthood, insistence on patrilineal lineage, and reliance upon the Samaritan rather than the traditional Masoretic text of the Bible. Before the establishment of the state of Israel, Samaritans were divided regarding their geopolitical affiliations and attitudes toward Zionism. Having now been absorbed into Jewish Israeli society, almost none identify with elements of the Palestinian national movement. Israel's Orthodox establishment considers them of Jewish descent but, as it does with members from other marginalized communities (such as the Beta Israel), requires a symbolic conversion process into rabbinic Judaism for those who wish to acquire a comprehensive confirmation of their Jewish identity.

The Judaizing communities described above, which are not accepted automatically as normatively Jewish by mainstream rabbinical authorities, help to provide a representative glimpse into the nature, location, and substance of other marginalized Jewish groups whose ultimate recognition often hinges upon financial and geopolitical considerations. Their inclusion has been intended to contextualize and augment—in the geographical, textual, theological, and ritual aspects—the more in-depth analyses of the three major communities profiled in later chapters.

One final note: I have purposely excluded in this section a discussion of the descendants of Jews from the Iberian Peninsula who were forcibly converted to Christianity and/or dispersed during the Spanish Inquisition. Sometimes called "Crypto-Jews" in English, *Conversos* (converted ones) or *Maranos* (damned; figuratively, "pig") in Spanish, or *'Anusim* (coerced ones) in Hebrew, these communities often clandestinely preserved remnants of their Jewish heritage while living in the midst of Christian communities in Europe and the Americas.[69] Aside from considerations of space, no overview of these communities has been given because, unlike the major groups discussed in later chapters, their Jewish normativity was never put into question prior to their persecution and dispersion in the thirteenth century CE. Additionally, despite the fact that the mixing between members of these dispersed communities with the indigenous West Africans among whom some Jews found themselves has been substantiated by a number of sources, no published scholarship yet exists on the possible influence of mixed-race descendants of Jews from the Iberian Peninsula on contemporary West African Judaizing movements.[70] Parfitt, however, is currently conducting research on the topic. His eventual findings will certainly shed much light on what role, if any, the Iberian Jews who settled in West Africa had on the formation of contemporary Judaizing communities in those areas.

ON THE OUTSIDE, LOOKING IN

Germane to the subject of the marginalized substrata of conventional Jewry is the matter of groups whose members self-identify as Jews, whether through genealogy or spiritual volition, but who are not recognized as such by any Orthodox rabbinical institution. Such groups make up the major case studies of chapters 2–4. In preparation for the discussions on those groups, the religious movements related to them, and the sociopolitical conditions in which they have developed, let us examine a selection of similar "fringe" communities whose claims of Jewishness have been met with even more skepticism than those mentioned above.

In recent decades, several such self-declared Jewish communities in Africa have garnered much attention in the international press. In fact, so much has been written in popular media about the phenomenon of black Africans who discover their Jewish roots that a 1994 April Fool's Day radio prank, in which an Israeli broadcaster told his listeners about lost Jews from the west-central African nation of Gabon being airlifted to Tel-Aviv, was taken seriously by hundreds of well-meaning listeners, who offered their services in order to help acclimatize the newcomers.[71] The hoax, as it turns out, was more prescient that comical, for a Judaizing community (the Neutralist Jewish Community of Gabon) does in fact exist in Gabon today, and is discussed in chapter 3.

One major Judaizing movement in Africa is centered in southeastern Nigeria, among the Igbo people.[72] The Igbo are perhaps most well known in the West as victims of the genocidal policies perpetrated against them during their unsuccessful attempt to secede from Nigeria during the Biafra War (1967–1970), and for the depictions of their precolonial existence in Igbo author Chinua Achebe's seminal postcolonial novel, *Things Fall Apart*.[73] Daniel Lis, who has written the most comprehensive study to date on the Jewish origins of the Igbo, estimates that around forty thousand of approximately twenty to thirty million Igbo, the majority of whom are Christianized, are active Judaizers who trace their ancestral lineage to the lost Israelites, specifically to the tribes of Gad and Ephraim.[74] According to Remy Ilona, an Igbo scholar who has amassed an impressive number of oral histories and heritage narratives that ostensibly link the group with ancient Israel, the customs of the Nri priestly clan of the Igbo bear a striking resemblance to those of the Levites.[75] Although American Jewish groups are beginning to pay particular attention to and, in some cases, practically and financially support the efforts of the Igbo to join mainstream world Jewry, Israel's rabbinical authorities have thus far rejected their appeals for recognition.

Another African group that self-identifies as Jewish in origin is the Lemba, a Bantu-speaking people found mainly in South Africa and Zimbabwe, with smaller numbers in Malawi and Mozambique.[76] Parfitt, the first scholar from the West to take an active interest in researching the Lemba's Judaizing practices and oral narratives, has been instrumental in documenting three significant aspects of their claims. The first is their possible derivation from the Jews of Yemen, a group of whom might have traveled southward from the Gulf of Aden down the coast of East Africa to their present locations. The second is their possession of the sacred *ngoma lungundu* (the drum that thunders), purportedly a replica of the original Ark of the Covenant that they carried with them from Arabia.[77] Third, and most famous, is the discovery that the patrilineal genetic markers of their priestly *Buba* class correspond to the markers of the "Cohen modal haplotype" gene, which indicates their common point of origin in the Levant and links them to Jews descended from the Levites, the Aaronite priestly class. This finding was the subject of a groundbreaking 1998 article coauthored by Parfitt in the leading scientific journal *Nature*.[78] Unlike the Igbo, the Lemba have not submitted a formally organized request for recognition of their Jewishness, and the state of Israel has not issued a public declaration about them.

Other claims of Jewishness have also proven quite resilient, and some have nothing to do with genealogy or heredity. Take the case of the Abayudaya, which is the generic term for "Jews" in Lugandan. This spiritual community of around two thousand people in Uganda is probably the emerging Jewish group about which the most has been written in the popular press. It is also the only emerging community to date to be officially recognized by the Jewish Agency for Israel, an international organization that works in tandem with the Israeli Ministry of Immigrant Absorption. An ethnic Baganda community, the Abayudaya started practicing some approximate kind of Judaism around one hundred years ago, when their ancestor and military leader Semei Kakungulu (1869–1928), dissatisfied with the colonialists' interpretation of the Bible, left the syncretistic Bamalaki Christian sect, circumcised himself, and proclaimed his status as a Jew.[79]

Like Kakungulu, the modern-day Abayudaya make no claim of Israelite ancestry. Rather, they wish to live their lives as Jews based on the spiritual principles of the Hebrew Scriptures. Unlike more recent Judaizing communities, their knowledge of Judaism has benefited from more or less consistent interaction with Jewish foreigners in Uganda since the early part of the twentieth century. Many hundreds have been formally converted to Judaism through the efforts of rabbis from the American Conservative movement. In the early 2000s, the community was shaken when a breakaway group of some 1,500 decided to align itself with those who favor bringing Israeli-style, modern Orthodox Jewish practice to Uganda. The old maxim about Jewish sectarianism, according to which "two Jews need three synagogues," is apparently true everywhere.

Gershom Sizomu, the current leader of the Abayudaya community, is the first Sub-Saharan black African to have obtained his rabbinical ordination at a *yeshiva*, a Jewish seminary, in the United States (the Zeigler School of Rabbinic Studies at the University of Judaism in Los

Angeles). The seminary he now directs near the city of Mbale—the only such Jewish seminary in Sub-Saharan Africa—hosts other black Africans who wish to be instructed in the Jewish religion but who cannot afford to study in Israel or the United States. A parliamentarian for the Bungokho North constituency and the brains behind several different development projects in his district, Sizomu has said that his dream "is to make Africa Jewish."[80] The recent formation of several new Jewish communities affiliated with the Abayudaya in neighboring Kasuku, Kenya, may bring Sizomu's dream one step closer to reality.[81]

The Igbo, Lemba, and Abayudaya are all examples of organized groups whose members have taken formalized steps to (re-)integrate themselves into the worldwide Jewish community. Outside the realm of such organized efforts, however, there are many instances of diverse African ethnicities whose members' heritage and customs have been conspicuously compared with those of the Israelites of old, but without any expression of desire for recognition or reintegration. Such groups include the Amazigh (Berbers), Baluba, Bantu, Fon, Fulani, Masai, Meru, Nga, Shona, Soninke, Tiv, Tutsi, Xhosa, Yibir, Yoruba, and Zulu, among others. Outside of Africa, others often cited as having links to ancient Israel include the Pashtuns of Pakistan and Afghanistan and the Maori of New Zealand. These comparisons have their rationale in alleged similarities in life-cycle events, heritage narratives, dietary and vestimentary codes, and cosmological perspectives. But none of these people are "Jewish" per se, in that the vast majority of them self-define as Muslim or Christian. Many practice syncretistic combinations of those faiths and animism, ancestor worship, or indigenous belief systems.

One such claim of descent from Jewish ancestors came from the now-defunct cultural association in Timbuktu, Mali, which went by the Hebrew name of *Zakhor* (Remember). What began as a search for roots among local Muslims starting in the 1990s ended when Salafist Tuareg rebels took over the northern part of the country in 2011, and claims of Jewish parentage or contact with Jewish groups overseas became an existential liability.[82] The same was true for the residents of the eastern Senegalese Muslim village of Bani Israel, meaning "Children of Israel" in Arabic, whose Wolof and Mandinka members claim to be descended from Jews from Egypt who arrived in the area via Somalia and Nigeria.[83]

Dougoutigo Fadiga, the community's president, has said: "We don't like to talk too much about our Jewish background, but we don't hide it, either."[84] Fadiga has also noted: "We are all practicing Muslims and we don't want to become Jewish."[85] Given the potential fallout from such claims, such malaise is understandable. One way in which these declarations have harmed the community is that it has become difficult for its members to obtain clearance to go on the *hajj* pilgrimage to Saudi Arabia. According to a contact of mine, when the Senegalese press recently caught wind of the Israeli ambassador's visit to the Bani Israel community, the villagers denied that any such meeting had taken place.

Other groups seem to be cashing in on the interests of Western Jewish and Christian tourists to visit regions in Africa where ancient Jewish practices are rumored to still exist. For example, during a research trip to Ethiopia, I noticed an advertisement targeted at such tourists. The poster advertised a "cultural workshop" led by leaders of the Kemant, an Agaw people who practice an Abrahamic religion and live in the vicinity of the lands formerly inhabited by the Beta Israel.[86] When I met with one of the leaders to see what was included in the advertised package, he told me that I would need to pay $1,000 to witness the slaughtering of a sheep "just like Abraham and his men used to do it." I respectfully demurred. The same leader insisted that their manner of circumcising young men was "just as Moses had invented it." I decided not to point out the discrepancy in the attribution. Most incredibly, he informed me that the Kemant were part of the same lineage as the Beta Israel. This declaration is quite revisionist, given that prior to the mass exodus of the Ethiopian Jews to Israel in the 1980s and 1990s, these two ethnic groups had traditionally been bitter enemies and had refrained from intermingling. Even as minority groups in the dominant Amhara culture, both were clearly distinct peoples, easily distinguishable to everyone in the region. Piggybacking on the recognition of the Beta Israel seems to be a way for some in this marginalized group to improve their socioeconomic situation. While historically unsound, it is also entirely understandable, given the systematic disenfranchising by the Ethiopian government of Kemant language, religion, and culture.

Outside of the spheres of genealogy or of the spiritual desire expressed by ethnoreligious movements from specific micronations to bind themselves to the Jewish narrative, there are many Christian groups whose adherents wish to be part of the "spiritual Israel" by binding the cycle of their daily lives to the observance of select Old Testament rites, but without abandoning the basic tenets of Christian theology. Such groups include but are not limited to Adventists, Christadelphians, Messianic Christians (and Jews), Hebrew Roots Apostles, Latter-day Saints (Mormons), Rastafarians, Sabbatarians, and Subbotniks. In the postcolonial contexts of the communities profiled here, it may be helpful—especially for subsequent discussions of Africa-centered Jewish movements—to provide a bit of background regarding so-called "indigenous," "initiated," or, more commonly, "independent" churches in Africa. Such churches are a fundamental component of religious movements that preach an "African Reformation" through a return to "nativism."[87] The congregants of these independent churches, who choose to privilege the Old Testament over the New, frequently do so after having drawn parallels between their pre-Christian, precolonial customs and those of the Hebrews or Israelites of the Bible.[88] Bringing such church movements into the discussion helps to contextualize the situational motivations for the more Jewish-centered movements explored later.

Initially referred to by missionaries or by the leadership of mainline European-based churches as "syncretistic" or "separatist," independent, domestically administered churches began to form in Africa around the beginning of the twentieth century. Part of their success lay in the ability to tap into the growing sense of resentment over white ecclesiastical leadership and the perceived insensitivity to local cultural norms. Harold W. Turner, one of the first scholars to explore these native religious movements, has defined an African Independent Church (usually capitalized in the scholarly literature as a distinct category) as "a church which has been founded in Africa, by Africans, and primarily for Africans."[89]

According to Gailyn Van Rheenen, one of the principal characteristics of such churches is that they endeavor to communicate, in opposition to churches founded by Europeans, a theology that emphasizes "patterns of interaction common to those who live within that [i.e., local] culture."[90] In that vein, they differ from mission-established churches in that they seek to synthesize theological viewpoints rather than establish clear lines of demarcation between them. In Allan H. Anderson's terms, this makes them largely "concordistic."[91] Kofi A. Opoku notes that the founders of such churches are well positioned to respond to the frustrations of dissatisfied parishioners, since they have themselves previously belonged to the mission churches, but "separated from them at some crisis-point."[92] Opoku points out that, for the leadership of such churches, Jewish rituals and customs "constitute a veritable prototype."[93]

Frequently, such locally centered initiatives have been met with scorn by the mission church hierarchy. The latter considers the desire of those in the native churches to incorporate elements more amenable to local worldviews as giving way to "apparently incongruous cultural syntheses," such as the veneration of ancestors or polygamy.[94] For example, Bengt G. M. Sundkler, a Swedish Lutheran missionary to Africa, refers to such initiatives as "the bridge over which Africans are brought back to heathenism."[95] More recently, in many regions of Africa, such valorizations of indigenous rites have been seen as a threat to localized forms of evangelical Pentecostalism (imported mainly from the United States), which now competes with global Islam for adherents.[96]

The emphasis on Old Testament mores and practices has not only recently ignited the ire of European churches seeking to inculturate the African. In fact, long before the establishment of African Independent Churches, even during the Age of Exploration and the Scramble for Africa, when large unexplored portions of the continent were seen as one "great mission field," missionaries were cautious about how much of the Old Testament to emphasize in their teachings. Sundkler has described these European tutors as "genuinely perturbed by the [natives'] incessant interest in the Old Testament."[97]

Godfrey Edward Phillips touches upon this potential point of contention in his words of wisdom to missionaries entering the field. (Significantly for our discussion, his advice is destined to those evangelizing in both Africa and India.) Phillips counsels his church members to heed "the need for caution in the use of the Old Testament, lest the church should be more Jewish than Christian."[98] For his part, William D. Reyburn insists that "one of the most subtle and pervasive tensions in the Christian African scene is the relation of the Old Testament to the life of the African church."[99] Observing that many in the mission field wished to delay or even prevent the translation of the Old Testament into local languages, Reyburn writes of the fear that the Old Testament would "sanction pagan ways of life."[100] Paradoxically, this hesitance actually seemed to work against the exertions of the early missionaries. Because there was a delay in allowing unfettered access to the Old Testament narratives, many converts to Christianity expressed indignation that knowledge about practices and beliefs so fundamentally close to their own were withheld from them for so long.[101]

Which practices and beliefs resounded with the native cultures? There exists an array of scholarly literature on the subject.[102] What Magdel le Roux calls "numerous points of convergence" between African and Old Testament practices include the following: prohibitions on consuming the flesh of "unclean" animals, such as snakes, rodents, monkeys, and pigs, as well as on the consumption of blood or of meat from an edible animal that has been killed improperly; marriage practices banned by most modern Christian denominations, such as polygamy and bride inheritance; burial taboos; animal sacrifices; libation-pouring; harvest festivals; male circumcision; patriarchal rule; and menstrual seclusion.[103] According to Phillips, the "legalism" and "outward sanctions" connected to the observance of these codes resound more strongly with the "native" than the moralistic messages of brotherhood in the New Testament, which favor the exaltation of grace over the adherence to basic laws.[104]

As Dickson points out, stories about ancient Israel tend to involve, on a more symbolic level, the move from oppression to salvation, which is a motif demonstrated most notably in the story of the Exodus.[105] These stories represent a salient point of commonality with peoples who have known slavery, persecution, and the travails of living under colonial regimes. If, therefore, such peoples identify more easily with the figure of Moses than with that of Jesus, should this come as a surprise? The view of Philip Jenkins, who is one of the world's most esteemed scholars on Christianity in the developing world, is especially instructive on this point. For African Christians, Jenkins writes, it comes as a shock that they are expected to interpret certain parts of the Bible, such as the resurrection, "with absolute literalism," while other parts of the Old Testament "must be treated as no more than instructive fables."[106] Jenkins's next rhetorical question on this superimposed dichotomy illustrates the paradox nicely: "Who made that capricious decision?"[107] Some so-called "Zionist" churches in South Africa (with no connection to the Jewish nationalist movement), which combine elements of African religion with Christian faith and dogma, are answering this question by forming branches that often refashion for their members a self-consciously Jewish identity as Christians. They do so without any claims of historicity, but rather with "a declaration of spiritual authenticity" that links them to the Israelites' chosen lineage.[108]

This discussion of African Independent Churches whose members find particular value in the Old Testament is relevant to the topic of Judaizing movements for the following reasons.[109] Some decades ago, the Judaizing movements profiled here may well have ended up, or simply been classified as, African Independent Churches. Before the advent of the Internet—and before newly Christianized African communities would have had the ability to contact any significant number of Jewish persons overseas—the access to normative Judaism, complete with its postexilic dynamics and its insistence that the Messiah has not yet arrived, would simply not have been possible. Obviously, there are possible exceptions to this deduction, especially in the case of the House of Israel movement in Ghana, as chapter 2 demonstrates. Notable earlier examples include, as mentioned, the self-defining communities of Ethiopia and Uganda, both of which had significant contact with overseas peoples of Jewish extraction prior to the recent period.

The point is that globalization has provided Judaizing movements with an unprecedented array of rubrics through which they might take upon themselves the practice of normative Judaism, as opposed to simply finding an affinity with the Old Testament or entertaining the idea of possible provenance from a Lost Tribe. Turner unknowingly anticipated this shift while writing his 1979 volume on religious innovation in Africa. In this volume, Turner lays out a typology for such movements, which he labels as "Hebraist." According to Turner, such movements "have made a radical transference from the primal faith into the world of the Bible, especially into that of the Old Testament, but . . . reject the Christian church and usually the New Testament, or else have no Christology."[110] Turner notes that their religious mind-set "seems to correspond closely to that of [ancient] Israel."[111] It is possible that many of the movements profiled in this book—including the Indian case study, whose context and possible analogues to the African Independent Church movement will be explored in chapter 4—would have remained "Hebraist" and not "Jewish," had they existed in a more static and stationary era. They would have likely continued to pursue an Old Testament–centered agenda, with possible ambiguity about, or even rejection of, the figure of Jesus, but they would have done this without the context of postexilic Judaism available to them as a mold from which to form a specifically normative Jewish identity.

TO EMBRACE, OR NOT TO EMBRACE? PROPONENTS AND NAYSAYERS

As several previous examples have briefly highlighted, and as the information in subsequent chapters will further demonstrate, certain groups and individuals within conventional Jewish communities around the world are opposed to recognizing nascent Judaizing movements. Those who contest these groups' inclusion may be divided into several different categories of opposition. The first category is made up of those who fear that encouraging the religious "antics" of millions of impoverished, self-identifying Jews from developing countries could promote copycat communities of other potential immigrants to Israel, which the Israeli state's already-taxed social welfare system would ultimately be unable to handle. Perceptions among some Israelis that the immigration of the Beta Israel was a mistake only reinforce the rationale of such concerns.

Those who convey trepidation about Israel being overrun by underprivileged immigrants often reference the difficulties posed by the deep socioeconomic divide between Sephardic immigrants from North Africa and the Middle East and Ashkenazi immigrants from Europe. According to this argument, the situations are comparable because Sephardic immigrants to Israel have customarily occupied more working-class roles than those occupied by the Ashkenazis, who arrived in Israel earlier and whose mores and mind-sets were shared by the founders of the state. Given the resultant Eurocentric cultural norms that held sway in the early days of the state, Sephardic Jews had great difficulty acclimatizing in their new home country. This cultural malaise was exacerbated by the fact that Ashkenazi Israelis viewed the eventual adaptation of their Sephardic brethren to the dominant way of life as the desired end-goal, tended to exploit Sephardic labor, and dismissed organized movements for the cessation of state-sponsored discrimination. This attitude was expressed in a brusque fashion by the first prime minister of Israel, David Ben-Gurion, who said of the Jews from Arab countries: "We do not want the Israelis to be Arabs. It is our duty to fight against the spirit of the Levant that ruins individuals and societies."[112]

Concerns about taxing the economy of the state are fair enough. But there is a major difference between the unexpected influx of Sephardic Jews to Israel in the 1950s and the potential influx of Jews of color from the developing world. The difference is this: most self-defining Jews from developing countries do not understand the possibility of immediate naturalization in Israel. Unlike the Sephardic Jews, who were forced to quit their native countries due to the pan-Arab backlash against the founding of the state of Israel, unrecognized and isolated Jewish communities are for the most part unaware that the possibility of immigration to Israel even exists. For most, the Jewish state is simply an abstraction, and knowledge about the modern geopolitical entity of Israel is perhaps on the level of the average Missourian's familiarity with the Botswanan periphery. Even if they are aware that an option exists for immigration to the Holy Land, almost none of the people with whom I have conversed want to explore the possibility. Obviously, this may change as links with overseas Jewish communities develop, but the manner in which such changes may take place is unpredictable. The central motivations for embracing Judaism seem to have nothing to do with a desire to one day immigrate to Israel. This book's subsequent chapters provide examples that describe in detail those fundamental motivations.

A related category of naysayers is comprised of those who fear that neo-Jewish communities are simply seeking to profit financially from the goodwill of affluent Jewish donors from overseas. Naturally, there are some crooks who wish to exploit the advantages offered by connections to foreign benefactors, and I have met several. They, however, are in the minority. Most of the people whom I have met want nothing more than to recuperate what they see as traditions lost to imperialism and modernity. The relationships with their overseas coreligionists are but one way to help recover those traditions. That, to my mind, is the essence of the partnership, feelings of affection and mutual provenance notwithstanding. Many from isolated Jewish communities actually accentuate their already-precarious financial positions by choosing to follow Judaism, since they are unable to work on Saturday, must sustain a physical infrastructure different from that of the surrounding communities (i.e., building and maintenance of facilities such as ritual baths, kosher kitchens, separate schools, etc.), and adopt modes of dress and behavior that cause them to stand out from their immediate neighbors. The notion that everyone from a developing country who wishes to join the Jewish fold is an opportunist is, to my mind, a contemptuous banality devoid of any real understanding of the motivations, sincerity, and intellectual and spiritual capacities of millions of people, the likes of whom such naysayers have probably never personally encountered. That there is more to life than material gain may not go without saying to some, but to many, it certainly does.

Besides those who base their concerns on perceptions surrounding economic opportunism, why do others refrain from encouraging Judaizing communities in their attempts to live Jewishly? The remaining category of naysayers usually justifies its hesitations by citing two supposed factualities. They maintain that, first, Jews have traditionally refrained from proselytizing; and second, that one's Jewishness must be established either by verifying the Jewishness of the mother, or by corroborating that one has undergone a formal conversion ceremony. The problem with both of these claims is that they ignore that such stringent definitions of Jewish belonging are only common to the postexilic period, and were, to a large extent, necessitated purely by the harsh conditions of the umbrella civilizations of Christianity and Islam under which Jews lived. For example, after the Second Temple Period, especially during the times in which Jews were under the yoke of hostile powers, the notion of matrilineal descent was simply the only way to verify Jewishness, owing to the many occurrences of rape, forced conversion, and the destruction of entire communities.

In the Hebrew Bible, ethnic heredity is established by patrilineal rather than matrilineal descent, and concepts like "conversion" or "intermarriage" do not really exist (see below the explanation on the figure of Ruth).[113] Proselytizing, in the way that the notion is understood today, would have been an anomaly to any one of the patriarchs. Slaves owned by Jews were forced to worship the God of Israel, and conquered nations who did not were put to the sword.[114] The famous story from Exodus 12:38 of the "*erev rav*" (mixed multitude) that left Egypt under Moses is an early instance of foreign peoples being allowed access to the Israelite way of life without any verification of pedigree or obligation to undergo a stylized ritual procedure. After the conquest of the Twelve Tribes, Jews frequently had mixed marriages, despite the stigma that such unions later carried.[115] To join the fold, men had to be circumcised; it is not known what other ceremony, if any, was demanded of women. On this point, Shaye J. D. Cohen notes that, in the second century BCE, "Judeans/Jews opened their boundaries and allowed outsiders to enter either by accepting the God of the Jews or by becoming citizens in the Judean state."[116] The biblical story of Ruth the Moabite, who is often considered to be the first convert, testifies to the ease with which one could join the nation. Ruth simply says to Naomi, her Israelite mother-in-law, "Whither thou goest, I will go; and where thou lodgest, I will lodge; thy people shall be my people, and thy God my God" (Ruth 1:16).

After the Destruction of the Second Temple, the process for joining the Jewish people becomes more complicated. Instructions for *giyyur* (conversion) in the Talmud (*Yevamot* 47a–b; *Keritot* 8b) and in post-Talmudic literature (*Gerim* 1:1) stipulate that there are separate measures to be taken for those who wish to convert for reasons of kinship, and for those who wish to convert by integration into Jewish praxis. Three elements are required for the (male) proselyte: acceptance of adherence to Jewish law; circumcision; and immersion in a *mikveh* (ritual bath). (For women, only the first and third apply.) Regarding proselytizing, the Talmud instructs Jews to be convivial toward potential converts, because the Mosaic covenant forged at Sinai ostensibly included all the souls of those who would eventually convert (*Shavuot* 39a). The community of Makhoza, for example, had many such converts to Judaism among its citizens (*Avodah Zarah* 64a; *Kiddushin* 73a). Later sages, such as Maimonides, agreed that Jewish converts had been accepted since the beginning, but that in times of Jewish political sovereignty, potential proselytes had to go through a more rigid set of requirements, lengthening the process (*Issurei Biah* 13:15–25). The point to be emphasized here is that, as Yeshayahu Leibowitz has noted, all the Jews alive today need not be thought of as literal descendants of the "people of historical Judaism."[117]

Today, conversion requirements and processes vary according to the different denominations. In Israel, where the ultra-Orthodox establishment controls the certification for all life-cycle events (birth, marriage, divorce, burial, etc.) for its Jewish citizens, as well as conversion, the requirements involve, among other things, years of study in Jewish law under the supervision of a rabbinical court. More liberal denominations of Judaism outside of Israel, such as the Reconstructionist, Reform, or Conservative streams, which do not recognize the adherence to Orthodox interpretations of Jewish law as necessary for Jewish belonging, follow more symbolic rites of initiation. These conversions, however, are not recognized by Israel's rabbinical establishment, which means that a person converting to Judaism outside of an Orthodox framework who wishes to obtain Israeli citizenship will not be allowed to do so.

According to Israel's amended Law of Return, originally codified to assist those seeking political refuge, a Jewish person who is not born of a Jewish mother but who has at least one Jewish grandparent—the same criterion for Jewishness used by the Nazis—is eligible for immediate naturalization. Paradoxically, such a person will not be seen as completely Jewish by the rabbinical establishment in Israel, due to the procedural differences that exist between the Israeli national criteria for obtaining citizenship, and the separate rabbinical criteria according to which a Jew may be considered completely kosher. One can, therefore, be a newfound holder of Israeli citizenship and yet suffer, as a non-Jew, from a variety of discriminatory measures in the infamous Israeli bureaucracy—unless, of course, one yields to the pressures of the religious authorities and agrees to undergo a conversion process and/or stylized legitimating ritual procedure, including (for men) adult circumcision.

A further point to emphasize regarding the "authenticity" of Jewish descent is that there is no racial or biological basis for claiming any kind of common Jewish heritage, despite the longevity of this assumption. Part of the reason that Jews have been considered a race can be traced back to Paul of Tarsus, who, in taking away from Christians the obligation to follow Jewish law, inadvertently made the Jews into a racial group based on the "sign" of circumcision. However, to say that race is a determining factor in establishing Jewishness is erroneous. Raphael Falk, a biologist by training, refutes the racial supposition quite clearly, maintaining that persecution and insular marriages are responsible for "caus[ing] them [the Jews] to form gene pools that were somewhat isolated from their surroundings."[118] This explains the frequency of the oft-cited "Jewish" diseases, such as Tay-Sachs, Gaucher, and Mucolipidosis type IV, among Jews of Eastern European extraction.

Concerning the makeup of Jewish gene pools, we find that, according to Richard Goodman, "interpretations of genetic data about the Jews stress two themes: (1) an intrinsic admixture of different non-Jewish populations with Jews, which resulted in great heterogeneity among Jewish groups, and (2) a common Middle Eastern origin."[119] Alain F. Corcos underscores that studies done in Israel in 1948 show that "'genetic distance' among major Jewish groups of diverse geographical origins were often smaller than the distance between Jews and non-Jews of the same regions."[120] More recently, the exciting DNA studies conducted by researchers such as Egorova and Parfitt have added much new information on the genetic origins of many Jewish populations throughout the world, while providing nuanced perspectives on what those genetic origins mean in the larger picture of Jewish identity and belonging.[121]

A final note regarding the naysayers. It should be pointed out that, for some, allowing so many new Jews into the fold risks creating additional schisms in the global Jewish body by further exacerbating the rifts between already sharply divided Jewish denominations. According to this reasoning, because there is no central governing authority to dictate religious policy (outside of the Israeli Rabbinate, which only has jurisdiction in Israel, there is no formal or centralized mechanism for recognition of one's being Jewish), polemics and misunderstandings between Jews with regard to belief and praxis have become the norm rather than the exception. Judaism in the modern period has thus become a "soft" religion subject to changing cultural trends, rather than a fixed way of life based on a nomocratic (i.e., law-driven) code. This variation on the "too much democracy is a bad thing" argument often functions as a basis for the idea that welcoming Jews from the developing world who are culturally dissimilar from their counterparts in the West will only heighten this tension.

And what about the people on the other side of the debate? Who supports the inclusion of Judaizing communities whose members do not conform to the standard religious, ethnic, or hereditary definitions by which Jewishness has conventionally been established? Like the naysayers, the proponents can be divided into several categories. Among them are nonpartisan Jewish groups from the West that are committed to inclusiveness; Christian sympathizers, frequently Zionists, who see the appearance of emerging communities as an eschatological sign of the impending Messianic Age; and certain religious bodies in Israel that wish to aid in the Ingathering of the Exiles and/or to boost the Jewish demographic majority vis-à-vis the Arabs.

Two pluralistic American Jewish organizations, *Kulanu* and *Be'chol Lashon* (Hebrew: "All of Us" and "In Every Tongue," respectively), belong to the first category and are worthy of mention here; they are also discussed more in the following chapters.[122] Both organizations strive to bring about awareness of the cultural diversity that they view as an inherent component of Jewish peoplehood. Both see the inclusion of Jews of color and Jews from emerging communities from around the world as a potential injection of much-needed dynamism into the existing tradition. To a certain extent, both also see the possibility of millions of individuals who wish to join the Jewish people as a way to make up for the devastating demographic losses to world Jewry due to the events of the Holocaust. Concerns about social justice, women's rights, economic development for vulnerable populations, and interfaith relations also occupy their respective agendas. However, their aims, philosophies, and organizational strategies diverge in a number of significant ways.

Kulanu was formed in 1994. Its purpose, according to the organization's website, is to "support isolated and emerging Jewish communities who wish to learn more about Judaism and (re-)connect with the wider Jewish community."[123] Unrecognized Jewish groups that make contact with Kulanu have the possibility of benefiting from donations of "educational materials, Jewish ritual objects and prayer books," and, occasionally, from the services of volunteers, teachers, and rabbis, whose travel to such overseas communities Kulanu facilitates.[124] Kulanu neither encourages nor discourages potential immigration to Israel. Rather, it focuses on strengthening the communities with which it works on their own turf. According to Rabbi Bonita Sussman, vice president of the organization, Kulanu hopes to create an "expanded Jewish Diaspora" for "a stronger Jewish future."[125] Sussman expresses the wish that new "pockets of Jews who will develop their own ways" will "add to the beautiful pastiche that makes up the Jewish people," and thereby "change the course of Jewish history."[126] All of the communities profiled in this book have extensive contacts with Kulanu.

Be'chol Lashon, founded in 2000 as an initiative of the earlier-cited Institute for Jewish and Community Research, strives to "build networks of global Jewish leaders, strengthen diverse Jewish communities around the world, educate Jews and the general public about Jewish diversity, and increase the Jewish population by encouraging those who would like to be part of the Jewish people."[127] Although Be'chol Lashon has worked to help emerging Jewish communities overseas (particularly among the Abayudaya in Uganda), its primary focus is on advocating for inclusiveness and educating about diversity in an American context, especially for "younger and unaffiliated Jews who want Judaism to reflect the global community in which they live."[128] The organization "seek[s] to overcome the significant organizational, cultural and ideological barriers to growth in the Jewish community" by debunking the idea that proactive conversion should be seen as taboo.[129]

Much of the impetus behind this central aspect of Be'chol Lashon's work stems from the legacy of Gary A. Tobin, founder of the Institute for Jewish and Community Research. In Tobin's groundbreaking treatise, *Opening the Gates: How Proactive Conversion Can Revitalize the Jewish Community*, he defines proactive conversion as the "open, positive, accessible, and joyful process of encouraging non-Jews to become Jews."[130] Tobin is careful to stipulate that encouraging potential converts does not mean actively proselytizing. Rather, it means that there should be a series of practical mechanisms in place to smooth the process of conversion for certain "target groups," such as "non-Jewish spouses of Jews; individuals with Jewish heritage; children of mixed marriages; individuals with no religion; [and] individuals dissatisfied with [their] current religion."[131]

Among Zionist or philo-Semitic Christian groups, the overwhelming tendency has been to support only those emerging Jewish communities with claims to Hebraic or Israelite lineage. There is therefore a clear demarcation among evangelicals between supporting communities whose members claim Lost Tribes status—an outlook that Allan Heaton Anderson calls a "particularly undiscerning approach to biblical prophecy relating to Israel"—and condoning the indiscriminate abandonment of Christianity by many recently Christianized peoples in the Global South who are simply disenchanted with their spiritual lot.[132] Since, for many Christians, the establishment of the state of Israel in 1948 is already one step toward fulfilling the prophecy of Jeremiah 23:3 regarding the coming of the Messiah ("I will gather the remnant of my flock out of all countries whither I have driven them"), it naturally follows that supporting the Ingathering of the Exiles would be undertaken unreservedly. Strictly Christian organizations involved in such initiatives include the Ensign Foundation and B'nei Ephraim International (no connection to the Children of Ephraim movement discussed in chapter 4). Organizations committed to these goals whose supporters are either Jewish or Christian include the United Israel World Union, the World Biblical Zionist Venture, iTribe.us, the Restoration of Israel, the International Fellowship of Christians and Jews, and *Kol Hator* (Hebrew: "Voice of the Turtledove").

Israel-based Jewish organizations committed to locating and facilitating the return of lost Jews around the world have sometimes worked alongside, and sometimes against, the directives of the Jewish Agency for Israel. Early examples of such associations include the Society for the Lost of Israel, the World Union for the Propagation of Judaism, and, most notably, *Amishav* (Hebrew: "My People Returns"), the original organization out of which Kulanu (formerly, Amishav USA) and Shavei Israel developed. Founded by Rabbi Eliyahu Avichail in 1975, Amishav welcomes *gerei tzedek* (proselytes by conviction), but its main purpose has been to facilitate the return to Israel of those who can provide "evidence" of descent from the Lost Tribes.

Unlike many in the religious community, Avichail (who died in 2015) did not believe that there are any potential descendants of the Lost Tribes in Africa. What takes the "form of Jewish practice" there is, in his words, "just a different style of circumcision." According to him, the true remnants of Israel are only to be found in the East, in places such as Afghanistan, Pakistan, India, China, Myanmar, and Japan. Throughout his life, Avichail was categorically opposed to the genetic testing of people who wish to verify their Jewish roots in that way, arguing that Jewishness cannot be established by hereditary signifiers, but rather "by the way people lead their li[ves] and by signs of cultural identity."[133]

Some established Jewish organizations have managed, at least for now, to sidestep the issue of emerging Jewish groups. For example, I know of emissaries from Chabad (an ultra-Orthodox, charismatic Jewish renewal movement) who encourage "wannabe Jews" to become Noahides, or "righteous Gentiles," instead of explaining to them what it takes to fully enter the Jewish fold. Noahides are non-Jews who embrace the seven laws that, according to the Talmud (*Sanhedrin* 56a), God gave to Adam and Eve in the Garden of Eden (Gen. 2:16) and then to Noah after the Flood (Gen. 9:4–6).

Most self-defining Jews from the developing world consider this approach a slight to their sincerity, since it assures neither acceptance nor assistance in the proper instruction of Jewish law. But the vast majority of ultra-Orthodox in the West seem concerned that advocating anything other than adherence to the Noahide Laws could be playing with Third World fire. Indeed, most devout followers of Mosaic monotheism do not relish the possibility of Torah-believing Jews in far-removed locales being an *or lagoyim* ("Light unto the Nations"), as per Isaiah 49:6.

In the grand scheme of things, such concerns may not matter much at all. Essentially, official recognition of one's Jewishness is subject to local and denominational criteria. What's more, in an increasingly interconnected digital age, the absence of proximity to one's coreligionists no longer poses a major problem. Communities can choose to self-define, seek out the information they need, and live as Jewishly as they like. No one needs permission to do this.

DEFINING "JEWISH": IMPOSSIBLE EPISTEMOLOGIES

A good Jewish mother who has read this far into the text may still insist on asking: "But are these people *really* Jewish?" A man whom I met at an academic conference, who identified himself as "a concerned member of the local Jewish community," demonstrated his incredulity somewhat differently by asking me, "Would you still call them Jews if they were flesh-eating cannibals?" While I do not wish to legitimize what I hope, at least in the second instance, is runaway hyperbole, let me offer here some final thoughts on why I think that the claims of Jewishness put forward by the groups profiled in this book should be taken seriously. Again, I wish to stress that this research approaches the topic of Jewishness inductively, in that it builds upon the data taken from these case studies to investigate the explanatory logic of claims of Jewish identity. It does not rely on the criteria of categorical or religiously assumed standards regarding how Jewishness should be presumed. Rather, it examines, without measurement or judgment, how the typology of each group may either conform to or go against existing intellectual perspectives on what constitutes Jewish identity in the modern world.

How to define "Jewish"? There is, of course, no one correct answer to this long-standing inquiry. That identity is fluid has become somewhat of a cliché. Nuanced, critical, and nondoctrinarian responses to such queries regarding "true" identity depend greatly upon the conceptual frameworks, cultural variables, and locational criteria associated with the people doing the defining. To borrow a metaphor from Isaiah (64:8), we are all clay in the hands of our potters. Jewish communities the world over have always been strongly identified with, and influenced by, the environments that surrounded them. Indeed, many Jews with whom readers of this book will be familiar—such as David Ben-Gurion, Connie Chung, Sammy Davis Jr., Alfred Dreyfus, Bob Dylan, Sigmund Freud, Heinrich Heine, Franz Kafka, Primo Levi, or Karl Marx—are frequently held up as examples of Jewish individuals who were influenced just as much by their local cultures as they were by any kind of common Jewish background. And yet, on the most essential level, there is something that all of the people listed above have in common: they self-identify (or have self-identified) as Jews. The same is undoubtedly true for earlier kinds of Jews (Hebrews, Israelites, and Judeans included as precursors, for the purposes of the example), like Abraham of Ur, King Solomon, Paul of Tarsus, Rabbi Akivah, Benjamin of Tudela, or Maimonides, all of whom would not find much in common with their modern Jewish compatriots mentioned above. After all, most senses of belonging are dictated by context.

If we consider attitudes toward Judaism as a part of the cultural cauldron in which individual and collective identities are formed (and therefore as the product of a certain historical sensibility), it seems logical that perceptions of Jewishness would differ from person to person, even if each person purports an allegiance, or possesses some connection, whether contested or not, to the Jewish people. These differences would be codetermined by several key environmental factors. These factors include geopolitical affiliation; degree of religious observance; attitudes regarding gender roles; and notions of ethnicity.

Any study purporting to probe the issues of ethnocultural diversity or notions of identity among Jews must take into consideration the accepted categories of what constitutes a Jew in the first place. In this study, I investigate Jewishness by means of three primary assumptions. The first is that the Jewish people can only be comprehended in terms of processes of transfer, adaptation, and reconfiguration, as opposed to any specific, fixed content. While many ideas surrounding Jewishness stem from the same common denominator, such associations may not be readily apparent, due to conflicting and divergent patterns.

The second assumption goes against the outdated thesis evidenced, for example, in the supposition of Yitzhak Baer that "Jewish history, from its earliest beginnings to our own day, constitutes an organic unit."[134] I dissent from such generalizing rhetoric and instead base my theoretical assumptions on current research in anthropology, sociology, and ethnography, according to which modern Jewry is made up of different and discordant groups, each of which "is characterized by a close approximation to the Gentile environment" in which its members reside.[135] The case studies of the new Jewish groups in question, presented in upcoming chapters, illustrate this approximation.

The third and most important assumption is that adherence to normative Jewish religion, especially in its conventional rabbinic iteration, is only one component of Jewishness, not its defining characteristic. This component must be examined in tandem with other components, in the context of their respective historical and environmental schemata. For even if we characterize Judaism as a religion with certain commonly held beliefs, there are still many stages in its religious development with very different emphases.[136] All of these stages of development project conflicting ideas about dietary laws, sin, marriage, theodicy, and so on. Moreover, besides the brief period of the Sanhedrin, there has never been any central religious authority in Judaism. Not to mention the utter pervasiveness of the secular Jewish character in the post-Enlightenment age, which is typified by what Raphael Patai calls "the absence of traditional religious inhibitions, or at least the kind of disregard for them which developed especially following the Jewish Enlightenment."[137]

For example, the medieval Jewish philosopher Maimonides's famous precept according to which a Jew must believe in God was a radical departure from rabbinic Judaism. The rabbis of the Talmud defined Jewishness biologically, based on matrilineality. Maimonides's precept appeared some six hundred years after the Talmudic criteria were established, quite late in the Jewish historical continuum (the twelfth century CE). Furthermore, it was greeted with considerable hostility by many of his compatriots—so much so, in fact, that Rabbi Jonah Gerondi (1200–1263) went so far as to ask the Franciscans and the Dominicans to burn Maimonides's books, on the grounds that he was a heretic. For the most part, historians understand Maimonides's assertion as having been influenced by the Nicene Creed, the dominant Christian profession of faith.[138] Today, though, Maimonides's precept is considered to be one of the unquestionable tenets of formal Jewish jurisprudence.

Jewishness is part of a complex hermeneutical process spanning a particular historical continuum. In this continuum, each person invested in Jewishness interprets elements differently based on his or her own particular subcultural praxis and individuality. Such a perspective might be explained by what Lawrence Rosen calls "a process of negotiation," in which cultural concepts are negotiable according to the terms in which they are conceived, rather than considered as intellectu-ally static ideas that maintain a fixed character across different historical and teleological continua.[139] This is why David Hartman, for his part, refers to Judaism as an "interpretive tradition" that often engenders exe-getical disagreements and results in games of discursive ping-pong.[140] Jewishness, then, is not a static signifier, but a spark that lights up dis-similar, contested meanings.

Following this line of thought, normative religion is only one com-ponent in the culture(s) of Judaism: e.g., Judaism is not a religion that has its own distinct culture, since the delineation of Judaism as a "reli-gion," as opposed to an ethical guide or nomocratic system, only dates to the modern era. Moreover, the different identiary groups that make up modern-day Jewry possess porous and ever-changing ideas about Juda-ism's religious functions. This supposition is similar to the argument of Mordecai M. Kaplan, founder of the school of Reconstructionist Juda-ism. According to Kaplan, Judaism is to be understood not as a religion, but as a series of evolving societies in which Jewish religion (usually) plays a major role—even if customs that had their genesis in religious functions have become an integral part of the modern secular psyche *without* having retained their original signification.[141] Els van Diggele puts it somewhat more lightly: "Judaism is a culture in which religion is only a part. This works out quite well because if you tell children today that Judaism is a religion, they want nothing to do with it."[142]

As Eliezer Ben-Rafael points out, the idea that Jews (as well as their culture and religion) share fragmented, yet somehow existential, associ-ations with one another possesses a parallel with Ludwig Wittgenstein's theory of "family resemblance."[143] According to this theory, many ideas stem from the same common denominator, although such associations may not be readily apparent, due to the conflicting and divergent pat-terns, both great and small, within the "family."[144] This theory might therefore explain why one of the most devout and influential of the twentieth century's Jews, Martin Buber, was unable to give a precise definition of what constituted a Jew, positing that the Jews simply resist any classification.[145] Even Freud himself, the Moses-bashing assimila-tionist, took a similar approach, stating that he could not help but feel connected to his Jewishness, due to "many dark emotional forces, all the more potent for being so hard to grasp in words, as well as the clear consciousness of an inner identity, the intimacy that comes from the same psychic structure."[146]

Regarding the treatment of Jewish cultural praxis, I am indebted in this study to one of the foundational texts in new Jewish historiography: Efraim Shmueli's *Shev'a tarbuyot yisrael* (*Seven Jewish Cultures*).[147] In that book, Shmueli proposes the idea that Jewish "unity" as such does not exist in either historical or ontological patterns; rather, it is a construct, a perceptual structure similar to Etienne Balibar's idea of "fictive ethnicity" or Benedict Anderson's notion of "imagined communities" as necessary for providing social cohesion in the modern-day nation-state.[148] In order to illustrate the differences among the above-mentioned patterns, Shmueli proposes that the span of Jewish existence be divided into seven historical phases, or systems, which he calls "cultures." He then categorizes the seven cultures in the history of the Jewish people as the following: Biblical culture; Talmudic culture; poetic-philosophic culture; mystical culture (and its offshoot, Chasidism); rabbinic culture; the culture of the Emancipation; and the national-Israeli culture.[149] The probable millions of people practicing some form of Judaism in the developing world may very well constitute an eighth "culture" in the next phase of this historical continuum.

When one considers in this fashion the history of Jewishness, it becomes clear that there is not one culturally uniform Jewish identity, religious or otherwise, which might be highlighted in any way other than by the reliance upon (certain) Hebrew Scriptures as symbolic and/or pragmatic points of reference—and even that, in an age of secularism, is no longer a given. These factors are particularly relevant for a study of differing Jewish subcultures because, as Shmueli notes, "In each culture a certain set of experiences had a decisive impact upon the imagery and conduct which became unique to that particular culture."[150]

The slippery nature of Jewish identity in the post-Enlightenment era has endowed the modern individual with unprecedented freedom, and has thereby fractured long-held notions of uniform normativity. These notions are hardly unimpeachable in and of themselves, because of the flexible nature of the conceptual frameworks in which they were formed. As Leon S. Yudkin observes, the post-Enlightenment position of the Jew "was no longer a permanent datum within a rigidly patterned . . . culture. Henceforth, he was to be a Jew (to whatever extent) and something else too, whether national or international, unitarily cultural or cross-cultural."[151] If Jewish identity has always been a construct, then the fragmentation of identity in the modern world has only made this construct all the more pronounced. From that perspective, I am in full accord with Dan Miron's theory, according to which "one of the inherent and most significant characteristics of Jewish history in modern times is that it produced no one Jewish culture but many variants of possible Jewish cultures or sub-cultures."[152]

Where does that leave us? If we assume that the Jews are not a specific race, ethnicity, or religious group, then what are they? I am inclined to agree with the supposition of Aviv and Shneer regarding the best way to define "Jewish" in the modern world. According to Aviv and Shneer, the idea of "'the Jewish people' means not that all Jews are one but, rather, that all Jews share one thing and one thing alone—they identify as Jews, whatever that may mean."[153] To my mind, their laudable approach, devoid of doctrinarianism or biased moral stringency, offers us an appropriate methodological means for probing the substrata of Jewish identity—including those of emerging or heretofore unrecognized Jewish communities—in the modern sociocultural, intellectual, and geopolitical context of our increasingly globalized world. Its genius, like many out-of-the-box concepts, lies in its resistance to binaries and in its embrace of that most inescapable quality of the human experience: ambiguity.

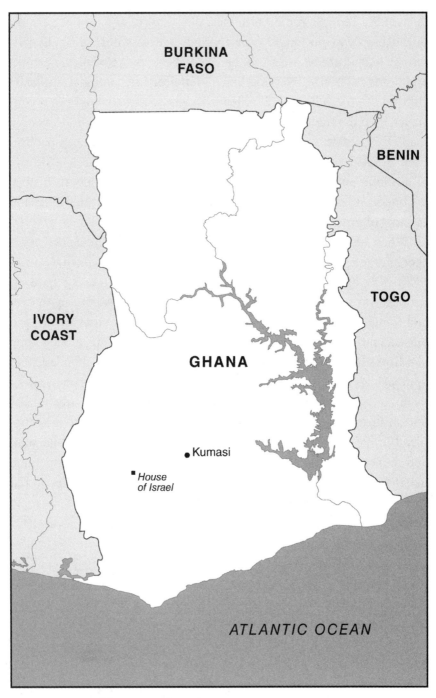

BURKINA
FASO

BENIN

IVORY
COAST

TOGO

GHANA

• Kumasi

■ *House
of Israel*

ATLANTIC OCEAN

MAP 2. Location of the House of Israel
community, Ghana

Structuralizing Nostalgia in Akanland

2

The "House of Israel" of Ghana

As the book's first systematic presentation and analysis of a neo-Jewish case study, this chapter focuses on a region and ethnic group that had, prior to the genesis of the contemporary "House of Israel" community, been long suspected of having Hebraic origins. The reader will recall that, as indicated in "Edward's" anecdotal depictions of his Judaizing neighbors, even many Sefwi who do not belong to the current practicing Jewish community in Ghana still show great esteem for its efforts and activities. This is because they find an inherent logic in its claim that the traditions of the Akan—the largest ethnic group in Ghana and the Ivory Coast—are ultimately of Hebraic provenance.[1] Moreover, since "glocalized" religious movements in Ghana (which combine elements of Judeo-Christian theology with the preservation of indigenous moral norms and codes) have become so widespread, one more syncretistic amalgamation of the global and the local does not seem to pose a threat to the existing multidenominational mélange.

On the one hand, then, this particular group of self-declared Jewish adherents is part of the much larger mix of philo-Semitic, prophetic, and millennial movements that have sprung up alongside sites of conventional Christian practice in Ghana, many of which privilege a kind of Old Testamentism. On the other, it is part of a growing web of, for lack of a better term, "traditionalists," who are clamoring for what Kofi Appiah-Kubi has called a "revaluation" of identity in Ghanaian and, in particular, Akan society.[2] In Appiah-Kubi's estimation, these traditionalists are involved in "a desperate search for identity, an identity that has [its] roots in tradition," while simultaneously attempting to "capture the capacity and the right to practice the full arc of Akan culture," which, according to him, "is considered more satisfying than Western patterns."[3] This "revaluation," then, is both a response and an addendum to the introduction of colonial belief systems. But it also reflects a general, collective malaise over what Paul A. Silverstein refers to as the loss of "cultural integrity," which seems to have been "uprooted by the conditions of post-colonial modernity."[4] Seen in this way, adopting Jewishness as a religious or ethnocultural marker of identity is but one of many possible reactions to the fragmentation of *Akanman* (the nation of the Akans). Other reactions, some competing and some not, are explored over the course of this chapter.

The realization that there are multiple ways of culturally enmeshing oneself in the spirit of the Hebrew Scriptures, without ever taking on the yoke of normative Judaism, struck me smartly across the face over the course of a phone conversation that I had with the former leader of the House of Israel community during my fieldwork in Ghana. David Ahenkorah, the former leader, had been voted out of the House of Israel community in the Western Region's town of New Adiembra in 2008, apparently for "undemocratic" behavior. Some of the congregation had left with him.

I had heard from a former neighbor of his in Sefwi Wiawso, the larger town on whose outskirts New Adiembra lies, and where most of the Jewish community members reside, that David was now a member of the Black Hebrews. Also known as the African Hebrew Israelites of Jerusalem, the Black Hebrews, founded by Ben Ammi Carter as an African-American separatist movement in Chicago in 1966, have been active in Ghana since the turn of the last century.[5] Their successes in attracting those in official governmental bodies as well as the general public at large have been many. Part of their positive image has been due to publicity generated by organizations such as the African Hebrew Development Agency. A continent-wide organization, active notably in Liberia and Kenya, it has existed in Ghana since 1995. According to its mission statement, the agency "specializes in providing technical assistance, training, and consultancy in essential areas of human development and capacity building such as health, agriculture, rural development, environmental maintenance and related fields."[6] The Black Hebrews, whose international base lies in Dimona, Israel, have one such training center in Sefwi Ahwia, a settlement neighboring Sefwi Wiaswo and New Adiembra. Unfortunately, despite my numerous attempts to make contact with representatives from the group, they were not, as my informants in Sefwi Ahwia told me, willing to meet with a "white foreigner" like me. One person suggested to me that their reluctance to meet may have stemmed from the fact that some of their training centers were known to be places of refuge for "fugitives from the law." I was never able to corroborate this allegation.

That David had joined the group intrigued me. For several years prior to my visit to Ghana, I had been reading many accounts given by David about the ritual activities of the House of Israel, with particular emphasis placed on how such activities were linked to the ancient cultural and religious heritage of the Akan. Consequently, I was eager to hear about the reasons behind David's move to a competing spiritual interest group that also had as its focus the replication and resurrection of Old Testament–style practices.

To that end, I asked some of my contacts in the House of Israel community if they would be able to connect me with David. They were hesitant to do so, given the level of intracommunal strife brought about by his departure. Understanding their concerns, and not wanting to make anyone uncomfortable, I decided to wander around town by myself to see if anyone outside of the Jewish community might have his contact information. Sure enough, the owner of a photography shop whom I approached (I knew that David had once worked as a photographer) happened to be David's nephew, and the young man gave me the former leader's cell phone number. During a quiet moment, I called.

When David picked up, I explained to him that I was an American-Israeli researcher working on the subject of Ghanaian Jews, and that I had gotten his phone number from his nephew. I told him that I was currently staying in Sefwi Wiawso, and inquired as to whether he would be open to meeting with me. David said no, that unfortunately he was in Cape Coast, the site of one of the Black Hebrews' main centers in Ghana. I then asked if I might interview him over the phone about his perspectives on the Hebraic origins of the Akan, and also about why he left the Jewish community. I added that, since he had been a close acquaintance of the original founder of the House of Israel movement, and was therefore a part of the Judaizing group long before they were even aware of the existence of coreligionists on other continents, his views on the progression of the community over the years were of great interest to me. He agreed to talk to me for a few minutes.

David began with a correction. He was not an acquaintance of the founder, as had been widely reported in the international Jewish press. *He* was the founder. His journey to Judaism had started, he said, when he and a small group of friends decided to meet regularly to read the Bible. Very quickly, they noticed odd parallels between precolonial Sefwi cultural practices and those practices described in the Old Testament. Some members insisted that they must be descended from a Lost Tribe. Others maintained that their presence in Ghana could have come about after having left the Holy Land at a much earlier stage. While the precise details were muddled due to the passage of time, all of them believed that they had finally found a record of how their forefathers' lifestyles had been circumscribed.

Up until this part of the conversation, our interaction had been pleasant. Then, little by little, David's tone began to change, and his voice got louder. He apologized for sounding angry, but emphasized that what he was about to recount to me was greatly upsetting to him. Everything in the community had been going fine, David said, until they made the mistake of inquiring about other "lost Hebrews" at the Ministry of the Interior in Accra. The ministry, unsure of what to do, had sent them to the Israeli embassy in the Ivory Coast, since Ghana did not have diplomatic relations with Israel at the time. The staff at the embassy asked the Ghanaians to compose a general query letter, which would then be forwarded to the "appropriate address."[7] Inexplicably, this letter found its way to the Tifereth Israel synagogue in Des Moines, Iowa. From that point on, contacts with overseas Jews snowballed. According to David, this marked the beginning of the end for the pure return to roots in Sefwi Wiawso. Curious Americans started coming, he said, and finished by ruining everything.

"I am not angry at you personally," David assured me, "but you have to understand how we felt. Foreigners wanted to snap their photos. They asked to take our statements. But they were not of our people!" I asked David what he meant by "of our people." They were, he explained, not Jews at all, but "CIA spies" whose mission it had been to drive a wedge between him and his congregants. And it had, he lamented, worked. "But why would they want to do that?" I asked. "Because, just like the colonialists, they want to hide our true culture," David explained. "Do you not understand?" I confessed that I didn't, and asked if he might elaborate.

"The behavior of the people in Sefwi Wiawso shows that they are not real Jews," David clarified. "But it doesn't matter. I want nothing [to do] with them. I am now affiliated with the true Israel." I asked if the "true Israel" meant the Black Hebrews. "Yes," he confirmed. "Exactly. They follow the laws of our ancestors." "But," I said, "the founders of the Black Hebrew movement in Ghana are Americans, and their association was started as part of a black nationalist movement in Chicago. Are they not CIA spies, as well?" David laughed, and his tone mellowed considerably. "Of course they are not spies," he chided me. *They are black!"*

The conversation with David underscores three key components in the discussion surrounding the rationale of Old Testament–oriented movements in Ghana. First, it shows that the initial motivations for this particular religious group were, as with many similar such groups, focused on the recovery of solely indigenous knowledge. That is to say, they only sought out other lost Hebrews who would have been living in their general geographical vicinity, and who would therefore have been, presumably, of a similar seed and creed. Moreover, they did so out of mere curiosity, and only after their movement had been founded; there was no need to reach out for instructional or infrastructural support. Clearly, the possibility that the members of the House of Israel might be able to retrieve other, as-of-yet undiscovered details concerning which parts of their tradition had been lost and corrupted through the sands of time was an intriguing one. And yet, the concern about retrieving such information outside of biblical or local sources of knowledge was only negligible. By connecting with other affiliated groups, they would simply be helping others to rediscover the same lost heritage to which, paradoxically, the colonizers' Holy Book had directed them.

Second, the conversation with the former leader of the House of Israel demonstrates that, at least for David, the compelling justification for affiliating oneself with either a Judaizing or Black Hebrew movement has to do with the adoption of a lifestyle based on Old Testament, rather than on New Testament, practices and worldview. The former represents a return to tradition, presumed to complement and coincide with indigenous forms of knowledge, while the latter signals the move away from it. What's more, the former's dominant narrative of an oppressed but chosen people guiding the world by example rings truer, for some, than the latter's narrative devoted to reconciliation, acceptance, and submission.

Third, and most important, both aforementioned movements were marked by a total absence of white people—until, that is, white Jews from America began to influence the spiritual and political mores of the House of Israel in a way that, by its very definition, the Black Hebrew movement was largely immune to. The introduction of Westerners thus complicated the anticolonial attraction of the neo-Jewish movement. After all, if racial difference was a defining characteristic of Hebraic provenance, then what to make of supposed brethren whose European physiognomy indicated an origin from the same continent that had enslaved Africa?

The trajectory of the House of Israel as an indigenous movement mirrors the development of many other syncretistic methods of worship popularized in Ghana in the last half-century. Almost all of these have in common, among other elements, the notion of Hebraic, Israelite, or Jewish provenance. What is unique about the self-defining Jews of Sefwi Wiawso is their formal incorporation of normative, postexilic Jewish practices into what began as a kind of "living tribal religion," to borrow the title phrase from Harold W. Turner's volume on that subject.[8] The term "tribal" is not used here in a deprecating fashion, but rather as a way to differentiate between universalist religions, whose credos (usually existing in written form) purport them to be for all peoples and all times, and ethnocentric, "self-contained" religious movements of specific micronations, whose adherents, in Turner's view, "feel they belong together through sharing a common culture and set of values, a common territory and social organization, and probably a common language."[9]

CONTEXTUALIZING THE MILIEU

The Republic of Ghana is a developing West African nation located in the Gulf of Guinea. It shares borders with Burkina Faso to the north; with the Ivory Coast to the west; and with Togo to the east. The area of modern-day Ghana was the site of the first European trade outpost in Sub-Saharan Africa, used for both gold and slaves. Formerly the British colony of the Gold Coast (1867–1957), Ghana became the first African territory to achieve independence from a European colonial power. Its first president, Kwame Nkrumah, was a founding member of the Organization of African Unity and one of the most vocal proponents of Pan-Africanism. Even today, with many disappointments over its legacy in the realm of African solidarity, Ghana's attempt to foment unity on the continent remains a fixed motif in the annals of the decolonization movement.

Ghana has also been hailed as a beacon of intercommunal stability, given its successes in dealing with the challenges of culturally heterogeneous demographics (over one hundred major ethnic groups exist in the country). Its democratic record, while not perfect, is among the best in an intensely troubled neighborhood, especially since major multiparty reforms were carried out in 1992. United States president Barack Obama reinforced this perception when he chose Ghana as the only Sub-Saharan African country to visit during his first term in office. During that 2009 visit—which, it should be noted, was only for a day-long stopover—Obama said in a speech to the Ghanaian Parliament: "Here in Ghana, you show us a face of Africa that is too often overlooked by a world that sees only tragedy or a need for charity. The people of Ghana have worked hard to put democracy on a firmer footing, with repeated peaceful transfers of power even in the wake of closely contested elections."[10] Political machinations notwithstanding, Obama's statements pretty much hit the mark.

The country is religiously diverse, with 71.2 percent of the population professing Christians; 17.6 percent, Muslims; 5.2 percent, followers of traditional religions; and 5.2 percent, unaffiliated.[11] Political power-sharing among Christians and Muslims is so much the norm in Ghana that even to speak of it seems odd. When asked about the eventual possibility of a Muslim being elected as president, former president John Agyekum Kufuor angrily exclaimed: "I don't know how it could get into anybody's mind to say that a Muslim could not be the President of Ghana. It's a democracy; it's a secular nation which practices freedom of religion, perhaps we may even have a president who is not religious at all."[12] Although all of Ghana's presidents to date have been Christian, the Ghanaian president in office as of this writing, John Dramani Mahama, comes from a family of mixed Muslim-Christian parentage. Currently a practicing Christian in the Assemblies of God Fellowship, he has repeatedly prayed at mosques with Muslims during Islamic holidays and festivals during his term in office.

The neo-Jewish community of Sefwi Wiawso, which does not appear in any government census on religious demography, is made up entirely of individuals belonging to the Bia-speaking Sefwi (alternately romanized in many sources as Sehwi, Sahwi, or Segwi) subgroup of the Akan people. Inhabiting the northern districts of Anhwiaso, Bekwai, and Wiawso in the area of Ghana's Western Region, as well as in several scattered locations in the far eastern areas of the southern Ivory Coast that straddle Ghana's western border, the Sefwi are related to the Anyi and Baoulé peoples who reside on both sides of the frontier. As an ethnic group that, like the Jews, "spent most of its [recorded] history dominated by neighboring powers," the Sefwi's origins are obscure.[13] It is not known precisely when, or from where, they migrated to their present locations.[14] Prior to the seventeenth century, the areas in which they now reside were ruled by the Aowin tribe, another subgroup of the Akan, whose non-Hebraic heritage narratives suggest origins in ancient Egypt. It is estimated that the Sefwi lived under Aowin rule between approximately 1500–1700 CE.

What is known about the Sefwi is that, by the early eighteenth century, they were powerful enough to challenge Aowin dominance, to such an extent that they invaded the neighboring kingdom of the Ashanti (sometimes romanized as Asante or Ashantee), the largest subgroup of the Akan nation.[15] Eventually, the Ashanti staged revenge attacks and forcibly incorporated the Sefwi into their kingdom, beginning the process of heterogenizing the area's population. Kwame Yeboah Daaku, a scholar from the Institute of African Studies at the University of Ghana who, under the sponsorship of UNESCO, carried out the most extensive oral history project to date among the Sefwi, has noted the long-standing assimilation of peoples and clans in the three Sefwi states. Their territory, writes Daaku, "has served as a centre of refuge for people escaping from the political centralization policies of their neighbours to the north and east."[16] Daaku also posits that, as far back as the period of the Aowin rulers, there was an "open door policy" in effect in the area in order to increase demographic numbers—an attractive policy, no doubt, given the region's abundance of cocoa, timber, and gold.[17] According to Eva Meyerowitz, the founder of the current settlement of Sefwi Wiawso was "an Ashanti chief of the Ayoko clan who was awarded lands in return for services given in the war."[18]

Traditionally, the three Sefwi districts have been largely uniform, religiously and culturally speaking. The Sobore River is the common patron deity, a tutelary protector and grantor of fertility. All districts have an annual yam festival common to other Akan subgroups: the celebration of firstfruits, known as the *Alluolie*. All Sefwi, like other Akan peoples, are organized into *abusua*, matrilineal family units. In such units, it is believed that the community line is transmitted through *mogya* (blood) to the child through the mother, while the *ntoro* (spirit) is transmitted through the father.[19] The reader will note that the last two religiocultural components correspond roughly to ordinations regarding the Jewish Passover, also a harvest festival (see Exod. 11:4–7, 12:1–50, 13:1–9; Lev. 23:5; Numb. 9:1–5; Deut. 16:12), and to the postexilic method of establishing Jewish heredity through the mother. (The latter custom, however, does not support the claim of a pre-exilic link to the Jewish people.)

These components, along with similar beliefs and practices common to most of the Akan subgroups, have often been cited as evidence that the progenitors of the Sefwi were originally Hebrews or Israelites. The Ashanti, for example, have long been associated with such an ancestry, although there has never been an organized Judaizing movement among that subgroup; such observations have come mostly from colonial-era sources. But proponents of the Sefwi assertion of a biblical pedigree often draw on the associations with the Akan nation in general, and with the Ashanti in particular, to buttress their arguments.

For instance, frequently mentioned commonalities and parallels between Ashanti and Jewish customs include the belief in a supreme being, Onyame, the Creator-God who is said to have been born on a Saturday. Individuals are not allowed to beseech him directly, but should worship him by way of a Sabbath corresponding to the day of the week on which he was born. British captain Robert Sutherland Rattray, who was an assistant district commander in the Ashanti region and an early ethnographer of their nation from 1911 to 1930, surmises with regard to Onyame: "I am convinced that the conception, in the Ashanti mind, of a Supreme Being, has nothing whatever to do with missionary influence, nor is it to be ascribed to contact with Christians or even, I believe, with Mohammadeans."[20] Onyame, Rattray thus concludes, "is the Jehovah of the Israelites."[21]

Joseph J. Williams, a Catholic friar, relies heavily on the work of Rattray in his *Hebrewisms of West Africa* (1930). He also draws on a much earlier work by the explorer Thomas Edward Bowdich, *An Essay on the Superstitions, Customs and Arts Common to the Ancient Egyptians, Abyssinians, and Ashantees* (1821), which claims that the Ashanti originally hailed from Egypt.[22] *Hebrewisms of West Africa* is focused mainly on descendants of "Gold Coast Negros" in Jamaica, with whom the author spent five years.[23] Like Rattray, Williams supposes that Onyame equals Jehovah by deducing that "we have in Ashanti exactly that 'mixed religion' which we find among the Israelites of old. They worshipped Jehovah, but they worshipped other Gods as well."[24] By "mixed religion," Williams means that, in the Ashanti pantheon, there are, in addition to Onyame, numerous *abosom* (intermediary deities), as well as spirits and ancestors.[25] In the Ashanti belief system, Onyame also has a wife, Asase Ya, who is a fertility goddess of the earth. Pointing out other parallel customs such as marriage rites, food and burial taboos, circumcision, and menstrual seclusion, Williams posits that "somewhere in the dim past, a wave, or more probably a series of waves, of Hebraic influence swept over Negro Africa, leaving unmistakable traces among the various tribes, where they have endured even to the present day."[26] Williams reached these conclusions apparently without ever setting foot in West Africa.

Popular South African travel journalist Lawrence Green concurs with these hypotheses. Green maintains that indigenous West African peoples who display a corrupted version of the Hebraic legacy must have intermingled with waves of Jewish travelers in West Africa. Green posits that "many [African] tribes absorbed them and some of their Jewish customs may be traced in strange disguise to this day."[27] Despite Green's certainty, he notes that there will not likely ever be any definitive evidence of the possible intermixing between Jewish migrants and native West African inhabitants, because these traces, according to Green, were "swallowed up" by the sands of time.[28]

While none of the self-defining Jews from Sefwi Wiawso whom I met had ever heard of Rattray, Williams, or Green—the most popular proponents in the West of such ideas—the same practices upon which these writers seized as proof phenomena have long been singled out, among native populations, as the most prevalent of the supposed connections to ancient Israel. For instance, in addition to the beliefs and customs already mentioned, other supposed parallels with Jewish practice include: the reluctance to petition God personally, as opposed to collectively (common to almost all Jewish denominations, save the Hasidic Breslov sect); the mandate for New Moon observances; and specific ritual obligations for mourning. Also worthy of note is the linguistic resemblance between the second part of the name of the aforementioned earth goddess (Ya) and the Hebrew construct *Yah*, which is an abbreviated form of the name of God in the Hebrew Bible. Other similarities are discussed later in this chapter.

Is there a verifiable historical record of Jews in precolonial Ghana? Unfortunately, no detailed written sources exist. Similarities, however compelling, do not constitute proof. The "dim past" mentioned by Williams is indeed obscure enough that we will most likely never know the precise origins of the Akan subgroups. Nonetheless, there are a number of plausible theories as to how these groups arrived to their present locations and acquired their specific customs, beliefs, and mores. Some theories touch on possible Jewish links, while others do not.

As early as the Middle Ages, Saharan Jews and other peoples fleeing the Almoravid conquests (which finally brought down the Ghana Empire about 1075 CE) left traces in the areas of present-day southern Morocco, Mauritania, Senegal, Gambia, and Mali.[29] According to Charles Monteil, substantial numbers of black Africans, primarily blacksmiths and *griots* (traveling storytellers), converted to Judaism in the wake of these migrations.[30] Whether or not any Jews actually penetrated as far south as modern Ghana remains undocumented. Similarly, while there are viable historical records indicating that, in the sixteenth and seventeenth centuries, Portuguese Jews journeyed by sea to Senegambia, Guinea, and Cape Verde, no documentation exists as to their possible presence in Ghana.[31] In short, the written record is anecdotal at best.

Oral histories pointing to the existence of Jews in Ghana are similarly vague. Among Akan subgroups, the only reference to such a history occurs rather late, in 1935, upon the reinstallation of the position of the *Asantehene* (absolute monarch of the Ashanti), which had been forcibly discontinued by the British in 1902. In a note regarding a chapter from his compilation of Ashanti oral history, "The First Inhabitants of the Gold Coast," the fourteenth Asantehene, Osei Agyeman Prempeh II, proclaims: "I know it truly to be fact that in the ancient past Ashanti people lived by Jerusalem and moved little by little . . . to here."[32] Writing of the monarch's motivation for emphasizing his people's presumed Israelite origins, Tudor Parfitt has posited that Prempeh II, whose reign lasted from 1931 to 1970, was attempting to underline "his view that the Ashanti elite was distinct from and superior to the people it ruled."[33] Parfitt reasons that the Asantehene, as a Christianized Ashanti serving as a figurehead for the British, must have thought that "there could be no better way of legitimizing his rule and his right to rule than linking himself and the elite from which he sprang to the chief actors in the sagas of Western sacred history."[34] With respect to this inclination of the Asantehene, T. C. McCaskie has pointed out that, in a later heritage manuscript from the 1940s, also an assemblage of oral histories edited by the monarch, the privileged origins of the Akan play a prominent role, and that "the Hebrew connection continues to have an abiding presence in certain versions of Asante tradition."[35]

While the House of Israel community claims that Sefwi heritage narratives indicate a precolonial Jewish presence, there is no evidence that such narratives contained references to Jews prior to the 1990s. For example, the major oral history compilation project among the Sefwi referred to earlier, which was carried out by Daaku in 1970, indicates no traces of anything that might be even remotely connected to

Jewish history or custom, besides the emphasis on a Saturday Sabbath. In fact, in Daaku's anthology, the *Omanhene* (traditional district king) of Anhwiaso, Nana Kofi Adjai, is cited as vehemently contradicting the earlier account of a migration through Egypt, insisting: "The people of Anhwiaso have not migrated from elsewhere. They have never been a subject people. We have never, never served any people—nor another stool [throne]."[36]

My own research into early colonial records, newspaper reports, and transcriptions of Akan (and, in particular, Sefwi) heritage narratives at the National Archives of Ghana, in Accra, yielded similarly inconclusive results. Most records were simply what anthropologists call "cumulative accounts"—mainly, lists of royal lineages. Stefano Boni, who is the foremost living expert on the history of the Sefwi, confirmed this notable absence of Jewish tropes. "I have done research on oral traditions and Sefwi pre-colonial history," he wrote to me, "but have found no mention of the presence of a Jewish community neither in stool histories I recorded personally nor in the secondary sources I came across."[37]

The questionable veracity of historical sources, as well as their relative paucity, does not help to paint a clearer picture of any supposed Hebraic or Israelite presence in Ghana. Neither do oral histories, whose apparent newness seems to point toward modern, (post)colonially influenced notions of chosenness. Where, then, might other answers as to the origins of such influences lie? Proceeding chronologically, we may examine the possibilities of two separate series of interaction, both of which might explain the presence of Jewish narrative tropes or customs prior to Ghana's entry into modernity. (Other contemporary influences are discussed later on in the chapter.) The first is interaction with the discourses of Islam, and the second, with the discourses of Christianity.

Meyerowitz's claim according to which "the Akan civilization is essentially pre-Arab North African in character" is somewhat of a generalization, although it points to the group's probable origins in the Saharan and/or Sahelian regions.[38] Southward migrations from this region, followed by mixing with the local populations of present-day Ghana, began around 1100 CE. Some oral traditions among the Ashanti speak of migrations from a city likely to be Timbuktu, along the Niger River, to Gonja, "the Timbuktu of the South," in the northern area of today's Ghana.[39] These traditions are likely conflating the arrival of the Guans (who moved southward after the fall of the Songhay Empire around the end of the sixteenth century, and after whom the country of Ghana takes its name) and the earlier penetration, previously mentioned, of the Islamicized Berber Almoravids into Ghana around the end of the eleventh century.

The broad consensus regarding the impact of Islam on premodern Ghana is that the commercial and political effects were great, given that Muslim merchants controlled most of the trade routes that linked Ghana to Northern Africa; and that these routes had been under mostly Islamic rule since the eighth century. Similarly, many Muslims lived in the Kingdom of Ghana, which extended into the southern parts of present-day Mali. This kingdom enlisted the Muslims' aid for governmental projects and guaranteed them separate living spaces, since their scientific contributions to the region were significant. The Andalusian historian Abu 'Ubayd 'Abd Allah ibn 'Abd al-'Aziz ibn Muhammad ibn Ayyub ibn 'Amr al-Bakri, for instance, wrote of "salaried imams and muezzins, as well as jurists and scholars" living in the territory under the protection of the king, who "led a praiseworthy life on account of his love of justice and friendship for the Muslims."[40] Religiously, however, the impact of Islam seems to have been slight. No mass conversions to that religion are recorded until around the fifteenth century, and they are confined to the northern areas of the territory. Consequently, it is difficult to conjecture to what extent, if any, Jewish customs or lore, filtered through the lens of Islamic practice, may have impacted the native populations of the Kingdom of Ghana in the premodern period.

Christianity reached Ghana after Islam did, beginning with the Portuguese in the fifteenth century. Roman Catholic monks from Portugal established their first mission school in 1529, in the area then known as the Portuguese Gold Coast. Subsequent efforts to Christianize the natives followed the same pattern: the Dutch, Swedish, Danish, and German missions established ecclesiastical footholds after each nation had formally laid claim to its own slice of the mineral-rich territory. These efforts, however, met with minimal achievement, due to a combination of poor organization and repeated fatal sicknesses on the part of the Europeans, as well as hostile resistance on the part of the indigenous inhabitants. According to Jones Darkwa Amanor, these missions had so little success that, "by the beginning of the nineteenth century, very little headway had been made in the evangelization of natives."[41]

The turning point came with the arrival of a Swiss Pietist mission, the Basel Evangelical Missionary Society, in 1828. Although its activities in the early years were nearly as troubled as those of its predecessors, by 1917 the mission had converted thirty thousand native inhabitants and built some 180 schools, where ten thousand students studied.[42] Other missionary success stories included the Wesleyan Methodists and the Anglican Society for the Propagation of the Gospel, which worked primarily in the coastal regions.

In the interior of Akanland, missionizing proved a more complicated task. The Ashanti, in particular, were as vociferous in their opposition to the founding of Christian missions as they had been to becoming a British protectorate. The first Methodist church in Kumasi, in the heart of Ashanti country, was not established until 1842; and the first Catholic church, not until 1910, fourteen years after the end of the fourth and final Anglo-Ashanti War. The peoples of the interior, unlike those on the coast, were largely indifferent to the promise that mission schools would help to equip their children with the tools necessary to participate in the colonial economy of what had become by then the British-administered Gold Coast. Heaping scorn on their obstinacy to adapt, one historian states that, while the coastal peoples were learning to work with the British colonial system, "they [the Ashanti] were still drumming and dancing Kete [an indigenous dance ensemble] in the forest."[43] Because of their steadfast adherence to traditional ways, the region's inhabitants were mostly illiterate even up until the beginning of the twentieth century. As a result, they were also ignorant of the gospels.

The Sefwi, even more physically isolated than the Ashanti, echoed this strong Akan resistance to change. The first government school was not built in Sefwi Wiawso until 1915, and this was done against the wishes of the Omanhene, who had also objected to the establishment of foreign religious associations in the area.[44] Until 1930, only one teacher at this school was a native of the region; the rest did not even speak Sefwi.[45] An Anglican bishop visiting the Sefwi districts in 1925 found the locale very inhospitable to the "good news" of the Christian religion, as he reported not meeting even one person who was interested in hearing about the gospels.[46] In fact, in the court records of Sefwi Wiaswo, the village in which the House of Israel community was founded, there are few mentions of any local converts to Christianity prior to the mid-1940s.[47]

In time, things began to change. By 1943, there were approximately twenty-six churches in the region. This can be attributed to the rapid increase in primary schools, which came to be seen, albeit grudgingly, as a necessary evil for procuring eventual employment.[48] Between 1929 and 1950, at the colonial government's initiative, a total of sixty-three schools were opened in the region, nearly all of them run by missionaries. In comparison with Islam, then, the spread of Christianity in the regions of Akanland came very late, indeed.

Given these considerations, it is highly unlikely that any of these early forms of institutionalized Christianity—which, as far as we know, did not contain any notably philo-Semitic dispositions—influenced the development of Judaism in the House of Israel community. However, it is worth pointing out that, since 1957, the year of Ghana's independence, many other Christian missions, especially those run by Adventists and Pentecostals, have set up shop in the Sefwi areas. Various African Independent Church movements have also become popular.

While precise numbers of adherents to specific religious denominations in Sefwi territory are hard to come by, a set of governmental statistics on religious affiliation in Ghana's Western Region (the population of which is 10.9 percent Sefwi) is telling. According to the survey, 81 percent of the population professes to be Christian; 8.5 percent, Muslim; followers of "traditional African religion," 1.5 percent; and those having no religion, 8.2 percent.[49] Of the Christian population, Pentecostals make up 26.1 percent; Protestants, 19.5 percent; Catholics, 19.4 percent; and "other Christian groups," 16.1 percent. Based on figures provided by the House of Israel community, there are approximately fifty "practicing" Jews among Sefwi Wiawso's 1,500 people. (There are 139,200 people in the entire Sefwi District.[50]) As mentioned, Ghanaian Jews do not appear on any official census.

Despite uniform declarations of formal affiliation to these various religions, traditional social norms (and to a certain extent, cosmological worldviews) still hold considerable sway among much of the self-professing Christian population of Akanland. As K. A. Busia has noted, even devout Ashanti Christians frequently "retain their own [i.e., indigenous] interpretation of the universe and the nature of man and society," despite outward appearances of Christian piety and deference to convention.[51] As Kwesi A. Dickson underlines, the same is also true for Akan-based philo-Semitic prophetic or millennial movements. With his tongue in his cheek, Dickson questions the "Hebrew Scripture fancy" among such ancestor-centered movements, remarking glibly that a "predilection for the Old Testament . . . must not be equated with a correct understanding of its meaning."[52]

The "predilection" among many such groups for adducing Old Testament propriety as a justification for maintaining certain local traditions is, dare I say, a rather "Western" way of legitimizing the recovery of an indigenous identity. In terms of postcolonial discourse, the performance of such legitimization essentially boils down to the colonized mimicking the perceived values of the colonizer, by appropriating an integral part of the colonizer's foundational text. Such mimicry, however, almost always results in a "blurred copy" of the original—one that, as Homi Bhabha reminds us, may be ideologically advantageous to the indigenous parties in question, but a far cry from any intended primary meaning or context.[53]

In the following sections, we shall see that the religious activities of the self-defining Jewish community of Sefwi Wiawso are also, in many ways, bound up with notions of recovery and customs of performed appropriation currently in vogue among other traditionalist movements in Ghana. The ancestor-oriented Old Testamentism of the House of Israel, which has slowly (and surprisingly) evolved into Western-style normative Judaism, is still presumed to complement and coincide with indigenous forms of knowledge. To what extent these stylized constructions are conscious or unconscious is beside the point.

Also beside the point, in my view, is any intimation that the recognition of such constructions takes anything away from the validity of the House of Israel's Jewishness. Indeed, most of its members are living much more Jewishly, ritually and religiously speaking, than many "authentic" secular Jews in the West, whose Jewishness is taken for granted day in and day out. The reader will observe that the Ghanaians' self-identification and spiritual commitment come at a great cost, both socially and materially. Since this is the first case study covered, allow me to press the point, again: the intellectual exercise of critically analyzing the discourse of this community—of examining the *how* and the *why* of their heritage narratives and notions of ethnoreligiosity, as opposed to focusing on a blasé (and Eurocentric) "true/untrue" dichotomy—should not in any way suggest that the construct of their Jewishness is illegitimate. On the contrary: "The proof of the pudding," as the expression goes, "is in the eating." The ways in which the Sefwi Jews partake of this proverbial pudding suggest that their Jewish roots are no less real to them than any other of their primary identifying characteristics.

LOST AND FOUND: COMMUNITY BEGINNINGS

Although stories about the community's beginnings vary slightly, it has been possible to reconstruct a fairly detailed description of how the founders of the House of Israel began their journey to normative Judaism. The account that follows represents the testimonies of several of the founding members. It also draws upon information supplied by current House of Israel members, some of whom were among the first to join the founders' initial group. Finally, it references versions of such testimonies already published in popular venues (websites, newspapers, etc.), as well as those recorded by both scholarly and amateur researchers. I have attempted to verify, to the best of my abilities, all conflicting accounts of the community's origins.

The story is as follows. In 1976 or 1977, a Sefwi man named Aaron Ahomtre Toakyirafa had a vision about the pedigree of his people. In this vision, God told him that the Sefwi were one of the Lost Tribes. Accounts diverge as to whether Aaron believed the Sefwi to be from the tribe of Dan or from another tribe. Aaron understood from this divine message that God wanted him to practice the religion of the Jews, a people about whom he had only vague notions.

Since Aaron was not a Christian—he had dabbled in both Islam and animism, according to most accounts—he was unsure of where to begin. At his mission school, he had been taught only select parts of the New Testament, as well as some of the Psalms. A friend recommended that he start with the Five Books of Moses, which Aaron began studying seriously. He would later claim, as have many among colonized micro-nations in Africa, that educational missionaries neglected to teach the Sefwi anything substantial from the Old Testament, fearing that it would lead to the rediscovery of the native peoples' privileged lineage.

Aaron was struck by the similarities that he noticed between the traditional customs of the Sefwi, which the colonial authorities had done their best to obliterate, and those of ancient Israel. Circumcision eight days after birth, burial and food taboos, the ritual slaughter of animals to be consumed, an annual harvest festival (of yams, in the Sefwi case), a Saturday Sabbath, and menstrual seclusion were points of commonality between the two traditions. He concluded that the Sefwi must be among those lost Israelite tribes that were scattered by the Assyrians. This narrative of exile, he thought, coincided with the Sefwi oral history according to which his forefathers had, approximately four hundred years earlier, migrated from Mali and the Ivory Coast before arriving in Ghana. Because they, too, were a group that had been forced to migrate repeatedly due to religious discrimination, Aaron reasoned that the relative isolation of Sefwi Wiawso must have been part of the underlying motivation for their ancestors to have chosen it as a safe place for permanent settlement.

At this time, Aaron's friend, Samuel Busampim, was also searching for the correct spiritual path in his life. Samuel was intrigued with Aaron's take on the links between Jewish and Sefwi history. Samuel invited another friend, David Ahenkorah—the same man who would later lead the community, and then leave it for the Black Hebrews—to listen to what Aaron had to say about this lost Sefwi religion. Both David and Samuel became convinced that Aaron was onto something big. David recalled the period thus:

> At the beginning I was not in the community. I was moving all around with Samuel Busampim. We tried to move with the Muslims, so we had conversations with them, heard of Islam, but what we are after is different, so we left. I found Christianity.

Their activities and belief was the same way as the Muslims do. They don't share our fate. They believe Jesus Christ is the one. It is not a pure religion. Same for Muslims, with Mohammad. If I join the group, it will never help my future or children. I decided to see about pagans, if they were good, but they also worshipped idols, deceiving people, so I avoided and did not practice. In my dreams I found the right religion to follow. I heard about Aaron Ahomtre and I decided to meet him. That day all he told me was of the Old Testament and whatever he said was of the same practice as our ancestors that had been abolished by people. I made my mind, Aaron's message was how I had to follow. The Old Testament pointed out that was the real religion. We moved onwards until he died in 1991.[54]

Several older people in the community who first witnessed Aaron preaching in Sefwi Wiawso told me that what he said had struck a chord with them. One person, echoing David's sentiments, related: "I realized that he was right, this was the way we had been looking for." Another man said that what Aaron explained to them about Hebraic customs reminded him of the practices of his parents and grandparents.

"They were Christians, but not really," this man said of his relatives. "They have gone to church and the [Christian] schools because of reasons of money. But in their hearts, they have the old tradition." Another veteran member of the movement, Kofi Kwartang, told me that the love of Israel and Jerusalem had been inculcated in Sefwi children of his generation by their parents and grandparents, but that the children did not really understand these places to be actual physical locations—they were just "in the sky somewhere." When his elders talked about going to Jerusalem, he understood it to be like "going upward."

Many Sefwi from both the Muslim and Christian communities, as well as those who practiced some form of traditional religion, decided to join Aaron's movement. One original member of the group, Nana Ahowi, explained to me that people just knew in their hearts that this Judaism was "already in them," because they believed "in one God, the God of Israel." Since Christianity had "three gods," the people finally realized that it must not be true. Ahowi summed up the enthusiasm for Aaron's movement by saying, "If you know your history, you won't get lost."

But not everyone was so charmed. Some local villagers decided to protest against this new religion. The dissenters beat those who self-identified as Jews and handed them over to the police. The Christians were especially incensed, David noted, because "they thought we had come to destroy their way of worshipping. The Christians condemned us by saying that Judaism had been abolished, and that we were trying to create confusion."[55] Fearing for their safety, the new group decided to move to the Ivory Coast, to the area from which their ancestors had migrated. However, the group encountered the same problems there with Christianized Sefwi Ivoirians who objected to their ideas. And so, after only a short period on the other side of the border, the members of Aaron's movement picked up and moved eastward, back to Ghana.

Fortunately, the Religious Bodies Law of 1989 had just been ratified, which included an important article stipulating freedom of religious practice for non-mainstream congregations. (The later 1992 Ghanaian Constitution would contain modified legislation that specified these freedoms in more detail.) For caution's sake, the group decided to make their home base just outside of Sefwi Wiawso, in the village of New Adiembra, which was somewhat removed from the area of their former hostile neighbors. In New Adiembra, they built a synagogue adjacent to the compound of Kofi Kwarteng. Aaron and David preached widely in Sefwi lands, hoping to bring people back to their precolonial customs by educating them about the Hebrew Bible and the "cultural genocide" inflicted by the Europeans. They made use of the widespread perception according to which Christianity would never have taken hold in Akanland, had everyone realized the lack of autonomy that would accompany it. Aaron and his followers insisted that the Europeans' imposition of an alien way of thought—Christianity—also masked the truth about the Sefwi as a special people chosen by God.

Aaron Ahomtre Toakyirafa died in 1991, and David Ahenkorah formally took over leadership of the movement in 1993. Although the precise dates are unclear, David's journey to inquire about other lost Hebrews at the Ministry of the Interior in Accra, and then at the Israeli embassy in the Ivory Coast, happened sometime in the mid-1990s.[56]

As mentioned earlier, the query letter that he and his coreligionists composed at the Israeli embassy somehow found its way to a synagogue in Des Moines, Iowa. In 1996, after the synagogue sent a representative to report on the goings-on in this new African community, word got around that Ghana—at the time, the African country probably considered the safest for foreign tourists, and one with many Jewish Peace Corps volunteers, to boot—was the site of a heretofore unknown Jewish community.

The community began to receive a flood of Jewish American visitors, most of whom were from the Reconstructionist and Reform movements, or from the liberal branches of the Conservative movement. Ahowi told me that they were "stunned" by these unexpected visits, calling the interaction with their "Israelite brothers and sisters" a "miracle." Among these visitors was Daniel Baiden, a naturalized American citizen of Ghanaian origin, who had formally converted to Judaism in the United States. Taking advantage of a few free days during a family visit to his native country, Baiden journeyed to the Western Region to meet with the Sefwi Jews.

Baiden's remarks about the Sabbath spent in New Adiembra, which were eventually widely disseminated in the American Jewish community, are particularly attention-grabbing. Baiden writes that many community members "stayed at the synagogue all day to make it easier for them to avoid such Sabbath prohibitions as watching television."[57] He also notes that the meal they shared "was cold because they do not cook on *Shabbat* [the Sabbath]," and that women and men maintained a physical separation in the improvised synagogue.[58]

Why should the observance of the aforementioned Sabbath customs not be taken as a self-evident step, which logically follows the volition to adhere to proper Old Testament–style Sabbath rites? The answer lies in the community's complete lack of a postexilic Jewish context—that is, in their total disconnect from the foundational Talmudic sources on which they could have drawn for clarifications regarding appropriate Sabbath procedures. Indeed, what is remarkable about these particular observances, which are followed by almost every observant Jewish community the world over, is that all three ritual procedures cited above are, in fact, only practiced as proper Sabbath protocol because they are specified as such by postbiblical explanatory addenda to the Sabbath laws. Possessing only the Hebrew Scriptures as a guidepost, the Ghanaian community would have had no knowledge about such homiletic methods of exegesis, which seek to disambiguate certain biblically mandated systems of conduct.

A series of explanations on this subject is perhaps in order. For nearly 1,500 years, organized Jewish communities around the globe have been able to rely upon the explanations given in the Talmud regarding the thirty-nine kinds of activity forbidden on the Sabbath (grinding, sorting, gathering, sowing, etc.), not to mention the endless records of later rabbinical debates regarding the finer points of the area under discussion. For instance, in addition to the three aforementioned procedures, the Ghanaians guessed that starting a car—which basically entails setting off a chain reaction in an internal combustion engine—would violate the sanctity of the Sabbath by constituting what the Bible (Exod. 20:9) calls "*malakhah*" (work). The Ghanaians, who could not have known the difference between what is known in Aramaic as *mitzvot deoraita* (commandments from the Torah) and *mitzvot derabbanan* (laws instituted by the rabbis) had to rely on gut instinct.

Mainly, they got it right. Community members had inferred, from the rather vague instructions in the Torah (Exod. 20:7–10 and 31:13–17; Deut. 5:11–14) regarding the Fourth Commandment, that the act of lighting a fire in order to cook food would constitute some kind of "work," hence the preference to eat their food cold on that day. By the same token, watching television (obviously a new Jewish problem, given its only recent invention) would violate the spirit of calm intrinsic to the day by willfully undertaking an activity antithetical to the peace of body and soul. Not to mention that hooking into a television signal or turning on electricity would also be akin to some kind of "work."

Similarly, on the issue of separating men and women in the synagogue, they reasoned that having the sexes separated during prayer time preserved the congregants' attention for God. This is in fact the same rationale for the practice given in the first major redaction of Jewish Oral Law, the *Mishnah* (*Middot* 2:5), which the Sefwi did not have access to or even knowledge of. Their careful consideration of how to best observe all components of the Sabbath was both a product of dedicated reflection

on the scriptural plane and a self-conscious re-enacting of the precolonial Sefwi practice (explained more fully below) of a Saturday "Free
Day" whose observance was mandatory, as in ancient Israel, upon pain
of death.

With regard to other forms of postbiblical practice, Baiden points
out that the miniature Torah scroll he brought with him, donated by
an American Jewish organization, came as a complete surprise to the
community. Previously, they had only been familiar with codex forms
of the Scriptures. Another item Baiden brought with him was a package
of modern prayer books, whose existence the community had also been
unaware of. Prior to this gift, the textual portion of their service consisted of, as I was told, "mostly read[ing] the Old Testament together."
Still another new element that Baiden introduced was a linguistic one.
Namely, he read out loud the weekly Torah portion in Hebrew, because
he "wanted them to experience an authentic Torah service emotionally,
even if they could not understand it," and because "every synagogue in
the world was reading the same Torah portion that same day."[59] With
these revelatory introductions, Baiden helped to plug the House of
Israel into the worldwide Jewish grid.

After similar such visits from overseas Jews, the nature of the House
of Israel movement changed considerably. In addition to the transformation of the community's Sabbath services, which now more or less
mimicked those of liberal Jewish communities in the United States, they
began to learn Hebrew and to arrange correspondence with American
rabbis on questions relating to proper ritual procedure. They acquired
Jewish ritual objects and prayer accessories from visitors and through
the post. With some reluctance, they decided to forego their custom
of slaughtering sheep for the Passover *seder* (traditional ritual feast),
as mandated by the Hebrew Scriptures (Exod. 12:1–14, 24–28; Numb.
9:1–3). David eventually yielded his insistence that the Sefwi "practice an
ancient form of Judaism that includes slaughtering," after learning that
no mainstream Jewish group has continued with this practice since the
Destruction of the Second Temple.[60] The American volunteers argued
that to perpetuate this observance would make the Ghanaian community heretical in the eyes of established Jewish groups overseas. Apparently also discontinued was the custom of widow inheritance (similar

to the Levirate marriage practice mandated in Deut. 25:5–6), although no one would give me details on precisely when the practice ceased. During the time of my visit, at least, there seemed to be recognition that this custom was taboo among Western Jews.

Significantly, they also stopped proselytizing among other Sefwi, once an American Jewish rabbi had impressed upon the leaders how antithetical such a practice was to postexilic, normative Jewish law. The cessation of proselytizing, however, did not mean that their neighbors stopped hearing about the House of Israel's activities. In fact, the presence of foreign visitors interested in the community—a veritable rarity in this part of rural Ghana—actually contributed to the community's legitimacy in the eyes of other residents. The foreigners, after all, were not from the former colonizing nation. And their presence was a significant boon to the economy. When Florence Gbolu, a young Ghanaian journalist who visited Sefwi Wiawso in 2004, asked the town's tribal chief how he felt about the new Jewish community, he told her: "We, the custodians of the land, see no problem [living] together with the Jewish [people] here in Sefwi Wiawso."[61] He also added that the Jews' beliefs and practices were, in many ways, the same as those of the traditional Sefwi.[62] No longer beaten, imprisoned, or driven away from their homes, the members of the movement that sought to educate Sefwi about their true origins now had official approval from the tribal chief of the area—a major improvement over the kind of treatment that the community had endured at the hands of its neighbors in the previous decades.

With regard to narratives surrounding Sefwi history and heritage, two new emphases were developing. One was on their provenance from the tribe of Dan, and the other, on their arrival to Ghana via a river called "Sabbaton." The reader will recall from chapter 1 that the tribe of Dan is, according to legend (and, per the historic ruling of Israeli chief Sephardic rabbi Ovadia Yosef), the same tribe to which the Jews of Ethiopia belong. The reader will also note that the name of the aforementioned river, Sabbaton, sounds very much like the Sambation, the mythic "Sabbath River" mentioned in chapter 1, which ceases to flow on the Sabbath, and beyond which, according to rabbinical sources, lie the Ten Lost Tribes of Israel. Although I asked many times for specific details about provenance from the tribe of Dan, no one could provide me with any particulars, save some members' claims that their ancestors must have migrated from Ethiopia and the Sudan through to West Africa. To what extent this assertion is a way of taking advantage of the successful recognition of the Ethiopian Jews is impossible to ascertain, just as it is impossible to determine if the name of the Ghanaian community—the House of Israel—was intended to mimic the name of the Ethiopian Jewish community.

With regard to the Sabbaton River, however, there was much to be said. For instance, Ahowi told me that, according to his grandfather's story, the Israelites came to Ghana "because of the war." Which war it was remains unspecified, but it was the Sabbaton River that led them on their long migration westward. When the Israelites got to the current Sefwi lands, they started calling the river "Sobore." He then pointed to Sefwi Wiawso on the hill in the distance, and said that the Israelites knew to stop there because the landscape "looked just like Jerusalem." One person accompanying us confirmed this resemblance. He had, he said, once seen a picture of the Holy City on a postcard. When I inquired from Ahowi as to whether or not the Sabbaton/Sobore River ever stops flowing, he thought about it for a moment, and then said, "It's not a big river." Apparently, he thought I was asking if the river ever dried out.

Another elder told me the same things about the river, but stressed, without my posing the question, that the river stopped flowing on Saturday. Other magical attributes were associated with the river, as well. In one battle, the elder said, the seven guns of the Sefwi had turned into seventy once they were deposited in the river. Because the river's magic was so strong, the warriors needed no bullets. Rather, they used marbles as ammunition to drive the Ashanti from the land. Another story he recounted told how, at one time, the king of Ashanti wanted to collect a tax on everyone crossing the river. The river, appearing in the form of a man, refused. "I came because of Jewish people, not for your taxes," the river said. Then, the Sefwi fought the Ashanti all the way up to the border with the Ivory Coast. Just to make sure I understood, the elder told me that the river "hates Ashantis."

Nana Tano Kumah, a member of the royal family living in New Adiembra, informed me that he did not know if the river ever stopped flowing, and insisted that such an attribute was of no importance. Instead, he wanted to impress upon me that the river demanded certain kinds of behavior from people. For example, no one should work or pump palm oil on the Saturday "Free Day." One should not shoot a pregnant monkey. When, in ancient times, the people still had "small gods" (idols), the river instructed the people not to worship them. When the river's commandments are followed, it protects the Sefwi whenever they fight another people. When wronged, the river retaliates.

To illustrate, Tano told me of the time when the British colonists came to conscript Ghanaians to fight on their side in World War II. The locals, concerned for their young men, went to consult the river, asking whether or not they should resist. The river said that it would protect the larger group of men, but that one person would have to die in battle. Tano confirmed that this was indeed what had happened. (In the absence of proper records, I was unable to verify this assertion.) When I asked Tano about possible symbolic associations between some of the figures he mentioned and famous characters in the Bible, he told me that he didn't know much about the Bible, besides what his grandfather had told him "about Sefwi history."

According to the standard community narrative, the Sefwi Jews no longer worship the river. I did not find any evidence to the contrary. Community elder Samuel, when asked about the river, did not make the connection to the mythical Sambation. According to Samuel, "When our ancestors were worshipping, they don't know the Bible. Our ancestors were practicing idolatry through the river, but they didn't know it was wrong."[63] Eager to learn more, I asked a local cab driver if he would take me to the river. He politely refused. He said that he knew the man in town who was its guardian, and that I should talk to him if I wished to have an audience. Other non-Jewish Sefwi with whom I consulted did not know of any connection between the river and a Jewish narrative.

Has the introduction of a foreign and long-term Jewish presence into Sefwi Wiawso—not to mention foreign Jewish visitors' expectations about "lost" Jews—contributed to these discursive shifts in the foundational heritage narratives? It seems quite likely, although it is impossible to provide direct evidence that this is so. Local residents claim to have learned a lot about the Lost Tribes from student rabbis sent by the

Reconstructionist Rabbinical College in Wyncote, Pennsylvania, who stayed with the community for several months at a time.[64] Apparently, in addition to normative Jewish history and practice, stories about the Lost Tribes in the world came up often as a conversation topic.

Contacts with overseas Jewish groups brought material changes to the House of Israel, as well. The community's relationship with Kulanu, the American Jewish outreach organization mentioned in chapter 1, has been particularly noteworthy. Through its website, Kulanu has helped the community to sell embroidered covers for *challah* (a braided bread eaten on the Sabbath) and *talitot* (prayer shawls) made from traditional Ghanaian *kente* (interwoven silk and cotton) cloth. These items are man- ufactured in a workshop with industrial-strength embroidery machines, which also were provided through a loan system by Kulanu. Profits from the sale of these goods, channeled through a bank account that representatives from Kulanu helped the Ghanaians to set up, have gone toward the expenses of constructing a guesthouse for foreign visitors, health insurance for community members, and other internal needs.

As David indicated to me in our phone conversation, not all of the changes to the community could have been foreseen. Neither were all of them welcome. Their exposure to overseas Jews and the transition to normative Judaism gave them an entity to belong to, but numerous things had to be (re-)learned. The whirlwind of foreign visitors and ideas, and the unexpected obligations that came with them, caused many rifts in the heart of the community. One such example had to do with the level of hospitality accorded to visitors. In local custom, one does not host modestly, and the expenditures incurred can be quite significant. In the same vein, one does not leave guests to wander around by themselves. Taking off work or school to accompany guests represents a noteworthy sacrifice. More often than not, foreign visitors to Sefwi Wiawso are not aware of the extent of such sacrifices made by community members, and do not offer to adequately compensate families for their troubles. Unsurprisingly, a simmering resentment developed among those community members who, by way of possess- ing more spacious living quarters, or whatever other circumstances, had frequently played host to foreign visitors. I was told repeatedly of this ever-present problem during my time in Ghana.

On the question of mores, there were also sharp divisions. Casual sexual activity between white visitors and black residents, even if both self-identified as Jewish, was not considered a simple pedestrian matter. Several such affairs were condemned with the utmost gravity. The reason for the community's anger was not that premarital sex—quite common in and of itself among young people in the Western Region—was condemnable. Neither was a potential romantic union between foreign Jewish guests and community members unwanted. In fact, community members had thought it beneficial to attempt to arrange marriages with foreign Jews, due to problems finding enough suitable single people in Sefwi lands who were willing to live Jewishly. Rather, their anger stemmed from the fear that careless liaisons would lead to biracial pregnancies out of wedlock. The children produced from these encounters would, in turn, leave the community disgraced in the eyes of their non-Jewish neighbors by the very foreigners who, oddly enough, had contributed to their movement's eventual acceptance in Sefwi Wiawso.

The most painful fissure in the community occurred in 2006, when David was forced out of the position of spiritual leader. This, too, stemmed directly from the changes brought about by the foreign Jewish presence among the Sefwi. David, who had accompanied Aaron, the founder, throughout his many travails, had assumed the position of leadership upon Aaron's death only after he experienced a prophetic vision of his own regarding his place in the community. Neither man was ever elected as leader. Both were religious autodidacts with no formal theological training. In response to a question about how religious leaders would be appointed in the future, David had said: "Thus far it has been [decided] by the grace of God."[65] But, in time, with foreign funds pouring in and new, liberal American ways of conceptualizing "community" disturbing previously held ideas about hierarchical propriety, members began to demand more of a say in decisions that affected them.

For those who benefited from the old system, the unprecedented expectation that community decisions regarding spiritual direction and the distributions of funds would be agreed upon "democratically" was, to put it mildly, a controversial one. In his role as spiritual leader, David was in a position of power somewhat analogous to that of a Sefwi tribal chief and/or fetish priest. Neither position has ever been beholden to the whims of the masses, let alone to junior members or to women. Nonetheless, enough of the members were dissatisfied with the system of governance that they demanded their voices be heard. Isaac, an elder of the community, has stressed that every person, no matter the age, should be able to participate in community decisions.[66] An American Jewish rabbinical student who lived with the Sefwi noted approvingly that this view was "a great example of the community's commitment to democracy."[67]

As we already know, David was voted out, with the official reason being for his "undemocratic" behavior. How many people left with him out of loyalty or disapproval of the direction of the House of Israel is unclear, but it may have been almost half of the congregation. Many of these former members whom I interviewed still consider themselves Jews, although they do not attend services or take part in any community activities. As of this writing, David's current association with the Black Hebrews is apparently a personal decision only. Unlike the situations of other Judaizing groups whose schisms resulted in the formations of separate communities, there is no alternative in Sefwi country to American-style, normative Jewish life. For those simply searching for precolonial roots, however, there is an entire series of alternatives closely related to Aaron Ahomtre Toakyirafa's original Old Testamentism, prior to its near-transformation by foreign elements. Those alternatives are discussed later in this chapter.

THE HOUSE OF ISRAEL, REDUX

Among community members and their nonpracticing Sefwi neighbors, current perceptions about Jewishness, Judaism, and Jews fluctuate wildly. The uniting thread among almost all of these perceptions seems to be the belief that Judaism is a kind of return-to-roots countermovement that decries the culturally devastating effects of institutionalized Christianity—a variation on the Sanskrit proverb according to which, "the enemy of my enemy is my friend." Taken together with the descriptions of previous and recent forms of religious practices in the community (and their supposed historical predecessors), these perceptions—a representative selection of which is given below—can aid us in our comprehension of the reigning motivations and metaphysical paradigms of the Ghanaian Jewish movement. Let us begin first with the perspectives of the community elders.

When asked what Judaism means to him, one senior member, J. K. Ahoing, said: "Being Jewish is knowing the difference between the Old Testament and the New Testament. The Old Testament is a long life. The New Testament is a short life."[68] Joseph Armah, one of the founding members, responded to the same query thus: "I feel free, I feel proud to be Jewish! In the name of God, I am very good. I have asserted myself from the Christian way."[69] Another older man, a recent member of the community, answered the question by taking a swipe at the idea of the Trinity: "Judaism is one people, one God." He then incorporated the genealogical trope into his justification, maintaining that "if you give everything in the world to me, I would never turn my back on Judaism, my grandfather's worship."[70] The same man claimed that not drinking alcohol was part of his grandfather's worship—a peculiar assertion that may perhaps be attributed to his confusing Judaism with Adventism.

Kofi, a veteran member mentioned earlier, echoed the previous interviewee's reservations about Christian hypostases: "Judaism brings me closer to my roots, closer to God, I am direct with God, there is no intermediary in the way."[71] Another elder explained that he is aware of the superior powers of the one God due to a dream that he had. In the dream, he heard a voice that asked him to choose between God, Satan, and Jesus. He chose God, and awoke realizing that he had made the right choice.[72] Several other elders told me that they "had accepted Moses [i.e., not Jesus] as [their] savior."

Another elder who offered his perspective on the essence of Jewishness is Nana Ahowi, cited earlier. Ahowi was part of Aaron's original group but left the House of Israel out of loyalty to David after the schism. Although he no longer attends any community events, he still considers himself Jewish. When I asked what Judaism meant to him, he claimed, "Judaism has kept me strong because I keep the commandments," and then repeated a phrase that I heard frequently during my time with the community: "Judaism is a soldier." Because of the strength Judaism gives him, he said, he can still take care of his own garden, even at his advanced age (he was eighty-two years old at the time). My practicing Sefwi companions, echoing what is usually seen as the "utilitarian" nature of Akan religions, agreed that this must be the reason for the old man's lasting physical vigor. These comments elucidate how symbolic performances of ethnohistorical identity in the Ghanaian community are inextricably linked to physical notions of what Vanessa L. Ochs calls "the materiality of lived-out beliefs and habits of conviction."[73]

In terms more biting than those employed by his compatriots, Ahowi expressed to me his reservations about Christianity. He began by saying that the axiom, "Love your neighbor as yourself" (Mark 12:31), has "kept African people down" and that "Christianity is just a lie." He then told me a story about how he had gone to see the last Ashanti king (at the time of my visit, the stool was empty), in order to demand that the Christian Sabbath be revoked and the Saturday Sabbath be reinstated. Ahowi warned the king that God would strike him down if he did not comply. The king refused, according to Ahowi; two weeks later, at the end of Ahowi's ultimatum, the king died of mysterious causes. Ahowi lamented the fact that things had changed so much since his childhood, when the Saturday Sabbath was still properly observed by everyone.

Younger people associated with the community have other concerns. Many of them are reluctant to "define" what Judaism means to them, since Sefwi Jewishness is the only identity that they have ever known. Two such younger members of the House of Israel, university students in their twenties, seemed, like David, more concerned about foreign Jews meddling in the community's internal affairs than about any problems posed by Christianity. Referring to American Jewish visitors to the community, one young man said, exasperated: "They want us to come meet them, so they can tell all their friends about Jews who are black. But what do we get from this? Nothing!" Then he added, quite astutely, "Many of them do not even keep the commandments!"

I wanted to know more about their feelings in regard to connections with Jews outside of Ghana. Did they desire these connections at all? Yes, they did want some kind of connection to the outside world, so that they could "share [their] knowledge"—that is, *Sefwi* knowledge—but not much more. They did not need anyone's money, they stressed, and loathed the idea that any Sefwi might be seen as some "poor African" looking for a handout, especially in the eyes of those who were less Jewishly observant than they.

Neither was I personally spared any of this criticism. In fact, although both of these young men had agreed to meet with me, their mood was combative from the beginning. They spent much of our meeting together, which took place at a shopping mall in Accra, trying to tell me what Judaism *really* is, despite the fact that I had introduced myself as a professor of Jewish Studies. No matter. Like most Americans, I was most likely "misinformed" about what Judaism is all about. Israelis, they claimed, were somewhat more intelligent than Americans, generally speaking, but were still poorly informed about Judaism.

Looking to break the ice, I mentioned that I was actually a dual citizen of both America and Israel. I then asked if, in light of this information, they might end up liking only half of me. No smiles. I then recounted the following anecdote about my coreligionist, Groucho Marx (no relation to Karl, I indicated), about whom they had never heard. I told them that Groucho was rumored to have said, in response to the objections of the anti-Semitic owner of a Gentiles-only country club, that his half-Jewish son should be allowed to go into the club's pool—but only up to his navel. I had to explain the joke's significance to the theme of being only partly tolerated. Again, no smiles. But all was not lost. Later, when I thanked the two for their time in an e-mail exchange, one of the students conceded that, despite my Americanness, I was a "nice, simple person."

So what was Judaism to them? Questions regarding "feelings" or "perspectives" about Judaism fell flat, so I asked a series of functional questions. The answers they gave about Jewish rites followed fairly standard Conservative (American) protocol, which is not surprising, given the influence of the ceremonially normative Jewish environment that had existed in the community ever since their childhoods. One functional question, however, elicited an interesting response. The question was: How did they worship while at university in Accra, away from their home village?

The query was taken with some offense. "You don't need a synagogue to be Jewish," one of the young men said, because "it's all in your heart." When I asked about the Mishnaic mandate of a *minyan* (prayer quorum) of at least ten male congregants for "sanctification" to take place (*Megillah* 4.8), the response was: "The Mishnah isn't a part of the Bible, so it's not part of Ghanaian Judaism." This, they said, was also the reason that Sefwi Jews have never felt compelled to follow the Talmudic practice of wearing *kippot* (skullcaps) (*Shabbat* 156b). When I mentioned that all the men whom I had seen at the synagogue in their home village had been wearing them, they conceded that most men did this in the house of worship in order to show penitence. But it was not really a commandment.

Everything considered, they admitted, Accra was indeed missing some kind of "learning center"—not a synagogue, per se—but a meeting place for people from "all of Ghana" who were interested to come learn about Judaism. "Many people are curious about Judaism," one of them said. "But they don't have any formal place for [learning about] it." I asked if they weren't worried about encouraging conversion, which the leaders of the House of Israel had been warned about by their American sponsors. The response: "If we know that people [will] convert easily, why should it be discouraged? Who says it's discouraged?"

For the sake of argument, I summarized the Talmudic passage (*Yevamot* 47a), which essentially dissuades potential converts from taking upon themselves the yoke of adherence to Jewish law. The passage reads: "Our Rabbis taught: If at the present time a man desires to become a proselyte, he is to be addressed as follows: 'What reason have you for desiring to become a proselyte; do you not know that Israel at the present time are persecuted and oppressed, despised, harassed and overcome by afflictions?'" The young men's response to the citation of this passage mirrored the earlier reaction to Talmudic directives: "Our ancestors did not write the Talmud." I asked if they were not concerned that encouraging conversion among people who did not understand what it means to be part of a worldwide Jewish community might delegitimize their cause among outside Jewish observers. The only response was a shrug of the shoulders.

I decided to shift the topic a bit. What about marriages, I asked. Did they have any plans to be married after they completed their studies? With some hesitation, both said they would have to marry non-Jews, because most of the young people in the community are somehow related. However, Seventh-day Adventists were a good catch, they explained, because they do everything like Jews—the only drawback is their belief in Jesus. When asked whether or not they could marry only Sefwi, one told me, with no slight amount of contempt, that all Akan people were Jews. When I expressed surprise about this divergence from the older generation's Sefwi-centric rhetoric, the only reaction was a second shrug of the shoulders. In response to a question about the long-standing enmity between the Sefwi and the Ashanti, the rejoinder was: "Those conflicts are no longer relevant." When I finally inquired what, if anything, they would like to communicate to the outside Jewish world, the response was: "If you would like to help, we thank you. But you do not need to. You can also just leave us alone."

A much less confrontational stance regarding the needs and inter-ests of the House of Israel community is espoused by current spiritual leader Alex Armah, a thirty-something former protégé of David Ahen-korah. Alex's journey to Judaism began when his older brother, Joseph Nippah, was introduced to David by a mutual friend in the early 1990s. Joseph began to study with David and Aaron, and even stayed in Aaron's house for a time. Alex recalled to me that, around 1992, while visiting his brother in New Adiembra, he, too, became enamored with their nascent Jewish practice. Alex has described his attraction to Judaism as stemming from what he saw as "purpose and responsibility" in the laws of the Torah.[74] He set about reading some of the books on Judaism donated to the community, such as Rabbi Ronald H. Isaacs's *Becoming Jewish: A Handbook for Conversion*.[75]

Both brothers are former Christians, and several Catholic priests count among their other male siblings. These siblings, as well as their parents, have no problem with Joseph's or Alex's decision to embrace Judaism. Neither does Alex's second wife, a Seventh-day Adventist who, he was happy to point out, observes the Saturday Sabbath faithfully. His first marriage ended in divorce after his wife would not respect the customs associated with his lifestyle. "She was not a Jew, so we had to quit," Alex explained.[76]

As one of the closest people to David, Alex was asked to lead services during a lengthy period in 1998, when David was forced to flee the area due to fears for his life following a family feud. "David," Alex said to me, "taught me everything." When David was voted out, he requested that Alex replace him, and the community agreed. The two remain on good terms. Even before David's ouster, as early as 1996, Alex had known that he wanted to become a rabbi. In the meantime, though, economic necessity dictated that he learn a trade, so he became an electrician.

In 2008, the stars aligned for Alex. A sponsorship from Kulanu allowed him to spend four months studying in Uganda at the seminary of Rabbi Gershom Sizomu, the leader of the Abayudaya community mentioned in chapter 1. Uganda was the only country to which Alex could receive a visa for seminary studies, after Israel and the United States both turned him down. While there, Alex became the first (and, to date, only) member of his community to formally convert to Judaism. A visiting team of Conservative American rabbis performed the conversion. Alex took the name of *Aharon ben Avraham* (Aaron, son of Abraham).

After this initial four-month stay, the American Jewish outreach organization Be'chol Lashon, also mentioned in chapter 1, decided to sponsor Alex with an educational fellowship as he worked toward his "Certificate of Introduction to Rabbinics" in Uganda. After obtaining the certificate in 2012, Alex returned to Ghana, now certified in methods of kosher slaughter and ritual circumcision. Today, Alex is the spiritual leader of the Jewish families in and around Sefwi Wiawso—the only certified teacher of the only indigenous, self-defining normative Jewish community in Ghana.

When asked about his mission and priorities for the community in the future, Alex said that he is very keen on bringing lost Sefwi Jews back into the fold. Alex told me that many practicing Sefwi Christians acknowledge the historical links between their ancestors and ancient Israel, but are hesitant to openly reject Christianity, for fear of professional or economic sanctions. This, he said, represents a marked difference from the more traditionalist-oriented atmosphere prevalent in Sefwi lands at the beginning of the movement, when the Sefwi were closer to the religion of their ancestors and not afraid to critique Christianity. In the old days, he recounted, one could easily find "Jews worshipping [and] doing Jewish things," whereas today, one must actively seek out such activities.

When I asked Alex to clarify whether he wanted to reach out to all Ghanaians, or just to Sefwi in particular, he said that anyone who wanted to be part of the Jewish religion was welcome. Muslims also "know the facts," he insisted, although none had yet approached him about becoming Jewish. When I wondered aloud if he wasn't afraid of proselytizing, he answered that he only wants to be able to "advertise" to those people who are "Jewish but not living Jewishly"—for instance, to people who still practice ancient customs, such as pouring libations to the ancestors.

How would he know who was genuine in the desire to embrace Judaism? If someone wants to come "back to Judaism from [his] own free will, not for economic matters, to worship the one God, he is free to come," Alex told me. "We will teach [him] Judaism again, and, when the time comes, we'll convert [him]." Ostensibly, one or two years studying would be required before such a conversion. When asked about whether the community could allow in people who recognize their Jewish roots but who do not wish to give up their previously acquired styles of worship, Alex told me that, because so many former Jews are Christians, he would have to explain to them that "Jesus is no good"—they cannot believe in Jesus and be Jewish at the same time. "One slave cannot have two masters," Alex said with a smirk, quoting an expression from the New Testament (Luke 16:13; Matt. 6:24).

When I asked Alex about the possibility of immigration to Israel, he was noncommittal. At this point in time, he stated, people don't know much about Israel, and they wouldn't want to move from where they are. They would like to visit, but no one has the monetary means to do so. Moreover, he said, it is unlikely that anyone would qualify even for a tourist visa, given the lack of funds. What was needed, he stressed, was community growth and sponsorship that would provide an infrastructure to keep the community intact. When asked what he feels the community needs most, he responded immediately: "The three most important needs of our community are to connect with the outside world; for our community to be officially converted; and to be recognized by the state of Israel." Alex also noted that, as the spiritual leader, he is in dire need of financial support, since the meager contributions of local community members do not add up to a living wage.

Alex's remarks recall similar viewpoints that I heard regarding Israel. Responding to my questions on that topic, people frequently called the inhabitants of that state "Israelites" and said that they had "returned to the land," but only a few young people knew more than that. One older person told me that I looked like Yitzhak Shamir, the former Israeli prime minister, who was described in one obituary as a "short, stubby man with the physique of a Graeco-Roman wrestler."[77] I failed to see the resemblance, and intuited that the comment was simply a way to name-drop.

To date, the community's interaction with Israelis has been limited mostly to visiting with trekkers on their post-army West Africa tours. Alex told me that one Israeli "military man" had visited the community several years prior to my visit. The man had promised to return so that they could carry out DNA testing to prove the Jewish origins of the Sefwi. Alex never heard from him again. Interaction with Jewish foreigners other than Americans is very limited, and members of the community do not seem to know much about Jewish life and settlement in other parts of the world. Even the Holocaust, which created the largest worldwide dispersion of Jews since the Destruction of the Second Temple, was only a marginally familiar subject. Out of all the people with whom I spoke, just one young person knew about the mass extermination of European Jews and the exodus resulting from that event.

On the topic of secular Judaism, no one was enthusiastic. I inquired: "What would the community say about accepting people into their ranks who were not practicing another religion, but who wanted to identify with the House of Israel movement solely on the basis of cultural heritage, without attending synagogue or strictly observing the commandments?" Alex, for his part, shook his head and indicated that there was no secular option to be Jewish in Ghana. Unlike in the West, where one could separate culture and religious practice, Ghanaians would never accept such a thing. Variations in denominations could be possible, as long as the commandments were observed. On that point, Alex noted that he personally feels a debt to the Conservative movement, which trained him, but his practices are decidedly more Orthodox—at least the ones that he is able to follow, given the lack of proper Jewish infrastructure in Ghana.

Alex's statements about the decidedly problematic nature of secular Judaism in a Judaizing environment mirror many similar statements that I heard from others in the community. The reasons for this position were quite logical. Every person with whom I spoke stressed to me that claiming to be of Jewish heritage but not agreeing to observe the commandments is simply counterintuitive, given that the observance of Jewish codes is seen as the most significant way to bind oneself to the world of one's ancestors. In other words, one comes closer to one's ancestors by practicing the customs that made their cosmological world go round. Because the transmission of oral narratives has waned greatly with the onset of modernity, the Hebrew Scriptures are seen as the most reliable reconstruction of this lost cosmological world. With respect to such reconstructions of Sefwi history, Boni has noted that these "are often driven by a hegemonic aspiration that leads to strategic representations of the past, often far from licit historiography."[78] Indeed, one honors the unspoiled past by actively participating in the re-creating of it. But the extent to which such participation actually parallels the actions of the ancestors remains to be seen, since no reliable records exist.

The Ghanaian community's lack of interest in, and engagement with, the modern-day state of Israel sets it apart from the other communities profiled in this book. It also reflects the "strategic essentialism" of this particular ethnoreligious Sefwi movement, which sees its engagement with the larger Jewish world as a mere byproduct of its quotidian efforts to return to the roots of its precolonial ancestral heritage.

ILLUSTRATIONS OF DAILY LIFE

As mentioned earlier, customs such as circumcision eight days after birth, burial and food taboos, the ritual slaughter of animals to be consumed, an annual yam harvest festival, and the observations of a Saturday Sabbath and of menstrual seclusion are all points of commonality between ancient Sefwi and normative Jewish traditions. The House of Israel community practices these customs with much more fervor than the customs mandated by rabbinic Judaism, whose only real adherent seems to be Alex. When I asked Alex if there is any pushback to rabbinic

Judaism on the grounds that it is postbiblical, he simply stated, "It's important for all Jews to follow the same religion." I didn't mention the comments of the two young men in Accra about the Talmud not being part of Ghanaian Judaism.

Outside of the weekly synagogue services, which are conducted almost as they would be in any Conservative North American synagogue, rabbinic Judaism is rarely seen in community activities. Similarly, knowledge of postexilic Jewish customs and festivals is scant, with the major exception of Hanukkah. That postbiblical festival, introduced to the community by overseas Jews, has proven quite popular, in part because its narrative (1 Macc. 4:36–59; 2 Macc. 10:1–8) involves the celebration of tenacity and religious freedom in the face of persecution.

Besides the significance of the Saturday Sabbath, which has already been discussed, the Jewish custom held up as being the most important to the community is that of menstrual seclusion. In precolonial times, the violation of this custom, along with childbirth taboos common to most Akan tribes, was punishable by death.[79] Elizabeth Amoah, describing the restrictions of Akan women during their menstrual periods, observes that they were forbidden to enter the houses of men, and were prohibited from cooking any food that men might eat. According to Amoah, an Akan woman "even had to leave her own home and live alone in the *bra dan*, the 'house of menstruation' on the outskirts of the village."[80] Such a woman was called *w'ako mfikyre* ("she [who] has gone to the outskirts of town").[81]

Today, Sefwi Jews still practice this custom, although the punishment for the desecration of the custom is no longer in place. Sefwi women who are menstruating must sleep in quarters separate from their husbands and can neither enter the synagogue nor perform the normal wifely duties of cooking and cleaning. Community member Gladys Armah spoke of the custom in these terms: "No synagogue, no cooking, then after seven days, you wash everything, when the sun goes down, you are free to pray to God."[82] Samuel confirmed the community's adherence to the practice in modern times, stating, "And now too, when my wife is in that mood, she doesn't come to my house."[83] The Sefwi Jews are clear about the parallels between their ancient customs and the prohibitions in the Hebrew Bible, and often quote the laws in

Leviticus 15:19–33 and 18:19 regarding the regulation of the behavior of the *niddah* (menstruant).

Several people outside of the practicing community also remarked to me, with obvious approval, that the Sefwi Jews still uphold the tradition, while others have let it slide. Tano Kumah, for instance, told me that, in the old days, menstruating women had to seclude themselves and avoid touching anything in the house. Because they followed the tradition, it made the men strong. "They [the men] go to war, come back alive," he said. "Compared to today, men are so weak. Because women are unclean, so our things become dirty." He then complained that "today, they don't even tell us when they're menstruating, so when we see them on the street, ride beside them in the taxi, [it] makes us weak." The introduction of Christianity was what changed the adherence to the custom, he lamented, and then added, "The river [Sobore] doesn't want these dirty things."

As in most observant Jewish communities, the most important part of the collective life of the Sefwi Jews takes place in the synagogue. The synagogue itself, a concrete structure adjacent to Kofi's home, is painted blue and white. During religious services, women and men sit separately, although there is no *mekhitzah* (partition). Only Alex has *tefillin* (phylacteries) and a *tallit* (prayer shawl), which were presumably donated to him by his overseas sponsors; the cost of these items is prohibitive to most Ghanaians.

The Sabbath services in which I took part followed a typical Ashkenazi-style service, beginning with the standard *shakharit* (morning) prayers; a Torah reading, followed by a sermon (given by Alex); the *haftarah* (reading from the Prophets) portion, which is thematically related to the weekly Torah portion; the ʿaleinu (closing) prayer; and, finally, the prayer of the mourner's *kaddish* (in honor of the deceased). On the morning that I was there, I counted at least forty people, around half of them children.

The prayer books with which the community conducted the service were donated copies of the *Sim shalom* (Create Peace) Conservative standards, originally published by the American Rabbinical Assembly in the 1980s, and by far the most widely used prayer books in the Conservative movement. When reading biblical passages for the weekly portion and for reciting Psalms, most members used missionary "Good News" Bibles in Twi translation, the dominant Akan dialect of the region. Although the community had a miniature paper Torah that they took out of the "ark," Alex read the Torah portion aloud from one of these volumes in Twi. One person carried with him a small book of Psalms and the New Testament in English translation—a volume frequently seen in Ghanaian homes.

While congregants could read only the transliterated Hebrew from the prayer books, Alex did his best to read straight from the Hebrew text itself. When I asked Alex about the use of Hebrew during services, he told me that he would like for the congregation to be able to read things mostly in Hebrew, but for now, they have to manage with English and Twi. Weekly Hebrew lessons are intended to help move the community toward this goal, but the responsibilities of daily life and the dearth of pedagogical resources complicate the mission.

The weekly Torah portion on this particular Saturday was the Life of Sarah, from Genesis 23:1–25:18, and the haftarah portion was from 1 Kings 1:1–31. The Torah portion deals with Abraham's efforts to buy the cave of Machpelah as a burial place for Sarah, who dies at the age of 127. In Alex's sermon on the Torah portion (which he gave in Sefwi, and which was translated into English for me simultaneously by a teenage congregant), Alex spoke about how, significantly, Abraham decided to pay for a place to bury Sarah, even though he could have obtained the land for free. The lesson to be learned from this story, Alex preached, is that Jews have to make sure to acquire things fairly, because if one prays only for material gain, acquires it, and does well in business but forgets about God, he has gained nothing.

The weekly haftarah portion, which dealt with King David ensuring the succession of his son, Solomon, was read; but the meaning of the passage, or its relation to the Torah portion, was not discussed. Instead, Alex's brother, Joseph, got up and acted out for the children the story of David and Goliath (1 Sam. 17:1–50). Joseph explained to the children that the most important thing to remember from the story is that David's strength came directly from God. One of the children, presumably linking the only white person in the room (me) to the faraway characters from the biblical tale, inquired as to whether or not there were any Goliath-like beings where I lived. I shook my head.

Before the closing of the service, I was invited to teach a few things to the children. Since they had enjoyed very much the action in the scenes from the David and Goliath story, I decided to perform for them some key elements of the story of Ehud and Eglon, from Judges 3:12–30. My Hebrew-language students had always enjoyed this tale, which was featured in one of their textbook lessons. Although I had never acted it out myself, I fondly recalled them doing so.

The biblical text recounts how the crafty Ehud, son of Gera and a judge of Israel, eviscerates the Moabite king, Eglon. Ehud is left-handed and is thus able to conceal from Eglon's guards the dagger, tucked away on his (unsuspected) right hip, with which he ultimately kills Eglon. But this is only the beginning of the fun in this graphic account. Eglon is so obese that Ehud elects to leave the dagger in the guts of this "Moabite Humpty-Dumpty," as one irreverent blogger has referred to him, while he steals out of the chambers.[84] The king's servants, who smell the waste leaking from the king's spilled intestines, assume that he is relieving himself, and don't come in until it's too late. By that time, Ehud is long gone, and another enemy of Israel has been vanquished.

My goal was not to tell the story with a specific meaning in mind; I only wanted to amuse the children. The women in the crowd thought it was hilarious. Unfortunately, among the children, the attempt fell flat: no laughs, and almost no reaction. To save face, I tried to provide a moral: even good can come out of bad people. This is evidenced in the fact that one of Eglon's descendants was Ruth, the first convert, and thus part of the line of the venerable King David. Still no reaction. I then mentioned that, in Ehud's time, being left-handed was seen as some kind of disability. But it didn't hinder this person, who eventually led the Israelites to conquer Moab and usher in a period of eighty years of peace. The children were still nonplussed. Alex rescued me from embarrassment by wrapping up the service, teaching the congregation the Hebrew prayer *Aiyn keeloheinu* (There is none like our God). He then quizzed them on some other Hebrew prayers that they had been trying to memorize, and, finally, declared the service ended.

The women and the children left the building. As the men huddled together to talk about some administrative matters, a group of Sefwi Christians walked in. Among them was a young man who said that he wanted to ask me about the Apocrypha. (Afterwards, Alex told me that the fellow was a disgruntled type who had come and gone in the community several times.) This man, who had heard about my visit, wanted to know if Jews in the United States believe in the Apocrypha. He didn't think that the Apocrypha was Jewish, because, he said, it is part of the Catholic Bible; and that, according to him, was "older" than the Protestant one. But he wanted to be sure.

Not wanting to step on the toes of my guests, I deferred to them to answer the man's question. Alex and the others were visibly flustered. Alex tried to explain to him that the Apocrypha is not part of the official Bible, but that parts of it are Jewish. What did "official" mean, the man wanted to know? Why, for instance, do the Jews observe the festival of Hanukkah, if the Books of the Maccabees are part of the Catholic Bible, but not the Jewish one? Several of the older men in the synagogue were able to tell the intruder about the chronology surrounding the Maccabean revolt and the formation of the canon, although they were a bit unclear on the exact dates. The man then demanded that someone explain to him why Jews don't consider Daniel a prophet, even though he prophesized.

The men in attendance pointed out, quite correctly, and almost certainly based on intuition (as opposed to familiarity with the commentary), that Daniel's function was that of a sage, or even a seer who predicted the future, but that his role was not that of a prophet because he spoke to the people during the captivity in Babylon. The trespasser was not satisfied with these answers, and kept looking at me for a response. Finally, one of the elders said to him, "It seems that you want to know what our white brother thinks." The man nodded in agreement. Now that I had the formal go-ahead, I told the man that I concurred with the elders' statements, and then added a few comments about dates and Talmudic discussions on the topics, with which no one in the audience was familiar, besides Alex. Alex then tried to explain to the man the importance of the Talmud, pointing to one elder, and saying, "You see this old man here? If you tell him a story and he repeats it, it will come out differently. That's why you need another text to confirm what's right." The outsider did not react to Alex's comment. Instead, he wanted to know if I had ever heard of the Crusades. I told him that I had. He wanted to know when they took place, and how long that was after the Jewish scriptural canon had been codified. I told him.

Again, for whatever reason, he was not satisfied. Instead of responding to what had already been said, he quoted to me 1 Corinthians 2:4: "My message and my preaching were not with wise and persuasive words, but with a demonstration of the Spirit's power, so that your faith might not rest on human wisdom, but on God's power." One of the older men, now in a rage, asked if I knew how to defend against such Christian "propaganda." He wanted to help prove that "they [Christians] don't know anything." Several of the younger Jewish men rebuffed the elder for his outburst, chastising him for being so confrontational. I didn't have time to respond before an argument between them escalated into a shouting match. The stranger left in a huff, and the men remaining in the synagogue split up into two groups. Later on in the day, I joined Alex and the two groups of male congregants at Joseph Armah's house, where Alex offered a "prayer of reconciliation" before the men discussed, and finally resolved, their argument from that morning in the synagogue.

I later learned from Alex that the friction between the men may have been due to some lingering hard feelings over a disagreement about the meaning of the Torah portion the week before (Gen. 18:1–22:24). Some of them, Alex told me, thought that Abraham must have had sadness in his heart when he was called to sacrifice Isaac, while others said that part of the greatness of the patriarch's character lay in the fact that he did not grieve for what God had commanded him to do. Beneath that disagreement lay another, more personal point of contention: they had also had an argument over what to do about one of the congregant's brothers, who had been "tricked" into going back to Christianity. Alex lamented that this man's heart must not have been "full of faith."

Since Jews rarely speak of "faith" in God per se (the reader will recall the discussion from chapter 1 about Maimonides's famous precept), this comment struck me as very Christian-sounding. That some of the Sefwi Jews' rhetoric sounds Christian should not come as a bolt from the blue, given that almost all of the people in the current congregation once lived as at least nominal Christians. And yet, the frequency of such rhetoric—especially on the paradigmatic Christian themes of love, faith, and reconciliation—did in fact surprise me.

For instance, when I asked one person why he had joined the House of Israel, he pointed at the sky and replied, "Love [for God] brought me here." Ostensibly, this could have been an innocuous comment with little symbolic significance, simply referring to the joys of being in community with like-minded others. However, I saw it then—and still see it today—as part of the larger dispositional Sefwi matrix of viewing Jewish religion as part of a personal relationship between the individual and God. This brand of theology is different from the conventional Jewish view, which sees God's will as being manifested through the collective destiny of a select group of people. Indeed, if we recall the words of the young man in the mall in Accra, who told me that Judaism is "in one's heart," then the emphasis on the relational aspects of collective ritualistic action—one of the ways in which Jewish adherence is distinguished from that of Christian practice—somehow falls by the wayside. Instead, what emerges is a reenvisioned, faith-based Judaism, not unlike many Christian ways of looking at the world. Still, following the customs of the ancestors, which, to the Sefwi, are synonymous with the customs of the Jews, allows for proper interaction with the cosmological realm.

Significantly, this individually focused way of looking at the role of faith in religious life is also very Protestant. As Marcus Borg has noted, the Reformation, which laid the intellectual foundations for Enlightenment thought and modern conceptions of the self, "emphasized that our relationship with God is primarily about faith."[85] Notwithstanding the issues of the divinity of Jesus and adherence to the Mosaic "works of law" (Rom. 2:15 and 3:20; Gal. 2:16) that the early Church dismissed as unnecessary for salvation, Borg's comment is instructive for elucidating the perceptions about how one interacts with the divine in the Sefwi mind-set.

The popular, modern way of viewing religious experience as "a kind of inner disposition," as Brent Nongbri puts it, owes much to Protestant ideas.[86] Significantly, Judaism as a religious experience is no different. Reform Judaism has long been associated with a Protestant influence, inasmuch as the adherence to "Jewish sacraments" (life-cycle and initiation events, ritual feast days, laws, and taboos), not to mention rote liturgy and knowledge of the Holy Tongue, are seen as merely optional components of something more spiritual and individual at its basis.[87]

To be clear, I am castigating neither the Sefwi form of Jewish practice nor the Reform Jewish one. I am simply pointing out that much of the Sefwi Jews' Christian-sounding rhetoric may be traced to the pervasive influence of Protestant thought in Ghana, just as many ideological components of Reform Judaism may be traced to Enlightenment-based European ideals, which, in turn, may be traced to the varied intellectual revolutions brought about by the Protestant Reformation. This does not make components of either religious system any "less" Jewish. It does, however, situate the Jewishness of the Sefwi in the domain of similar ethnoreligious movements that have broken away from, or are in competition or conflict with, institutionalized mission churches in Ghana.

ALMOST JEWISH: OTHER GHANAIAN EXAMPLES OF OLD TESTAMENTISM

The previous sections of this chapter have showcased the ways in which the members of the House of Israel relate conceptually to their Judaism. This section outlines how similar racial or ethnic-based religious movements in Ghana, among the Ewe and the Gadangme, have utilized the Hebrew Scriptures to buttress esteem for their own narratives and customs. It also demonstrates how these groups both resemble and deviate from the self-defining Ghanaian Jews. Because of space considerations, only brief overviews of each group are given. That more detail is granted to the Gadangme stems only from the fact that I have spent considerable time with them; it does not privilege their position vis-à-vis any of the other groups profiled. (Incidentally, the Sefwi expressed no opinion on any of the Ewe or Gadangme origin claims.)

The patrilineal Ewe people, who live primarily in the eastern Volta Region of Ghana and in parts of Togo and Benin, attribute their provenance to Jewish sources.[88] According to several oral heritage narratives, their founding ancestor, Gu, who was a descendant of Noah, joined a settlement in the Nile Valley comprised of different peoples who had been forced out of Canaan. Gu's people intermingled with the Israelites, who also had a settlement there, and eventually retained many of their customs, such as male circumcision and widow inheritance. When Moses led the Jews out of Egypt, a new leader, Mi, guided the Ewe through Sudan and Ethiopia, eventually migrating westward toward the region between Akanland (Ghana) and Yorubaland (Nigeria).

The reader will notice that this migration story mirrors that of some subgroups of the Akan, which, as mentioned, also claim provenance from Egypt. While it is almost certain that Egypt and Noah are recent additions to the Ewe migration saga—likely added under the influence of colonial-era writers and administrators, not to mention Christianized Ewe seeking to reconcile their origins with the grand narratives of their colonial occupiers—precise information as to when exactly they began to appear in these narratives is unclear.

As a genealogical heritage tale, the origin narrative of the Ewe privileges a liaison with the chosen people as a strategic method of finding a place-marker in the history book of the colonial mind-set. To my knowledge, it has not gone further than this. There is no organized neo-Jewish movement among them, although the mostly Christianized Ewe, many of whom still practice a syncretistic form of worship incorporating ancestral rites, often refer casually to such origins during discussions surrounding the Hebrew Scriptures. Aside from the aforementioned customs—which, as indicated, are common among many different African peoples with no connection whatsoever to Jewish heritage—nothing in Ewe history or cosmology provides substantive evidence of a connection that is anything other than arbitrary.

While many Ewe with whom I have spoken are proud of their Jewish heritage, some find the attempt to link Ewe ethnohistory to that of the Jews insulting. For instance, one blogger on a popular site dedicated to African thought decries the trend that "tries to legitimize Ewe history by synergizing it with biblical personages and places."[89] Another concurs with this view, affirming that "Ewes should hold the banner of their 'Eweness' proudly and bury this 'Ewe Jewishness' milage [sic] nonsense now."[90] This same blogger explains his assessment of the motivation behind the adoption of the "Jewish Ewe" trope:

It seems the Ewes were trying to grab on to something, anything that will elevate their status in Ghanaian society as the crème de la crème of the tribes in Ghana and why not Jews? The Jews might be the most successful people in the world both economically and the will to survive despite being surrounded by enemy countries in Isreal [sic]. . . . Definitely, there might be one or two similarities between the Ewes and Jews [as there] are some similarities between Jews and other people around the world so the similarity between the Ewes and Jews is not unique. . . . Don't you dare try to pick up a proud and dignified African tribe, such as the Ewes are, and make them appendix of someone's race and tradition. My candid opinion is you do more harm than good. You are making my people the butt of [a] joke to another race.[91]

The blogger's expressions of consternation are insightful, as are his reservations about jumping on the Jewish bandwagon. He rebukes the Jewish-Ewe connection while reproducing commonly held stereotypes about Jews (i.e., their supposed economic and military superiority), but does not descend into outright anti-Semitic generalizations. Notably, he does not reference any of the heritage narratives that point to such connections.

Another people historically and politically linked to both the Ewe and the Akan whose name has been frequently associated with the Jews are the patrilineal Gadangme (alternate spelling: GaDangbe), an ethnolinguistic group that inhabits the eastern parts of Ghana and certain areas of Togo.[92] Divided in Ghana into the two major subgroups of the Ga (located primarily in Central Accra and Nungua) and the Adangme (in Osu, Krobo, and Ada), the majority of Gadangme are practicing Christians, their forefathers having converted under the influence of the Basel Mission. Modernity has not erased all adherences to traditional practices, though, and customs such as libation-pouring and divining remain popular. My analysis here focuses mostly on the Ga subgroup, since they are the group with which I have spent the most time.

Like the Sefwi and the Ewe, the Gadangme have much in their heritage narratives and precolonial customs that suggests a racial and historical link with ancient Israel. While there are currently no Jewish-centered religious initiatives among the Gadangme, there is a wide community consensus—based on my fieldwork, even wider than that of the Ewe, or even that of the Sefwi—that the Gadangme people are descended from ancient Israelites.

The oral narratives of the Ga and Dangme peoples recounted to me indicate that their provenance is from the tribes of Gad and Dan, respectively. Just how they arrived in present-day Ghana varies according to the particular version of the story told. Some say that they came by sea, while others indicate that they came overland, through Sudan and Ethiopia, and finally, from present-day Nigeria to their current areas. Regardless of the Jewish question, no one disagrees that the ancient Yoruba city of Ileife was the last major point of migration of the Gadangme to their present location.

Every person of this group whom I interviewed said that "the ancestors came from Israel," although few had detailed descriptions of how that happened. Some suggested that I "look in Genesis" for answers, while others told me that I could find the history "in Deuteronomy." Many asked if I "had read Dr. Mensah's book"—the most widely available English-language publication on the topic—which goes into the reasons for the forced migration.[93] Indeed, I had, and it prompted me to learn more about Gadangme culture. Through it I was also introduced to several community leaders with whom I have since become friends.

Joseph Nii Abekar Mensah, a son of the former Ga King Nii Larbi Mensah II (1912–1969), is the president of the Gadangme Heritage and Cultural Foundation. Mensah has compiled the Gadangme oral heritage narratives into an English-language volume, which is the book referred to above.[94] Mensah calls the Gadangme "Descendants of Authentic Biblical Hebrew Israelites"—but not Jews. Mensah traces the Gadangme migration according to the aforementioned pattern, noting that a familiar saying among his Ga elders was, "*Awusa eshwie wo*," meaning, "The Arabs sent them [the ancestors] into exile."[95] According to Mensah's oral history, the Gadangme "migrated from Israel about 6th Century B.C. through Egypt, then to Ethiopia, having been expelled or exiled by the Assyrians."[96] When I inquired from an associate of his why there is a gap of around two hundred years between the accepted date for the dispersal of the Ten Tribes and that of the Gadangme ancestors, the associate told me the reason was because of "chaos" at the time.

Mensah also adds an unexpected detail that would lend credence to an Israelite origin. In Ethiopia, Mensah writes, the Gadangme dwelled in the city of Gondar, which is widely known as the home region of the Ethiopian Jews.[97] Nikasemo Asafo supports Mensah's thesis, positing that the Gadangme "are either directly descended from ancient Jews who settled in Goshen or were the result of inter-marriage between Goshen and Ethiopian Jews and who married with various Negroid peoples both in upper Egypt and Abyssinia as well as on their migratory journeys."[98] What's more, Mensah claims that the Gadangme are "believed to be related by blood to the Igbos of Nigeria."[99] As the reader will recall from the description in chapter 1, the Igbo are a group that maintains perceptions of shared Israelite origins, although those origins have not been officially recognized. Anticipating that many will dispute the factuality of these claims, Mensah proposes that DNA testing should be conducted, writing that "it will be helpful if the oral tradition of the Gadangmes of Ghana is backed by science (geneticists) as in the case of Lemba of Southern Africa."[100]

Aside from the said heritage narratives, there are a certain number of customs that supposedly corroborate the professed Israelite origin. One custom symbolically tied to the migration saga is the annual millet harvest festival of the Ga subgroup. This religiocultural feast corresponds roughly to the Jewish Passover, which is also a harvest festival mandated in tandem with commemoration of a forced migration. Known as the *Homowo*, which literally means "shouting at hunger," the Ga festival is similar to the Akan yam festival held to celebrate firstfruits.[101] It also possesses commonalities with the Igbo *Iwa Ji* new harvest yam festival, which, among the Igbo Jews, as well, is held up as a substantiation of the claim to a Hebraic or Israelite pedigree. According to Hubert Nii Abbey, the name *Homowo* came about because of a "severe famine" that the Gadangme had to endure during their exodus.[102] However, the food shortage forced the people "to embark on massive food production exercises which eventually yielded them a bountiful harvest enabling them to survive."[103] They later held a feast at which they mocked and "hooted at hunger."

This event is now memorialized in the annual re-creation of that initial feast. In addition to the harvest component of the festival, the

Gadangme place *ntsuma* (red clay) on the doorposts or the entry doors
of their houses in order to drive away evil spirits. This resembles the
section of the Exodus story according to which the Israelites placed the
blood of the paschal lamb on the doorposts of their homes, in order to
escape God's decree that each firstborn in Egypt would be put to death.
(According to Mensah, the replacement of clay for the lamb's blood was
instituted when many families could no longer afford to sacrifice a lamb
on that occasion.)[104] *Kpekpele*, a steamed corn meal dish, is also eaten,
which, according to Mensah, "more or less represents unleavened bread
in accordance with Jewish tradition."[105] In a variation on the Passover
custom, family and tribal elders leave palm-nut soup and fish outside
for ancestral spirits to consume.[106] Marion Kilson, the Western scholar
who has done the most wide-ranging work on the Ga (although not on
the Jewish question per se), points out that "all people who consider
themselves Ga participate in *Homowo*, except for those very few belonging to exclusionary Christian sects."[107]

Other common practices among the Ga thought to be of Semitic
origin include the practice of circumcision, sometimes on the eighth
day (accounts vary as to when exactly this should be done); a twelve-
month lunar calendar; certain rites of menstrual seclusion (not uni-
formly practiced); the prohibition on eating pork; the tradition of priests
wearing white (supposedly modeled on the high priests of the Temple);
the injunction to remove sandals before entering a shrine (supposedly
based on the passage from Exodus 3:5, whereby Moses is instructed to
remove his sandals when God calls to him from the burning bush);
libation-pouring to the gods and the ancestors (schnapps is the libation
of choice, supposedly conforming to the "drink offering" or "oil" mentioned in Genesis 35:14); and the practice of *kpojiemo*, or "outdooring,"
the ceremony in which a child formally receives a name.[108] Despite the
lack of precise correlations between these customs, David K. Henderson-
Quartey sums up the prevailing opinion on the matter by stating that
the Ga's "religious and moral culture [is] parallel to Judaism prior to
Christianity, which the Ga still hold in its pristine fashion."[109]

During my fieldwork in Accra, I was fortunate to meet many Ga spiritual leaders, among them the current Ga king, Nii Tackie Adama Latse II,
as well as the current Ga high priest, Nuumo Adwaa Mensah III. During

an audience with the king, whose role entails "functions of a law-giver, judge, administrator, prime minister, war leader or supreme commander, supreme defender as well as ritual function," I heard many of these generalities about the Gadangme's' Jewish origins reiterated, both by the king and by his advisors, oracles, and linguist, all of whom accompanied him to our meetings.[110]

When I asked the king about where the Gadangme came from, I first received a perplexed look. Then, a one-word answer: "Israel." With regard to customs of ancient Israel that persist among the Ga to this day, the king said that the customs "pertaining to what they really do as rabbis [is] what the prophets do here . . . the way they dress, move, affiliate, the same thing they do here," including funerary customs and treatment of widows. He also noted that kings and clan heads were descended from Old Testament priest-kings. I inquired as to whether the Gadangme feel a kinship with modern-day Jews. "The simple answer is yes," the king told me, again, rather annoyed at the question. He then emphasized how both peoples are "discriminated against, pushed around, and persecuted." Also, he noted, the Ga people were great fighters, just like the people of Israel. He asked if I knew of former International Boxing Federation welterweight champion Joshua Clottey. As a longtime boxing fan, I said that I certainly did. Everyone in the king's entourage was pleased.

One of the king's oracles also told me, apparently referencing historical anti-Semitism (the knowledge of which, I later verified, was scant), that opposition from the institutionalized Church was something that both peoples had in common. To illustrate, he complained about how most Protestant denominations, of which almost all of the Ga in Accra are members, object to pouring libations to the ancestors. The Church, he said, discourages this, branding it "evil worship." Was this veneration not just like the Catholics honoring the saints, he wondered? As long as the Supreme God was honored, what was the problem? He then referenced the *derba* (rally) for forthcoming peaceful presidential elections that I had attended the day earlier, and over which the king had presided, remarking how both a traditional Ga priest and an Anglican bishop were asked to consecrate the event. After witnessing that, he fumed, how could any discerning mind claim that the traditional and Christian components of Ga identity were incompatible? The Church was simply practicing a form of neocolonialism. One of the king's advisors added that libation-pouring and polygamy, the two "most Jewish" of their customs, were the practices under the greatest threat from the Church.

Uncomfortable with the heavy mood that had descended upon the meeting, I questioned aloud whether using a more traditional drink for libations, such as palm wine, might send the signal that foreign-made schnapps was no longer *de rigueur* for the ritual pouring. Might this not help to underline the sought-after respect for traditional values while simultaneously indicating that neocolonialist intrusions would not be tolerated? Unfortunately, no one got that I was making a joke. "The fact that it's British schnapps is of no consequence," one advisor told me. "But didn't the British introduce it to Ghana?" I asked. "No," he said. "The Dutch, then?" I ventured. Again, a no. "So it was introduced to the country by the Portuguese?" I asked. "We've always had schnapps," the oracle said, not amused at what was finally recognized as my attempt at humor.

This exchange amplifies some of the fissures in modern Ga identity brought about by the forces of modernity and globalization, in particular with regard to the status accorded to ritual practice. On the one hand, adherence to traditional religion is seen as compulsory—a kind of antidote to the numbing uniformity of Western cultural impositions. On the other, Christian beliefs are espoused almost universally, and being considered a "good Christian" is tantamount to wearing a universally recognized badge of honor.

One area, however, in which time-honored ritual practice takes precedence over alternative, colonially inspired systems is that of the penal code. Based upon Ga religious law and enforced by the Office of the High Priest of Accra for civil or criminal disputes below the level of murder (theft, physical assault, etc.), this accord regarding punitive measures is part of an arrangement sanctioned by the Ghanaian government. The terms of this arrangement allow specific micronations such as the Ga to exercise broad autonomy when dealing with infractions in their jurisdictions, by granting legal legitimacy to traditional methods of social control outside of the state police apparatus.

I had the opportunity to witness the traditional Ga penal system in action when my main contact among the Ga in Accra, Prince Afotey

Laryea, suggested one day that I accompany him to the high priest's office, where he wished to lodge a complaint against a man who had attacked his son (the son did not retaliate physically in order not to harm an elder). When we entered the office, Afotey was asked to describe the nature of the dispute. He then paid a small registration fee, the confirmation of which he received in the form of a written receipt on official stationery. Afterwards, the court bailiff then led us outside to hail a taxi. The taxi, paid for by Afotey, took us to the man's house, where he was served with a subpoena to appear before the high priest.

I was amazed that the Ghanaian police were not involved for even a moment in the entire affair. "What if the man just decides not to come? What will happen to him?" I asked. Afotey responded: "He will come. Everyone must, or he will be struck down. This is not a secret." Afotey then related a story about a man who had failed to appear before the high priest. Apparently, the man had turned into a snake on the very day during which he was to be wed. Afotey himself had not seen it happen, but everyone knew that the high priest was able to influence disembodied spiritual forces at will.

As we see, the influence of long-established religious beliefs and mores upon Ga society is still strong. And yet, many Ga, such as Joseph Nii Abekar Mensah, think that "a reorganization of the entire traditional structure of [the Ghanaian] government on Christian principles may be desirable."[111] If so much anger exists at institutionalized Christianity, then why is this so? Namely, because many Ga already see themselves as existing outside of the realm of the umbrella state. They are a micronation within a larger structure with which they do not identify, are largely not beholden to legally (save for taxes), and which, from their perspective, exists only to exploit. A Christian superstructure at least has checks and balances, and would ideologically unite most Ghanaians.

Strangely, this desire for a Christian umbrella state does not affect the pride that stems from the perception that the roots of Ga culture are Jewish. For instance, many of my contacts among the Ga end their e-mails to me with statements such as, "Blessings in Jesus's Name," unaware of the fact that Jews do not accept Jesus as a savior. When alerted to this divergence, responses generally tend to be along the lines of, "Well, Jesus was a Jew, and that's the important thing." Similarly, one of the king's advisors told me, "Before the Europeans came with the Bible, we were doing things that we know now were from Israel, just like Jesus. This proves the affiliation between Jews and Gadangme."

A final illustration of Ga perceptions regarding Jews is in order. One meeting I had with the Ga high priest, Nuumo Adwaa Mensah III, at his office in the Bokum shantytown section of the Jamestown neighborhood of Accra, was particularly insightful for understanding how the Ga inner circle relates to claims of Jewishness. Again, I was fortunate to have the connection to Afotey, who used to play football with the high priest, before the latter gave up his profession as a manicurist and pedicurist in order to assume the hereditary role. Their prior relationship allowed me a unique kind of access to certain aspects of Ga cosmology, not to mention to certain forms of Ga material culture that, they claimed, no white person before me had ever seen.

When Afotey and I arrived at the meeting, the high priest and his counselors greeted us warmly. They began by giving an explanation of the high priest's role in Ga society. Just like the great heroes of Israel, they said, he was a priest, prophet, and judge all at the same time. From the moment the high priest takes on the role, he gains the powers to diffuse anything going wrong in the Ga state. To carry out his task, he communicates with spirits, and also with "God Almighty." One advisor among the assembled reiterated the same logic about spirits that the king's oracle had previously indicated to me: as long as one worships the Supreme God, there is no problem dealing with intermediaries. When I asked how Christianity, Judaism, and traditional Gadangme cosmology each play different roles in their identity, one subpriest present told me: "We are all three of these. We know that we came from Israel. Our practices are the same. We believe in Jehovah. We have knowledge about the Old Testament [i.e., as reflected in Ga ritual] that the Christians don't have."

To demonstrate the point, the high priest and his men led me into a room adjacent to the courtyard that contained a small sanctuary. Before entering, we were instructed to remove our shoes. This is the space, they said, where they perform all of the rites as the high priests did in the Israelite Temple, such as sacrifices and the pouring of blood. Farther inside, in an antechamber, they pulled back a set of white curtains to reveal a replica of what they called the *kpanmo adeka* (the Ark of the Covenant), which they claim their ancestors carried with them from Egypt to Ghana. Although they did not possess the original ark, this one was modeled exactly on the instructions from Exodus 25. The original had been lost and its location was unknown to them. The replica was made of palm branches (a local substitute for Acadia wood), was rectangular in shape and, as far as I could tell, had measurements that seemed approximate to the one and a half cubits in width and height and the two and a half cubits in length of the original ark.

How was this ark different? It was not plated in gold, and did not have the four rings attached to the bottom in order to facilitate its transport. There were no figures of cherubim on top. Inside, there were no replicas of the Tablets of the Law, which, according to Jewish custom, were the only items kept in the ark (1 Kings 8:9). Neither was there a replica of the jar of manna, nor of Aaron's staff, as posited in the Christian tradition (Hebrews 9:4). Rather, there was, they claimed, water from the Nile and from "the sea" (presumably, the Red Sea) which, after all these years, had not dried up. Another significant deviation from Israelite practice was that libations were regularly poured onto the replica, evidenced by the empty bottles of (British) schnapps littering the floor of the room. The sanctuary of the ark purportedly marks the place where their ancestors had first settled in Ghana after their long migration, and was thus the founding-stone for the city of Accra.

It is impossible to enter into a full-fledged discussion on the history and symbolic significance of the Ark of the Covenant here, but a few remarks about this decisive "proof phenomenon" of biblical material culture are worthy of notation. First, the reader will notice that the idea according to which Gadangme ancestors carried the ark with them from Goshen to Ghana mirrors the Ethiopian legend according to which Menelik, the son of Solomon and the Queen of Sheba, visited Jerusalem and came back with the ark to the Kingdom of Cush. In the Ethiopian tradition, the ark still rests in Axum. Second, other African peoples who claim a genealogical connection to the Israelites have similar legends about the possession of duplicates, or replicas, or even of the original ark itself. The most famous among these is the claim made by the Lemba, as mentioned in chapter 1.

It seems that tying this esoteric trope to the Gadangme heritage narrative, as well as to the quotidian, utilitarian character of a libation altar, is a relatively recent occurrence, because none of the scholarly or testimonial literature mentions such a replica. Symbolically, this is a very powerful move, given the representational role of the ark in the Hebrew Scriptures. That the Bible describes the ark as the physical protector of the Israelites during wartime and their motivator in times of trial seems especially significant, given that the sanctuary for this ark lies in the middle of the Bokum slum. Bokum is an area rife with disease, poverty, petty crime, and hopelessness—an ugly reminder of public disenfranchisement. Moreover, since God's holy presence is said to emanate from the ark, the object provides a material manifestation of the power of the high priest, who, in Ga cosmology, is equivalent to God's human agent on earth. Finally, the privilege of possessing a carbon copy of the long-fabled object adds yet another layer of legitimacy to the claims of chosenness.

Is it possible that the Ga ark story is modeled upon similar tales emanating from other locales in Africa? Based on my conversations with the high priest and his advisors, it appears unlikely. They seemed genuinely unaware of similar claims—as unaware, in fact, as they were of anything to do with modern-day Jewry. In my estimation, the entry of the ark trope into the Ga consciousness represents a very recent attempt to reinvigorate the status of, and justifications for, the office of the high priest among the Christianized Ga. The ark lends a sign of Christian legitimacy and adds structural value to traditional cultural transactions, such as those made by the high priest. Even if such transactions are couched in terms of their relation to precolonial customs, they remain an integral part of the colonizers' religious history. The fate of the Lost Ark is mythological quicksand in the Western imagination, and a mystery that the colonizers themselves have never been able to solve. Maintaining a replica of the original ark may, in some fashion, provide a way of one-upping the Christian Church in terms of legitimacy by appropriating a foundational component of one of its enduring psychodramas. And by simultaneously using the replica for a traditional rite publicly frowned-upon by the Church—libation-pouring—the Ga hierarchy can extend the proverbial middle finger to those who critique its alleged impropriety, thus manipulating to their advantage the free-floating molds of a globalized religious environment.

To a certain extent, this inclusion of Jewish tropes in the conceptual realm of the Ga mirrors a similar process among the self-defining Sefwi Jews, although the Ga have come nowhere near an outright abandonment of Christianity or an attempt at full-scale Old Testamentism, as have the Sefwi. This may be due in part to the Ga's longer association with the Christian religion. It may also be tied to aspects of their rapid urbanization in the country's capital city, as opposed to the humdrum, backwater province routine of the Sefwi, whose isolation was a major factor in the organic development of its Judaizing movement.

Another difference between these movements is that the Sefwi were not forced to contend with that great taboo of newly Christianized societies—the dreaded "animist" label—since they were not really Christians to begin with. Nor did they seek any recognition from the Christian Church. They simply described their practices as a return to the ancestors' "traditional religion," which, in this case, happened to be called Judaism. As Appiah-Kubi affirms, this focus on a slightly different version of the "veneration of ancestors," who are seen as "the custodians of law, morality, and ethical order of the Akans," places the Sefwi movement in line with other independent religious movements in Ghana, several of which are profiled below.[112]

ANTIDOTES TO CULTURAL AMNESIA

Outside of the ethnoreligious movements of specific micronations, many so-called "indigenous" or "independent" churches in Ghana choose to privilege the Old Testament over the new, often drawing parallels between native Ghanaian customs and those of the Hebrews or Israelites. Bringing such churches into the discussion helps to contextualize the situational motivations for more Jewish-centered movements.

For example, a growing number of independent Ghanaian churches mandate the observance of a Saturday Sabbath, drawing a parallel between the Akan holy day and the Israelite day of worship. These include the Apostolic Revelation Society and the African Faith Tabernacle

Church (both originally Presbyterian); *Memeneda Gyidifo* (The Saviour Church; also called "Saturday Believers," originally Methodist); and the Church of the Twelve Apostles, a prophetic-spiritualist church considered the forerunner of Pentecostalism in Ghana, alternatively known as the Church of William Harris (after William Wade Harris, the Liberian prophet who preached in Ghana) or the Nackabah Church (after its cofounder, John Nackabah).

These churches, as well as scores of others with broad ecumenical bases, belong to the "Sabbath Association of Ghana" and work on behalf of the umbrella *Kristo Asafo* (Christ Reformed) Church. An organizational body more than a church per se, its members endeavor to convince church leadership across Ghana to adopt Saturday as the mandated day of rest, using traditional Akan notions of the Saturday Sabbath as a springboard.[113] The Saturday Sabbath remains high on the agenda of many churches in Ghana due also to the wide-ranging activities of Seventh-day Adventists, who have been active in the country since 1894. Many Adventist groups, including those located in the Sefwi areas, have taken their Old Testament practices a bit further than the norm, and now observe a significant number of Levitical practices, including menstrual separation and ritual immersion.

Other churches, such as the *Mussama Disco Christo* Fellowship (formerly Methodist), follow Old Testament food taboos, such as avoiding pork and common forms of bush meat like rat and monkey, animals killed by strangulation, and the ingestion of blood.[114] They also practice animal sacrifice, hold an annual "Peace Festival" modeled on the Passover, allow "controlled polygamy," favor hereditary succession, and, like the Ga, have a model Ark of the Covenant, kept in the *kronkronbea* (the Holiest Place), to which only their high priest is allowed access.

Such perceived psychological, symbolic, and practical affinities with Hebraic and Israelite history, combined with a decidedly anticolonial (and therefore anti-European Christian establishment) atmosphere, create a situation in which finding one's past in the story of another "Other" becomes very attractive. The attempt of the Sefwi to "structuralize nostalgia," as indicated in the title of this chapter, links their movement to similar initiatives in postcolonial Ghanaian society. Given the dearth of reliable records and the lack of familiarity with a disappearing oral culture, the sources upon which one relies are, paradoxically, those supplied by the colonial powers.

My use of the term "structural nostalgia" owes much to the ways in which Michael Herzfeld in particular discusses it. According to Herzfeld, it is the "collective representation of an Edenic order—a time before time—in which the balanced perfection of social relations has not yet suffered the decay that affects everything human."[115] Israel Gerber, for his part, has noted in regard to the similar self-archiving project of the Black Hebrews, that "[they would] engage in another strategy to circumvent the shortcoming imposed upon them. They would align themselves with an existing group already blessed with a well-established background and heritage. This approach would immediately add substance to their lives, would help them escape the reality of the present, and would elevate their status."[116] Granted, the Black Hebrews are coming from another kind of imperialist project: that of institutionalized slavery in the United States. But the substance of the movement is the same. For, in aligning oneself with the slaveholders' (or the colonialists') spiritual foes, the Jews, and following their "Old Law," rather than practicing the grace and submission proscribed in the New Testament, the downtrodden cease to be, in Frantz Fanon's terms, the "wretched of the earth." Instead, they become its inheritors.[117]

T. C. McCaskie's masterful essay on "Asante Origins, Egypt, and the Near East" shows how, outside of a Jewish context, such historical refashioning is gaining ground all over Ghana. The focus of his discussion centers on certain popular texts like Osepetetreku Kwame Osei's book, *The Ancient Egyptians Are Here*, which argues that all Ashanti origins lie in ancient Egyptian civilization.[118] McCaskie notes that Ghanaian university students in Kumasi with whom he discussed the book were "skeptical about the particular case but asserted the general case that sabotage was used to create African cultural amnesia, loss, and underdevelopment [by the colonial powers]."[119] His comment that "the quest for origins is driven on by needs much larger than academic ones" is a fitting one to reflect upon as we end our discussion of the Sefwi case study.[120] Indeed, while the academic historicity of Sefwi heritage narratives can neither be proved nor disproved, the motivations behind their (re)creations are, indisputably, as sound as they come.

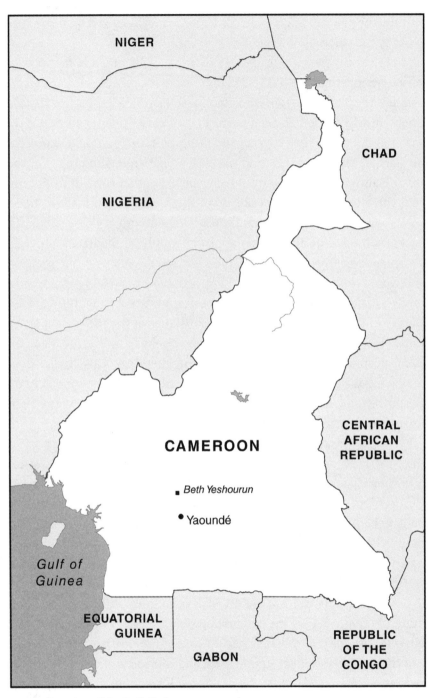

MAP 3. Location of the Beth Yeshourun
community, Cameroon

Online Spiritual Volition   **3**

The "Internet Jews" of Cameroon

VIRTUAL OTHERNESS

The previous chapter on the Ghanaian case study has demonstrated the prevalence of the genealogical trope as a decisive motivating factor in the emergence of neo-Jewish communities. As we have seen, perceived commonalities in heritage narratives, rites of passage and life-cycle events, preserved remnants of material culture, physiognomic traits, and alimentary and hygiene taboos are among some of the "proof phenomena" employed to reveal the supposed hereditary links between the Hebraic or Israelite pedigree of the Bible and that of the ancestors of the communities in question.

One community in rural Cameroon, however, began its journey toward Judaism without taking into account any such apparently inherited similarities. Its discovery of the postbiblical Jewish religion came about by chance, when some of its members started surfing the Internet in the late 1990s. Inspired by a deep spiritual desire based on their online experience, the members of this community, who eventually decided to give their congregation the Hebrew name of "Beth Yeshourun" (the House of the Righteous), began to practice Judaism according to information found on the Internet. One of the first known communities to have discovered normative Judaism in such a fashion, these "Internet Jews" sought contact with their coreligionists from the outside world only after the decision to adopt an Old Testament–style identity predicated solely on faith-based concerns.[1]

In the context of Judaizing movements, this community is unique in two fundamental ways. First, its founding members do not claim to ever have been "lost" from the hereditary Jewish fold. As we have seen, references to the genealogical trope occur almost across the board in the discourses of modern Judaizing movements, with very few exceptions. (More recent members of the Cameroonian community have, however, begun to embrace the idea of a lost Jewish genealogy, with varying degrees of acceptance from the others; this subject is discussed later on in the chapter.)

Second, their adoption of the Jewish discursive system of religious thought via online means, without any prior personal interaction with other Jews whatsoever, makes them one of the first established examples of a neo-Jewish community evolving from improvised Old Testamentism to postexilic, normative Jewish practice, via the digitally globalized matrix that Heidi Campbell calls "networked religion." Building upon the work of Manuel Castells and Jan A. G. M. van Dijk, Campbell notes that the forms of religious practice garnered through this medium, as well as their eventual interpretations by Internet users, are "increasingly flexible, transitional, and transnational," insofar as access to a particular praxis or worldview is now almost entirely decentralized.[2]

On the level of the nation-state, this is especially true in the Cameroonian case, since access to Internet technology came about without any assistance from official governmental powers. In fact, the main meeting site of the approximately sixty-person Jewish community, in the village of Saa, still has only sporadic, state-supplied electricity—available solely for the most well-off of its residents—and has never had telephone lines. Only modern communications technology (computers connected to the Internet at first with dial-up, and then, cellular modems, followed more recently by smartphones) supplied by mainly Chinese migrant merchants has allowed the members of this group to enter into such a decentralized communication paradigm.

Just as the process of economic globalization creates virtual marketplaces that are monetarily interdependent, with little concern for geopolitical ideology or human geography, so does the process of cultural globalization necessitate a symbolically interdependent marketplace of ideas from which analogues and corollaries of lived experience may be, for lack of a better term, "consumed." As the example of the Cameroonian community shows, the patterns of such spiritual consumption driven by technology are rapidly evolving in tandem with new agents of social change, such as international migration, diffused sectarianism, and other associated factors. Stephen Ellis and Gerrie ter Haar's astute comment that "the blooming of religious movements has created international networks that bind groups of [culturally dissimilar] people, often without reference to states," is particularly fitting for this case study of a neo-Jewish movement in Cameroon.[3] This is because, for many, the principles of Jewish religion, broadly defined, are quickly eclipsing popular manifestations of earlier political liberation ideologies or alliances. Those ideologies, such as Négritude, Pan-Africanism, Afro-Radicalism, and plain regional partisanship, have, in many cases, fallen by the wayside as widespread corruption and economic inequality erode confidence in local or continental governmental systems.

However, as mentioned in chapter 1, and as I demonstrate below, there is a strong associative tie between this new Cameroonian Jewish theology and other theologies common to independent African Christian movements. Most important among these is the so-called "theology of decolonization," discussed at length in this chapter. A philosophy that Byang H. Kato calls a "defensive theological system," comprising elements of Ethiopianism and African-American "Black Power" movements, the neo-Jewish form of this theology combines preexisting misgivings about colonially transmitted modes of thought with the promotion of indigenous moral norms and codes.[4] The liminal space of the Internet encourages the hermeneutic mélange of such philosophies, rather than demarcating the borders between them.

Any notion that this estimation of the political nature of Judaism in Cameroon smacks of hyperbole is easily squelched by the following musings of one of Beth Yeshourun's leaders. "There are probably about eight million potential Jews in Central Africa who have had enough of our rotten, neoimperialist regimes," this person told me, referring to supposedly like-minded people in Equatorial Guinea and Gabon (the sites of two additional neo-Jewish communities inspired by the Cameroonian movement), as well as to his native Cameroon. When I inquired as to what kind of regimes he would instead like to see come to power, he mentioned that something akin to the House of David would be desirable, provided it had the same degree of celestial support. The man noted that such divine backing, coupled with the accountability created by the unprecedented ease of communications facilitated by e-mail and cell phones, would spare those in the nascent Jewish Central African fraternity from suffering the same fate as his cousin, the folk hero Félix-Roland Moumié, who was assassinated for his activities as chairperson of the *Union des Populations du Cameroun* (Cameroonian People's Union), an anticolonial political party.

Whether or not the social agendas of new Jewish religious movements and anticolonialist freedom struggles are intrinsically comparable, or even politically and intellectually responsible, the point has been made: Judaism in Cameroon is a political phenomenon whose genesis and potential reach have been made possible, to a great extent, by the latest communication technologies. How fast, how far, and how profoundly Judaism will take root in Cameroon, and in Central Africa in general, remains to be seen. What is certain is that its members have high hopes for its eventual diffusion. Their reasons for believing so are detailed below.

PERCEPTIONS OF JEWISHNESS

In May 2014, during my fieldwork in Cameroon, the thirty-something spiritual leader of the Beth Yeshourun community, Serge Etele, told me the following story to illustrate the kinds of general perceptions about Jews that exist in his country.

A few days earlier, after the end of the Sabbath, Serge had been traveling with a friend by car from Saa to Yaoundé, Cameroon's capital city, when they were stopped by police at a roadblock. Tensions were high in Cameroon over the continued incursions into the north of the country by Boko Haram, the Nigeria-based Islamist terror group. With Cameroonian Independence Day approaching, the police were especially alert to any suspicious activity around the capital.

"Where are you coming from just now?" one of the police officers asked Serge. "From the synagogue," Serge answered. "The *what?*" the officer inquired, unfamiliar with the term. Serge explained to the policeman that a synagogue was like a church, only for Jews. "You're Jewish?" the officer asked, confused. "Yes," Serge said. "But you're black!" the officer protested. "Yes, I'm black, *and* I'm Jewish," Serge told him. The officer looked over Serge's papers a bit longer, and then radioed his superior for instructions. A short exchange ensued. Still hesitant, the officer finally said, "Okay, go ahead," waving them through the checkpoint.

Serge's story is educative for two reasons. First, the policeman's lack of familiarity with the term "synagogue" signals his inability to conceive of such a meeting place in modern-day Central Africa. This is in spite of the likelihood that, given the mostly Christianized population in and around Yaoundé, the policeman had probably heard the word used before in the context of New Testament readings. Second, his bewilderment over Serge's insistence that one can be both black and Jewish points to the widespread notion among Cameroonians that Judaism, a foreign faith with no roots in native historical memory, is a religion of white people only.

That perception is changing as knowledge about Judaism in Cameroon grows. Serge's community, which numbers around sixty regular members and many more affiliated individuals, has meeting places in Yaoundé as well as in Douala, the country's largest city. Its home base is still in the village of Saa, about an hour's drive from Yaoundé, where the large front room of Serge's family home doubles as the community's makeshift synagogue. In all of these places, interested visitors are welcome to attend study sessions or religious services. They may also ask to simply converse with community members about what exactly it means to lead a Jewish lifestyle.

While word of mouth is one manner in which people come to know about the community, the most common way is through the same medium that the founders of Serge's community first used in order to learn about Judaism: the Internet. To that end, the Beth Yeshourun community has created a comprehensive website dedicated to its activities, with versions in both French and English.[5] Serge estimates that more than 90 percent of people who learn about the community do so via the Internet. Interested readers can use the site to learn about Jewish religion, history, and law. Links provided on the site direct the user to online versions of the Torah, the Talmud, and other sacred Jewish texts. A weekly blog looks at issues germane to the particular moment in time through a Jewish lens. Answers are given to many Frequently

Asked Questions, especially to those regarding the differences between Jewish and Christian religious beliefs.

For example, under the section entitled, "Du Christianisme au Judaïsme: nos raisons" (From Judaism to Christianity: Our Reasons), topics include "Les paraboles de Jésus" (The Parables of Jesus); "Les prédictions de Jésus" (The Predictions of Jesus); "Les difficultés du nouveau testament" (The Difficulties of the New Testament); "Bref aperçu sur l'apôtre Paul" (A Brief Overview of the Apostle Paul); and "Pourquoi les juifs ne croient pas en Jésus?" (Why Do Jews Not Believe in Jesus?).[6] All of these appear to be original compositions, although they are heavily reliant upon more well-known sources. From a cursory Google search (in French) using selected quotations from these articles, dozens of instances of citations from the Beth Yeshourun website appear in different chat rooms, news site talkbacks, and Facebook pages frequented by Cameroonians. Persons using the site who wish to know more are invited to contact Serge via the e-mail addresses provided, or by calling one of several cell phone numbers. Many such queries result in a face-to-face meeting with one or more community members. Significantly, this method of communication has also resulted in the recent formation of two other Central African Jewish communities: one in Gabon, and the other in Equatorial Guinea. Originally begun as "Friends of Israel" cultural associations, these communities, whose members now attempt to live Jewishly the best they can, look toward the senior members of Beth Yeshourun as their spiritual mentors. Serge travels frequently to these two communities as the resident Central African expert on Judaism.

I was fortunate to witness one such face-to-face encounter between Serge and a prospective member during my time in Cameroon. One day, in Yaoundé, Serge indicated to me that he had received two requests by phone for in-person meetings on the subject of joining the Jewish community. I was invited to attend these meetings in order to witness firsthand how Judaism is explained to potential congregants. Both meetings were arranged in the bar area of a hotel near the commercial center of the city. Besides Serge, three other members of the Beth Yeshourun community, who had been with us during the day's activities, elected to stay on to meet the interested parties.

Only one of the two people who had called showed up: a university student in his twenties, whom I shall call "Dominique" (not his real name). Serge began by introducing himself and the others who accompanied him, including me, to the potential congregant. He then asked Dominique why he was interested in learning more about Judaism. Dominique, who was obviously from Cameroon's privileged class, told us that, while studying at the London School of Economics on a foreign exchange program, he had befriended an Israeli student, with whom he was still in contact by e-mail. He had also become friends with an American Peace Corps volunteer in Cameroon who was a dual American-Israeli citizen. Discussions with both of these acquaintances had sparked his interest in Judaism. Dominique, raised in the Protestant faith, had recently become dissatisfied with his spiritual life, and was informally studying Kabbalah (the repository of Jewish mysticism) online. He wanted to know what was expected of one who wished to live Jewishly, and how the commitment, if undertaken, would play out in community life with the others.

Serge answered all of Dominique's questions in a matter-of-fact fashion, neither encouraging him to, nor dissuading him from, joining the community. Serge explained the laws of the Torah and their application in normative Jewish ritual practice, stressing that following the Law entailed certain lifestyle inconveniences, not to mention the possible ostracization from one's family. For this reason, Serge said, many people who had joined the community eventually left because they felt the way of life to be too much of a hassle. Serge spoke of the "generosity" expected of members, who needed to collectively bear the financial burden of providing a Jewish infrastructure. He also noted that self-defining as Jewish entailed a certain risk, since radical Islam in neighboring Nigeria seemed to be taking off in ways that were heretofore unprecedented. When asked for clarifications on the scriptural plane, Serge provided the standard Jewish rationale for the reasons that Christianity was not a suitable way of coming to know God, and suggested several print- and web-based sources for Dominique to consult if he wished to have further information. Technically speaking, I did not find anything lacking in the explanations that Serge gave. It was extraordinary to think that almost all of Serge's knowledge of Judaism, scriptural and otherwise, had been gleaned from the Internet.

Serge also used me as an example of the strength of Jewish people-hood, emphasizing to Dominique how Jewish community transcends national and racial boundaries. Serge told Dominique that nothing else but an inherent sense of common destiny could explain why I, who had never met him or anyone in his community in person prior to my visit to Cameroon, would—unlike other jittery Westerners who had recently cancelled their plans to visit the country—journey all the way to Central Africa under the threat of Boko Haram simply to have brotherly fellowship with them. (Serge neglected to mention that I was actually in Cameroon to conduct research on his group; and, wanting to see how the conversation would play out, I did not attempt to correct him.) As another example of Jewish solidarity, Serge mentioned how, in 2011, Israel had agreed to swap one thousand Palestinian prisoners for one single kidnapped Israeli soldier: Gilad Shalit. Dominique was visibly impressed.

After Serge had finished his explanations, Dominique asked several of those in attendance about their reasons for joining the Jewish fold. Each man present told of the feeling of having been "duped" and "deceived" by Christianity, which, according to them, encouraged political passivity vis-à-vis imperial interests, and promoted foreign ideals that were ultimately incompatible with the African worldview. One of the community members in attendance, Frédérick Ndawo, commended Dominique on his interest in Judaism, emphasizing that he was among the many in Cameroon who were coming "closer to the truth." No one mentioned the burgeoning supposition, discussed later in this chapter, according to which some tribes in Cameroon are descended from Hebrew or Israelite stock.

Somewhat to my embarrassment, Dominique was especially interested in my own spiritual quest—correctly guessing, presumably based on my demeanor, that I was the only secular one among those assembled. To that end, he asked me whether or not Jewishness could be transmitted hereditarily as well as spiritually, referencing the argument of John the Baptist, who proclaimed that simply being the "spiritual seed of Abraham" (Matt. 3:9) was not enough to ensure the inviolability of the

Remnant of Israel. Instead of going into my own complicated opinions on religious faith, I decided to don my Jewish Studies professor's cap, and offered an explanation as to how definitions of Jewishness (patrilineal, matrilineal, etc.) had varied over the millennia in response to changing situational concerns.

Most of the group seemed uncomfortable with these fluid designations, and Serge hastened to add that, whatever the societal process may be that determines the "true Israel," once one becomes Jewish, one can "never go back." Serge also insisted that Jewishness is conveyed through the father's line, which is the biblical, preexilic way of determining Jewishness. I found this inaccuracy rather curious, since Serge undoubtedly knew the conventional Jewish norm of matrilineal descent. Was he saying this in order to assuage fears about possible issues surrounding religious inheritance, which, among most ethnic groups in Cameroon, usually follows the father's line? Whatever the reason, I did not attempt to address this instance of misinformation—the only one on Serge's part that I witnessed all evening.

The episode with Dominique demonstrates the ease with which people are able to access details and testimonies about a religious way of life that, until 1998, had never existed in Cameroon. Granted, Dominique had a prior, albeit perfunctory, familiarity with Judaism before meeting with us. But Dominique is an exception, both because of his privileged social status (most of the members of Beth Yeshourun are agricultural laborers of very modest means) and, because of the overseas connections made possible by that status, in that he knew what to look for when researching Jewish topics on the Internet. Most people who encounter the Beth Yeshourun website without a referral do so by accident, while researching unrelated issues of Christian denominational specificity or questions about scriptural interpretation, both of which the information provided on the site addresses.

This encounter is also worthy of mention because it illustrates the paradox of recruiting new community members in a land where no real Jewish infrastructure exists. As noted, Jews are forbidden to engage in proselytizing. And yet, it may be argued that the Beth Yeshourun website does in fact do just that, albeit in a roundabout fashion. By strongly debunking long-held notions about the biblical veracity of the Christian tradition, it implicitly encourages prospective local "converts" to Judaism. This is in spite of a sort of disclaimer about proselytizing on the French version of the website. Entitled "Conversion au Judaïsme" (Conversion to Judaism), it offers the following declaration: "Bien que le Judaïsme ne soit pas une religion fondamentalement prosélytiste, il accepte néanmoins ceux qui, sincèrement et de leur propre gré, souhaitent et s'efforcent d'adopter la foi Juive" (Although Judaism is not an inherently proselytizing religion, it nonetheless accepts those who, sincerely and of their own free will, wish and endeavor to adopt the Jewish faith).[7] To put it another way: After providing an explanation as to why Christianity is the problem, the information offered on the website then provides the solution—Judaism—by way of demonstrating adherence to the "correct" tradition. This may not be the conventional, pavement-pounding method of seeking converts that Jewish law expressly forbids, but the outcome is, to some extent, the same. In fact, in Cameroon, it is working astonishingly well.

SETTING THE STAGE: THE CAMEROONIAN COMMUNITY IN CONTEXT

Often referred to as the "Crossroads of Africa," or "Africa in Miniature," the Republic of Cameroon is a developing country situated in West-Central Africa. It is bordered by Nigeria in the west; by Chad and the Central African Republic in the east; and by Equatorial Guinea, Gabon, and the Republic of the Congo in the south. The only country in Africa to have been colonized by three different European imperial powers—Germany, England, and France—Cameroon has over two hundred major ethnic and linguistic groups, making it among the more culturally diverse nations in Africa.[8] Religiously, the population is around 50 percent Christian, 25 percent followers of indigenous beliefs, and 20 percent Muslim, with many syncretistic combinations of native belief systems and conventional religions, as well as uncategorized beliefs, present.[9] The Muslim population lies mainly in the north of the country. The Christian denominations in the south of the country have traditionally been predominantly Catholic, but are beginning to slide toward a Protestant majority. Pentecostal and Revivalist churches are increasing their activities and drives for converts, but their followers still make up less than 10 percent of the population.[10]

With the exception of the self-defining Beth Yeshourun Jewish community, there has never been any record of an indigenous, organized Jewish community in Cameroon—nor of any substantial foreign Jewish community, for that matter, save the intermittent gatherings of expatriate Israelis working in the country during the years since Cameroon's independence. (Several colonial accounts do, however, suggest traces of Portuguese Jewish ancestry in Cameroon.[11]) Chabad, the ultra-Orthodox, charismatic Jewish renewal movement, does not have a presence in Cameroon; its hub in Central Africa is in the Democratic Republic of the Congo.

First exploited by the Portuguese in the fifteenth century, the area of present-day Cameroon proved a difficult region in which to maintain a steady European colonial presence during the Age of Exploration, due to its high rate of tropical diseases. In a territory that might be called "the white man's grave" par excellence, the presence of cerebral malaria—the deadliest strain of the disease on the planet—was a particularly strong impediment to long-term colonization. Thus, European powers did not have a strong foothold in Cameroon until quinine, the first widely used malarial suppressant drug, became available in the late nineteenth century. The establishment of Christian missions and trade outposts in Cameroon soon followed. The initial colonial presence during the Scramble for Africa, mostly by the Germans, disturbed the long-established Fulani dominance in the northern part of the country. For centuries, the Fulani had been using that region as their trafficking hub for the Islamic slave trade network in West Africa.

In 1884, Germany formally took control of most of the area of modern-day Cameroon, which it held until its defeat in the Kamerun Campaign of World War I (1916). After the war, the League of Nations divided the administration of the country between Britain and France. Respectively, these powers ruled the northern and southern areas of the former German protectorate as parts of their overseas empires until after World War II. Self-rule was granted to French Cameroon in 1958, and after a protracted political struggle, full independence was achieved in 1960, resulting in the birth of the Federal Republic of Cameroon.

In 1961, by popular referendum, the British enclaves in the south of Cameroon voted to join the emerging state, while the British areas in the far north elected to become part of Nigeria.

As with many former colonial territories struggling with the trials of independence, Cameroon's national challenges have been many. Due to the repressive policies of Cameroon's first authoritarian president, Ahmadou Ahidjo, a de facto civil war reigned between 1962 and 1970, when fighters backed by the communist Cameroonian People's Union agitated against what they decried as neoimperialist hegemony, pervasive corruption, and ethnic favoritism toward Muslim Fulani northerners of Ahidjo's background. Ahidjo was nonetheless credited with modernizing Cameroon's economy and integrating, at least somewhat successfully, the British and French infrastructures. Ahidjo resigned for health reasons in 1982. He was succeeded by Paul Biya, a Christian and ethnic Beti from the south.

Despite repeated accusations of political cronyism and human rights violations, Biya has ruled Cameroon since 1982, currently serving his sixth term as president. Like his predecessor before him, Biya rules in large part thanks to a system of what the French call *dosage*: an ethnic balancing act whereby positions of power in the regime are distributed to representatives from the country's major cultural and religious groups.[12]

Although freedom of the press and freedom of speech are tightly constrained by the government, religious freedom has been a constant in Cameroon since independence. As one of the African countries known for its religious tolerance, Cameroon, by way of its history and geographical location, has always been at the crossroads of intersecting systems of belief. Encompassing Sahelian and equatorial territories at the intersection of West and Central Africa, it straddles regions both traditionally Islamic and animist.

Because of its diverse colonial history, various streams of Christianity, from Roman Catholicism to Adventism, have long existed side by side in Cameroon. Missionary groups, Anglophone and Francophone, are still very active in the country. The public revulsion among large segments of the population—including among Muslims—regarding the ideology of the terrorist group Boko Haram, and its besmirching of

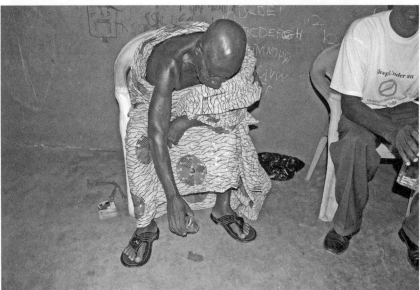

FIGURE 1. Alex Armah, spiritual leader of the Ghanaian community, in the synagogue in New Adiembra.

FIGURE 2. A Sefwi man pouring libations to the ancestors in New Adiembra.

FIGURE 3. Sefwi elders in Sefwi Wiawso.

FIGURE 4. Delegation of the Ga king, Nii Tackie Adama Latse II, led by his linguist, during a peace rally in Accra.

FIGURE 5. Oracle of the Ga king (center) pouring libations to the ancestors, Ga Palace, Accra.

FIGURE 6. Residence of the Ga high priest, Nuumo Adwaa Mensah III (seated, second from left), in Bokum, Accra.

FIGURE 7. The Cameroonian community outside the synagogue in Saa, after having received their first Torah scroll.

FIGURE 8. Cameroonian community members outside the synagogue.

FIGURE 9. Cameroonian community members during a religious service.

FIGURE 10. Cameroonian community members celebrating the arrival of the Torah scroll.

FIGURE 11. Cameroonian community members dancing outside the synagogue.

FIGURE 12. Cameroonian community members taking a break to surf the World Wide Web.

FIGURE 13. Cameroonian community members meeting with a delegation from the Celestial Church of Christ in Yaoundé.

FIGURE 14. Indian community members in the Guntur district synagogue.

FIGURE 15. Indian community members with the author (center) in Vijayawada, studying Hebrew via Skype.

FIGURE 16. Indian community members outside the synagogue in Machilipatnam.

FIGURE 17. A community member standing outside the synagogue in Machilipatnam.

FIGURE 18. A Hindu man in Vijayawada holding the fruit from which bitter chutney (a mixture supposedly akin to the bitter herbs eaten during the Jewish Passover) is made.

FIGURE 19. Shmuel Yacobi (standing at the table) leading a study session for Noahides in Tadikonda.

the tolerant Cameroonian image with its activities in northern Cameroon, has been widely publicized.

As in many parts of Africa, the notion that one would not belong to an organized religious community is considered anathema in Cameroon. This may explain part of the early missions' depiction of their successes in the region as the "Cameroonian miracle," referring to the rapidity of the spread of Christianity. On the subject of Cameroonians' natural propensity toward religiosity, Tatah H. Mbuy has declared, "What we can therefore call a Cameroonian worldview is that view which sees man as intimately caught up in a triangle of relationships with God, community, and self. It is a view which shuns atheism, abhors disunity, and sees the individualistic concept of a person as repugnant."[13] One informant in the neo-Jewish community echoed the essence of this statement when he told me: "In this country, a person without a religion is like an animal—it means that he has no soul. Secularism is not part of the Cameroonian worldview." Then, paraphrasing the more general expression about pan-African religiosity made famous by Zambia's first president, Kenneth Kaunda, the man said: "Part of the fundamental makeup of people in Africa is our attitude about 'the mysterious depth in life.'"[14]

Unlike the case of Ghana, where the genesis of the self-defining Jewish group coincided with a perceived recognition of links to Old Testament practices in precolonial heritage narratives, the Jewish *religious* experience was the sole impetus behind the formation of the Cameroonian community. As former Christians, the Cameroonians relate to their Jewishness, in some way, as a sort of conscious denial of a previous identity. In a sense, then, they see themselves as "a people bound together as much by their refusal of faith as by blood"—curiously, the same way that, as Fran Markovitz has noted, Jews under medieval European Christendom saw themselves.[15] But, because the Cameroonians have taken on their Judaism as an "ontological given" (again, in Markovitz's terms) for strictly religious reasons, their Jewishness does not necessitate the shared genealogy fundamental to the Ghanaian example.[16]

Whatever the reasoning may be for embracing the Jewish mold as their own, neither of these groups has had any ascertainable epistemological or hermeneutic basis in the Jewish experience. Neither do they share many preconceived philosophical commonalities with modern (Western) Jewish cultural or political thought, which has its roots in liberal, Enlightenment-based ideals regarding emancipation, assimilation, and, more than anything, secularism. As we shall see, this tension between the philosophical liberalism of the Western Jewish worldview (especially as it is articulated among Jews in the United States) and the more conservative moral perspectives in Cameroon presents an interesting prism through which one may view the continued, and possibly delicate, interactions between established and emerging Jewish communities.

BEGINNINGS OF A COMMUNITY

The Beth Yeshourun community was formally founded in 1998, after a group of about one hundred evangelical Christians who had been meeting regularly for Bible study became concerned with what they saw as apparent disparities between Old and New Testament worldviews. Since the formal study of the Hebrew Scriptures had been discouraged by their mainstream Christian churches, this group took it upon itself to figure out why. What, they wondered, was this Jewish faith that Jesus lived by? Why did some people refuse to become Christians after his death and resurrection, and what happened to them and their descendants? Why did the Church encourage its congregants to follow in the footsteps of Jesus, but not in those of the characters revered in the Old Testament, with whom many of the Cameroonian Christians felt, as one person said, "certain psychological affinities"? On this point, one of the first members of the study group told me: "During my days as a Christian, I was confused as to why I wasn't at all attracted by the figure of Jesus. But I was deeply moved by the stories about other people in the Old Testament, like Noah, Abraham, Isaac, Jacob, Joseph, Joshua, Samson, Samuel, King David, and King Solomon . . . but most of all, it was Moses whom I wished to emulate."

In addition to questioning the Church's marginalization of Old Testament figures, many members had begun to despair of the "Promise

of Heaven" theology that they saw within much of evangelical Cameroonian Christianity. In the opinion of one contact, many of those responsible for formulating the public discourse in Cameroon have taken to
replicating a theology whose doctrine of salvation focuses on the world
to come, while ignoring the political time-bomb of crushing poverty
and governmental neglect. Was Christianity, the members of the study
group questioned, just another ploy on the part of Cameroon's leaders
to make them weak and submissive?

As mentioned in earlier chapters, this questioning by African
peoples of the motivations of institutionalized Christianity is not new.
The Kikuyu proverb, "*Gutiri mubea na muthungu*" (There is no difference between a missionary and a settler), is perhaps the most oft-cited
simplification on the topic. In the Cameroonian context, many ethnic
groups, in particular the Bassa, had traditionally been hostile to Western
Christianity, although a large portion of this demographic did eventually
embrace (nominally, at least) the indigenized Christian doctrines of
various African Independent Churches.

Not surprisingly, Christianization in Cameroon has time and again
been equated with colonization. This is especially true with regard to
the tactics of the French during their period of colonial rule, although
the French were not the first to introduce Christianity to the natives.
My contacts in Beth Yeshourun maintain that, even more than the other
European colonial powers, the French used conversion and mission
schools as the proverbial carrot to "civilize" the native inhabitants of
Cameroon, all the while employing the very real stick of the in-situ
French regime. The Germans and the British did the same, but the
anger on the part of Cameroonians toward them is largely absent, due
in part to what they see as the particularly brutal way in which the
French colonial regime initially attempted to suppress independence
movements. The fact that France is now clearly the neocolonial power
only reinforces these negative perceptions.

Whatever the historical truth about comparative levels of colonial
brutality may be, the collective rage against the French colonialists—
as well as toward their perceived post- and neocolonial cronies, who
remain glued to the former colonial power in the dysfunctional relationship often referred to as *Françafrique*—is palpable in nearly every

corner of Cameroonian society.[17] A few illustrations of this sentiment are in order.

The time of my fieldwork in Cameroon coincided with the marking of the twentieth anniversary of the 1994 Rwandan genocide, in which approximately eight hundred thousand people, mainly ethnic Tutsis, were slaughtered by their Hutu neighbors. While listening to the radio one day, some Beth Yeshourun community members and I heard the accusation by Paul Kagame, president of Rwanda, that the French had played an active role in helping the Hutu militias to carry out the genocide. This declaration signified a notable ratcheting-up of the rhetoric surrounding France's complicity in the massacres, which had, prior to that time, been mostly confined to allegations of diplomatic ineptitude. My companions were quick to agree with Kagame. They also pointed out that the French were responsible for a wide variety of ills on the continent, such as the downfall of Libyan president Muammar Gaddafi; the introduction of the Ebola virus into West Africa, and the AIDS virus into Central Africa; and the disintegration of the Central African Republic. In all of these instances, they said, France was acting to further its exploitative interests by maintaining a form of neocolonial control of the continent, all under the guise of "humanitarian aid" and concerns about supposed democratic processes. Why should these things be surprising, they asked, when it is well known that the French hastily left many Sub-Saharan colonies with few university-trained public servants or manageable systems of infrastructure, precisely in order to ensure that those territories would remain needy and reliant? Since their departure, my companions claimed, the French have ruled in Africa by a kind of proxy colonialism.

Several congregants vowed that, should they ever journey out of the country by plane, they would circumvent Paris at all costs. I recounted to them a story about my maternal grandfather, a World War II veteran who detested the French with the utmost gusto for what he thought was their hasty capitulation to the Germans. I told them how, when he and I were on a trip from Spain to England, he had refused to leave the train station during a daylong mandatory stopover in Paris, while waiting to board the Eurostar to travel through the Chunnel. Though I mentioned the incident in a tongue-in-cheek fashion, expecting to elicit a few laughs, an elder looked at me solemnly and stated, "Your grandfather was right to do that."

In my continuing efforts to lighten the mood, I told a few of my usually better-received jokes about the French, which I had happened to learn (from French friends, it should be said) during my year as an undergraduate exchange student in Bordeaux. A representative sample follows. Question: "How are French children born?" Answer: "With their hands up!" Question: "Why are French weapons in such good condition?" Answer: "Because they've only been dropped once!" Question: "Why do French soldiers have name badges on their buttocks instead of on their chests?" Answer: "So they can recognize each other as they run away!" And so on. These were met with similar grave expressions and shaking of heads, but not with any laughter.

My companions also noted that any doubt about France's thoughts on whether or not Africans are capable of governing themselves was removed by former French president Nicolas Sarkozy's now-infamous "Dakar speech," given in Senegal's capital city in 2007. In that address, Sarkozy claimed that "Africa is partly responsible for its own misfortune." Then, sidestepping the responsibility of the colonial powers, he added, "The African peasant only knew the eternal renewal of time, marked by the endless repetition of the same gestures and the same words. In this realm of fancy . . . there is neither room for human endeavor nor the idea of progress."[18] After such an insulting and duplicitous speech, they asked, what further proof was needed in order to understand that the French had nothing but contempt for the Cameroonians' precolonial way of life?

My time in Cameroon also coincided with a series of anti-Semitic demonstrations in France, which were broadcast on Cameroonian radio. Listening to the reportage, which included recordings of protestors chanting, "Juif, casse-toi, la France n'est pas à toi!" (Jew, get out, France is not yours!), I watched my interlocutors shake their heads in dismay. My companions lamented the fact that France allowed its Jews to be treated so poorly. The French were ignorant of the Jews' divine mission, they said, due in part to the faulty translations of the Hebrew Scriptures into French. They told me they had learned to be especially wary of Louis Segond's *Édition de Genève*, the most widely disseminated

French translation of the Bible, which had been given to them by American Presbyterian missions. Many important truths about the Jews were purposely kept hidden in this translation, they asserted.

This trepidation was deeply ingrained, despite having no knowledge of historical anti-Semitism in France. For instance, no one I met had heard of the historical examples most often cited during discussions of discrimination against Jews in France, such as the Dreyfus Affair or the anti-Semitic legislation of the Vichy regime. Conversely, they knew nothing of the brighter sides of Jewish life in France, such as the fact that the celebrated Rabbi Shlomo Yitzchaki (1040–1106), more commonly known as Rashi, hailed from Troyes; or that the Napoleonic Emancipation was largely responsible for granting civic equality to Jews in the modern period.

To return to the subject of the community's beginnings: Most of the founding members of Beth Yeshourun were from the Cameroonian branch of the *Mission Evangélique du Christ* (Evangelical Mission of Christ), a Baptist-oriented movement based in Saint-Nazaire, France. The group eventually split up into three separate camps. One, despite its misgivings, decided not to leave the church. Another sought out a Messianic Jewish congregation, which would allow it to incorporate Old Testament–style worship practices without leaving Christianity altogether.[19] Finally, the last camp, which was led by Serge's father, Clément (Nachman) Etele, who was a pastor in this church at the time, decided to explore a "third option": to try their best to live by the laws of the Old Testament. The details of that option were not yet fully understood, since it was unclear precisely what kind of model the approximately one hundred people were searching for. Enter the Internet.

Since Nachman's son, Serge, had a greater ease navigating the Internet, he took it upon himself to do the lion's share of searching about how one might follow Mosaic Law in the present day. (Serge already had a working knowledge of English and a background in information technology, having worked for a time for the Cameroonian government as a freelance webmaster.) In time, Serge became the de facto "spiritual leader" of the community, as he calls himself, due to the ever-present necessity of accessing, and then making sense of, information obtained via the Internet.

Between 1998 and 2010, Serge spent a lot of time in Internet cafés. He succeeded in procuring for the community an impressive amount of material about those who, as he thought at the time, "still follow God's law to the letter": the Jews. In particular, Serge accessed a wealth of useful information from instructional sites run by Chabad, which are intended to bring nonpracticing Jews back into the religious fold. These sites are among the first to appear in a Google search on Jewish topics. What's more, they have French versions and are easily intelligible, since they presuppose no specialized knowledge of traditional practice. Other sites frequently visited include www.torahbox.com, which gives its mission of purpose as "diffusion du judaïsme aux francophones" (spreading Judaism to speakers of French), as well as www.hevratpinto.org, a site dedicated to the memories and teachings of two famous Moroccan rabbis, Haïm and Moshe Aaron Pinto.[20] Another popular site is www .akadem.org, a site jointly funded by the Paris-based *Fondation pour la mémoire de la Shoah* (Foundation for the Memory of the Holocaust) and the *Fonds social juif unifié* (Jewish Social Service Fund), which calls itself "un opérateur majeur dans le domaine de la diffusion de la culture juive" (a major player in the field of the propagation of Jewish culture).[21]

As their knowledge of normative Judaism increased, so did their numbers. People who had not been part of the original group heard about it through friends, family members, or, starting from 2011, by way of Google searches that led them to the community's website. The site describes the group as "une communauté de personnes pratiquant le Judaïsme, unies par le même lien d'amour du Dieu d'Israël et d'attachement à Ses commandements (Mistvot)" (a community of people who practice Judaism, unified by the same relationship of love for the God of Israel and the attachment to His commandments [*mitzvot*]).

Some brought their entire families with them. One woman mentioned to me how she joined the community when her younger brother began to read Hebrew prayers to her while she was ill; she claims to have, thereafter, miraculously recovered. Another noted that her family reacted positively to her interest in Judaism because "serving God as the people of Israel served him must be a good thing." Others were ostracized from their families because of the shift. For example, one young woman reported being left alone with a baby and no support system because her husband was convinced that she had "become part of a cult." Still others left due to internal discord. One such former member later attempted to form his own congregation and, to that end, traveled to meet with rabbis in France and Germany for support. Because of problems verifying the outcome of his story, I have decided not to include it here.

All of the persons thus far who have joined Beth Yeshourun are former Christians, although some of them had been practicing a syncretistic form of Christianity, combined with indigenous religions and/ or ancestor worship, prior to their adoption of Judaism. Several such individuals mentioned to me that, although many newcomers expressed exasperation with the cumbersome food taboos necessitated by Jewish law, those who had previously been following ancestral rites in combination with Christian practice were used to being "picky" about their food. One man told me: "I was not at all surprised by the Jewish lifestyle, especially the kosher laws, since from the time I was a child I had systematically refused to eat almost everything prohibited by the Law."

What kinds of people were drawn to this fledgling group? One was a Benedictine monk-in-training who was going through a crisis of faith. After stumbling across a copy of the Zohar, the "Book of Splendor" (the most important work in the Kabbalah) in a used book store, he asked his superiors at the monastery why "Jewish mysticism" was not anywhere in the New Testament. They explained to him that those who decided not to follow Christ had formed a heretical philosophy, akin to witchcraft. When he pressed them for more information, they told him to drop the subject, as it was not important for his studies.

An aside here is in order. Informal study of the Kabbalah by non-Jews—at least in its pop-culture iteration—is considered by many in Francophone Africa to be a very hip activity. Online Kabbalah study groups abound, as do in-person group study meetings. Major Kabbalah Centers exist in Benin, Cameroon, and the Ivory Coast. Cameroon in particular has a relatively long infatuation with Kabbalah, ever since President Paul Biya, who originally trained as a seminarian, was supposedly taught its esoteric secrets by an Algerian-born rabbi. Patricia Balme, a communications officer for the president, writes that Biya "a toujours été mystique" (has always been a mystic), and that he is "féru d'esoterisme" (crazy about esotericism).[22] As we have seen in the case of Dominique, religious seekers online frequently find their way to sites promoting mystical practices of some sort, often loosely labeled "Kabbalah." Another member of Beth Yeshourun who had been to Israel for business purposes was studying Kabbalah online when he realized that, as he told me, "I wouldn't be able to understand anything about Kabbalah without knowing the fundamentals of Judaism." This man's acquaintances in Israel helped him to search online for other Jewishly oriented venues, and were able to find information on Serge's community, to which they directed him.

Another young man who joined the community was the son of a Pentecostal pastor, and a pastor-in-training himself. He reported that part of the initiation rites of the seminary that he attended included the need to find one's "own language": in other words, to speak in tongues. He recounted to me that he felt like this was "complete bullshit." Providentially, this realization ended up marking the beginning of his path toward Judaism. Once he had admitted to himself that this part of his church was a show, giving up Jesus was not so hard. His crisis of faith also coincided with an introduction to the community via a friend.

Frédérick, whom I have mentioned earlier, joined the community in 2013, after hearing about it from an acquaintance at the Russian Cultural Center in Douala. Unlike the two young men mentioned above, Frédérick was not going through a crisis of faith. For most of his life he had been an active member of a Cameroonian branch of the *Église du Christianisme Céleste* (Celestial Church of Christ), a prophetic church based in Benin and Nigeria. An ethnic Bassa, Frédérick was attracted to Beth Yeshourun's practices because, as it seemed to him, the community had succeeded in uncovering "the true religion of the ancestors." The first proponent of the genealogical trope among Beth Yeshourun's members, Frédérick eventually felt compelled to give up his long-standing membership in the church. His two sons now want to become rabbis and, according to him, are even "more Jewish" than he is. The proof? Whenever the boys' sisters are menstruating, the sons insist that their sisters stay in their rooms and not touch any communal food. A separate discussion about Frédérick and the supposed shared genealogy with the Bassa people follows later in this chapter.

CONTACTS ABROAD

A milestone moment for Beth Yeshourun occurred in March 2010, when Serge began exchanging e-mails with Kulanu. Serge had come across their website during one of his online searches, and was interested in knowing more about the outreach work they did for emerging African Jewish communities. After an initial series of introductions, he invited representatives from the organization to visit Cameroon whenever they could do so. Husband and wife rabbis Gerald and Bonita Sussman accepted the invitation and visited Cameroon in July of that year.

The particularity of the way in which this meeting was achieved merits a special revisiting. So let us recap: An emerging African community of former Christians begins to self-identify as Jewish, despite the fact that none of them has ever met a Jew in person. They spend over ten years gathering information about their new religion from the Internet. They do this using desperately slow technology on personal laptops in a village with very little electricity, or make a special schlep to the nearest urban locale in order to access the World Wide Web at Internet cafés. They make contact with an association located almost six thousand miles away. That association sends two emissaries to assess the situation. And so the formal recognition of the Beth Yeshourun community begins.

The Sussmans, for their part, were deeply impressed by what they discovered in Cameroon. According to the Kulanu website, they found "a thriving and dedicated community practicing the Jewish faith in a knowledgeable and highly motivated manner. Their [the Cameroonians'] grasp of Jewish ritual and law and the sophistication of the questions they asked . . . reflected the depth of their knowledge."[23] Bonita Sussman informed me that she and her husband expected to find a community "in progress," but, instead, found "a group of already-made Jews."[24] Unlike other emerging groups, they did not need much help with their Jewish learning. What they needed, she said, was infrastructure.

Upon their return to the United States, the Sussmans agreed to serve as the community's online spiritual mentors. The Sussmans also assisted in facilitating a loan made to the community via Kulanu, for $22,500, with the aim of establishing the aforementioned infrastructure.

Specifically, the funds were earmarked to buy land for a very large cocoa farm. (Cameroon is a global leader in the production of cocoa, after the Ivory Coast, Indonesia, and Ghana.)[25] Kulanu's website describes the loan to Beth Yeshourun thus: "Although Kulanu rarely engages in economic development projects, the board decided to help the community advance these goals through an agricultural development project."[26] With the profits from the farm, which the community members will work themselves, they hope to be able to erect a permanent synagogue (the existing location, in Serge's family home, happens to be sandwiched between two very loud Pentecostal churches), a kosher butcher shop, ritual baths, a learning center, and a guesthouse for foreign visitors.

In the winter of 2012, at the invitation of Kulanu, Serge visited the United States. He spent six weeks giving lectures about his community at synagogues, universities, and Jewish community centers along the East Coast. Most significantly, Kulanu helped arrange Serge's formal conversion to Judaism, which was conducted by three American rabbis (two Conservative and one Orthodox). Serge took the Hebrew name *Yisrael Amir* ("Israel" and "treetop," respectively). During his time in the United States, Serge was hosted mainly by organizations connected in some way to Kulanu. Harriet Bograd, the president of Kulanu, told me that she initially was worried that Serge would not feel comfortable in the homes of people who were presumably less observant than he was. Serge eased her fears by reassuring her that he followed the principle of *minhag hamakom* (literally, "the custom of the place"; figuratively, an accepted community practice). In other words, he would ease his orthodoxy as required, depending on the tendencies of his hosts. Harriet found this impressive, considering that Serge had, prior to the visit, never met other (Western) Jews in his life, save the Sussmans.

In the face of growing interest and recognition, it was obvious that Serge would eventually need some kind of accreditation in his role as spiritual leader. Again, the online option was the one that provided an imperfect, albeit temporary, resolution to the problem. Upon his return to Cameroon, and with the financial support of a Canadian Jewish congregation, Serge enrolled in online classes in the *Pirchei Shoshanim* (Rose Blossoms) Seminary, an initiative of the Shema Yisrael Torah Network College Credit Program. According to the seminary's website, the program offers "comprehensive courses on extensive topics" and "provides meaningful learning opportunities for individuals who are seeking to develop and expand their knowledge of, and commitment to, Jewish law."[27]

Why did Serge not elect to travel abroad to attend seminary, as did Gershom Sizomu, the leader of the Abayudaya Jews of Uganda? Serge told me his reasoning was as follows: Even if Kulanu, or other Jewish groups, could have financially supported Serge (as they did Rabbi Sizomu) with a scholarship to come to the States to study, the course of study would have been six years—far too long for his community to hold together without a leader. As an only child and one of the main workers on his family's cocoa plantation, an absence of six years would not have been feasible.

As an alternative to a long-term stay in the United States, Serge hoped to be able to spend several months at a time studying in Israel. But this plan was complicated by the fact that the Israeli embassy in Cameroon had not yet agreed to issue him a tourist visa. Even the British embassy denied Serge a visa to attend the *Limmud* (study) conference, an annual global Jewish convention held in the United Kingdom. The official reason for these refusals? Serge could not provide proof that he would willingly return to Cameroon.

The more likely reason—at least on the part of the Israeli authorities—is the fear that a growing number of impoverished, potential black African converts to Judaism will want to immigrate to Israel, thereby putting untenable pressure on Israel's social welfare system. Several members of the Beth Yeshourun community told me that they were also denied tourist visas to Israel, and that the Israeli embassy staff had been quite rude to them. The community was invited once to a Hanukkah celebration at the embassy, but had not been contacted after that event. They were perplexed as to why the staff of the Israeli embassy made continued overtures to Christian Zionist churches in Cameroon, but not to the people who had elected to live out their lives as Jews. I attempted to make contact with the Israeli embassy in Cameroon to verify these stories and to hear the staff's impressions of the Beth Yeshourun community. My calls and e-mails went unreturned.

The Internet, for all its miracles, is still a poor substitute for real-life interaction. As the community developed, Serge realized that he would need to physically attend classes in ritual circumcision and methods of kosher animal slaughter in order to be certified for these two basic Jewish practices, which are essential elements for any semblance of Jewish communal infrastructure. During my fieldwork in Cameroon, Serge lamented that he had been unable to obtain a tourist visa to Israel in order to become certified in the two aforementioned ritual practices, despite years of efforts and promises from the Israeli ambassador to Cameroon. He told me that he had briefly considered going to Morocco for the certification, since it would be easier to obtain a visa to somewhere in Africa; but he feared that the Orthodox rabbis there would be disinclined to recognize his conversion from the United States. The same problem of recognition prevented Serge from applying for possible study with Rabbi Sizomu in Uganda. Sizomu, who is Conservative, would have given Serge accreditation only recognized in select parts of the Jewish world—the same paradox that befell Alex Armah from Ghana, as mentioned in chapter 2.

The last day of my stay in Cameroon, Serge finally received a renewable, two-month tourist visa to Israel, which he used to study circumcision, ritual slaughter, and other Jewish topics at the Ohr Torah Stone Seminary, located in the city of Efrat, in the West Bank. The seminary is run by American-born Shlomo Riskin, the chief rabbi of Efrat, who has a Zionist, Modern Orthodox perspective on Jewish law. Riskin is well known in the Israeli public, and in Jewish circles in general, for two things in particular: advocating for women's rights; and campaigning for the decentralization of the practice of conversion in Israel, which is currently controlled by the ultra-Orthodox state Rabbinate. Bonita Sussman made this announcement about Serge's acceptance to the seminary on behalf of Kulanu: "We are thrilled to report that Rabbi Shlomo Riskin . . . has agreed to partner with Kulanu to help develop Jewish life in Africa."[28] Riskin, a very influential figure in Israeli political life, apparently put pressure on the Israeli authorities to issue the visa for which Serge had been waiting for so long. As of this writing, Serge spends several months in Israel every year studying under Rabbi Riskin, with the eventual aim of obtaining his rabbinic ordination.

PRAXIS AND WORLDVIEW

On the operational level, the members of Beth Yeshourun follow normative Jewish religious practice as closely as they possibly can, a proper local infrastructure notwithstanding. If one takes away the rural African setting and the linguistic or physiognomic specificities, witnessing a religious service at the Beth Yeshourun synagogue might seem almost identical to witnessing a Conservative or Modern Orthodox service at any synagogue in Europe, Israel, or the Americas. In the age of selfies and YouTube, this should not prove surprising, since, even before the arrival of the Sussmans, the congregation had meticulously studied online videos of Jewish services overseas. They had also learned traditional Hebrew melodies and classic Israeli patriotic songs to sing during services and festivals. "*Hatikvah*" (The Hope), Israel's national anthem, and "*Yerushalayim shel zahav*" (Jerusalem of Gold) are two favorites.

The members of Beth Yeshourun have their own prayer books. These are essentially assortments of printed material in French, which have been downloaded from the Internet and then bound together. Hebrew prayers are listed alongside a French transliteration. The weekly Torah portions are read from French Bibles given by missionaries. The congregants pray three times a day, and meet twice weekly for Bible study. Women and men sit separately, except when young mothers need help with their children. There is no partition. Most of the rites are Sephardic, because of the influence of the Francophone sites, largely run by and for Sephardic Jews, from which the community takes the majority of its information. According to the community's website, their practices "tendent vers l'orthodoxie" (lean toward Orthodoxy).[29] Despite this tendency, women are currently allowed to form part of the *minyan* (prayer quorum), although the community wishes to change this practice once they are able to ensure a presence of ten adult males at every gathering.

Although the men wear skullcaps and prayer shawls during religious services, they rarely wear them outside of the synagogue. Most men are not bearded. Some wear ritual fringes, but others have not been able to locate any to purchase. No one eats meat outside of the community because they know it has not been properly slaughtered. The Sabbath is kept without question. Women practice menstrual seclusion, and the nearby river functions as the *mikveh* (bath for ritual immersion), for purposes of ridding oneself of impurity. Circumcision is almost universally practiced in Cameroon, due both to the Muslim presence, as well as to the history of the custom in traditional tribal ritual; and so ensuring adherence to this procedure is not a problem. However, before Serge's certification as a trained ritual circumciser, community members elected to have their newborn sons circumcised on the eighth day by a doctor in the hospital, where they gathered to hold a circumcision ceremony. When there is doubt about how best to carry out any one of the ritual obligations, the community consults with rabbis or persons versed in Jewish law via e-mail.

Their numerous contacts with Jews overseas during the past few years have somewhat changed the ways in which they relate to their Jewishness. Whereas the Hebrew Scriptures were once the sole basis of their practice and belief, they now possess a greater understanding about postexilic Jewish life and practice, thanks to online discussions about seminal texts such as the *Pirkei Avot* (Sayings of the Fathers) or the *Shulkhan Arukh* (Code of Jewish Law). In recent years, many members have also begun to use Facebook to "friend" Jews from abroad, including those from France, Israel, and other emerging African communities. Those who have televisions watch I24 News, a Jewish-oriented Francophone television station based in Israel. Other popular outlets for news about Israel include Judeo-centric Francophone websites such as www.juif.org/tv. As of this writing, only one person from the community besides Serge has visited Israel (the same individual mentioned earlier whose acquaintances in Israel were the ones to direct him to Beth Yeshourun).

Although there is now an entire generation of Beth Yeshourun that knows only Judaism as its way of life, this knowledge comes strictly from the home. For, even if they could afford to staff an entirely Jewish school, the community does not yet have a critical mass for such a venture. Children in the rural area of Saa attend local schools out of necessity, while those in Douala and Yaoundé attend either public schools (not the best option, due to the poor quality of education) or, funds permitting, private Christian schools (a better educational option, despite the religious conflict of interest). Several members have elected to enroll their children at Adventist schools, since there, they claim, the children will at least gain a proper understanding of Old Testament practices.[30] Also, Adventists in Cameroon are among the most vocal in their support for the state of Israel. A comment from an Adventist minister on this point is telling: "Israel is obviously the strongest nation in the world," he said to me. "Who else could say no to Obama a million times and keep getting such copious amounts of aid?"

A similar problem of critical mass affects the community in the realm of marriage. There are simply not enough regular members of marriageable age to go around. So, when pressured to choose between remaining eternally single (not an acceptable choice in Cameroonian society) or taking a spouse who does not agree to live Jewishly, assimilation is the only option. A frequent point of contention is the prohibition against working on Saturday, which, for men in particular, carries heavy economic consequences. Many members explained to me that this was one of the key obstacles to keeping the community intact, and, on that topic, wanted to know about possibilities for arranging marriages between Beth Yeshourun members and Jews overseas.

Persons who have come to Judaism after having been married, and whose spouses do not wish to embrace Judaism, are not required to divorce. With regard to his Catholic wife, one man told me, "She wants to know more before making a big leap. Because I don't want to proselytize, I don't force her hand. I know that one day she'll join me, though, because my [Jewish] soul acts like a ray of light for her." With regard to the children of mixed marriages, the community does not currently discriminate between children who have only one Jewish parent, be it the father or the mother. One practicing parent is enough. (It is worth noting that this custom, based on demographic necessity, is considerably more flexible than the other mostly Orthodox practices that they have adopted.) Wherever possible, the community follows the convention accepted by most religious communities in Cameroon, according to which children (especially male children) are raised in the religious setting favored by the father.

Beth Yeshourun's stance regarding Israel is, at least on the surface, typical of many observant communities in the Jewish Diaspora, in that criticism of the Jewish state is kept to a relative minimum. When asked about their opinions regarding Israel, respondents offered the following statements: "Jews there feel free because they are no longer in exile, and this makes us proud"; "Although we are far from there, we feel its joys and its sorrows, because we feel connected to those who live there"; "The creation of the state of Israel constitutes a very important part of my belief system . . . it announces the end of the exile of the Jews." When pressed for an exact reason as to why Israel is important, one man remarked, "We need Israel because Jews are persecuted in most of the other countries." To illustrate his point, he told me that even in the United States, Jews are not safe. He related that the United States government had accused Dominique Strauss-Kahn, former director of the International Monetary Fund, of sexual assault only because he is of Jewish origin. Of course, the man emphasized, the French had their role to play in the affair. That conversation then drifted back to various criticisms of the Fifth Republic.

Like those in many diasporic Jewish communities who have little real-life experience of modern-day Israel, members of Beth Yeshourun also have some difficulty processing the very secular nature of many aspects of Israeli life. When asked about the system of values that reigns supreme in that country, one person noted, "Israel as a modern state is firmly based upon the law of *Moshe rabbeinu* (Moses our teacher)." Another member, who had followed Serge on Facebook during Serge's time in Israel, and had seen profile pictures of some of the scantily clad Israeli females who had "friended" Serge, expressed shock at Jewish women being allowed by the state to dress in such a manner. He then alluded to a possible moral lapse on the part of Israel, which, he said, was becoming increasingly westernized because of globalization. "The leaders of Israel," he said, "should really take into account the commandments of the Torah, which are the foundation of the state."

This lack of nuance regarding the state of Israel also manifests itself in how the community views the Israeli-Palestinian conflict. Although the Cameroonian Jews profess to have no problem with their Muslim neighbors—and, as far as I could tell from the many conversations that I had with them, they have no problem with Muslims in general, anywhere—their overwhelmingly negative perceptions of the Palestinians closely toe the line of most right-wing, pro-Israel media outlets. This is not surprising, considering the places from which they obtain the majority of their news about Israel.

There is also a localized rationale for these views: namely, preexisting sentiment in Cameroon about the prowess and moral superiority of the Israeli military. Most Cameroonians are aware that, since 1989, when President Biya was almost ousted in an attempted coup, the president's personal security apparatus has been staffed by former Israeli commandos. Many are also familiar with the figure of Avraham Avi Sivan, former defense attaché at the Israeli embassy in Yaoundé, who helped to found Biya's *Battalion d'intervention rapide* (Rapid Intervention Battalion), an elite combat unit. Sivan is also credited with persuading President Biya never to vote against Israel in the United Nations, thereby helping to provide a positive image for the Jewish state in Cameroon, despite the country's important Muslim population. Significantly, in 2012, Cameroon was one of the few African countries (along with Rwanda, Togo, and the Democratic Republic of the Congo) that abstained in the vote on whether to let Palestine have nonmember observer status in the United Nations.

Several postings on Facebook by members during 2014's "Operation Protective Edge," in which Israel invaded the Hamas-ruled Gaza Strip in order to stop rocket fire against Israel, demonstrated a categorically conservative stance. One person posted: "Ces Palestiniens veleunt nous détruire à l'indifférence du monde. C'est à Israël que nous appartenons et nous lui sommes solidaires" (These Palestinians want to destroy us, and the world is unmoved. It's to Israel that we belong, and with which we are united). In a Skype conversation around the time of this operation, another person told me that he had stayed up all night in order to hear the latest news about missing Israeli soldier Hadar Goldin, whose death was later confirmed by DNA testing. He said: "We've just lost one of our boys, which a cancer has taken from us." He then added the traditional Hebrew response to the news of a Jew's death, "*Barukh dayan haemet!*" (Blessed is the True Judge!). Note the unilateral expressions of solidarity: the fallen soldier is one of "ours," and it is "us" that the Palestinians, who are a "cancer," want to destroy. To be sure, I am in no way mocking these sentiments about a shared destiny. They are genuine. The pain that members of the Cameroonian community feel at the loss of Jewish life is real. However, the practical lengths to which this Zionism may be taken, and the extent to which such sentiments are even minimally reciprocal, are other matters entirely.

Do the members of Beth Yeshourun desire to immigrate to Israel? At the time of this writing, the answer is a definitive "no." They do not, they claim, wish to follow the example of the Ethiopian Jews. They mention the self-defining Igbo Jews from Nigeria as a possible model. The Igbo, they say, who are increasing their numbers within Nigeria, are helping Israel to be, in the words of Isaiah 42:6, "a light unto the nations" from afar. What's more—and, as strange as it may sound to Israelis, or to Jews from the West—the Cameroonian community does not think that it needs Israel. (The heavy groans of Israeli skeptics, who are convinced that any group of black Jews-in-the-making is only plotting to take advantage of Israel's generous social network for new immigrants, are readily audible as I write this.) The contrary is actually the case: the Cameroonians think that Israel needs *them*. I repeat: they only want to support Israel, and do not want anything material from it. When I first heard their stance on Israel articulated in such a fashion, I confess that my thoughts went immediately to the image of a popular tee shirt worn by Israelis, as a kind of snub to patronizing American Jewish tourists. The tee shirt, in English, reads: "Don't worry, America—Israel is behind you!"

I mentioned earlier the rough estimate given to me of around eight million prospective Jews in Central Africa, which, I assume, is based on expected interest from those hailing from the Bassa and Beti ethnic groups (more on that below). Beth Yeshourun's senior leaders told me that Israel therefore has a potential "reserve army" of approximately eight million people (their estimate) in Central Africa, who can be called upon to defend the Jewish state in a time of crisis. With so many Arab countries demographically outnumbering Israeli Jews, they stress, this is not an offer to be sniffed at. Training of reservists would begin in Israel once the community and their expected millions of adherents were officially recognized by the Israeli Rabbinate. On this subject, one member asked me, since I am a former officer of the Israel Defense

Forces, if I might arrange for him to send his son to Israel for military training before the official recognition comes. I had to admit that I was unsure of how such a process might work.

A Western visitor to the Beth Yeshourun synagogue, who shall remain unnamed, pointed out that Serge's daughter has been given the Hebrew name of *Aliyah* (literally, "ascent"; more figuratively, "immigration to Israel"). This is proof, he fumed, that the members' true intention is to follow in the footsteps of the Ethiopian Jews and immigrate en masse to the Jewish state. He also noted how, in their synagogue, the American and Israeli flags are positioned more prominently than the Cameroonian flag. Allegedly, this is proof that the Cameroonian Jews' national alliances were shifting. Serge's study in Israel would just be the first drop in a flood that would overwhelm Israel in the long run.

Based on my extensive contacts with the community, I disagree with this man's predictions for two major reasons. The first is that, unlike in the case of the Ethiopian immigration, there is no prejudice against the Jews in Cameroon; and, given the country's social makeup and particularly diverse history, there is never likely to be. Second, there is a wide ideological gulf between the worldview of the Beth Yeshourun community and the religious (and not to mention secular) Israeli communities with which they would be enmeshed. Despite their love for Israel on the abstract level, in practice, this gulf will not be easily bridged. I illustrate why with a few examples given below.

During my time in Cameroon, I repeatedly heard two unfailing, albeit vague criticisms of life in Israel that were clearly labeled as deterrents from wanting to live there. According to one person, Israel had become "too democratic." Allowing Palestinian citizens of Israel to vote was a dangerous precedent, as was the ease with which women could leave their homes and lead independent lives. So many political parties made elections every few years an unstable but constant component of political life. A divine kingship would be a better thing for Jewish sustainability. One man's comment that "in Israel, the system is Greco-Roman, and that is foreign to our mind-set" speaks volumes.

Another telling criticism of life in Israel, as alluded to earlier, is that the regime, under attack by the loose mores of globalized media, allows for too much secularism. For example, when I confirmed as true the rumors about whether pork is sold in Jerusalem, or that buses do indeed run on the Sabbath in Tel-Aviv, the revulsion was palpable. That said, I was never asked why I personally did not wear a skullcap, why I traveled on Shabbat, or why I ate meat that I could not verify as kosher. I was also referred to as an "angel" that God had sent to the community, despite my obvious secularism.

Put simply, the possibility of being naturalized in Israel is not something that occupies the thoughts of most community members. Unsurprisingly, the most pressing Jewish issue remains the current lack of infrastructure, which effectively prevents them from living as observant Jews. On the one hand, this is a strictly financial, and therefore theoretically solvable, problem. On the other, it is a problem complicated by the larger issue of recognition, or lack thereof, on the part of major Jewish overseas communities, since it is unlikely that Beth Yeshourun will ever be able to develop a Jewish infrastructure entirely on its own.

How will they gain the recognition they so desire? Formal conversion appears to be the only way. Menachem Kuchar, a colleague of Rabbi Shlomo Riskin, who was the third Western Jew to visit the community in February 2014, spoke to me about the problem regarding their conversion. Prior to Kuchar's visit to Cameroon, he had been counseling the community online regarding queries related to Jewish law and custom. According to Kuchar, the logical move to make would be for all the community members in Cameroon to be converted, not just Serge. Why? Because if Serge is the only Orthodox (read: recognized by Israel) member of Beth Yeshourun, then the Cameroonian community is still, in the eyes of many, just not Jewish enough. This is in spite of the fact that Kuchar thinks they are already living in an Orthodox fashion. Upon his return to Israel, Kuchar wrote on his blog:

> As much as I felt at home with them, and as much as I respect their conviction to *Hashem* [God] and His Torah, I know their path to orthodox conversion will be long and arduous. First there is no established community in Cameroon; this is often a prerequisite for conversion. I don't believe this should make much of a difference with these people. What they have managed to learn and are practicing on their own, mainly using the Internet as a

resource, shows that they are able to function and grow without an existing, external community. Of course we should be coupling this with periodic visits from the outside, as well as bringing their members to Israel for further education and experience.

The second and major problem is what can only be described as a racist attitude by Israeli government officials. The proposed changes in the conversion law are supposed to make conversion easier; but will this effect our situation? When senior officials can say, "We're not racist, but you know that these people have many relatives," and "We'll give you a visa for your person to come to study, on condition that you do not convert him," then I believe there is a problem. Or, "Use the new conversion law to convert people who will be of benefit to Israeli society," the implication being obvious, I can only feel great shame being Israeli.[31]

The dilemma as articulated by Kuchar boils down to the following paradox: most Orthodox rabbis, especially those from Israel, will not want to convert a community whose members cannot live Jewishly due to a lack of infrastructure. Recognition connotes sufficient means. The Cameroonian community has neither. Infrastructure will not come until they are recognized, and recognition will not come without infrastructure. If conversions are to be performed, money needs to be raised either to (1) bring rabbis to Cameroon to perform the procedure; or (2) bring all the Cameroonians to Israel, the United States, or a third country, for an extended period of time necessary for the conversions to take place. Both scenarios are unlikely. That said, after the recent conversions of over one hundred people in Madagascar to Orthodox Judaism in May 2016 (an event facilitated by Kulanu and discussed at length in this book's conclusion), the first option is not out of the realm of the possible.

While some of the members of Beth Yeshourun see the idea of conversion as insulting, most are willing to do it if it helps them to gain recognition and to live more Jewishly. One person, who scoffed at the idea that conversion should be necessary, told me that "conversion is just an artificial and political formality." Another person, in an e-mail, put a variation of such an opinion to me like this: "Je demeure persuadé qu'on naît Juif et qu'on ne le devient pas du jour au lendemain. Je considère la conversion comme une pure formalité qui ne peut m'empêcher dans aucune mesure d'observer les *mitzvot* dans la mesure de mes possibilités." (I remain convinced that one is born a Jew, and that one does not become Jewish from one day to the next. I consider conversion to be a pure formality that does not prevent me, in any way, from observing the *mitzvot* [commandments] to the best of my abilities.)

On the economic plane, the community has many plans to increase its wealth in order to become as self-sustaining as possible. Many agenda items have to do with the feasibility of different business ventures. These include ideas such as using the profits from the cocoa plantation sponsored by Kulanu to launch a "fair trade Jewish chocolate" initiative; marketing the CDs of several community musicians to overseas Jewish audiences; starting a gold-panning business; forming a tour agency that would cater to overseas Jewish visitors to Africa; opening a center for the study of Hebrew and Aramaic, which would attract local Christians; starting a poultry farm to compete with the Chinese hegemony in that industry (community members are convinced that people would want to buy eggs from a store with signage in Hebrew); building a retirement home for Jewish pensioners from abroad, much like the kind that exist already in Central and South America; and starting a Jewish university (to compete with the Islamic university being constructed in Yaoundé by the Turks) that will draw upon "Jewish values" in order to attract Adventists and other philo-Semitic Christian groups.

Many members of Beth Yeshourun express the desire to go into business ventures with Israeli and American Jewish businessmen, since, according to them, "people will want to do business with their brothers, because they know they won't be cheated." To that end, the community has set up a business fund called Magen Co., Ltd., which will be the umbrella investment organization for such efforts. In an e-mail to me about the establishment of the fund, one person wrote, "Il est temps que nos hommes d'affaires viennent conquérir l'Afrique Centrale qui a été maintenue dans l'obscurité par la France et les catholiques" (It's time for our [Jewish] businessmen to come and conquer Central Africa, which has been held down in darkness by France and the Catholics). Pondering the astounding transformations of these former Christians who now self-identify as Jews, I couldn't help repeating to myself the glib saying about stereotypical Jewish entrepreneurship: "Jesus saves, but Moses invests!"

In the nonprofit arena, community members are talking about starting a center for the study of the Holocaust. Taught by overseas volunteer staff via video feed, the center would offer classes to local people about the history of that catastrophe, as well as classes on genocide prevention. Because of the history of slavery and the legacy of colonialism, Beth Yeshourun members say, Africans would be able to easily relate to this catastrophe. What's more, some are likely to become attracted to Judaism because of it, drawing on the trope that Vittorio Lanternari has called "an image of anguish and successful survival," which is one "with which the [Cameroonian] natives [would] wish to be identified."[32] The center would also help in the realm of public relations for the state of Israel.

When polled about their hopes for the future, community members express the desire to see both economic and "inter-fraternal cooperation" with Jews from the outside world. One member commented, "Given the relatively weak economic situation of the community, it would help, if possible, that we be supported economically." Another said that the outside Jewish world could help by "avoiding exclusion and negative thoughts, and by going beyond unhealthy stereotypes that always make one think that, because we are African and black, we are looking to convert in order to improve our lot." He then added that, above all, "we need the good wishes of other communities in the world, because we all have the same priorities."

One has to wonder how far such cooperation and goodwill are liable to go, given the deep ideological dissonance between the Emancipation-based, Enlightenment-infused, neoliberal worldview of the Israeli and Western groups that (potentially) support Beth Yeshourun and encourage their embrace of Judaism, and the more "traditional" worldview of the Cameroonians. It is not at all certain, at least from my impressions, that any shared priorities go beyond surface-level considerations, despite the reciprocal feelings of affection and general expressions of goodwill.

How are the worldviews of the Cameroonians essentially different from those of their overseas coreligionists? As with all the other groups profiled in this book, there is a deep lack of understanding on the Cameroonians' part about the essential links between secular culture and modern Jewish points of view. This stems, in large part, from their adoption of Judaism as a discursive *religious* system divorced entirely from notions of cultural belonging. In turn, this lack of understanding about the emphasis on the cultural components of Jewish life is exacerbated by the fact that the sources from which they learn about modern Jewish civilization are almost all invariably religious sources, written by and for religious people. These same sources often frame modern Jewish life in reactionary terms of two options: proper religious observance, or hedonistic indulgences that invariably lead to assimilation.

On the subject of observance, for example, several people in the community asked me to explain the differences between Reform, Conservative, and Orthodox movements, about which they had read briefly online. When these people learned that Reform Judaism does not require anyone to keep the Sabbath, to follow food taboos, or to observe purity laws, the reaction was one of incredulity. How then, they wondered, can such living be called "Jewish"? When I tried to offer a bit of background by explaining the reasons for which many Jews in the nineteenth century had revolted against the tyranny of the rabbis and tried to bring about civic integration and equality, the reaction was one of disbelief. Why, they wondered, were Jewish observance and modern life so mutually exclusive?

To illustrate further, I used the example of my maternal great-grandfather, who was a bacon-eating, card-carrying communist from the Ukraine. As a new immigrant to the United States, he refused to send his son (my grandfather) to Hebrew school, fearing that a parochial education would condemn the child to a life of provincialism and limited opportunity. Instead, he sent his son to a secular Yiddish school, where he would learn about Jewish (read: Yiddish) *culture* from the Old World. Angry both at the rabbis who decried Jewish emancipation and self-reliance as ungodly, and at the anti-Semitic authorities that perpetuated the same structural inequalities that had forced him to leave Europe, my great-grandfather did not need religion to remind him of his Jewishness. It was who he was, plain and simple, because of the culture in which he had grown up, and because others would always define him that way. He had adopted heartily the words of advice given by Yehuda Leib Gordon, which became, in effect, the maxim of the Jewish Enlightenment: "Be a Jew at home and a man on the street."

This story did not impress my listeners. Nor did the emphasis on relating to Jewishness as a culture *sans* religion seem to make any sense. Whatever social challenges that living Jewishly might entail, interpreting the Law metaphorically, or relating to biblical stories simply as legends with laudable moral content, sounded too "Catholic." By "Catholic," what they meant was a perspective too symbolic to be truly meaningful. Many reproach the Catholics for advocating a doctrine that tends to allegorize and typologize the Hebrew Scriptures, rather than following them to the letter. The idea that "metaphorical truth" might be another possible paradigm also fell flat.

To be clear, I am not suggesting that the Cameroonian worldview is backward in any way. I only wish to point out that there are significant ideological differences between the perspectives of this emerging community and their established backers and benefactors. These differences are often glossed over, since, upon first glance, Cameroonian Jewish customs closely model the worship styles and textual praxis of recognized Jews from the West. But rote memorization and mimicry based on careful observation does not equal true insight about common inner dispositions. Mimesis, by definition, is not reality.

THE GENEOLOGICAL TROPE, AFTER ALL?

Although the beginnings of the Beth Yeshourun community were not tied to claims of descent from Hebrew or Israelite stock, there are a growing number of voices that now support such assertions. This shift in emphasis, if it does end up occupying center stage, will have a major influence on the ways in which the group is received.

Despite the fact that there are no traces of established Jewish communities in Cameroon in the premodern period, legends about the biblical origins of current-day inhabitants of the country, particularly involving Bantu groups, abound. According to one popular story, which I have heard from several non-Jewish Cameroonian friends, the ancestors of the Cameroonian peoples were the Israelite slaves in Egypt, who, after escaping from the forces of the Pharaoh and settling in Nubia, journeyed southward to avoid the Islamic conquest from Arabia. A supposed precolonial practice that establishes this link (which I have been unable to verify) is the custom of separating milk and meat. Another legend, perhaps more likely, but similarly unverifiable, has to do with Jewish traders from the Sudan bringing Judaism to Central Africa in the Middle Ages. Unfortunately, there is no existing material evidence of Jewish settlement in Cameroon that would lend credence to any of these claims, despite the interesting similarities in narrative patterns and common folkloric typology.

Legends are one thing, and attempts at recognition are another. One such group whose awareness of possible Jewish roots has moved from the realm of legendary to the realm of the real is the highland Bamileke, a people of the "Grassfields Bantu" ethnicity. Dieudonné Toukam, in his *Histoire et anthropologie du peuple bamiléké* (*History and Anthropology of the Bamileke People*), recounts that the oral traditions of the Bamileke trace their ancestors' origins to Egypt. According to these traditions, the Bamileke migrated to what is now northern Cameroon between the eleventh and fourteenth centuries. In the seventeenth century, they migrated farther south and west to avoid being forced to convert to Islam.[33]

Beth Yeshourun has several members of Bamileke origin, one of whom has recently relocated to France, where she is undergoing a process of formal conversion to Judaism. Her children, who remain in Cameroon, are studying with Serge's family. This member's Facebook page includes a link to a social media group dedicated to exploring the Jewish origins of the Bamileke. Several Western visitors to Beth Yeshourun have also been taken to meet with Bamileke leaders, in order to hear their Jewish heritage narratives firsthand. To date, though, the members of Beth Yeshourun are not promoting this origin theory in any way, and simply treat it as an interesting but ultimately unverifiable possibility.

The most famous proponent of the "Jewish Cameroonian" theory is Bodol Ngimbus-Ngimbus, now known as Rabbi Yisrael Oriel. Oriel claims that the "Israelites" in Cameroon, mainly (although not exclusively) hailing from the Bassa tribe, numbered 400,000 in 1920, but that only 167,000 were left in 1962, due to colonial missionary activity.[34] (More information about claims of Bassa-Israelite origin is given below.) The members of Oriel's family, who identify themselves as Levites descended from the Mosaic line, are said to have built the last synagogue in Cameroon, the material traces of which are now nonexistent.

Oriel is a former Cameroonian political dissident—the "only nonviolent and noncommunist Central African opposition leader," as he puts it—who left the country for France in the 1960s by way of a UNESCO scholarship.[35] After moving between European countries as a persecuted political refugee, Oriel converted to Judaism and immigrated to Israel in 1998, later achieving his rabbinical ordination. Subsequently, the Sephardic Spiritual Court in Israel appointed him chief rabbi of Nigeria, where he served for several years. Although I have attempted to make contact with Rabbi Oriel to verify his claims, his current whereabouts are unknown. People in the Beth Yeshourun community have heard of him, but dismissed him as a mentally unstable paranoid, noting that his curriculum vitae reportedly states his birth date as "The Year of the Beginning of World Redemption."[36]

Other famous Cameroonians who employ the genealogical trope include Saa Kameni, a writer and political activist based in the United States, and the American-born actor Yaphet Kotto, whose father immigrated to America from Cameroon in the 1920s. Kotto appeared in films such as *Alien* and *The Running Man*, and in television series such as *Roots* and *Homicide*. Kameni, for his part, speaks on behalf of Cameroonians everywhere, claiming that "nous sommes conscients d'être des Hébreux" (we are conscious of being Hebrews).[37] Their duty, according to Kameni, is to "chanter, écrire, enseigner et répandre la connaissance au sujet des tribus Hébraïques relocalisées au Cameroun" (sing, write, teach, and spread the knowledge about the subject of Hebrew tribes resituated in Cameroon). Kotto, who passed away in 2008, claimed in his autobiography that his father was a "crown prince" in the area of Douala who spoke Hebrew.[38] In a 1990 interview, he said, "My father was slated to become king of his nation, but he had to get out, because the Germans were taking over."[39]

Most of the veteran members of Beth Yeshourun place no importance on the possibility of shared hereditary ancestry. Out of all the people with whom I spoke, only one veteran member told me that her decision to embrace Judaism had to do with a possible common phylogenetic heritage. A more representative opinion can be found in the following response, which was an answer to my question as to whether or not Judaism as a genetic heritage or as a legal and moral code was most important. The man answered: "Since we don't have any viable historical sources, Judaism as a legal and moral code is how we see it—at least until God reveals to us another of his miracles [regarding such origins]."[40]

Part of the reason that many veteran members of Beth Yeshourun may not be entirely enamored with the possibility of a shared genealogical heritage stems from the fact that most are from the Eton ethnicity. The Eton are a subdivision of the Beti ethnic group, which is centered in southern Cameroon, Equatorial Guinea, Gabon, and the Republic of the Congo. This group has very little in the way of Hebraic ancestry narratives, in spite of possessing the same nearly universal Hebraic-like customs as other groups in Central Africa, such as widow inheritance and circumcision.[41] According to their oral tradition, the Beti came from Ethiopia, crossing the river Sanaga on the back of a giant serpent called Ngang Medza.[42]

I found only one minor heritage narrative—in a printed compilation based on this Ethiopian trope—that suggested a Hebrew origin of the Beti. No one in the community had heard of this particular story.[43] Then again, no one in Beth Yeshourun's original group had been a fully practicing traditional religionist, and so no one could point to the relevancy or irrelevancy of any of the Beti heritage narratives. My questions on the subject were usually answered with noncommittal shrugs. The only element significant to them was that most historical accounts describe the Beti as having been originally monotheistic. Aside from any possible Hebraic or Israelite origins, this may explain, in part, the group's quick embrace of Christianity relatively early on in the period of colonial evangelization.[44]

The only group whose supposed Hebraic origins are largely corroborated by members of Beth Yeshourun are the Bassa (alternately

romanized as Basaa or Basa), a group of around half a million ethnic Bantus located mainly in the coastal, western part of Cameroon.[45]
Widow inheritance, circumcision, monotheistic cosmology, a lunar
calendar, menstrual seclusion, a Saturday Sabbath, and the Ten Commandments (which they claim were in their possession prior to any
encounters with missionaries) are some of the customs that the Bassa
share in common with ancient Hebrews (and other Bantu groups).

According to Bassa oral tradition—which, until recently, has been
closely guarded by a select few—their Israelite ancestors, led by Mabimeleck at the Exodus from Egypt, feared that Moses and those who
followed him did not stand a chance of surviving by going into Canaan
through the desert.[46] In fact, many Bassa claim that, before the arrival
of missionaries to Cameroon, their priests all assumed (as did Sigmund
Freud in *Moses and Monotheism*) that Moses had been killed in the desert by his own people.[47] The followers of Mabimeleck elected instead
to follow the Nile southward, benefiting from the fertile land alongside
the river.

After stopping at Lake Meroe in Upper Nubia for forty days, they
built a stone shrine to God to show their gratitude for having been
saved from the clutches of the Pharaoh. They eventually mixed with the
inhabitants of Nubia, who were darker than they. They subsequently
divided into four clans. One clan followed the Blue Nile in the direction
of Ethiopia. Another followed the White Nile to its source in the region
of the Great Lakes. Another, Baah, son of Soh (the name "Bassa" apparently derives from this lineage marker), took his clan southward toward
Mozambique. The last clan journeyed to the far west of the continent,
around the swath of land that today makes up the territories of Mali,
Guinea, and Liberia.

At some point, the descendants of this clan migrated back eastward,
finally forced from the area of present-day Nigeria down to their current
location in Cameroon. All this time, they thought that they were the only
vestige of Israel that had survived, because they knew nothing of post-
Egyptian Israelite or Jewish existence. When contact with the Bible via
missionaries challenged this assumption, it did not really matter. Their
understanding about the fate of those descendants of Abraham who
had not accepted Jesus as the Messiah was relatively nebulous. They

assumed that everyone had died out, and so, to their knowledge, there was no remaining remnant with which to be affiliated.

In the modern period, the Bassa have been known in Cameroon for being at the forefront of the anticolonial movement (the Bassa-Bakoko region was the headquarters of the armed struggle for decolonization), and for their initial resistance to the adoption of Western cultural norms, including European Christianity.[48] They are also known as Cameroon's perpetual political gadflies. Many high-profile Bassa party leaders, such as Thong Likeng and Ruben Um Nyobe, have been among the most outspoken and active participants in the Cameroonian People's Union. Other Bassa agitators have focused their ire on what they see as a passive government stance toward recent Chinese economic hegemony across the country. Many Bassa continue to believe, despite the long-standing discrimination against them in the political realm, in a *Nka kunde* (a liberation toward independence).[49] It is commonplace for Bassa leaders who speak about the political suppression of their ethnic group to start the discussion with the phrase, "The problem for us, the Jews, is . . . ," thus connecting the fate of their community to that of (Western) history's most reviled ethnic group.

The relations between the Beth Yeshourun community and leaders of the Bassa ethnic group have only recently become large-scale. These relations have been facilitated in large part by community member Frédérick Ndawo. Frédérick, who met Serge in Douala while studying architecture at the Russian People's Friendship University, was attracted to Beth Yeshourun's practices because, as it seemed to him, these new Jews had uncovered something significant about the Cameroonian past.

A fiercely energetic fellow and one of the wealthier members of Beth Yeshourun, Frédérick makes his living as a private entrepreneur. At my suggestion, he took the Hebrew name *Yirmiyahu* (Jeremiah), after I pointed out his tendency to showcase the sins of the people, his repeated refrains about the Ingathering of the Exiles, and his self-proclaimed connection to Moses, who, Frédérick noted, was also fond of castigating those who transgressed. His role in the community, as he calls it, is "development officer." He is in training with his tribal elders to become a *mbombock*, a traditional Bassa priest and medicine man, a status passed down patrilineally. Frédérick hails from a long line of well-known freedom fighters and politically relevant Cameroonians of Bassa origin.

Frédérick is in the process of conveying to the Bassa leadership and to prominent tribal members what he considers to be the recently uncovered truth about their Jewish heritage. Needless to say, Frédérick is not alone in this venture. I have met many other Bassa, from cultural associations and from various indigenous church movements, who claim Jewish origins as their own. Frédérick, however, seems to be the first to actually encourage the organized inclusion of the Bassa, on an official level, into the worldwide fold of normative Jewish life and practice.

In conversations with prominent Bassa holy men, I found that most priests can orally trace their parentage back to the Exodus from Egypt. For instance, one Bassa holy man, going back to the beginning, asserted that they were all Hamites, but "without the curse." Others not of the priestly class often claim to be descended from the tribe of Judah, despite the obvious anachronism. Frédérick described to me his first realization about the roots of the Bassa thus:

When my mother died, I was four years old, and my little brother, two years old. My father had resolved to let me and my younger brother sleep with him in his room and when he prayed at four o'clock in the morning, he woke me up to pray with him, despite my young age. This is how he prayed: "Lord of Heaven and Earth, our ancestors called you Elohim. Help me to raise these orphans. When I die, in my next life, take my soul back to Israel to our land." His way of praying was strange to me, and one morning, when I was five or six years old, I asked him to please explain to me why he talked about Israel and death? This is what he told me: "We, the Jews, are the people of God. Our family is the caste of priests, and my father [Frédérick's grandfather had been killed during the struggle for independence] asked me to pray that all of the souls of the Bassa should return to Israel, their land of origin, after their deaths." Then he said to me: "You are still young, I will tell you the rest when you are older, but know that the Bassa are

Jewish in blood, and one day, we will return to Israel at the hour chosen by Elohim!" It wasn't until many years later that I thought about this incident carefully.

During the time of the anticolonial uprisings, after the supposed slaughter of three hundred and fifty Bassa priests, Frédérick's father was the only *mbombock* left in their village. Frédérick claims that hundreds of thousands of Bassa were killed in the anticolonial struggle, which, in his terms, was their own "Holocaust." (This number is impossible to verify, given the paucity of written records during the mid-century period.) His grandmother, who is over one hundred years old, purports to remember the first sight of the Germans at the beginning of the twentieth century, and characterizes that day as the beginning of the end of the observance of their ancient customs. Clearly, the rhetoric surrounding the Bassa's Israelite origin narratives betrays a very livid anticolonial bent, a theological "chosenness," and the persistent motif of victimization. Part of their attraction to Judaism, it seems, is that the recognition of this belonging promises to free the Bassa from the bonds into which they have been cast, echoing Deane W. Ferm's statement that many political theologies in Africa are "deeply concerned with racial oppression."[50]

Much of the politicized anger on the part of the Bassa is also directed against European Christian institutions, which, it is widely believed, instructed their priests to fire on Bassa parishioners during the struggle for independence. To illustrate the betrayal they feel by the churches to which they had been (sometimes forcibly) converted, one Bassa man repeated to me the celebrated musing of Jomo Kenyatta, Kenya's first president: "When the missionaries arrived, the Africans had the land and the missionaries had the Bible. They taught us how to pray with our eyes closed. When we opened them, they had the land and we had the Bible."[51] Another man, speaking of the duplicity of the Western Christian missions in Cameroon, quoted to me a similar saying of Um Nyobe's with which I was unfamiliar: "Ainsi la grande loi ordonnée par Jésus: 'Tu aimeras ton prochain comme toi-même' se transforme en cet autre slogan: 'Tu protégeras les intérêts de la colonisation au détriment de la liberté de ton frère'" (Thus, the great law commanded by

Jesus, "Love your neighbor as yourself," is transformed into this other slogan, "You will protect the interests of colonization to the detriment of the liberty of your brother").[52] Many Bassa elders also expressed their certainty that European missionaries had been aware of their tribe's Israelite origins but suppressed those origins and emphasized the New Testament instead, in order to "keep the Bassa weak politically." As Kato notes, this is a recurring trope in many African philosophies of decolonization, as the tendency to brand "biblical concepts as colonialist or neo-colonialist" is a direct response to abuses by the Church hierarchy.[53] This emphasis on the colonialists' violations of the Bassa also informs their understanding of the motivations and moral foundations of Western Christianity.

It should be emphasized that most Bassa are not anti-Christian; many are simply against the institutions of European Christianity, due in large part to the reasons listed above. Frédérick's life experience provides, again, an illuminating illustration of the areas in which Bassa theological energy is directed. Frédérick, like approximately 80 percent of his Bassa compatriots, was an active member in his African-founded prophetic church, the Celestial Church of Christ, for twenty-six years. Frédérick is the only one of his brothers who decided not to enter the priesthood, and the first elder in his family to ever leave the church.

A few details about the Celestial Church of Christ may help to contextualize Frédérick's decision. Founded in 1947 in Benin by the pastor Samuel Bilehou Joseph Oshoffa, it is a prophetic movement that broke away from the colonial Methodist church. As a part of the ecclesiastical community known as "Aladura" (meaning, in Yoruba, "praying people"), it is often considered to be in the same theological category as churches such as the Faith Tabernacle and Christ Apostolic Church. Like many Pentecostal churches, the Celestial Church of Christ places great emphasis on the powers of prayer and faith healing.

In his monograph on the Celestial Church of Christ, Albert de Surgy points out that its adherents "se sentent de plain-pied avec les Hébreux de l'Ancien Testament" (see themselves on the same level as the Hebrews of the Old Testament), and that "ils trouvent dans l'exposé des coutumes juives la justification d'interdits, d'attitudes et de rites demeurant très proches de ceux de leur religion ancestrale" (they find, in the presentation of Jewish customs, the justification of taboos, attitudes, and rites that closely resemble those of their ancestral religions).[54] Indeed, the church combines elements of African traditional religion with Adventist-like concerns, forbidding certain impure foods and maintaining menstrual taboos. Other traditional African and Old Testament–like practices mandated by the church include the celebration of a harvest festival; the presentation of newborn males to the temple eight days after their birth (this ceremony, however, does not culminate with the circumcision of the infant, which takes place later); the separation of men and women during worship; and the careful consideration of dreams as potentially prophetic visions.

Not all congregations of the Celestial Church of Christ have the same emphases, as Christine Henry stresses in her work on the subject. Henry distinguishes neo-Pentecostals, who have a mainly "globalized" (i.e., heavily American) style of worship, from other groups (such as the branches of the church in Yaoundé, which I visited) that insist on incorporating elements of traditional African religion.[55] Neither should it be assumed that such legalistic rites, which often resemble those found in the Hebrew Scriptures, are an automatic precursor to an affection for Judaism. As M. L. Daneel correctly points out, the emphasis on ritual legalism in most independent churches "relates to tribal laws that had to be upheld for the well-being of the tribe and the principle of reciprocity in the kinship structure, according to which all human relationships are governed by certain rules."[56] In the eyes of many, legalism seems to trump grace.

It was indeed the Law, rather than grace, that was on the minds of the pastors and elders of several different parishes of the Celestial Church of Christ with whom I conversed during my time in Yaoundé. More specifically, their concern was how to understand the Law better. To that end, they were all, to my great surprise, very pleased that Frédérick had made the connection with Serge's community, since Frédérick would, by that association, help all of them get closer to the "real meaning of the Law." Their Bassa forefathers knew this meaning, but had forgotten it during the long migration from Egypt. Serge, they pointed out, was already helping them to brush away the corruption of the Hellenized ideology of the New Testament, as well as the imperialist ideology of the French translations of the Bible with which they had to contend, in his weekly study sessions with them on the Hebrew Bible for Christians. One of the pastors had been so inspired by these sessions that he founded and became the president of the Cameroonian Noahide Association.

What's more, my Bassa contacts stressed time and again, Jesus had never abolished the Law. The words of Jesus as recorded in the verses of Matthew 5:17–18 were quoted to me on several different occasions: "Do not think that I have come to abolish the Law or the Prophets; I have not come to abolish them but to fulfill them. I tell you the truth, until heaven and earth disappear, not the smallest letter, not the least stroke of a pen, will by any means disappear from the Law until everything is accomplished." Obviously, there are many reasons for which other professing Christians might disagree with the supposition according to which correct ritual observance did not change with the death and resurrection of Jesus. These include the idea that Jesus's crucifixion did away with the old ceremonial law because his sacrifice was the culmination, or "accomplishment," of God's plan for humanity; or that people are now to be saved from death by grace in Jesus, as opposed to attaining salvation by carrying out the laws of the Torah to the letter.[57] Whatever the arguments to the contrary may be (and there are many), the members of the Celestial Church of Christ, like those in many other African Independent Churches, believe that Mosaic Law is still binding—at least, to a certain point.

To know the Law better, the Bassa elders said, they needed the perspective and assistance of Serge and other Jews. They expressed, like many Bassa, a veritable rage against the colonial authorities, and against the Catholic Church in particular, for having suppressed their Israelite roots in order to lord over them more easily. When I questioned whether the issue of Bassa heritage might be separated from their concerns, as clergy people, about proper textual and ritual interpretation, the response was carefully articulated. The Bassa are clearly Jews, the pastors told me, but this realization could not be separated from proper ecclesiastical conduct, since both the Church as an institution, and the Bassa as a people, were concerned with following the correct form of the Law.

The founder of the Celestial Church of Christ, who was not a Bassa, had broken away from the colonialist church because he saw that the ideology of the church was incompatible with the African worldview. He realized that the Old Testament is the basis for everything, and that the time spent in Africa by biblical figures (Jesus included) was crucial to the Israelite frame of mind. Those realizations in and of themselves were telling. But the founder might not have gone far enough, precisely because he was not a Bassa. "We need to leave the ignorance and obscurity put upon us by the colonialists" was a phrase repeated by one senior pastor as his explanation for taking these additional steps.

To that end, this same senior pastor wanted to know: Could I procure for his congregation a copy of the French translation of the Hebrew Scriptures used by Jews, given that they didn't trust the French (Christian) translations of their Bibles? Could I provide them with a way of knowing what in the New Testament was a Greek or Roman fabrication, and what was "authentic"? (I later sent them copies of the standard Jewish Bible in French translation, as well as a copy of Amy-Jill Levine and Mark Z. Brettler's *Jewish Annotated New Testament*, which showcases the Jewish context and background of Jesus and his times.)[58] They also wanted to know about Jewish perceptions of Jesus, which I shared with them, paraphrasing Daniel Boyarin's argument in *The Jewish Gospels*. They were thrilled to hear Boyarin's take on conventional Christianity, namely, that it "hijacked not only the Old Testament but the New Testament as well by turning that thoroughly Jewish text away from its cultural origins."[59]

One elderly pastor, from the English-speaking part of Cameroon, added that the one thing Boyarin had left out was how traditional African heritage, itself infused with Old Testament laws and dispositions, had also been hijacked by Christianity. To illustrate, he approximated the Kenyan theologian John S. Mbiti's remarks on the subject to me. I later looked up the entire passage, which is as follows:

> In contrast [to being taught the Bible from missionaries], we opened the Scriptures in our own languages and saw the Jewish people in the Bible as a mirror in which we viewed ourselves. This insight was something contrary to the image that colonial and missionary presence projected about us. For us, the Bible had a greater authority than that of colonial rulers, anthropologists,

and missionary preachers. We could find anthropological refuge and protection within the pages of the Bible, and nowhere else. Furthermore, it was and is the word of God, the very God that we knew and trusted through traditional religion long before missionaries arrived. Africans already knew something about the same God and offered worship to the same. The Bible accepted and described that same God, which was something that foreign presence had denied us. In the pages of the Bible, the people identified themselves together with God the Creator of all things.[60]

The pastor's reference to Mbiti—who, in a Kenyan context, expresses many of the Cameroonians' same sentiments—demonstrates not only a selection of pan-African views surrounding Old Testament laws and their applicability to everyday life. It also points to the fact that the reverence for Jewish custom predates an association with the organized Jewish movement in Cameroon. That they were familiar with the works of Mbiti, but not with those of Boyarin, or of Levine and Brettler, is not unusual, considering the regional, linguistic, and commercial practicalities of the distribution of such literature to Cameroonians. Most of them belong to a generation that is still uncomfortable navigating the Internet. But their children do not share those limitations. One of those children, a former choir leader, is the son of a senior pastor in the Celestial Church of Christ. He has recently been sent to study with the members of Beth Yeshourun, in the hopes that he will become a cantor. Will he eventually convert to Judaism and leave the church? No one seemed to be concerned either way.

Initially, I was as baffled by this as I was by the fact that the church leadership had encouraged Frédérick on his own path toward Judaism. The situation seemed most peculiar: a respected, long-serving elder in the church leaves, joins a new movement that openly rejects the divinity of Jesus, and is encouraged by his fellow elders to do so. Then, the son of a high-ranking pastor is sent away from the church to study with the same group of Jews who coaxed the aforementioned elder away from his former spiritual home. Was this not odd? When I asked Frédérick's former spiritual mentors at the church how it really felt for them to lose such a valuable congregant, the lead pastor at one parish told me that they were, in fact, truly happy for him, because his departure was "ordained by God."

"And are you comfortable sending one of your sons to the same group that Frédérick has joined, despite the fact that this group does not believe in Jesus as the Messiah?" I asked. "Jesus lived as a Jew, and died as a Jew," the pastor told me. "The rest is unimportant." Recalling Ghanaian Alex Armah's observation about how Sefwi clergy know the truth about Jesus, but are afraid to admit it for fear of losing their livelihood, I began to wonder if Frédérick's comparable comment that many of the pastors would eventually "give up their collars" for Judaism would indeed prove to be, in accordance with the mission of his Hebrew namesake, prophetic.

Since the pastors seemed open to discussing sensitive topics, I decided, during one of our meetings, to push the envelope a bit. I said to the lead pastor that, given everything he had told me about his reverence for the Hebrew Scriptures, his belief that the Bassa are genealogically connected to the Israelites, and his suspicions regarding the veracity of the New Testament narratives, it sounded to me like he was, already, almost as Jewish as the people in Serge's group who self-define as such—if, that is, we took away the one small matter of the belief in the divinity of Jesus. Could he ever see himself joining Beth Yeshourun, or another similar Jewish community? With a smile, the senior pastor waved his hand and said he had no need for such strict definitions. "We are all brothers," he said. He then quoted to me Romans 2:28–29: "A person is not a Jew who is one only outwardly, nor is circumcision merely outward and physical. No, a person is a Jew who is one inwardly; and circumcision is circumcision of the heart, by the Spirit, not by the written code. Such a person's praise is not from other people, but from God."

Whether or not the pastor was sidestepping my question is beside the point. The real query of importance is this: Will the Bassa members of the Celestial Church of Christ, or Bassa people in general—many of whom I have been in contact with outside of this Beth Yeshourun connection, and almost all of whom have categorically embraced such philo-Semitic attitudes and notions about shared origins and adherence to the Law—be content to remain enamored with Jewish narratives and customs from afar? Or will their enthusiasm, coupled with interaction with those from Jewish and Noahide movements, push them to take the final leap, joining the Jewish body politic, as Frédérick and some others think they will?

Seen through the eyes of the Bassa, the Judaism of the Beth Yeshourun could easily become both a spiritual and ethnoculturally motivated institution. In that case, the genealogical trope would sustain and preserve identiary continuity, as opposed to solely spiritual volition. In this way, it would mirror the "universal vocation" of the African prophetic churches in Cameroon, which, as Séverin Cécile Abega has demonstrated, address themselves to the widest possible audience by appealing to the idea of a return to time-honored customs.[61] In that case, Judaism would double as a "traditional religion." In order to ease the transition, indigenous churches like the Celestial Church of Christ might maintain their preference for the Old Testament, but go even further by declaring Jesus a prophet, as opposed to the Messiah. In another scenario, a kind of syncretistic practice might develop, combining elements of traditional folk religion with selected Jewish customs. This would be, instead of an African Independent Church, an "African Independent Synagogue." It would incorporate the enthusiasm for returning to traditional practices with the theology of decolonization. It would offer hope to the disenfranchised, by joining what Henry calls the indigenous churches' drive against "la bureaucratie néocoloniale" (the neocolonial bureaucracy).[62] Because Africans have already "seized on the idea of the Bible as an object with living energy, which as such can be disembedded from the missionary's vision of Christianity," as Matthew Engelke has noted, it seems entirely possible that doing away with the New Testament in favor of the Old would provide a space for this "living energy" to be harnessed toward traditionalist concerns.[63]

This kind of syncretism may not be far off. But will it be Jewish? Éloi Messo Metogo's incisive typological method of categorizing African Christianities—"What concept of salvation do they hold?"—provides an interesting mold for categorizing the varying iterations of African Judaisms.[64] For now, the genealogical trope responds to Metogo's basic question in that it provides a way of dealing with the anxieties and inequalities of cultural expressions voided and devalued in (post) modernity. Seeking comfort in the return to one's roots is one way of finding salvation in the here and now. Perhaps in spite of itself, Beth Yeshourun's spiritual volition has already blazed the trail. It is likely that other Cameroonians, maybe Jewish, or maybe not, will follow their lead.

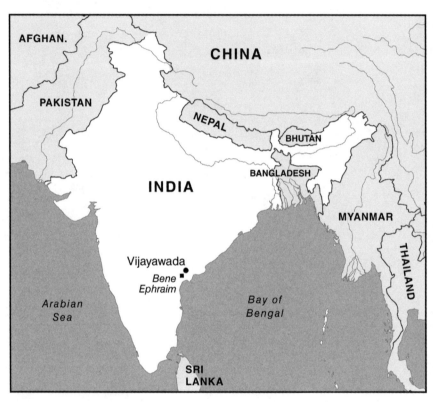

MAP 4. Location of the Bene Ephraim
community, India

Political Revivalism as Religious Practice

4

The "Children of Ephraim" of India

UNTOUCHABLE, YET CHOSEN

In most of the geographical regions profiled in this book, no historical evidence of a purported Jewish presence has ever been sufficiently established. In contrast, the lengthy presence of Jews on the Indian subcontinent has never been in dispute. In fact, several recognized Jewish subgroups have existed in that territory over a span of at least four centuries. The voluminous scholarship published on those subgroups has covered almost every conceivable aspect of Jewish life in both pre- and postpartition India (and, to a lesser extent, Pakistan).[1]

With regard to Judaizing movements in India, much has recently been written on the "Children of Manasseh" movement from the Mizoram and Manipur regions of the northeast, as mentioned in chapter 1.[2] Several publications by Yulia Egorova and Shahid Perwez provide masterful and wide-ranging contextual examinations of the history and religious dynamics of another Judaizing community: the *Bene Ephraim* (Children of Ephraim) of South India, the group of formerly Christianized "untouchables" on which this chapter also focuses.[3] Although my fieldwork among members of this Indian movement was completed nearly a year before the publication of Egorova and Perwez's culminating monograph on the Bene Ephraim, I had followed their project closely for several years prior to that time. Enthusiastic about their findings on the community whose adherents claim descent from the aforementioned Lost Tribe, I hoped to find additional areas of inquiry, outside the realm of those distinguished anthropologists' intellectual purviews, which would be worthy of exploration for my own research project.

Owing to a number of factors, including several new developments in the community that occurred following the departures of Egorova and Perwez, it became clear that three was not a crowd.[4] It also became clear that, despite the different ethnic, religious, and locational circumstances that separate the Indian example from the two African case studies on which I had elected to concentrate in this monograph, an inquiry into the Bene Ephraim movement stood to greatly enhance the comparative significance of my research on new Jewish communities from the developing world. I am grateful to both Egorova and Perwez for encouraging me to pursue these connections, as well as for their graciousness in sharing drafts of their works-in-progress.

A few points intended to buttress the suitability of comparing the Bene Ephraim with the other groups profiled in this book are perhaps in order. The first has to do with the Bene Ephraim's status as citizens of a former British colony. Like the previous case studies of Judaizing groups in Ghana and Cameroon, the members of the Bene Ephraim community inhabit a distinctly postcolonial paradigm. The daily challenges that they face regarding endemic corruption, poor or nonexistent infrastructure, and reliance upon foreign entities for regulation of health, education, and legal or civic-based concerns mirror those of other formerly colonized peoples elsewhere. Moreover, in spite of the fact that India did not experience chattel slavery or colonial subjugation on the same scale as did (black) Africa, the Bene Ephraim's near-lowest ranking in the hereditary hierarchy of their region's "Scheduled Caste" structure has resulted in systemic oppression and suffering on a scale that, in the very least, may explain some of the symbolic affinities their members feel with the Judeo-Christian world's archetypal sufferers. Unlike the Jewish communities of Ghana and Cameroon, however, their anger is not directed at the former colonial power. Rather, it is directed at the conational instigators of an oppressive system. This specific feature of their struggle notwithstanding, their sentiments regarding perceived injustices by a greater power situate them firmly within the thematic contexts of the other Jewish movements profiled in this book.

The second reason for which the Bene Ephraim's Judaizing initiatives merit inclusion here is that their religious worldviews, like those of the other individuals and communities already described, have been profoundly shaped by the discourses of Christian missionary activity. Anecdotal accounts consistently suggest that members of the Madiga caste (the caste from which most Bene Ephraim hail) were long suspected by the colonial-era missionaries who converted them from nominal Hinduism of having ancestral ties to ancient Israel, although I have not been able to find any primary sources that would attest to that viewpoint.[5] Customs prohibited to those from higher-level Hindu castes, such as the consumption of buffalo meat and burial of the dead, as well as supposed physiognomic differences between the Madiga and their neighbors, led to the Europeans' speculation about that group's possibly dissimilar provenance. How much, if at all, such speculations were internalized is impossible to determine.

Another way in which the Bene Ephraim's Judaizing initiatives constitute a reaction to Christian missionization has to do with more recent expressions of dissatisfaction with Christian liberation theology. This is especially true with regard to perceived exploitation by bodies connected to the institutionalized Church in South India.[6] Among many, such dissatisfaction has led to a grassroots reckoning of sorts with the religion that initially seemed to offer lower-caste peoples a way out of perpetual maltreatment.[7] In Jason Francisco's view, many converts or descendants of converts from Hinduism feel that the "trappings of deliverance" promised to Christians in India "more closely reflect the sheen of Western investment than the imminence of the Second Coming."[8] For the Bene Ephraim, embracing normative Judaism seems to offer a way to chosenness that neither Hinduism nor Christianity has been able to provide. In Egorova and Perwez's terms, this embrace of Jewish identity constitutes nothing less than a "project in communal self-empowerment."[9]

Audiences predisposed to the rhetoric of such self-empowerment are not confined to formal members of the Bene Ephraim, whose community comprises a hundred or so families in and around the district of Guntur in the southeastern state of Andhra Pradesh. Taken to its logical conclusion, the application of the genealogical trope in this instance would necessitate the inclusion of all those who belong to the region's Madiga—by most approximations, at least six million people—a guesstimate often cited by jittery officials from the Israeli Ministry of Immigrant

Absorption.[10] Other Dravidian and Telugu-speaking lower-caste peoples, particularly those from the neighboring Mala caste, are also a target audience for this kind of "Jewish Sanskritisation," which reenvisions their place in society by augmenting the prestige of their genealogical origins.[11] Astonishingly, the manner in which almost all such individuals have become exposed to the idea of a noble Jewish ancestry can be attributed to the efforts of one man: Mukthipudi Samuel Sundara Raju, a former Christian preacher who now goes by the Hebrew name of Shmuel Yacobi.

Shmuel has described himself alternatively as an "Israelite," a "Bene Ephraim Jew," an "Elder of the Telugu Semitic Community," a follower of "the traditional *Halakhic* [Jewish law-based] Bene Ephraim Telugu Jewish nationalistic culture," or the leader of "the Council of Eastern Jewry." Most recently, he has begun calling himself "a citizen of *Eretz Ephraim*" (the Land of Ephraim), a future nation that Shmuel hopes to found as a "sister state" to Israel, in the region (currently located in the West Bank) originally inhabited by the biblical tribe of Ephraim. The impetus behind the public disavowal of his earlier religious affiliation and subsequent embrace of Judaism came in 1986, when he experienced a vision about the Israelite pedigree of his forefathers. (He would later claim to have held previous, albeit incomplete knowledge about this ancestry, which was passed down to him orally by his parents and grandparents.) Determined to spread this awareness among his fellow lower-caste compatriots, Shmuel made a risky decision: In 1991, after having quit his job as a preacher, he publicly renounced the American-sponsored Baptist movement that had educated and employed him.

Shmuel's older brother, Aaron, and his younger brother, Sadok, followed Shmuel's lead. So did Shmuel's wife, Malkah, and their three sons: Yehoshua, Yacob, and Dan. Other family members wished to join their charismatic relative but feared for their livelihood, as they, too, were employed by Christian organizations. In 1993, during a trip to Israel, Yehoshua was admitted to a Jewish seminary. Much to everyone's surprise, he was granted the opportunity to formally convert to Judaism, subsequently receiving Israeli citizenship one year later. He is the only member of the Bene Ephraim to have been allowed such options by the Israeli state.[12]

Since his fateful revelation, Shmuel has proven himself to be much more than a religious leader whose theology has shifted. He is widely acknowledged as a talented scholar, a popular lecturer and teacher, and a resourceful entrepreneur and Renaissance man. In his efforts to disseminate the idea that many South Indians are genealogically connected to the Lost Tribe of Ephraim, Shmuel has employed diverse categories of media. These include musical productions, compositions of prose and poetry, historiographic treatises, a motion picture (still in the making at the time of this book's composition), and, most importantly, pedagogical outreach tools.

To date, the most notable successes of Shmuel's outreach initiatives have been linked to the activities of his Hebrew Open University Research Study Centre, which Shmuel describes as "the first Semitic cultural educational institute in India." This primarily distance-learning institute offers "theological courses in the Bene Ephraim community perspective" to "Hindus, Christians, and Muslims of all denominations."[13] According to Shmuel, most students who enroll at the institute are from lower-caste Christian backgrounds. Among them are those "vexed with their denominational interpretations and beliefs" who wish to know "the original cultural meanings from their translated sacred Bibles."[14] Others are "excited to sincerely support our [the Bene Ephraim's] cause and bless us without expecting anything from us."[15] For those students who come from philo-Semitic Christian backgrounds, such as Messianics or Adventists, there is also an element of prestige involved in being affiliated with the centre. Shmuel claims that, in the past, many Christian clergy people who "studied this new perspective" at his institute were able to supplement "their theological degrees and [subsequently] got promotions in their churches" because of the integrity of the "authentic knowledge" offered there.[16]

A good number of students decide to enroll in the centre's correspondence courses after having met Shmuel at one of the many Bible Study lectures that he delivers at lower-caste Christian congregations throughout Andhra Pradesh. Over the years, hundreds of such congregations have invited him to speak as the resident expert on the topic of "Hebrew culture." These lectures represent not only valuable economic opportunities to further the activities of the centre, whether through honoraria or eventual tuition fees, but also the possibility to gain new adherents for the Bene Ephraim movement. This is in spite of Shmuel's assertion that such meetings are not directed at "promoting religious conversions." When I asked him about the likelihood that such encounters might indirectly encourage a move toward Judaism, Shmuel assured me that there is "no proselytizing involved" because people have paid to gain the information that he is contracted to provide. He has written elsewhere on this subject that "all humans must stick to their own religions and religious beliefs without poking their noses into others' businesses unless asked for."[17]

A CAPTIVE AUDIENCE

During my fieldwork in India, I was privy to several encounters that testify to the success of what one journalist has referred to as Shmuel's "Judeo-revivalism."[18] One particularly memorable case in point was a lecture given by Shmuel at a prayer meeting in the village of Tadikonda, to which he had been invited by a fellowship of independent pastors. The leader of the fellowship was a Baptist preacher who had been ejected from the church due to his increasing Judeophilia, nurtured in large part by the association with Shmuel. The preacher had asked Shmuel if the visiting American-Israeli researcher (me) would like to observe the interaction between Shmuel and his audience at the planned lecture. I eagerly agreed.

The pastoral (pun intended) setting of the prayer meeting reminded me of a revival assembly in the American South. The tent under which the audience was waiting had been set up in the middle of a vegetable field owned by the Baptist pastor's sister. Placed upon tarps along the edges of the tent were stacks of English and Telugu Bibles and a PA system that had seen better days. Shmuel had been there since the previous evening, when he instructed the pastors in proper ritual slaughter by, as he put it, "koshering" a sheep for them. The adults' cries of "Hallelujah!" met me upon my entry into the tent, while the children pointed at my (at the time) long blond hair and beard, shouting, "Jesus! Jesus!" Around thirty people were in attendance, slightly more men than women. I later learned that I was the first Westerner that most of them had ever seen in person.

It turns out that I was also the first "Judean," as Shmuel introduced me, to have crossed these people's paths. Presenting me to the group, Shmuel explained that, although he and I were both of Israelite origin, I belonged to a tribe of the chosen people that had not gotten lost, as had the tribe of Ephraim. One pastor in attendance, intrigued by these differences in our histories, inquired as to whether I would approve of conducting a short Question-and-Answer session with the audience before Shmuel began his lecture. He said that they would benefit greatly from hearing my "Judean" perspective, since their only real knowledge about Jewish people came "from the Old Testament" and "from Shmuel," who was, after all, from a different branch of that nation. The man also mentioned that they wanted to know more about "modern Israelites," and thought I might help to clarify things in that regard. He said that, since 1991, when Israel and India established full diplomatic relations (a move the pastors attributed to the efforts of Pamulaparti Venkata Narasimha Rao, India's Telugu prime minister at the time), they had received only limited information on the return of the Jews to the Holy Land, gleaned largely from snippets of insufficient news reports.

I agreed to answer the pastors' questions, but emphasized that I could not speak on behalf of the Jewish people or of Israelis in general. I was, I explained, a completely secular person with regard to ritual practice. Consequently, my opinions on such matters were not representative of the perspectives of more religiously oriented Jews. Similarly, I had made a conscious decision to not continue living in Israel, partly because of personal misgivings with certain aspects of Israeli society. Therefore, my feelings regarding Israel's policies or future direction were those of a nonresident citizen. Neither the notion of secular Jewishness nor that of civic dissenter seemed to register, but I refrained from pressing the points. The only information that I would feel totally comfortable relaying, I said, would be connected to historical factualities given from my professional standpoint.

Despite the qualifying proviso, the first questions posed were ones from which I had to demur. Among them were: "How did Abraham feel when he was instructed to sacrifice Isaac?" "Does Ariel Sharon really think that Indian Jews are the nicest ones?" And: "Is it true that Hebrew letters contain magic formulae?" I had to admit that I could not properly answer any of those questions. One woman in the audience then asked a more straightforward, yet equally problematic question: Was I, as a Jew, in favor of Indian Christians becoming Noahides (righteous Gentiles)? She was part of a burgeoning movement of Indian Noahides for which Shmuel served as an advisor, and informed me that she and the others would very much like to have my blessing for this undertaking. I tried to remain neutral by generally extending my warmest wishes for good fortune in all of their lives' pursuits. Someone else, sensing that this line of questioning was going nowhere fast, asked if I would mind quoting a Bible passage in Hebrew. I complied, reciting the first few lines from Genesis. A roar of applause erupted. One pastor stood up and told the attendees that every living thing in the vicinity had undoubtedly been blessed by "those holy utterances," including the trees and the vegetables growing in the fields.

I suggested that we move on to questions dealing with more historical or sociocultural issues. Among the questions posed in this portion of the discussion were the following: What is the history of the Jews in India? (relatively straightforward); What is meant by the term "Holocaust," and why does the term always seem to upset Indian Muslims? (slightly more complicated); Which tribes had already gathered in Israel? (murky at best); When was the Israeli government planning to officially erect the Third Temple? (I audibly gulped); Why does the world always try to "whitewash the Arabs' crap"? ("Next question, please"); and, Does the Talmud contain information on how the tribe of Ephraim had made its way to India? (I deferred to Shmuel). While Shmuel was giving details on the Bene Ephraim's migration to the subcontinent, I moved away from the front of the crowd, hoping to shift the spotlight to the real invitee. I then sat down in the audience next to a young pastor who had agreed to translate the Telugu portions of the lecture for me.

Shmuel's remarks that day focused on two main themes. The first was the need for Telugu people to abandon the belief, propagated by Western missionaries, according to which "miracles can occur." Shmuel stressed that, because God is always in control and nothing is beyond God's power, the entire notion of miracles is silly. The emphasis on miracles among "rice Christians"—a pan-Asian derogatory term employed by some Bene Ephraim to refer to nominal Christians of lower castes, who only attend church services in order to receive their free bowls of rice—was nothing more than an amalgamation of hollow liberation theology and "Hindu superstition" that had filtered down to the Andhra (Telugu) people of South India. In Shmuel's estimation, breaking away from imposed superstition was a necessary step in order to leave behind both physical and intellectual servitude.

Shmuel cited two passages from the story of the Israelites' exodus from Egypt to illustrate his point: the parting of the Red Sea (Exod. 14:21) and the receiving of manna from Heaven (Exod. 16:1–36). He told the group that these two instances of supposed "miraculous" occurrences could be explained scientifically, by showcasing natural analogues to such occurrences in Teluguland. The first analog was the Gundlakamma, a seasonal river that can suddenly become shallow when currents change and the wind blows in a certain direction. The second was bamboo seed, which people in Andhra Pradesh are fond of eating. The seed shed from bamboo trees can descend quickly, seemingly out of nowhere, in the form of thick clouds of germ.

The Judaism of the Israelites was a logical religion, Shmuel said: a sacred covenant based on adherence to a particular set of laws. That relationship was special enough to justify God's preservation of the Israelites' well-being without having to resort to "supernatural" explanations. In the perspective of the Bene Ephraim, therefore, the Israelites never fled Egypt; they simply returned to their ancestral home after having made a collective decision to do so. They did this with the blessing of the Pharaoh. No miracles were needed.

The pastor next to whom I was sitting asked Shmuel if Jews had ever believed in the "possibility of miracles." The answer was as follows. Everything is part of God's plan. Thus, nothing "extra" need happen for God's plan to become reality. For instance, Shmuel noted that, in the oral laws of the Bene Ephraim, there are no such things as transgression or punishment. Postbiblical Christian conceptions such as original sin (Gen. 3), or rabbinical exaggerations of minor incidents, such as the making of the golden calf (Exod. 32:4), the Israelites' reluctance to enter Canaan (Num. 13), or the resulting motif of the punishment of the "generation in the desert" (Num. 14), are "non-Hebraic" ways of making sense of things ex post facto. "We must always remember the Covenant," Shmuel told the audience. "Nothing happens by coincidence. Not the actions of any person, and the not the reactions of *Hashem* [God]." In other words, transgression on the part of humans would suggest that something happens outside the will of God, "by coincidence." In the Bene Ephraim's view, this is illogical. Crucially, this stance also represents a categorical refutation of the reward-and-punishment rationale for the hereditary caste system in India, which is based in part on Hindu cosmological theories regarding sins committed in past lives (more on that below).

The second theme of Shmuel's lecture had to do with the problem of the "different Jesuses" mentioned in the New Testament. Shmuel told the group, somewhat bemusedly, that even though Jesus was initially thought of in India as "the god of Malas and Madigas" because those castes had been the first to convert from Hinduism to Christianity, the descendants of those early converts still had trouble identifying basic details about Jesus's existence. The audience acknowledged this observation with good humor. As a Bene Ephraim Jew, Shmuel said, he could provide a "Jewish context" in order to help them make sense of the many enigmas surrounding the figure of Jesus, such as the differences between the Gospel narratives about Jesus's birth and death, the typological reliance of New Testament dialogues upon their Old Testament precursors, the vagaries of the intertestamental period, and the rescinding of the Covenant by Paul of Tarsus. He then set about doing this by providing, respectively, an overview of the following: tropes connected to the many so-called "Jewish Messiahs," from Simon of Peraea to Shabbetai Tzvi; the process of canonization of the New Testament; the phenomenon of Hellenistic Judaism; and Jewish sectarianism during the Second Temple period.

By the end of the lecture, Shmuel had the audience eating out of his hand. Rightfully so: he is a compelling and articulate speaker who projects seasoned confidence. As one of the pastors in attendance explained to me, Shmuel's formal training in biblical languages and exegesis, Greek and Roman philosophy, and extensive knowledge of Indian history and culture (in particular, of Hindu religion and of the history of pre-Hindu coastal Andhra Pradesh) put him in the perfect position to explicate the Jewish context of the New Testament to lower-caste South Indians whose parentage is, at least from the Bene Ephraim's viewpoint, genealogically linked to that of the chosen people.

That Shmuel is a former Christian preacher does not hurt, either, both from the perspective of social status and from the perspective of familiarity with the relevant rhetorical devices. A woman seated near the front of the audience declared as much when, at the lecture's end, she exclaimed: "Mr. Yacobi is a person who leads you to follow him!" On the spot she enrolled in a correspondence course on Hebrew culture from the Hebrew Open University Research Study Centre. The process was quick and convenient, as the application forms had been carefully placed at the end of the table from behind which Shmuel delivered his remarks.

The interaction that took place at Shmuel's invited lecture in Tadikonda is informative on several levels. First, it demonstrates that on the part of many lower-caste Indian Christians, there is a sentiment of estrangement from conventional, mission-based churches, coupled with a thirst for other options of religious belonging. In effect, this growing exposure to alternative systems of thought mirrors the process of their forbearers' rejection of their pitiful position in the social hierarchy of Hinduism, and eventual move to Christianity, toward the end of the nineteenth century. For even if untouchable Christians of such backgrounds ultimately prefer to remain affiliated with their respective churches—and it should go without saying that, for clergy people such as those in attendance, breaking away entails a tremendous economic risk—the mere act of questioning the veracity of the New Testament implies the potential of serious rupture. After all, the head of the independent pastors' association was relieved of his official church duties due at least in part to his association with Shmuel.

The second reason for which this "revivalist" episode is worthy of mention is the indirect proselytizing fashion in which the instruction was conducted. Much like the explanations about the differences between Judaism and Christianity that are given on the website of the Cameroonian "Internet Jews," the ostensibly innocuous activity of highlighting the Jewish context of the New Testament, including the even

"light" debunking of miracles and/or narrative authenticity surrounding details of the Christian savior, may eventually lead to a deeper questioning of Christianity's fundamental truths. This is especially true if
such questioning takes place in tandem with the adoption of Noahide
observances, or, even more so, with a genealogical identification with
the Lost Tribes.

At the very least, such involvement almost ensures future support
for the cause of the Bene Ephraim, whether monetary or otherwise.
At the most, it provides a vast repository of potential "converts" to the
movement, despite the assertion by its leader that encouraging people
to join their fold is not part of the equation. It also explains in part how
the Bene Ephraim have managed to hold fast to their lifestyle for the
last quarter-century in the absence of any official recognition of their
Jewishness—be it from Israel, the Jewish world, or, for that matter, the
Indian state. As lower-caste people trapped in a highly discriminatory
structure, they have become used to doing everything in their power
to find a way out of that system. The stratified nature of life in the
Indian subcontinent has provided a strikingly appropriate analogue to
the experience of anti-Semitism for those Jews from other locales whose
Jewishness has never been in question, whether this is an intentionally
conscious parallel or not. Enlisting the support of fellow underprivileged
persons offers a solidarity that is practically as well as psychologically
advantageous.

UNITY IN DIVERSITY? THE PARADOX OF MODERN INDIA

The Republic of India, the world's largest democracy in terms of population, is a former British colony situated on the peninsular landmass
of South Asia. Its neighbors include Pakistan to the northwest; Nepal,
China, and Bhutan to the north; and Bangladesh and Myanmar to the
east. The site of the first major empire in the southern part of Asia—the
Indus Valley Civilization and its related Indianized Kingdoms—India
has always been a crossroads for the migration of peoples, goods, and
ideas. Inextricably linked by way of its location to European, African,
Middle Eastern, and Far Eastern societies, India has played a pivotal part

in the transmission and dissemination of scientific and philosophical knowledge the world over.

Although the country is officially recognized as a "developing" nation, this delineation is somewhat misleading. India has the world's fourth-largest economy, but the vast majority of its population—around 70 percent—is still agrarian and rural.[19] It boasts one of the world's largest armies, and is one of nine countries whose nuclear weapons capabilities have been established. However, many challenges remain with regard to perceptions surrounding bureaucratic ineptitude, especially regarding the powerlessness of the state's police service to mitigate harassment against women, migrant workers, and political protestors.[20] Positive international impressions regarding India's new generation of software developers and their rock-hard work ethic have led the country to be recognized as a leading offshore center for information technology companies. Yet, nearly 22 percent of all Indians live on less than one dollar a day.[21] To remedy such structural inequalities, the government has publicly declared its aspiration to transition from a "developing" to "developed" nation by 2020.[22]

The birthplace of Jainism, Hinduism, Buddhism, and Sikhism, India has always been a locus of religious diversity. Islam, the second-largest Indian religion in terms of adherents after Hinduism (approximately 13.4 percent versus 80.5 percent), has existed in the subcontinent since the seventh century of the Common Era.[23] Adherents to Christianity, India's third-largest religion, make up approximately 2.3 percent of the population.[24] Zoroastrians, Baha'is, Buddhists, Jains, and Jews count among India's other religious minorities, each group making up less than 1 percent of India's total population.[25]

Although interreligious tensions exist, the freedom to practice one's religion of choice is generally respected. The Indian state's particular brand of political "secularism" is intended to limit what India's first prime minister, Jawaharlal Nehru, called the country's inherent "separatist and disruptive tendencies," which have oftentimes resulted in outbreaks of severe group violence.[26] The official position is that the state is religiously neutral, in the sense that the government prefers, in theory, a strategy of nonintervention in the affairs of religious minorities. That said, the actual extent to which this approach ensures evenhanded treatment of individuals or communities based on their religion is a hotly debated topic, especially following the 2014 rise to power of the Bharatiya Janata political party, which espouses ideologies linked to Hindu nationalism.[27]

The Indian government generally carries out the formal classification of its citizens according to language, as opposed to race or religion, assuming that one's ethnicity and mother tongue are interchangeable. The country's major ethnolinguistic groups include Indo-Aryans (primarily in the north) and Adivasis and Dravidians (primarily in the south). The Deccan plateau often serves as the informal line of demarcation between them. The most important exception to this organizational practice is the policy of categorizing members of historically marginalized communities according to their hereditary caste or tribal association.[28] The motivation behind this formal categorization is for the purposes of affirmative action, in order to ensure equitable political representation and professional and educational opportunities for those who have been born into the lowest ranks of the social hierarchy.

Traditionally disadvantaged peoples belonging to the so-called Scheduled Castes continue to face routine discrimination, both officially and unofficially, despite long-standing legislation in the Indian Constitution forbidding such prejudicial conduct. Few would argue that the success of the Indian state, as a federation and a democracy, depends on the viability of guaranteeing communal safeguards to the most socially vulnerable of its citizens. And yet, almost half of those classified as belonging to the Scheduled Castes—around 16 percent of India's total population—live below the poverty line.[29] More than half are illiterate.[30] The popular perception is that, while some success stories do occur, most people born into a Scheduled Caste have little hope of ever breaking out of it.

The popular press in the West has often presented India's caste system as the most immoral component of the Hindu cosmological superstructure. But this is only partly true. The Hindu concept of *varna*, a Sanskrit term meaning "color" or "class," which dates from the Vedic era (1500–500 BCE), traditionally divided people into four categories: *Brahmins* (priests); *Kshatriyas* (noblemen); *Vaishyas* (commoners); and *Shudras* (servile laborers). The rationalization for one's status in one of those categories had to do with the moral value of deeds committed in a past life. The manner of an individual soul's transmigration was therefore a direct product of karma.[31]

A fifth category of people originally outside of the system, called "outcasts" or "untouchables," ranking even lower than the servile laborer class, later became part of the official Hindu religious hierarchy. According to V. B. Krishnaiah Chetty, this fifth category has traditionally "been associated with unclean occupations, social restrictions, poverty and exploitation by the strong and advanced sections of the society."[32] People hailing from this category were condemned to perform all the "polluting" tasks prohibited to those from other classes, such as the handling of dead animals or the cleaning of human excreta. Forbidden to enter Hindu temples or to travel on the same paths as their neighbors, they maintained strict public segregation upon pain of death. As a friend once remarked, ancient laws governing the treatment of untouchables resembled an "Indian series of Jim Crow laws on steroids."

During the period of British colonial rule (1858–1947) over the subcontinent (which includes the territories of present-day Pakistan and Bangladesh), social stratification took on a somewhat different form. Naturally, the educated inhabitants from the higher castes became the ones to serve as liaisons to the British Crown. They profited accordingly. The British colonial model of indirect rule exacerbated the already-existing gulf between the social classes in India, merging capitalist modernity with imperial exploitation. The British also projected popular European ideas about racial supremacy onto the Indian caste system. For instance, Herbert Hope Risley, a colonial administrator in India between 1873 and 1910, formulated and published a highly influential racial theory to explain the strict separation of classes that he encountered during his time there. He surmised that lighter-skinned Northern "Aryan" Indians, who had existed since time immemorial in "comparative purity," were "a higher race on friendly terms with the lower, but keenly conscious of the essential difference of type."[33] The "lower" race referred to—dark-skinned Dravidians—Risley considered akin to "monkeys."[34]

When India achieved independence in 1947, few mechanisms were in place to guarantee lower-caste peoples an equal role in the newly sovereign state. This is in spite of the many preindependence efforts of social activists such as (most notably) Mohandas Gandhi. Gandhi, who proclaimed that "a man's caste is no matter for pride [and] that no superiority attaches to any of the four divisions," thought that the issue of class would be the crucible of modern India.[35] In 1934, while campaigning for the rights of those whom he called by the Hindi term *Harijan* (Children of God), Gandhi surmised that, with the struggle for independence in full swing, untouchability was on its way out.

Other activists posited that, rather than depending on the state for protection, it would be better to convert to an alternative religion in order to escape the caste system. For example, Bhimrao Ramji Ambedkar, a legislator who criticized Gandhi for not going far enough to help the formerly untouchable *Dalits* (the more politically correct term for those belonging to the Scheduled Castes; literally, "oppressed" in Marathi), turned to Buddhism. This was a logical choice, historically, as Buddhism began as a rejection of Brahmanism.[36] Ambedkar's conversion to Buddhism in 1956 prompted millions of his fellow lower-caste supporters to follow suit. Of the caste system, Ambedkar said: "There cannot be a more degrading system of social organization than the *Chaturvarnya* [the classification of the four varnas]. It is the system which deadens, paralyses and cripples the people from helpful activity."[37]

Buddhism, however, was not the first religion to be seen as a method of escape. As noted, many Mala and Madiga converts to Christianity at the end of the nineteenth century—the first period in which these populations converted out of Hinduism in large numbers—saw their new religion not only as a means for economic advancement, but also as a way to guarantee, in the words of Ankur Barua, "recognition of their human dignity."[38] Today, it is estimated that between 65 and 70 percent of Indian Christians are from the lower castes.[39] To a certain extent, Islam had also provided a ticket out of the Hindu caste system, before Christianity became a possible alternative for doing so. But Islam in India existed in some places with a similar, albeit less extreme, form of social stratification.[40] For all we know, looking toward Judaism as an alternative affiliation is an extremely recent phenomenon, despite the long-term presence of Jews on the subcontinent.

KEEPING GOOD COMPANY: INDIA AS A JEWISH CORNUCOPIA

Historically, the experience of Jews in India has been fundamentally dissimilar from the experiences of Jews living under Christendom or in countries of Islam. Among Hindus, Jews were seen from the beginning as a people apart, and were consequently spared the pressure to convert or conform in a way that would compromise their spiritual identity. On the whole, the same is true for Jews living in regions of India that came under Islamic rule. Nathan Katz, the foremost scholar of Indian Jewry to date, emphasizes this point by using an apt pecuniary metaphor. Katz asserts that the "acculturation" of Jews on the Indian subcontinent "is not paid for in the currency of assimilation."[41] With the noteworthy exceptions of marauding Portuguese Inquisitors in South India and the mob violence directed at the Jewish community of Pakistan immediately postpartition, institutionalized anti-Semitism has more or less never existed there. Referring to the Jews of Cochin, India's oldest Jewish community, Katz and Ellen S. Goldberg underline the singularity of their historical experience by posing the following open-ended question: "What is the psyche of a Jewish community which has never tasted hatred?"[42]

According to various sources of legend, Jews have dwelt in the area of present-day India since Solomonic times. However, the only mentions of India in the Bible appear briefly, in the Book of Esther (1:1; 8:9), purportedly written during the period of Babylonian captivity (597–538 BCE). Describing the lands ruled over by Ahasuerus, King of Persia, the author of the Book of Esther notes that Ahasuerus's territory extended "from India even unto Ethiopia" (1:1). If Jewish exiles had dispersed throughout all of that kingdom's far-flung provinces, their entry into India would almost certainly be taken as a given.

Numerous other legends attribute the existence of Jews in India to remnants of the Lost Tribes, who had moved southward from Afghanistan. Authors of some contemporary religious texts (ostensibly documentations of such legends) posit that certain well-known Jews, such as the apostles Thomas and Bartholomew—and even Jesus himself—made their way to India to preach the New Covenant to those descended from

Israelites.[43] For the majority of the world's Jews, however, the notion of their brethren residing in India was not even a blip on the radar until after the establishment of the state of Israel. As Shalva Weil points out, the Jews of India were "numerically insignificant" compared to Jewish populations in other locales.[44] And, because they (with the exception of the Cochin Jews) had little contact with Jewish communities outside of India before the onset of modernity, they "remained relatively unfamiliar outside the subcontinent."[45]

The earliest reliable, albeit imprecise, records attesting to a Jewish presence in India date from the eleventh to thirteenth centuries CE, and describe Jews involved with trade missions.[46] We also have during this period numerous sightings of "black" Jews documented by medieval explorers, especially along the Malabar Coast near Cochin, on the southwestern side of the peninsula.[47] Sephardic Jews from Iberia fleeing the Alhambra Decree in the fifteenth and sixteenth centuries eventually made their way to Cochin, as well, where they settled and became known as the "white" Jews—a qualifier used to distinguish them from the site's earlier (and darker) Jewish inhabitants.[48] Beginning in the eighteenth century, the Jews of Cochin were in regular contact with Jews from Ottoman Palestine. During the early years of Israel's existence, the majority of the Jews who had remained in Cochin chose to leave India in order to move to the Jewish state. Today, it is estimated that only a few dozen Jews remain in Cochin.

India's largest Jewish community, the *Bene Israel* (Children of Israel), is concentrated in the western region of Maharashtra, India's most urbanized state. The Bene Israel, whose heritage narratives suggest origins in ancient Galilee, were "discovered" by Jewish traders from Cochin in the eighteenth century.[49] The latter were shocked to find that this group, made up of both "black" and "white" populations whose main occupation was pressing sesame oil, self-identified as Jews, but had no knowledge of Hebrew, the Bible, or rabbinic Judaism. Their only corroborable Jewish traits were circumcision, knowledge of the *Shema* prayer (the central invocation and the cornerstone of Jewish liturgy), and a Saturday Sabbath. The latter custom led them to be nicknamed "Saturday oil-pressers" by their Hindu neighbors. By the mid-nineteenth century, the practices of this group had been normalized, due to increasing contact with Jews from more established communities. Like the Jews of Cochin, the majority of the Bene Israel (at their peak, some twenty thousand) have moved to Israel.[50] Close to five thousand remain in India, mostly in Mumbai.[51] Despite their long-normalized practices, strong sense of Jewish identity, and official recognition by the Rabbinate in 1964, many Bene Israel continue to battle against nonrecognition on the part of some ultra-Orthodox authorities in Israel.

A "transplanted" Indian group known collectively as "Baghdadi Jews," whose members never made any claim to long-standing roots in India, first settled there after migrating in the eighteenth century from Syria, Yemen, Persia, and, as their name suggests, Iraq. As Jael Miriam Silliman notes, these Jews, who possessed "British colonial ideas about race," quickly became part of the "upper echelons" of the British colonial regime by "emphasiz[ing] their foreign origin and their religion."[52] In Egorova's view, the Baghdadi Jews' ranking as "Europeans" on the subcontinent (as opposed to the categorization of the Cochini Jews and the Bene Israel as "Indians") was due to the Baghdadis' status as "newcomers" to the region.[53] Most Baghdadi Jews, who may have numbered five thousand preindependence, left India for Anglophone countries in the 1950s. Very few immigrated to Israel. According to popular accounts, only several hundred Baghdadi Jews remain in India today.

What do modern-day Indians think about their nation's Jews? The answer is, not much. Approximately 85 percent of India's Jews left postindependence, and there are only around five thousand Jewish citizens of India remaining in a total population of approximately 1.3 billion. Indigenous Indian Jews are therefore so few that they do not constitute a major cause for discussion among most Indians. Israel, however, is another matter entirely. To generalize, there is a broad admiration for Israel among Christians, for the obvious reasons, while Muslims tend to be more critical, due to the Palestinian issue. Among middle- to upper-class Hindus, there is a respect for what one journalist calls "the cultural self-assurance of Israeli Jews," not to mention a feeling of solidarity with Israel regarding both countries' struggles against the menace of global jihad.[54] This is particularly true since the Mumbai terror attacks of 2008, in which at least 166 people were killed by Pakistan-based Islamic militants.[55] On the subject of religion, many Hindus do not readily differentiate between Jews and Christians, assuming that Jewish-ness is an ethnicity more than a type of religious belonging. The paucity of education in India about the Holocaust or the Jews' perennial status as the scapegoats of European Christendom has created a situation in which Israel, for many, is the only real point of reference regarding all things Jewish.

What do the Bene Ephraim think about (other) Indian Jews who come from established Jewish communities? The answer, again, is: not much. Bene Ephraim oral narratives do not mention any significant historical interaction with the Jewish groups described here. Aside from a relationship with Sharon Galsulkar, a Bene Israel Jew from Mumbai who has befriended the community, and limited contacts among those from the Children of Manasseh movement, dealings with other Jews have primarily involved those from Israel and the United States.[56] Those countries, after all, are host to the most influential Jewish communities in the world, and building connections with them is vital to any eventual recognition of the Bene Ephraim as a legitimate part of world Jewry.

BOUND TO A NOBLE LINEAGE

From whence do the Bene Ephraim come? The specifics are fuzzy, despite the seemingly exoteric nature of their heritage narratives. Some-times the details vary slightly, or not so slightly, based on the ways in which questions regarding the group's provenance are posed. In the same way, the addressee of the question also appears to make a differ-ence. Why is this so? Because besides Shmuel Yacobi, who is (among other things) the architect of the Bene Ephraim's media project, no one else in the community with whom I spoke could ever give a detailed explanation of the group's migration to India. The synopsis of their her-itage narratives as presented here thus relies heavily upon information taken from my interviews conducted with Shmuel. It also references his many print- and web-based publications in English, which, accord-ing to him, are intended for "family members, relatives, friends, and well-wishers."[57]

Although Shmuel's providential vision about the heritage of his ancestors did not occur until 1986, he claims that he "was always brought up as a Bene Ephraim," absorbing the sacred traditions passed down to him orally by his parents and grandparents.[58] The entire collection of these oral traditions is known as the *Cavilah*, a Hebrew substantive construction whose root connotes "binding," "restriction," or, more severely, "chained." (Before learning about this set of heritage narratives, I had never heard the term before. I recognized the Hebraic root, but the particular nominative construction sounded odd to me, something along the lines of a gauche neologism.) Shmuel has described the content of the Cavilah as "not [about] religion but [about] the constitution of our nation, history of our people and our cultural heritage." Such content must "be interpreted within our own national evolutionary context and not in the religious or theological context."

After Shmuel's decision to abandon Christianity and embrace his birthright, he decided that the best method to preserve and propagate the teachings of the Cavilah would be to "record [them] in a systematic fashion before [they are] forgotten"—in other words, to write them down. This was a radical departure from previous custom, which had dictated that "nothing be put in written form" in order to "keep it out of the hands of the anti-Semites." In the present age, Shmuel reckoned, it was worth the risk. Telugu people were becoming more and more aware that their true history had been "suppressed," and the time had come to stop being afraid. Moreover, even among higher-caste Hindus, it was an open secret that the Telugu "were not native to this place." The potential benefits outweighed the potential dangers.

Somewhat ironically, the linguistic medium first chosen to record the traditions of the Cavilah was the language of the colonizers: English. And yet, for all practical purposes, this choice was the logical one to make. All of Shmuel's higher education had taken place in English. Many of the scholarly sources that he had to consult were from tomes written in English. And his intended audience would be those outside of Andhra Pradesh who would not be able to receive the tradition orally: namely, American Jews, Israeli Jews, and non-Telugu-speaking Jewish Indians.

The preliminary result of this documentary effort was a typescript, produced in 2001, with the help of Shmuel's younger brother, Sadok.[59] The contents of the typescript were expanded during the following year, which Shmuel spent in New York City. Shmuel had traveled there with the specific aim of using resources from the New York City Public Library to properly contextualize the historical occurrences recounted in the Cavilah. The fruits of the year spent on this research yielded a book published in 2002, titled, *The Cultural Hermeneutics: An Introduction to the Cultural Translations of the Hebrew Bible among the Ancient Nations of the Thalmulic [sic] Telugu Empire of India.*[60] In 2004, Shmuel published a much-condensed version of this work in Telugu, divided into two booklets. One presents a concise history of the Bene Ephraim and their migration to India, while the other contains excerpts of spiritual teachings from the Cavilah.

When asked about the historical veracity of the texts in the Cavilah, Shmuel projects a nondogmatic approach. He qualifies the oral narratives as "exegetical," "apologetic," "pseudo-epigraphic," or "apocryphal," maintaining that "fictions, opinions, and ideas from forefathers" are important even if they are not necessarily true. He also refers to the Cavilah as the "Talmud *mizrakhi*" (the Eastern Talmud), ostensibly adding a third version to the two already-canonical compilations (i.e., the Babylonian Talmud and the Jerusalem Talmud). Deflecting the notion that appendages to the Jewish canon are heretical, he states that the world needs to know about a branch of the Jewish people whose ancient traditions are "not included in the present Bible or related writings." Moreover, Shmuel hastens to add, the Jews are a people, not a religion, so minor differences in textual understanding do not automatically disqualify a lesser-known group from belonging to the collective Jewish body.

While the Bene Ephraim have "never forgotten about stories from the Torah," they apparently had no knowledge of the Prophetic Books or the Writings (Hagiographa) until their encounter with Christianity in the late nineteenth century. This is because the texts that they and the other nine Lost Tribes carried with them upon their dispersal from the Land of Israel in 722 BCE only included what had been canonized up to that point: the Five Books of Moses. They carried these with them through Persia to Afghanistan, down to Kashmir (a mountainous territory now divided between Pakistan and India), eastward to Mizoram and Manipur (the location of the Children of Manasseh movement), and finally down to southeast India around 1100 CE.

Upon their arrival to the area of present-day Andhra Pradesh, they were "welcomed" by "the egalitarian Telugu people," some of whom may have included descendants of the "'erev rav" (mixed multitude) that had left Egypt under Moses (Exod. 12:38). Also believed to be present among the Dravidians were descendants of Pashtun tribal peoples named "Ephraim," who built the first synagogue at Machilipatnam, a city in coastal Andhra. In time, due to "wars and famines and foreign forces" instigated by the Aryans against the "bull-jawed Dravidians," the Bene Ephraim were "clubbed with the Telugu Sudra servant castes" and relegated to their present status. In *The Cultural Hermeneutics*, Shmuel estimates that there are about ten million descendants of these people living in Andhra Pradesh.[61]

Eventually, they lost the written records of who they were, but most never forgot that their common ancestor, "Ephrati," had been of noble blood. This remembrance persisted even after nearly all Madiga were converted to Christianity by the American Lone Star Baptist mission (from Pennsylvania, not Texas—who knew?) in 1872. Shmuel's father, Yacob, who served for fifteen years in the British army in an engineering battalion, was apparently the first person among the Bene Ephraim to make contact with Jews outside of India for over a thousand years. During his service in World War II, Yacob visited British Mandatory Palestine and recognized in the language and behavior of the Jews there traces of what had been lost over the course of his own tribe's isolation.

A few words on the significance of the group's provenance from the tribe of Ephraim are in order. In the Bible, "Ephraim" is not only the name of a specific tribe whose progenitor was blessed by Israel as the favored son of Joseph (Gen. 48:14). It is also a symbolic appellation for all of the Lost Tribes of the Northern Kingdom of Israel, just like the designation "Judah" refers to all of the "Jews" of the Southern Kingdom. The fate of the lost Israelites depends on the fulfillment of God's promise, as prophesized in Ezekiel 37:19, to "take the stick of Joseph, which is in the hand of Ephraim, and the tribes of Israel his companions" and "put them unto him together with the stick of Judah, and make them one stick" in the Land of Israel.

Shmuel admits that, given the ancient connections between India and the Near East, it is possible that not everyone among the Bene Ephraim is actually from that tribe. Indeed, the figurative aspect of the name does not escape him. He notes that, because of the "pride and arrogancy of heart" (Isa. 9:8) of that tribe, and the fact that the central cults of early Israelite religion were located in its territory, Ephraim appears in the Bible as an archetype of fortitude. Is it a coincidence, then, that the Bible's depiction of Ephraim vis-à-vis other peoples, closely resembles the Aryans' depiction of the Dravidians as "bull-jawed"? It seems unlikely. Referring to the indigenous peoples of South India as "Ephraim" makes them blessed but long-suffering; strong-willed but temporarily down. Most importantly, it signals that they will be instrumental to a redemption that will eventually restore them to their rightful place and status. Before that redemption happens, however, every descendant of Ephraim must know that "the Covenant compels you to suffer; you must be an instrument of suffering." Shmuel underlines that the knowledge of this suffering should not be equated with tolerating the wickedness of the caste system, which he has called "a monstrous social disease." Through his activities aimed at fostering awareness about South India's true heritage, he "has been fighting" against this "monster" by "stand[ing] up for the Bene Ephraim communities and for the other [Indian] victims of exploitation."

Shmuel argues that the typological similarities between sacred Hindu and Jewish texts may also be attributed to such "exploitation": namely, that the Aryans "stole" the narratives of the original Israelite inhabitants of South India. He claims that Hinduism, Buddhism, Jainism, Confucianism, Zoroastrianism, and most other religions born north of the Deccan plateau are all "offshoots" of Judaism, an influence that he dates to the sixth century BCE.[62] This dissemination of Israelite (Jewish) thought did not take place because of any proselytizing, he stresses, but because of the "moral high ground" of the Bene Ephraim that other groups eventually wished to emulate.

For example, Shmuel maintains that the myths surrounding the character of Manu, the ancestor of all Indian kings who survived a great

flood, and whom Hindus revere as the first human, are an Aryan corruption of the biblical story of Noah (Gen. 5–9). By the same logic,
Harishchandra, a central figure in several major Hindu religious texts
who demonstrates faith and moral uprightness in the face of tribula-
tion, is taken directly from Job. The story of Draupadi, who was the
most beautiful woman of all time according to the *Mahabharata*, finds
its inspiration in the tale of Merab, daughter of Saul, who was given
to Adriel despite having been promised to David (1 Sam. 18), just as
Draupadi was given to Yudhistara although promised to Arjuna.[63]
And so on.

How does the Cavilah compare to conventional Jewish writings?
The differences are few, but significant. In the same way that Reform,
Conservative, Reconstructionist, and other "alternative" streams of non-
Orthodox Judaism have reinterpreted seminal Jewish texts and doctrines according to Western humanistic and liberal traditions, it appears
that the Bene Ephraim have reinterpreted key Jewish stories, symbols,
texts, and tropes according to their own situational contexts. Overwhelmingly, they have done so along the lines of emphatically Madiga-
based concerns, accentuating existing themes and discourses while
marginalizing others.

The most significant revisions seem to be the near-total abandonment of traditional notions of subservience, punishment, and sin,
together with the embellishment of the notions of equality and justice. According to Shmuel, these themes prevalent in the Cavilah are
emphasized to Bene Ephraim children starting at a young age, in order
that they avoid being indoctrinated with theories of higher-caste Hindu
superiority or with Aryan or Christian "contaminations" of the Divine
Word. In that sense, Egorova and Perwez's comment that "the community's self-identification with the Jewish tradition is as much an expression of their pride in being Madiga as it is a protest against the caste
system" is especially relevant for an examination of the Bene Ephraim's
approach to Jewish textual praxis.[64]

The primary lesson of the Cavilah is that God does not "rule over"
anything. When God made man in his image, it was not in order that
man should have "dominion over the fish of the sea, and over the fowl of
the air, and over the cattle, and over all the earth, and over every creeping

thing that creepeth upon the earth" (Gen. 1:26). Rather, it was that man should be a *caretaker* of these creatures, just as God would be a caretaker of man. For instance, the Cavilah recounts that, after God made Adam, the first man, he did not "order" him to "do" anything.[65] Instead, God came "everyday, with angels, to teach him everything in a patient way." When Adam and Eve went against God's "recommendations," they were not expelled from the Garden of Eden. God "explained their mistake to them, and they understood." They were then turned into spirits—the only spirits in which the Bene Ephraim believe, because Adam and Eve are the parents of humanity—and were there to answer the prayers of God's subsequent human creations. Interestingly, there is no serpent figure in this Cavilah story. When I asked for clarification on whether or not Satan exists in the Bene Ephraim tradition, Shmuel jokingly answered in the affirmative: "Satan does exist. He is the Aryans!"

The Cavilah also "corrects common misunderstandings" about certain biblical events that might be seen as shameful or dysfunctional. For instance, the "fabricated" scene involving the incestuous union between Lot and his daughters (Gen. 19:30–38) does not appear in the Cavilah. Instead, the Cavilah tells of "shape-shifting demons" who coupled with Lot's daughters. The truth about the matter was discovered by Abraham, the first Jew, who knew that his "brother's son would never do such a thing." With regard to Abraham, the Cavilah also corrects widespread misconceptions about his actions regarding his sons, Isaac and Ishmael. Abraham, it seems, never intended to physically sacrifice his son Isaac (Gen. 22). This "near-sacrifice" is a corruption of the original tale, which was altered according to themes present in Babylonian mythology. Abraham merely "offered up his son to continue the service of the Covenant." Moreover, Abraham had never cast out his firstborn son Ishmael or the boy's mother, Hagar (Gen. 21). The two merely decided to dwell in a nearby "forest area," where they were visited frequently by Abraham and Isaac "during vacation times."

Abraham's descendants did indeed encounter misfortune, but none so great as is commonly believed. For example, Jacob, Abraham's grandson, did not "flee" to his uncle Laban in Haran (Gen. 28:10) due to the earlier threat of fratricide (Gen. 27:41–42). Instead, he was called there to be "Laban's commander-in-chief," and never worked as a shepherd.

Rachel and Jacob returned to Canaan with the blessing of Rachel's father, but not before Rachel encouraged Laban to "forget his idols." Note that, in this version of the story, Jacob does not suffer in bondage to Laban (Gen. 29–30), but chooses to leave of his own free will. Rachel, for her part, neither steals her father's idols (Gen. 31:19) nor defiles them by menstruating on them (Gen. 31:34–35). Rather, with a disapproving nod to the Hindu phenomenon of worshiping household gods, she calmly points out that such gods are "false ones."

However, not everything was rosy in the lives of Abraham's descendants. The Cavilah recounts that Jacob and Rachel's son, Joseph, was sold into slavery in Egypt, just as in the biblical account (Gen. 27:38). However, Joseph had requested that no one "ever publish the event," because, "it will ruin our relationships, as future generations will say to the descendents of Reuben and Judah, 'You are the ones who sold my father.'" Later, in Egypt, Moses, the assimilated Hebrew, had no idea about this ignoble occurrence in his people's history. In fact, he had not much of an idea at all about his own origins. He had been a content member of the "expatriate" Israelites who worked for the Pharaoh and paid taxes without molestation. When Moses became interested in his parents' ethnic background, he went to Midian, where he learned Cavilah with the elders from Goshen. He and the Israelites then made a collective decision to leave Egypt, but not under threat of death. The Pharaoh did not try to stop them, realizing that "because they came through the Covenant, they must leave through the Covenant." In the Cavilah, Moses is depicted as a "social reformer" rather than a liberator.

While journeying through the desert en route to the Promised Land, the Children of Israel learned "administration, handicrafts, and other useful things." They also received "the world's first constitution"—the Ten Commandments. As mentioned earlier, the instance of idol worship involving the golden calf and the so-called "generation in the desert" story are corruptions of the original text of the Cavilah. On those points, Shmuel insists that God forgave the small number of people who engaged in idol worship, and that the Israelites had to linger before entering Canaan only because that particular waiting period had been established by the Covenant long beforehand. The agreement had always been to sojourn in seven places of exile: Egypt, Assyria, Babylon, Persia,

Greece, Rome, and "all nations." After these seven exiles would be the long-awaited ingathering in Israel. This ultimate return to a common territory highlights the fact that Israel is a confederation, not a religion. Shmuel stresses that, according to the Cavilah, the people of Israel never did anything wrong. They were sent into exile only because "they were the instrument."

The Cavilah also contains legends and characters that are postbiblical in their chronology and context. For instance, the *golem*—an anthropomorphic figure from Jewish folklore, familiarized to the world mainly through its kabbalistic iterations—is part of the Bene Ephraim oral tradition.[66] However, unlike the conventional Jewish portrayals of the golem, in which the monster ends up turning on its creator and running amok, the golem in the Bene Ephraim tradition is an obedient watchman who possesses not only a corporeal body, but "free will," to boot.

Similarly, the postbiblical conception of the *Shekhinah* also appears in the Cavilah, albeit in slightly different form. Known alternatively as the "Divine Presence," the feminine counterpart of God, the "Sabbath Bride," the messenger of God, or the mystical representation of all the Jews in the world, this composite of the feminine attributes of God is said to have gone into exile with the Jewish people, destined to return only when they fully repent of their transgressions.[67] In the lore of the Bene Ephraim, however, the Presence has never left. "No matter how unclean the community is, she is always with us because of our Covenant," Shmuel says.

While listening to these histories, I had to wonder: If there is no sin, then what of the afterlife? Do the Bene Ephraim entertain the concepts of Heaven or Hell? According to Shmuel, the Cavilah does indeed tell of an afterlife, but not one that separates people according to good or bad deeds. Rather, everyone has "his own colony according to his own ethnic or religious group," and the soul "never rests until it finds likeminded people." The location of the afterlife is in a place called by the Hebrew name of *Har tzion* (Mount Zion), which was also the first thing that God created, even before the sun or the moon. The souls of the Bene Ephraim serve as guides there, showing other souls the way to go. The learning and instruction that they receive at Mount Zion "takes forever"—and this is what it means for a member of the Bene Ephraim to go home to the arms of God.

The dominant tone of these reenvisioned biblical stories is, in a word, *accepting*. This is not liberation theology in the traditional sense, but a redemptive narrative that provides a countermeasure to themes and discourses that have contributed to a sense of inferiority. In offering such an alternative, it recreates the perception of self and of one's place in God's creation. In that reenvisioned universe, there is little iniquity or ill will. God cares for his people and strives to show them the right way to live in a loving manner. The Covenant is in place forever and can never be rescinded. Everything is therefore part of a benevolent divine plan. As indicated, "miracles" as such are absent from these narratives, even in the realm of the afterlife, further buttressing Shmuel's declaration that the Bene Ephraim "do not fear hells, fires, judgments or any other religio-fantasies."[68] Also of importance is the trope of belonging to the Land of Israel, embodied by the mythical topos of Mount Zion as Heaven. This recasting of the primary diasporic signifier for the site of lost Jewish sovereignty (and eventual Jewish redemption) into the be-all and end-all address of Creation itself is highly significant, especially for a community whose leadership has made no secret of its desire to be "repatriated" to Israel.

OBSERVANCE AND WELTANSCHAUUNG

The Bene Ephraim follow several customs to which they point as associative evidence of their historical ties to ancient Israel. However, not all of these customs necessarily demonstrate an Israelite origin. Some of the customs, such as the consumption of buffalo meat and the burial of their dead, are seen as anathema by their upper-caste Hindu neighbors. But these are commonly practiced throughout Andhra Pradesh by many other lower-caste Telugu peoples.[69] Less "touchy" practices, such as the use of a solar-lunar calendar, are commonly acknowledged as throwbacks to the cultures of South India's original inhabitants. The observance of a Saturday Sabbath is increasingly in vogue among

Christianized former untouchables who belong to Sabbatarian, Seventh-day Adventist, Messianic, or Prophetic movements, despite the heavy economic consequences that such an observance carries.

Other rites, such as circumcision and ritual slaughter, are practiced by local Muslims, but have only recently been (re)introduced among the Bene Ephraim. Shmuel recounts that the Bene Ephraim elected to stop practicing circumcision in the eighteenth century, when Islam gained a foothold in Telugu country. This was done in order that they not be mistaken for Muslims. Unsurprisingly (and courageously), Shmuel has been instrumental in bringing these observances (back) to his community. At the age of twenty-nine, he underwent elective surgical circumcision. He has also endeavored to educate his compatriots about proper practices of ritual slaughter, helped along by contacts from overseas Jewish communities.

The Bene Ephraim deny that their practices may have been influenced by behaviors prevalent among their Muslim neighbors. In fact, the idea of such "contamination" by Islamic practices is not even entertained. The same is true for any supposed linguistic similarities. On that point, Shmuel insists that the approximately two hundred Hebraic-sounding words in the Telugu language should be attributed to the influence of Hebrew among the early settlers of Andhra Pradesh, and not to any influence from neighboring Islamic cultures. When Shmuel pointed out his theory of a vanished "Assyrio-Telugu" language, akin to proto-Hebrew, to the editors of the Telugu Historical Dictionary Project, the "Telugu pundits," as he now calls them, responded with a contemptuous silence.[70]

Certain customs surrounding issues of gender propriety, such as Levirate marriage and polygamy, are common among the *Adivasi* (tribal or aboriginal peoples) of South India, and are therefore not exclusive to the Bene Ephraim.[71] The laws of menstrual seclusion are said to be upheld according to the Levitical text, with the corporeal purification carried out in streams, rivers, or with the aid of wells or natural springs. Concerns about maintaining separation between menstruating females and other community members actually have much in common with mainstream Hindu ideas about corporeal propriety, according to which a woman must refrain from certain religious duties during her menstrual flow. The Bene Ephraim's insistence upon maintaining menstrual separation also resembles similar tribal customs common to South India, where menstruating females are, according to Dianne Jenett, "considered vulnerable" to possession by spirits and must therefore be isolated.[72]

Other supposed parallels between Telugu peoples and the Israelites have to do with the eating of bitter chutney during the Hindu festival of *Ugadi*, which marks the beginning of the Deccan New Year (similar to the eating of bitter herbs during the Jewish Passover); marking the doorframe on certain ceremonial occasions with the blood of a recently sacrificed goat (again, similar to the Jewish Passover); the pouring of libations; and excommunication. The similarities between these and other Madiga customs and "ancient" (which the Yacobis suggest actually means "Israelite") methods of worship were remarked upon as early as 1899 by the American Baptist missionary Emma Rauschenbusch-Clough, in *While Sewing Sandals: Or, Tales of a Telugu Pariah Tribe*.[73] When I asked Shmuel if the customs of the Bene Ephraim had ever been influenced by the Aryans, he admitted that there were *"goyishe"* (Yiddish: non-Jewish; Gentile-like) things absorbed because of the long sojourn in Teluguland. But these things, which he did not detail, were superficial, not fundamental.

Since the time that the Bene Ephraim began making extensive contacts with overseas Jewish groups, their observances have shifted somewhat toward normative Jewish practice. But access is still a problem. Besides the Yacobi family, few congregants possess the funds or the connections needed to obtain written materials from conventional Jewish sources. For Bible study, these individuals make do with Telugu Bibles (distributed by Christian missionaries) without the pages containing the New Testament, which have long since been ripped out. (The stubs of the removed pages were shown to me repeatedly as evidence of this unambiguous severance from previous religious affiliation.) For standard Jewish prayer services, Shmuel has transliterated into Telugu letters the basic Hebrew prayers, such as those found in the morning, afternoon, and evening Sabbath liturgies. Also in transliterated Telugu is the entire text of the Hebrew Scriptures—a monumental task on which Shmuel spent an entire year. Services usually consist of a reading of Psalms in Telugu, followed by an attempt at reading the Hebrew prayers. For the many community members who are illiterate—their precise number has been difficult to quantify—prayers in Telugu or approximate Hebrew consist of recitation and repetition. Partitions to separate men and women exist in two of the three community synagogues. Men wear skullcaps in the synagogue, but usually nowhere else.

Shmuel freely admits that most members of his community "do not pray much," although they do "observe the major commandments." Shmuel is ultimately able to discern who among the Madiga is a true part of the Bene Ephraim according to each person's "attempt to live religiously." Such discernment does not come about based on that person's level of worship or praise, because the "pure humanism" of the Bene Ephraim will inevitably cause one to refrain from "easily praising God like a habituated religionist." Instead, maintaining the necessary dietary restrictions, avoiding work on the Sabbath, and circumcision (for men) are the basic requirements to join the organized community. Learning the basics of Judaism as a matriculating student in community education classes is also recommended. With regard to marriage, Bene Ephraim may wed other Madiga who have been raised as Christians, since, ostensibly, all Madiga are, in Shmuel's words, "Jews who just don't know it yet." To be on the safe side, no "love marriages" are allowed, and any potential mate's family tree must be checked at least three generations back before the marriage arrangement can be formalized.

Those who wish to become formal members at any one of the three community synagogues must undergo a trial period of one year, after which God will "put in the heart [of Shmuel] who is a true part of the tribe."[74] That person may then take on a Hebrew name or its functional equivalent. (When I met a girl from the community and introduced myself to her using my Hebrew name, Natan, she proudly informed me that her Hebrew name was "Golda Meir," after Israel's fourth prime minister.) If anyone is found to still be practicing Christianity on the side, that person is immediately ejected from the community. One university-aged man whom I met during an audience with some younger Bene Ephraim openly challenged this policy, protesting in front of the assembled crowd that they were, as Shmuel has repeatedly said, "a nation, and not a religion." "Why," the young man asked, "are we not allowed to worship someone who lived his entire life as a Jew?" The man then left the meeting in haste, but was apparently pursued to the edge of town, where he was told not to show his face in the community again.

The most learned of the community are the members of Shmuel's immediate family. They also are the ones who officiate at religious services and community events. The original congregation in Shmuel's home village of Kothareddypalem, near the town of Chebrolu in the Guntur district, is led by Shmuel's younger brother, Sadok. Shmuel directs services at the improvised synagogue (sometimes called the Bene Ephraim Yeshiva Community Center) in the city of Vijayawada, while Shmuel's youngest son, Dan, frequently leads the congregation in the synagogue located in the city of Machilipatnam, where Shmuel's wife, Malkah, has a family plot. Shmuel's eldest son, Yehoshua, who still lives in Israel, usually holds weekly Skype sessions on Sundays with at least one of the congregations, teaching them about Jewish history, Hebrew language, and Israeli culture, in preparation for their eventual move to the Jewish state. At the time of this writing, there are only a few dozen fervently observant people in the community, besides those in the immediate and extended Yacobi family. None of them hold leadership roles in any congregational capacity.

Out of all the Judaizing communities I have visited, the Bene Ephraim were the least willing to engage in theoretical discussions about what being Jewish means to them. It seems that most perspectives on the matter are replications of the views held by Shmuel, whose opinions as leader hold almost ultimate sway. Moreover, since most interviewees did not have access to a diverse range of media about Judaism or modern Israel, their perceptions tended to be as "mythologized" as those of their fellow (Christianized) Madiga.

Responses to my questions about details regarding the community Cavilah were almost always answered with a request that I pose the questions to Shmuel himself. Answers to queries regarding proper Jewish practice among the Bene Ephraim focused on those basic customs that separate the Madiga from their higher-caste Hindu neighbors: burial, circumcision, food taboos, etc. This manner of responding seemed to be the case among both literate and illiterate persons. On occasion, out-of-context references were made to some of the more central pillars of Jewish religious life, such as the instance in which a well-meaning community member offered to pray for me (in Hebrew) during a particularly nasty bout of "Delhi belly," the local expatriate expression for food poisoning. The prayer turned out to be the blessing said over the Sabbath wine. Many times, my questions were redirected toward tangential comparisons regarding respective traditions of suffering under the yoke of more dominant powers. One man, surprised to hear that my Ashkenazi forefathers did not have "any Cavilahs," wondered what kind of "sacred wisdom" we held onto in order to resist complete surrender in the face of persecution.

Although many literate people knew that there had been a Holocaust of European Jewry, few had any idea about the details. One person asked if I had personally been affected during the course of those events, which he said happened during the 1990s. Another man, who made his living as a private tutor, asked how Hitler could have understood anything about the Jews in Germany if he was not "proficient in Aramaic—or was it neo-Aramaic?" One group of young men wondered aloud why European Jews had not used the self-defense techniques outlined in the Cavilah, which they equated with the famed Israeli martial art *krav mag'a* (contact combat). Another person, recalling an earlier question of mine about why there were not more Bene Ephraim interred at the local cemetery, referenced this tradition of self-defense and stated matter-of-factly: "You see, we are so strong—that's why we don't die enough!" An elderly woman who overheard this conversation asked why Hitler's victims did not try to use their amulets for an apotropaic effect. After all, as she pointed out, the spells of "Hindu witchdoctors" are known to be useless against the talismans of the Bene Ephraim. The same woman began to demonstrate to me the power of such charms to heal the sick, rubbing her amulet against the arthritic leg of another female community member. Shmuel's brother Sadok, who was present, quickly urged her to cease the demonstration.[75]

About modern-day Israel, knowledge is negligible. Some members with whom I spoke had heard of *kibbutzim*, the renowned collective farming settlements, and wanted me to help them build some of their own. Several referred to the current aggressors of Israel as "Philistines," by which I assume they meant Palestinians. A few dozen of the more

well-off members of the community who had been to Israel were familiar with the debates surrounding Israel's domestic and foreign policies,
but did not know much about Israeli life per se. One man, an electrician
by profession, had seen a news story about "feminist agitators" in Israel
and expressed shock over such behavior. When "the Ten Tribes return,"
he said, "all that crap will be washed away!" Another professional who
came to Israel to study professed the same discomfort with the behavior
of, as he put it, "secular, non-Orthodox Israelis." Harassed by the police
and the immigration authorities, who did not believe him to be Jewish,
he lamented:

> I came to the Land of Israel with pre-fixed thoughts that people
> and land will remind me [of] the biblical time with holiness,
> Torah, Shabbat, etc. . . . But I found myself in a different situ-
> ation. To say frankly at first I felt very sad with the ways going
> around there. I thought it is just another modern country. I was
> seeking some spiritual enlightenment. But it was just like another
> Hollywood movie this time in front of my eyes. I saw the people
> not keeping the Shabbat. Adding to this I went to a Conservative
> synagogue where I saw men and women sitting together in the
> synagogue and the *chazzan* [cantor] was a woman. I felt I was in
> the church, God forbid. I came across some young kids teasing
> with some very bad words. I was in [a] big dilemma whether I
> made the right decision or not.

By Shmuel's account, there have been at least twenty-five Israelis
who have visited the community since 1991, among them rabbis interested in knowing more about this potential "seed of Israel."[76] In the years
since post-army treks to India have become the rage among Israel's
adventurous youth, backpackers crossing through Andhra Pradesh have
also visited. So far, only one Israeli organization, an NGO called *Adam
leadam* (Person to Person), has maintained sustained contact with the
community. Shavei Israel, the Israel-based organization mentioned in
chapter 1, has kept in contact mainly through Yehoshua, whose project
on translating into Telugu selected Jewish pedagogical materials was
facilitated by the organization. According to Yehoshua, it also paid for

Sadok to study Judaism in an Israeli seminary for three months, and for Yehoshua to travel back to India for a brief period to offer classes on Jewish topics and Hebrew language.

Israel is seen as a source of protection against possible terror attacks. In 2004, when the local press reported that the Indian police had foiled an intended attack upon "Jewish families" in Guntur by the Pakistan-based terrorist group *Lashkar-e-Tayyiba* (Urdu: "Army of the Righteous"), Shmuel appealed to the Israeli Ministry of the Interior for assistance. Although no answer was received, some members of the community apparently believe that the Israeli security services are monitoring discontented Muslims in the area. One person told me of a Muslim who had "infiltrated" the synagogue in Machilipatnam, but then disappeared after the community confronted him about his identity. While nearly 80 percent of the people whom I polled expressed a desire to immigrate to Israel, where they "would be safe" from such threats, no one besides those in the Yacobi family has made any formal requests to that effect. Yehoshua despairs that no member of the Bene Ephraim movement will ever be allowed to obtain Israeli citizenship. He is convinced that the Jewish Agency, the body that oversees immigration, has made a conscious decision to marginalize the movement.

Contacts with the wider Jewish world have traditionally been infrequent, but are becoming more and more common as word about the community gets out through social media. Thus far, the only visit to the community by representatives from a major diasporic Jewish organization was the 2007 visit by Rabbis Gerald and Bonita Sussman, who came on behalf of Kulanu.[77] One of the results of this visit was the establishment of a small poultry business financed by Kulanu, which was supposed to yield profits that would then enable the community to develop a proper Jewish infrastructure. By the time I visited, in 2012, the farm had long since been shut down, primarily due to concerns about fiscal accountability. According to Egorova and Perwez, two factors contributing to this setback were that "none of the community members had any prior experience with raising chickens and only very few had the knowledge of microfinance."[78] Some community members were so embittered by what they perceived to be exclusionary tactics and economic mismanagement on the part of the project managers that they left the organized movement. Other projects funded by outside Jewish groups aimed at economic advancement for the community have fared poorly for similar reasons. And yet, more than one person informed me that the Bene Ephraim were blessed with "the Jewish head for business."

Among the community in Kothareddypalem, where the movement began, there is also a serious issue of trust vis-à-vis foreign Jewish organizations. Part of this trepidation stems from an incident that occurred in the mid-2000s, in which three young men from the village were sent to New York City for study along with Shmuel's son, Dan. Upon arrival, the supposedly trustworthy Jewish New Yorker who had invited the young men locked them in his apartment, declared himself the Messiah, and said that he would not let them go until they agreed to enlist in a branch of the Jewish Defense League in Uganda. The Indians eventually escaped and found refuge with other Jewish contacts facilitated by Shmuel, but the episode marked a turning point in the community's belief in the absolute benevolence of Jewish foreigners.

The affair also created a rift between much of the Kothareddypalem community members and Shmuel, whom they blamed for initiating such risky business. Moreover, the anger over their sons' lives being put in danger brought to the surface long-simmering frustrations. Some questioned the wisdom of persisting in Jewish observance when they had obtained almost no tangible results from their nearly thirty-year effort at recognition. As one community member told me: "We have many problems to confront in our daily lives that are bigger than Mr. Yacobi's genealogy."

For a brief period after the "New York incident," Sadok took over leadership of the Kothareddypalem community in order to heal the rifts. One change that Sadok made was to publicly advocate for formal conversion to Judaism, as opposed to Shmuel's more ambitious wish for ancestral recognition.[79] Eventually, Shmuel came to agree with Sadok's stance on conversions. While things cooled down, Shmuel formed new constituencies of Bene Ephraim outside of his home village—namely, in Vijayawada and Machilipatnam. Those two locations are now the main sites of activity for the Bene Ephraim movement.

The fact that there has not risen another leader for the Bene Ephraim outside of the Yacobi family has much to do with Shmuel's and Sadok's relatively privileged economic status. Because their father, Yacob, was able to escape many evils of the caste system by rising to the military rank of *Subedar* (the equivalent rank of a British lieutenant for colonial subjects), subsequently receiving training as an English teacher, purchasing land, and educating his sons, the Yacobis have linguistic and monetary means that most of their fellow Madiga do not. Even the plot of land on which the synagogue in Kothareddypalem sits is nearer to the town center than the other areas on the periphery traditionally reserved for untouchables. Shmuel supports himself with the activities of the Hebrew Open University Research Study Centre, and Sadok sells insurance. To be sure, they are by no means well-off. By Western standards, they are actually quite poor. But their particular background and experience are almost unprecedentedly more advantaged than those belonging to their religious flocks.

The number of "zealous" families belonging to the Bene Ephraim movement has not changed much over the years. Formerly enthusiastic adherents have backslid, new ones have come along, and others have gone for good. The pool of potential congregants has also remained the same: lower-caste Telugus looking for something missing in their current spiritual associations. The episode described at the beginning of this chapter, in which Madiga Christians excitedly signed up for the courses offered by Shmuel's Hebrew Research Centre, is but one illustration of the ways would-be Judaizers relate to the Bene Ephraim movement. Many become supporters or members, while others—a growing number, in fact—choose to explore other options. In their chapter on "The Other Bene Ephraim," Egorova and Perwez have perceptively discussed the phenomenon of those who have been inspired by the movement, but who ultimately pursue other ethnoreligious affiliations.[80] Two other such groups, profiled below, demonstrate possible alternative outcomes of interaction with the Bene Ephraim.

One group of non-Jewish supporters is an association known as the "Telugu Noahides," mentioned briefly at the beginning of this chapter. Noahides, as the reader will recall from chapter 1, are "righteous" non-Jews who choose to embrace the seven laws that, according to the Talmud, God gave to Adam and Eve in the Garden of Eden (Gen. 2:16) and then to Noah after the Flood (Gen. 9:4–6). In the view of Michael

Shelomo Bar-Ron, the process of this "semi-conversion" by Gentiles is seen as part of the "divinely-ordained legal, social, moral, and spiritual framework that non-Jewish human beings are born into."[81] Jews, for their part, are commanded to treat Noahides favorably and to provide for their welfare. There is therefore a kind of built-in reciprocity between Jews and Noahides.

The Telugu Noahides were established independently of the Bene Ephraim outreach and education movement, but later sought out Shmuel's advice on proper ritual procedure. Currently, Shmuel advises them in their activities when requested to do so, but does not do more than help with brainstorming, or, occasionally, advertising. Prospective Noahides are informed in announcements promoting classes on the topic that they can "learn Noah's seven laws" in order to live "life in peace," as well as be part of making "world peace through [becoming acquainted with] Hebrew culture."[82] Since 2014, Shmuel has served as a liaison for this association in partnership with the Jerusalem-based Noahide World Center, whose goals are to "disseminate the message of the Torah to the non-Jewish world" and "to help establish Noahide communities around the world."[83]

Ironically, the Noahide World Center does not consider any of the Bene Ephraim to be kosher Jews, save Yehoshua, who underwent a formal conversion in Israel. What's more, their objectives in this venture seem to be quite the opposite of Shmuel's, who stated in a Facebook posting that "the Telugu Noahides forgot their covenant with the Bene Ephraim Community, but they will remember it and become one people again." For the time being, however, the Bene Ephraim work with the Noahides only in a consultative capacity. Most Noahides in Andhra Pradesh are lower-caste Christians who are intrigued by the Bene Ephraim, and who may choose to support them morally or financially, but ultimately do not wish to join them. That they are portrayed by some as being "on the fence" with regard to any Judaizing intentions seems to be wishful thinking.

Another group of people inspired by the activities of the Bene Ephraim are proselytes by conviction and former members of the Telugu Noahides. Now part of an agrarian-style Judaizing commune outside of Vijayawada, they agreed to be interviewed for this book, provided that their anonymity be preserved.[84] Around sixty people live at the community, whose governing philosophy is described as "close to the spirit of a kibbutz." The leaders of the community, and many of the congregants, began their paths toward Judaism after taking Hebrew classes with Shmuel as part of the Noahide training module. All are of Madiga or Mala extraction, and all besides two (former nominal Hindus who come from mixed-religion families) are former Christians. The religious background of the formerly Christian members is largely uniform, centered on foundational experiences in Messianic, charismatic, or Pentecostal churches. Their break from Christianity occurred when they realized that "Jesus could not be God" based on the criteria of the Hebrew Scriptures.

Their decision to Judaize outside of the body of the Bene Ephraim community came about for several reasons. One reason, according to a senior member of the community, is that he felt it was impossible for "illiterate people" who had been "duped by sentimental reasoning" to call themselves Jews. To take on such a radically different spiritual identity, the man said, one must "really know what it means" and "not bother about so-called genealogy between Telugu and Israelite peoples." To ensure such understanding, their religious services consist of close readings of and discussions on biblical texts. Another reason to be independent, cited by several in the community, is that the hierarchical structure of the Bene Ephraim movement encourages authoritarianism and "dynastical privilege." They want to live as a true community, with no one person more advantaged than another. And this is in spite of the fact that they still "respect Mr. Yacobi's children very much."

The final reason for their decision to form a separate Judaizing collective had to do with their distaste for the increasingly Western- and Israel-centric nature of the Bene Ephraim's Jewish practice. For example, they did not buy into the notion that the customs of the Israelites had to undergo "necessary changes" between the time of those customs' documentation in the Hebrew Scriptures and the present day. They wanted to make burnt offerings and to "circumcise themselves" just as Abraham had done, but without modifying the rituals or consulting with any "pesky intermediaries." Because the Messiah has not come, they do not believe that the state of Israel has any divine legitimacy.

Consequently, they have no desire to move there. Moreover, several expressed concerns about safety "because of the wars between Israelites and Gazans." Unlike the Bene Ephraim, they are content to live out their communal Old Testamentism on Indian soil, without worrying about where they are going or from whence they came.

OUTREACH AND PUBLICITY EFFORTS

The two communities profiled above demonstrate that, in spite of notable successes, the Bene Ephraim are not always triumphant in their efforts to reach out to discontented lower-caste inhabitants of Telugu-land. But this has not stopped them from trying. Besides the obvious pedagogical contexts for such outreach efforts, other venues have been used in order to spread the word about the Bene Ephraim in Andhra Pradesh and beyond. These include "family wellness" consulting services; creative writing and historiographic/scholarly treatises; a motion picture (still in the works at the time of this writing); and musical productions. For a number of years, Shmuel also maintained a detailed website on community history and goings-on, but was advised by the Indian police to take it down after the terror threats of 2004. A new website is currently being constructed by the more tech-savvy Yehoshua.

Since 2013, Shmuel has been intermittently involved with Ayurvedic health clinics in Hyderabad, the capital city of the neighboring state of Telangana. His involvement has consisted of offering prescriptions of "spiritual nourishment," to be given in tandem with advice on ameliorating one's physical and mental health. He has also served as a therapist in the Hebrew Cultural Family Counseling Center, which promises help for "those lonely souls seeking for love and warmth and yearning to know the purpose and goals of their lives."[85] The center staff pledges to potential clients that they will "try to understand you and your human problems and share the Hebrew Culture so that you can have a fresh approach to your family life on earth."[86]

In the realm of writing and publication, Shmuel has been prolific. Indeed, in my first e-mail communication with Shahid Perwez on the subject of the Bene Ephraim, Perwez described Shmuel to me as "a radical Jewish writer."[87] Writings of Shmuel's in the creative category comprise poetry in both Telugu and English, including an epic "response poem," "John Milton at Pandemonium."[88] Dedicated to *Paradise Lost*'s author—who, according to Shmuel, "always liked to represent the downtrodden," and who "learned Hebrew and studied Jewish literature"—the poem deals with the Bene Ephraim's history and the transmigration of souls.[89] Shmuel's numerous prose compositions are also connected to themes germane to the concerns of the Bene Ephraim movement. For instance, his novel, *The Prince of Whales*, recasts the tale of Jonah in a modern, James Bond–style narrative, detailing the efforts at recognition of "isolated" Jewish people from the East.[90] His scholarly works and theological essays have explored similar themes, ranging from the "comparative ideo-genetics of all cultures" to explorations of the question, "What is prophecy and how is it fulfilled according to the Christian standards?" Some of these works remain unpublished, although almost all of them appear in abridged versions online. He has also composed a Hebrew language textbook for speakers of Telugu.

One noteworthy aspect of the Bene Ephraim's recent outreach activities has been the production and diffusion of digital video and sound media. This shift seems to stem from a conscious attempt on the part of Shmuel, its creator and instigator, to harness popular support for and create interest in the Bene Ephraim among those Indians who would not have the English language level, or the generational habitudes, to read his earlier scholarly treatises, fiction, or poetry. It also appears to have Western and Israeli Jewry in mind as potential audiences, especially those who fall into the "wired" age bracket.

One such example of this new method of outreach is the music and video combination set composed by Shmuel, called "Hebrew and Telugu Menorah Songs."[91] First released as a downloadable album via iTunes and other online stores in 2011, the songs were then uploaded with accompanying videos onto YouTube later that year, under the revised titles of "Tel-English Songs from South India" and "Hebrew Menorah Songs from South India." This combination of mostly Indian music, sung in Hebrew, English, and Telugu, contains new compositions, as well as modified tunes and lyrics first composed by Shmuel as synagogue standards in the early 1990s. As with Shmuel's creative writing, most of the content revolves around Bene Ephraim–related subjects, although several of the songs involve no Jewish themes at all. In the explanatory blurb given for each video on YouTube, Shmuel refers to himself as "Producer and Director of Eretz Ephraim Pictures."[92] Each video is listed as belonging to "Production No. 1," which is an "upcoming Telugu comedy movie" (more on that below) that Shmuel hopes to finance by "sell[ing] my movie songs." Almost all the videos were filmed at the compound of the community's synagogue in Machilipatnam.

Much of the footage in the videos is simply documentary-style reportage of the Bene Ephraim's bureaucratic problems, interspersed with images of community members going about their daily tasks. For instance, one video, with an accompanying soundtrack of Hebrew Psalms set to South Indian flute music, shows Malkah, Shmuel's wife, holding the long-awaited registration authorization for the construction of the Machilipatnam synagogue.[93] The scene then cuts to Malkah holding a letter from the Israeli Prime Minister's Bureau, dated 2004, informing Shmuel that the Ministry of the Interior is still waiting for information to complete his application for immigration, which had been submitted in 2001. (He eventually supplied the information, and is still waiting for an answer.) The writing on each document is easily discernable to the viewer.

Some of the same video footage is shared between dissimilar songs. For instance, two videos feature Shmuel's son, Dan, putting on a prayer shawl and then bringing a miniature Torah scroll out of an "ark" to a podium in the synagogue.[94] In both videos, the camera lingers lengthily on the Israeli flags and Indian flower wreaths hanging from the synagogue's ceiling. Several common shots follow Shmuel as he enters the synagogue, repeatedly signaling to the cameraman to focus on the *mezuzah* mounted on the door frame. (A *mezuzah* is the traditional marker of a Jewish home, made up of a decorative casing in which a piece of parchment containing biblical verses has been placed.)[95] One of the videos shows Dan reading from a prayer book.[96] Other scenes involve domestic images such as Malkah sewing, a chicken walking about in the yard, and the movements of a pet dog who is tied to a car.[97] The accompanying music includes the Hebrew chanting of portions from the Song of Songs and the Psalms.

Some of the Hebrew songs are essentially conventional Jewish hymns put to Telugu music, often taken verbatim from standard prayer books or from the Torah itself. One such Hebrew song starts off with the prayer for the "Blessing of the Sons" recited by the *cohenim*, the hereditary Jewish priests: "*Ya'asimkha elohim keefrayim vekhemenashe*" (May God make you like Ephraim and Manasseh). The singer then recites nearly verbatim the Song of Songs 7:1: "*Shuvi shuvi shulamiti, shuvi shuvi venekhezeh bakh; mah tekhezu bashulamit kemekholat, hamakhanayim*" (Return, return, O [my] Shulamite; Return, return, that we may look upon thee. What will ye see in the Shulamite? As it were a dance of two companies).[98] The accompanying video footage is made up of close, zoom-in shots of a Word document on Shmuel's computer, which informs the viewer about a Telugu "listening competition." The competition offers to reward Telugu speakers for identifying and making sense of the English words in the "Tel-English Songs from South India."

Another video starts out with a shot of Malkah reading a 2003 Telugu news article about the Bene Ephraim community. It then shifts to a series of long shots that pan over the same synagogue registration certificate and letter from the Israeli Prime Minister's Office.[99] The first Hebrew lyrics of the musical composition, which do not seem to come from any particular source, are "*Adonai emet torah emet moshe emet*" (God is truth, the Torah is truth, Moses is truth). Ensuing verses include lines taken verbatim from Psalm 136:1, "*Hodu leadonai ki tov: ki le'olam khasdo*" (Give thanks unto the Lord, for He is good, for His mercy endureth for ever); Psalm 118:26, "*Barukh haba beshem adonai*" (Blessed be he that cometh in the name of the Lord); Deuteronomy 4:44, "*Vezot hatorah asher sam moshe, lifnei bnei yisrael*" (And this is the Law which Moses put before the Children of Israel); and Deuteronomy 33:4, "*Torah tzivah lanu, moshe: morashah, kehilat ya'akov*" (Moses commanded us a law, an inheritance of the congregation of Jacob).

One of the most visually interesting videos also contains some of the most (inter)textually interesting lyrics. That video begins with a shot of Malkah indicating to the cameraman the title of the book she is holding in her hands: the classic Soncino Press edition of *The Pentateuch and Haftorahs: Hebrew Text, English Translation and Commentary*.[100] Although Malkah's voice is not audible over the accompanying soundtrack, the viewer understands that she is explaining to the cameraman the substance of the book. The camera focuses for a moment on the Table of Contents before showing Malkah turning to Genesis 1:1. At this point, Shmuel enters the room, a skullcap on his head, and turns to the text of Exodus 4:11. This is the passage in which God instructs Moses to return to Egypt to free his people, indicating the necessary rhetorical and decorative components of the task.

The next scene shows Shmuel holding up a copy of the December 2010 issue of the *Journal of the Film Chamber*, a local publication for aspiring filmmakers. Shmuel points out to the cameraman an article on financing for freelance and low-budget films. The shot then shifts to Shmuel holding a letter from the South Indian Film Chamber of Commerce, which details an enclosed refund of advertising charges. In the next frame, the viewer learns from the letter that Shmuel had asked the chamber for assistance in advertising his musical album, which would be the soundtrack for an eventual film.

The following shot follows Shmuel to his computer desktop, where the camera zooms in on a folder of files related to the forthcoming film. Shmuel opens the file containing the screenplay, which the viewer can read as the cameraman scrolls down. The introductory text informs the viewer, "This upcoming hilarious Telugu movie is about English education in the Telugu country." The film is described as suitable for "family entertainment" and promises to "inspire the audience to impart basic education to the illiterate masses among the nations." The viewer learns that part of the story "is a fiction based upon the daily news and common happenings among the human societies." But another part of it is about a nation that existed "about 2700 years ago," called the Land of Ephraim, whose inhabitants

> received a message from their God and went to all nations to deliver their God's message to all. They experienced great difficulties to deliver such a particular and peculiar message. The gist of the message was: Do not muddy, pollute or block Education. Man can use, misuse or disuse his freewill and can pollute any thing he wants and yet can survive. But if he begins to muddy, pollute or block Education, the whole human race will die and vanish from the face

of the earth once and for all. Do not dare to do that mistake! The recipients of that message went to all nations and began to deliver that message to one and all without any bars or discriminations.

There is much thematic overlap between the content and style of these video sequences and those of Shmuel's creative and scholarly writings. The associative approach of the shot formations, for example, is executed in the style of classic linear narrative, without much cinematized superimposition. The spectator's gaze is directed at almost all times on Jewish spatial signifiers that suggest equation with a Jewish spiritual or genealogical signified, which is the same method of concentrating the focus of the reader on Jewish-related subject matter, even in a seemingly dissimilar context. The textual indices in both configurations point to the Bene Ephraim's status as an embattled community that strives to maintain its moral codes in the face of discrimination, exile, and lack of recognition. Yet, the lyrical content assures the viewer/listener that, with God on the Bene Ephraim's side, all hope is not lost. One song's message alludes to their eventual redemption by first recalling the words of Isaiah 63:16, "*Ki atah avinu, ki avraham lo yad'anu; veyisrael lo yakiranu*" (For Thou art our Father; for Abraham knoweth us not, and Israel doth not acknowledge us), finally ending with an excerpt from the benediction for the Ingathering of the Exiles, "*Tek'a beshofar gadol lekheruteinu vesa nes lekabetz galuyoteinu*" (Sound the great horn for our freedom and lift up the ensign to gather together our exiles).[101]

Although Shmuel's film is incomplete as of this writing, I have read the screenplay and seen early edits. I am also familiar with details of the project from conversations with Shmuel and from online explanations of the venture, all of which go beyond the cursory information assembled from the aforementioned YouTube videos. The history of the project is as follows. Shmuel began to plan seriously for the making of a motion picture in 2007. Realizing that he would need to gain knowledge above and beyond what he had thus far studied only informally, he traveled to London for three months to complete a beginner's course for aspiring filmmakers. (Shmuel's prior awareness of cinematic technique had been gained chiefly through watching action movies; his familiarity with this genre was evident in our discussion of the finer points of Sylvester

Stallone's *The Expendables 2*, which we watched together during my time in India.) In order to pay for the trip and the film courses, Shmuel taught English literature classes via distance education for universities in Hyderabad for several years. While formulating a plan to make the film, which he hoped would both publicize the Bene Ephraim movement and bring about awareness of larger societal ills, he "prayed for confidence and approval."

Upon his return to India, with draft screenplay in hand and new technical capabilities at his disposal, Shmuel set up a production company that he called "Eretz Ephraim Pictures and World Peace Promotion." Shmuel describes the first movie to be made by the company, *Dr. Babel*, as a "historical Telugu/Hebrew/English movie that tries to define true education" and that "hopefully send[s] a message to all to work for world peace promotion by all channels of education."[102] Although the film would employ a light mood, focusing on "educational comedy content" to allow people to "at least taste the idea of true education that brings world peace, prosperity and well being of all living beings irrespective of caste, religion, color, class, gender, age, region, language or any other discriminatory superstitions," the marrow of its religio-historical subject matter would hardly be a laughing matter.[103] On that point, Shmuel commented to me that the "Jewish stuff" in the film "is meant to be subtle," but should nonetheless "make Telugu people think." Rejecting the idea that the intent of the film would be to convert the viewer to a new religion, Shmuel insists: "One thing is guaranteed: We do not beg anyone to believe what we say or show. We [only] present our Cavilah."

The plot of the film revolves around a series of interactions between a crooked educational administrator, who typifies the corruption in the Indian school system, and an outstanding but disadvantaged student, who happens to be a member of the Bene Ephraim community. In time, the Madiga student manages to overcome his economic hardships and the discriminatory behavior of the official, finally emerging triumphant at the film's conclusion. The lesson to be learned, according to the young member of the Bene Ephraim, is that scholastic inferiority among India's Scheduled Castes will not be eradicated unless everyone goes "back to the old system" of his forefathers, who circumvented reliance upon outside educational bodies by "hav[ing] their own management schools."

The title of the film, *Dr. Babel*, alludes to the biblical story of the Tower of Babel and the scattering of Noah's descendants all over the earth (Gen. 11:1–9). Evoking the legendary edifice whose construction signified the end of monotheism (not to mention the fall of King Nimrod), the title is a symbolic reference to the complexities of India's multilingual educational system, itself a microcosm of the state's poorly functioning public service sector. The implication is that the pathology of tyrannical rule is present in both narratives. Shmuel's film thus issues a warning to the "Aryan" educational system. The warning is this: Ours is a destiny that is greater than the force of your petty authority. Working against us will only ensure your eventual downfall. Even if you continue to deny us our due, deifying yourselves and willingly generating confusion, we will triumph over you in the end.

EPHRAIM, THE DARLING?

In Jeremiah 31:19, the tribe of Ephraim is referred to as God's "darling son," for whom the Lord's "heart yearneth" and upon whom he "will surely have compassion."[104] Whether other branches of God's chosen people will do the same for the supposed remnant of Ephraim in South India remains to be seen. Tudor Parfitt's observation that representatives from international Jewish outreach organizations have "not been especially moved" by the predicament of the Bene Ephraim—even though the Telugu Jews are, in his view, "as 'Jewish' as their cousins in Manipur [i.e., those from the Children of Manasseh movement]"— speaks volumes.[105] This is especially true when one considers that both Shmuel and his youngest son, Dan, underwent Orthodox conversions to Judaism in New York City. They did so in spite of Shmuel's earlier insistence that, since Judaism is a people, and not a religion, he and his followers should not need to convert to "another Jewish denomination." To no avail. Israel does not recognize these conversions, because they did not take place in the Yacobis' home country.

Why has the relationship between the Bene Ephraim and the international Jewish community not been closer? It seems that a variety of factors are involved. First and foremost is the widely held assumption that the community is, as Shmuel bitterly sums up the perception, "claiming their links with the Ten Tribes of Israel to escape from poverty and untouchable status and to go to Israel and live as happy rich Jewish converts."[106] Officials in Israel with whom I have spoken also acknowledge their fear, maintaining that a recognition of the Bene Ephraim would open the floodgates to literally millions of impoverished South Indians, who are far greater in number than their (mostly) recognized cousins from the northern part of the country. (As a general rule, members of the community outside of Shmuel's family can only obtain nonrenewable tourist visas to Israel for a maximum period of two weeks. Such an unusual measure is almost certainly reflective of a specific concern about this particular community.)

Shmuel's insistence on maintaining the nomenclature of "Bene Ephraim" and the specific provenance that it connotes also presents a problem for those connected to the Israeli state. Purportedly, representatives of Israel's rabbinical authorities have told community members to drop the claim of tribal affiliation and simply refer to themselves as "active Judaizers." According to the officials, that approach would offer the Bene Ephraim the opportunity to connect with other established Jewish communities in India, which would then put them in a more likely position to convert in a manner acceptable to the Israeli Rabbinate. No one has yet agreed to act on this advice, because of the ethnic, linguistic, economic, and cultural challenges inherent in making such a move. But even some in the Yacobi family quietly admit that insisting on the tribal claim was a mistake.

With regard to connections with the non-Israeli Jewish world, the tide seems to be shifting. In recent years, the Bene Ephraim have been featured in a documentary film on Indian Jewry, as well as on a CD showcasing music from nonconventional Jewish groups around the world.[107] Increasingly, they are the subject of both academic and popular publications. They maintain relationships with several American NGOs and Jewish volunteer organizations, but the extent of these relationships has been, as one person involved put it, "superficial rather than transformative." Part of the reason may lie in the disinclination of American Jews to actively assist the Bene Ephraim in achieving their goal of "repatriation" to Israel. Therefore, while such contacts may represent sources of potential encouragement, they do not necessarily translate into a tangible system of support.

One new development whose genesis seems to stem from frustration about the stalled immigration plan is a project aimed at bypassing the Israeli state apparatus altogether. As mentioned briefly in the beginning of this chapter, Shmuel is now calling for the establishment of *"Eretz Ephraim"* (the Land of Ephraim), a future nation that will be founded as a "sister state" to Israel, in the region originally inhabited by the biblical tribe of Ephraim. The diplomatic relationship between the two states would be modeled on the idea of a "confederation," similar to that of the Commonwealth countries. In his online postings, Shmuel has begun to urge "all the Diaspora Jewish and Israeli communities to take part in this historical event" proposed by "the Bene Ephraim communities of South India."[108] Interested people from "all tribes of Israel in exile" are now able to "register themselves as citizens" while the "awareness program" intended to "reach the world leaders and the UN authorities" is set in motion.[109] On the diplomatic front, this idea has not gained any traction, despite Shmuel's written appeals to several dignitaries and Western heads of state, such as Israeli Prime Minister Benjamin Netanyahu and British heir-apparent Prince Charles.

While waiting for yet another idea to be acknowledged by outside powers, the Bene Ephraim keep on keeping on. Weekly study sessions are held with Yehoshua via Skype. When the electricity goes out (an all-too-common occurrence), the study group has to make do with Yehoshua coaching them from Israel via speakerphone. Among the members of the study group are "second generation" Bene Ephraim—the children of those Madiga who embraced Judaism along with Shmuel in the late 1980s. Jewishness, or at least the Bene Ephraim's version of it, is the only identity that these young people have ever known. When I asked one of them if it had all been worth it, the person replied:

> I am very thankful to Shmuel Yacobi for everything he had done in his life because if not for him we would never have realized who is the source of everything: the one God, the God of Israel, God of my forefathers. . . . Even though he [Shmuel] had the opportunity to move to America with all his family he choosed [*sic*] to stay in

my place and educate the people in Judaism. I don't have any words to appreciate this kind of dedication to the community.

What will happen to the Bene Ephraim after Shmuel Yacobi, now in his late sixties, is gone? The future is anyone's guess. His eldest son, Yehoshua, no longer has Indian citizenship, and therefore would not be able to remain in India again for any extended period of time. Shmuel's younger sons have neither the theological training nor (as they admit) the requisite finesse with public speaking that would be crucial to carrying out Shmuel's role in the community. Given these factors, it seems likely that this Judaizing movement, which has been centered on the brains, heart, conviction, and doggedness of one man, may disappear when that man does. Then again, maybe—just maybe—Ephraim will prove to be God's "darling" after all, reunited with Judah not because of, but in spite of, the (re)actions of Jews elsewhere in the world.

Conclusion

5

THE THREE EXAMPLES of Judaizing communities presented in this book provide a limited albeit significant glimpse into the phenomenon of globalized religious movements. Through the field-researched case studies profiled here, I have tried to make sense of one particular aspect of this phenomenon: the Jewish one. Because empirical data related to perceived phylogenetic heritage were not part of the research concerns, my focus was on examining the practical and symbolic ways in which these new Children of Israel construct their ideas about what Jewishness means to them, as well as on understanding the situational factors that may influence dispositional views on the observance of Jewish law and custom. I wanted to know how their perceptions of and articulations about what it means to be Jewish are informed by particular social, personal, political, and historical circumstances, and what kinds of intercultural exchanges result from their encounters with Jews from other countries. I have tried to address all of these issues in the preceding chapters by providing detailed information on the genesis, configurations, and contexts of each Judaizing movement.

Having established the specific nature of each individual movement, let us now highlight some general points of commonality between them. First, the ancestors of each group (with the exception of the Cameroonians) were at one time thought of by travelers, traders, missionaries, or colonial administrators as exhibiting cultural practices that suggested either a foreign or possibly Hebraic or Israelite origin. Such practices included animal sacrifice; burial taboos; observance of a Saturday Sabbath and/or lunar calendar; harvest festivals; libation-pouring; male circumcision; patriarchal rule; menstrual seclusion; and prohibitions on the consumption of snakes, pigs, rodents, and monkeys. Oral histories often corroborate such perceived origins, although we have no way of knowing which oral accounts have been "contaminated" with ideas about Jews that stem from sources other than local ethnocultural or religious systems of knowledge.

Second, most members of each community (with the exception of some of the Ghanaians) have recent Christian theological backgrounds. Many have come to Judaism through Christian communities whose focus is primarily on the Old Testament, such as those from Sabbatarian, Seventh-day Adventist, Messianic, or Prophetic movements. In the two African examples, many hail from so-called "indigenous," "initiated," or "independent" churches. Part of the reason for which Judaism appears to be, as Timothy C. Tennent puts it, "theologically translatable" to previously Christianized peoples such as these in the Global South lies in the anger that many feel at the institutionalized Church (oftentimes equated with the colonial regime) over its exclusion of traditional native practices, such as ancestor worship, polygamy, or bride inheritance.[1] Contrary to the perspectives espoused by Pauline theology, the legalism required in Judaism is not seen by such persons as burdensome. Rather, it is viewed as a doctrine that complements precolonial mores, and not (as one person described it to me) "post-facto Hellenized mumbo jumbo." Such sentiments should not lead us to believe that all Jewish movements in postcolonial paradigms are nothing more than reactionary in nature. Nonetheless, by choosing Judaism, as opposed to (for instance) Buddhism or Hinduism, new adherents to this religion are in fact participating in a return-to-roots countermovement that, in their eyes, effectively removes the "West" from biblical conventions.

Third, each group alleges that its people have endured histories of oppression—not of anti-Semitism per se—but certainly of discrimination and degradation carried out by stronger powers. Put simply, they see themselves as Jewish in symbolic terms. As noted above, these avowals frequently take the form of anticolonial or anti-neocolonial rhetoric, although they may also be directed at the postcolonial power dynamics in various iterations of what has become known as the "failed state." Such rhetoric among those belonging to Jewish movements is part and parcel of a larger and newer microlevel drive to reform society through religion, rather than through frequently out-of-reach political or economic macromeasures.

Fourth, the members of each movement (with the exception of the Indians) insist on maintaining strict religious observance, in many cases putting themselves in grave physical and economic danger by doing so. For these people, secular Jewishness as a category does not exist. Ostensibly, this adherence violates utilitarian (Western) assumptions about how the world works, because, for such individuals, secular Judaism based on Jewishness as a mere hereditary signifier—what Joane Nagel calls "recreational" ethnicity—does not suffice for a formal declaration of belonging.[2] Such heredity may, however, serve as a symbolic means to elevate the status of the present-day downtrodden by connecting them to a prestigious, supranational past. Convincing one's own public of this "genealogical sophistication" may take the form of proselytizing, whether directly or indirectly. While certain individuals become convinced of the relationship, subsequently adopting normative Jewish practices and/or seeking out Jews from abroad for contacts or instruction, others prefer to stay on the sidelines. Some groups, such as the Noahides, become part of the larger Jewish matrix to a certain extent, but favor following a select number of ethical teachings rather than categorically adopting a new religious affiliation.

Fifth, globalized media and technology have played a major role in both the creation and dissemination of information on these communities. Just as the invention of the telegraph at the beginning of the nineteenth century had a profound effect on the development of the Spiritualist movement by furnishing its members with a heretofore unprecedented method of exchange, our digital era of globalized interconnectedness is transforming the ways in which self-defining communities from developing nations conceptualize what it means to be Jewish.[3] That the Cameroonians, for example, adopted the Jewish discursive system of religious thought via online means, without any prior personal interaction with other (Western) Jews whatsoever, points to the decentralized and transnational nature of the current globalized communication paradigm. On the level of the nation-state, it also points to the ways in which modern communications technology enables disenfranchised peoples to "leapfrog" other conventional forms of access and interaction (electricity, phone lines, etc.) previously unavailable to them in their home countries.

The reader will recall, for reasons explained in chapter 1, that I have refrained from establishing a typology of which groups should be considered "authentically" Jewish and which ones should not. The criterion for inclusion in this study—and what, in my view, sets each group apart from similar Old Testament–centered movements in their close geographical proximities—is the expressed desire on the part of each community to (re)connect with the wider Jewish world through the adoption of normative practice. Differences in ritual observance, lifestyle, ideology, or worldview that may seem incompatible with the norms formalized by Jewish institutions elsewhere have been shown to be, for the most part, not as extreme as one might initially imagine. Nor should such dissimilarities matter much, given that Jews in the West are free to self-define without a hereditary or organizational substantiation based on the burden of proof, the issue of Orthodox and/or Israeli state recognition notwithstanding. That it should be any different for Jews in the developing world is a gross double standard. When one acknowledges that Jewishness has always been a bricolage, it is in effect impossible to view issues surrounding conversion, intermarriage, and lifestyle choices as anything more than petty power struggles between different denominational interests. Jacob S. Dorman brilliantly sums up this point thus: "The mistake Ashkenazi Jews often make is to think we Jews have progressed from one purity to another. That's not the case, and no religious faith can claim that."[4]

As we have seen, the state of Israel is the proverbial elephant in the room in almost every discussion surrounding the future of these new Jewish movements. How will Israel react to the possibility of millions of impoverished immigrants beating down its door? In spite of Israel's recent recognition of the Abayudaya community of Uganda (a community which, unlike most others in the developing world, maintains ties to centers of normative Judaism in the West that go back decades), the answer is far from clear.[5] The words of Yisrael Yeshayahu, Israel's former Deputy Speaker of Parliament, who visited Ethiopia in 1958, are still appropriate for describing the ambiguity of the Jewish state's position vis-à-vis its long-lost brethren. In response to a question about Israeli policy on relations with the supposed remnant of the tribe of Dan in Ethiopia, Yeshayahu stated that "as Jews and as a country it is not at all certain how we should relate to the community of Falashas," because "one hand pushes away or recoils from the possibility that they may be considered Jewish," while the other hand "seems to bring this [possibility] nearer."[6] That both Jewish and Christian private organizations, as well as so-called "renegade" rabbis, are promoting ties with these new Jewish groups against the wishes of many in the Israeli state apparatus demonstrates that such indecisiveness is ever present.

The position of Israel, however, may ultimately end up being a moot point, given that most new members of these emerging communities do not want to move there. This should not be surprising, since for most of its history the Jewish experience has been a primarily diasporic one. In fact, it may be that the prophecy recorded in Isaiah 2:3, "For out of Zion shall go forth the law, and the word of the Lord from Jerusalem," could be considered applicable not only to Gentile nations whose members wish to follow the basic paths of righteousness, but to Jewish neophytes whose belonging to the chosen people happens almost solely in the virtual realm of cyberspace or on relatively isolated geopolitical or demographic peripheries. That pluralistic American Jewish organizations whose ideologies are somewhat post-Zionist count among these neophytes' most vocal supporters and collaborators speaks volumes about the Jewish world's shifting centers of influence, and not just with regard to issues of formal recognition.

To my mind, a question far more interesting than the extent of these groups' eventual relations with Israel is: How will these new Jews change the national, religious, cultural, and familial settings out of which they have developed? Clearly, there is an attraction for many to become enmeshed in the Jewish narrative of chosenness and ultimate redemption. What Dan Sperber calls the "epidemiology of representations"—in essence, the tendency for some ideas to "stick," taking hold in the manner of a contagion—seems particularly fitting for describing the pull of Judaism as an ethnic or religious category in the developing world.[7] Given this enthusiasm, it is unlikely that the already-impressive broadening of the Jewish world through new adherents will end up being a flash in the pan. As one rabbi who works in a Jerusalem-based institute that facilitates conversions told me: "Only Greenland hasn't yet called!" This growing inclination may counter Peter Berger's somewhat dated (and yet oft-cited) claim that there are only "two dynamic upsurges in the world today: the Islamic and the Evangelical."[8]

Might we anticipate, contrary to this assertion, that region-specific, politicized ethnocultural expressions of Jewish identity, diffused primarily through communications technology, will be a decisive factor in tomorrow's marketplace of religious ideas? In light of what we have seen, this possibility does not seem far-fetched. Indeed, the world has already witnessed in the cases of the "British jihadists" how transnational social media operates as a "soft" ethnic- or faith-based nonofficial diplomatic actor.[9] As Jeffrey Haynes perceptively points out, "What religious transnational actors principally represent is the capacity to influence international relations by their ability to disseminate *ideas* and *values*."[10] And so it is with new Jewish groups from the developing world.

Although the influence of transnational actors on the phenomenon of globalized Judaism seems likely, another (non-mutually exclusive) possibility exists on the level of local or national government: that of public conversions of high-level officials to Judaism. Such conversions could influence state policy in the same way that the conversions to Islam of Gabon's Albert (Omar) Bongo and the Central African Republic's Jean Bedel (Salah al-Din) Bokassa shifted allegiances toward Saudi money and supposed pan-African (Islamic) unity in the 1970s.[11] As noted in chapter 3, the current president of Cameroon, Paul Biya, is already a well-known Judeophile and would-be Kabbalist whose internal security apparatus is made up of Israeli Special Forces. If, as my contacts in Cameroon hope, Biya and his inside circle become enamored with the Beth Yeshourun movement and take their Judeophilia one step further, would the possibility of "an Israeli reserve army of eight million Central Africans" (a frequently cited wish among my contacts) move from the realm of the fantastic to the possible? Stranger things have happened.

ON A RESEARCH trip to Lusaka, Zambia, for a related project in November 2014, I was reminded of the possibility of the state-endorsed transmission of Jewish values during a meeting with former First Lady and Minister of the Environment Vera Tembo-Chiluba, to whom I had been

introduced by contacts in the local *Beit Talmidim* (House of Disciples)
Judaizing community. After assuring me that the African nations who
sided against Israel would be "cursed," she outlined one of the primary
policy goals for the future presidential mandate that she hoped to
secure. Pointing to my two companions who had served for some time
as her spiritual advisors, she told me that, if elected as head of state, she
would do her best to "make Zambia Jewish." Granted, she did not mean
normatively Jewish, as no one in the community had yet accessed the
discursive reservoir of Jewish culture outside of Zambia, but the principal reference in her remarks that day was to what she called "Torah-
centered values." As this book was going to press, similar statements
were being made by senior officials in the governments of the Central
African Republic, Gabon, and Equatorial Guinea, all of whom have
been influenced by the leadership of the Cameroonian community of
Beth Yeshourun. As the examples in this study have demonstrated, the
slope that leads the members of Tembo-Chiluba's Zambian community
(and others like it) from marginal toward normative Judaism may be a
slippery one.

Then again, it may not be. The example of the *Communauté juive
de Madagascar* (Jewish Community of Madagascar), a Judaizing group in
the former French colony to which one chapter of an earlier draft of this
book was dedicated, serves as a reminder that not all Old Testament–
oriented movements may necessarily lead toward Jewish normativity.
This Malagasy group, which ended up splintering into several different
rival factions between the time I conducted fieldwork there in May 2013
and the formal conversion to Judaism of 121 of its members in May
2016, lost about 90 percent of its original adherents.[12] Because most
of the people I interviewed subsequently left the normative-oriented
movement, I felt that I could not in good conscience include their stories
here. However, as an illustration of how such communities may evolve
in unanticipated directions, a brief exposition of this group's genesis
and ultimate fragmentation may be an instructive vignette with which
to conclude this discussion of the possible futures of Judaizing communities in an era of globalization.

In November 2012, while browsing the Internet for Africa-related
Jewish content from my hotel room in Ghana, I discovered the profile

of a former parliamentarian from Madagascar who purported to lead a "Judaist association" of individuals interested in the "cultural ties" between the Malagasy and Jewish peoples. Intrigued, I contacted him by e-mail and explained that I was writing a book on emerging Jewish communities from the developing world. I asked him if he and his cohort would be open to the possibility of participating in my research study. He answered enthusiastically in the affirmative. He also connected me with the leaders of a much larger group of Judaizers, whose objectives were more religious than cultural, and with whom I would eventually spend the majority of my time in Madagascar. Six months later, I met them all in Antananarivo, the country's capital city.

What I discovered in Madagascar far exceeded any expectations that I had previously entertained about organized Jewish life on the island. From the detailed scholarship of Edith Bruder on this topic's historical angles, I had already learned much about the centuries-old legends concerning the supposed Jewish provenance of the country's indigenous peoples, as well as the popular contemporary beliefs according to which precolonial Malagasy traditional religious practices were equivalent to those practices of the ancient Israelites.[13] I also knew that the state of Israel once sponsored frequent fellowships for Malagasy professionals working in the domains of agriculture and science, and that most of the members of the parliamentarian's "Judaist association" were veterans of such programs. What I did not anticipate was the formidable size and scope of the other association, which was made up of around a thousand people from all walks of life who were pursuing their Jewishness religiously. Although no one among the people in this group had visited Israel, all of them were practicing a fairly sophisticated form of normative Judaism that they had pieced together from informational sites accessed on the Internet.

Just like the individuals belonging to other groups profiled in this book, the members of the formerly Christian Malagasy community fully subscribed to notions about their descent from the ancient Israelites, which had first been disseminated by Arab explorers to the island, and later by colonial administrators and missionaries. They insisted that the precolonial customs practiced by their forefathers—customs that were "identical" to those mandated in the Hebrew Scriptures—had been carefully suppressed by the French colonial regime in order to hide the Malagasies' noble origins and thereby dominate them more easily. With the advent of the Internet, they were able to learn that Jewish religious communities did continue to exist after the time of Jesus, a fact about which they had previously been ignorant. To regain what had been taken from them by those affiliated with the French imperialist project, they resolved to recover their precolonial identity by learning about how other followers of the Jewish faith adhered to Mosaic Law in the present day. Curiously, no one thought at that time to connect with other Jews in countries outside of Madagascar. After all, the information gained online was enough for them to proceed, and the people with whom they most wanted to connect were fellow Malagasies who might benefit from such knowledge. And so, in 2011, the initial members of the Jewish community left their mainly Protestant churches to form the island's first organized Jewish community.

In addition to the widespread notions surrounding Israelite provenance, several other factors were responsible for the outpouring of interest in, and subsequent affiliation with, the community. First, the leaders of the new community had been active in church leadership roles during their previous lives as Christians. Consequently, many people from their prior flocks joined the new one. Second, one of the community leaders had a professional background as a radio and television personality, and he used his media influence to help spread the word about this new organization. Third, a preexisting cohort of Messianics, Adventists, and Kabbalah enthusiasts already had superficial knowledge about Jewish theology, and convincing them to take their interest one step further did not prove too challenging. What all of these people had once seen as precursory material for the Christian religious milieu now became reenvisioned as indigenous heritage narratives, whose enhanced sacrosanctity both perpetuated and substantiated the claim of genealogical chosenness.

This was the group that I encountered in 2013: a one-thousand-strong community of individuals from varied religious and professional backgrounds who wished to embrace normative Judaism because it brought them closer to the pure religion of the ancestors. I was the first Jew from outside of the island that any of them had ever met. As such,

I was besieged with requests for information, for help with contacts abroad, for clarifications about a wide array of Jewish issues. I stayed in close contact with a number of people from the community upon my return to the United States.

As early as 2014, fissures began to appear among those in the leadership. Some wanted to make concessions to the wishes of Messianic Jews, who represented a great number of new adherents, but who did not understand why worshiping a decidedly Jewish *Yeshua* (Jesus) and reclaiming the religion of the ancestors were incompatible activities. Many in the community felt a resounding antipathy toward the Messianics, based on the assumption (also held by many Jews in the West) that Messianic Judaism is an evangelizing subterfuge masquerading as an innocuous coopting of Jewish identity. Others wanted to put the emphasis of their postexilic religious practice more on the mystical teachings of Kabbalah than on those of the rabbis of the Talmud. And yet others began to absorb the fact that much of contemporary Jewish custom was "not religious enough," as one person told me, especially with regard to dietary observance, communal punishment of transgressions, etc. Eventually, the Messianics left. The Kabbalah devotees formed their own community, as did another group led by the former cantor, who swore off Internet usage and all contact with foreigners, claiming that the latter had "sullied" through their interference and "liberal" mindsets the nascent community's efforts to live Jewishly. Most of those who had formed the cell of the original group remained.

Now eager to be fully integrated into the worldwide Jewish community, the leaders of what remained of the normative-oriented movement began corresponding with rabbis from the American outreach group Kulanu in late 2013. By 2015, Kulanu had made the decision to bring a rabbinical court to Madagascar to formally convert the members of the movement to Orthodox Judaism, despite the fact that no one on the rabbinical court had ever met any of the potential converts in person. All of the preparation was done via e-mail, Facebook, and Skype. The eventual conversion of 121 people from this group (and a few rejoiners from the groups that had seceded) in May 2016 made headlines in a variety of international publications as an unprecedented instance of recognition of emerging Jewish communities.

Will those who left the normative community now be persuaded that this recognition of their Jewishness by foreign entities (not to mention possible future recognition by the state of Israel and/or financial assistance from donor sources) represents enough of a reason to join the movement anew? Or will this act of legitimization by white, European-descended Jews, whom some see as part of a neocolonial spectacle, push away for good other potential members of this nascent Jewish community? The arguments on the subject have already begun.

Just like the Ghanaians, the Cameroonians, the Indians, and the Zambians, it will be up to the Malagasies to decide which path to follow. Their predicament, in fact, is a microcosm of the existential situations in which all of the groups profiled in this book find themselves. Irrespective of whether other Malagasies opt for the acknowledgment and support of officially recognized Jews from the outside world, a seed has been planted. What will this seed yield? That is anyone's guess. One thing, however, is certain: the motivations that led the Malagasies on their Jewish quest are the same motivations shared by millions of other people around the world. Based on what I have seen, it is my estimation that, in this era of globalization, new Jewish communities will continue to appear and to multiply, the products of this same seed. They may very well be, in the words of Jeremiah 17:8, "like a tree planted by the waters that spreadeth out its roots," one that "shall not cease from yielding fruit."

NOTES

ACKNOWLEDGMENTS

1. Throughout this book, I use the term "developing world" to refer to mainly postcolonial nations transitioning from traditional to modernized societies whose qualities of infrastructure, Human Development Index scores, and Gross National Incomes lag behind those of industrialized countries. No intended pejorative value judgment is attached to this term.
2. For a description of study procedures related to the elimination of identifiable data, see the section on methodology in chapter 1.
3. Any use of the term "Old Testament" throughout this manuscript is intended to coincide with the mention of the Hebrew Bible in a Christian or nonnormative Jewish context. For Jewish contexts, I refer to the whole of these texts as the "Hebrew Scriptures."
4. According to Tudor Parfitt, the estimated number of nonrecognized "shadow Jews" worldwide may be between 13.5 million and 14 million. Cited in Judy Maltz, "Number of Wannabe Jews Equals That of Recognized Jews," *Haaretz*, November 4, 2014, http://www.haaretz.com/jewish-world/.premium-1.624585.
5. John S. Mbiti, *African Religions and Philosophy*, 2d ed. (Oxford: Heinemann, 1990), 2.
6. Charles Liebman, "Jewish Identity in Transition: Transformation or Attenuation?," in *New Jewish Identities*, ed. Zvi Gitelman, Barry Kosmin, and Andras Kovacs (Budapest: Central European University Press, 2003), 347.

CHAPTER 1

1. Throughout this book, I use the term "immigration," as well as its verbal and substantive variants, to refer to the resolute movement of Jewish individuals or communities to the state of Israel for purposes of naturalization. This usage follows the standard tendency to situate such a move to Israel firmly within the Jewish context of return, as opposed to the sometimes nonvolitional nature that the term "(e)migration" and all its variants convey.
2. To my knowledge, the only exceptions are the following: Edith Bruder's section on the Ghanaian community in *The Black Jews of Africa: History, Religion, Identity* (Oxford: Oxford University Press, 2008), 149–53; Janice Levi, "The House of Israel: Judaism in Ghana," in *African Zion: Studies in Black Judaism,*

ed. Edith Bruder and Tudor Parfitt (Newcastle upon Tyne: Cambridge Scholars, 2012), 117–35; and Bruder's brief sections on the Ghanaian (again) and Cameroonian communities in her *Black Jews: Les juifs noirs d'Afrique et le mythe des tribus perdues* (Paris: Albin Michel, 2014), 199–207 and 216–23, respectively.

3. See Yulia Egorova and Shahid Perwez, "Old Memories, New Histories: (Re)discovering the Past of Jewish Dalits," *History and Anthropology* 23, no. 1 (2012): 1–15; Egorova and Perwez, "Telugu Jews: Are the Dalits of Coastal Andhra Going Caste-Awry?," *South Asianist* 1, no. 1 (2012): 7–16; and Egorova and Perwez, *The Jews of Andhra Pradesh: Contesting Caste and Religion in South India* (Oxford: Oxford University Press, 2013).

4. See, in particular, the revised editions (in English translation) of Fanon's *The Wretched of the Earth*, trans. Richard Philcox (New York: Grove Press, 2004), and of his *Black Skin, White Masks*, trans. Richard Philcox (New York: Grove Press, 2008).

5. See the following representative works: Aijaz Ahmad, *In Theory: Classes, Nations, Literatures* (New York: Verso, 1992); Homi Bhabha, *The Location of Culture* (London: Routledge, 1994); Albert Memmi, *The Colonizer and the Colonized*, trans. Howard Greenfeld (New York: Orion Press, 1965); Ella Shohat, *Taboo Memories, Diasporic Voices* (Durham, NC: Duke University Press, 2006); and Gayatri Spivak, *A Critique of Postcolonial Reason: Toward a History of the Vanishing Present* (Cambridge: Harvard University Press, 1999).

6. Tudor Parfitt, "Hebrew in Colonial Discourse," *Journal of Modern Jewish Studies* 2, no. 2 (2003): 159.

7. Tudor Parfitt, *Black Jews in Africa and the Americas* (Cambridge: Harvard University Press, 2013), 103.

8. Bruder, *Black Jews of Africa*, 192.

9. Tudor Parfitt, *The Thirteenth Gate: Travels among the Lost Tribes of Israel* (Bethesda, MD: Adler and Adler, 1987), 3.

10. Pew Forum on Religion and Public Life, *Global Christianity: A Report on the Size and Distribution of the World's Christian Population* (Washington, DC: Pew Research Center, 2011), http://www.pewforum.org/files/2011/12/Christianity-fullreport-web.pdf.

11. Valentin Y. Mudimbe, *The Invention of Africa: Gnosis, Philosophy, and the Order of Knowledge* (Bloomington: Indiana University Press, 1985), 45.

12. John L. Jackson, *Thin Description: Ethnography and the African Hebrew Israelites of Jerusalem* (Cambridge: Harvard University Press, 2013), 17.

13. Caryn Aviv and David Shneer, *New Jews: The End of the Jewish Diaspora* (New York: New York University Press, 2005), 20.

14. Ibid.

15. Paul Hopper, *Understanding Cultural Globalization* (Cambridge: Polity Press, 2007), 29.

16. On this point, see Eric Shiraev and David A. Levy, *Cross-cultural Psychology: Critical Thinking and Contemporary Applications* (Boston: Pearson/Allyn and Bacon, 2007), esp. 17; and J. J. Goodnow, "The Socialization of Cognition: What's Involved?," in *Cultural Psychology: Essays on Comparative Human Development*, ed. James W. Stigler, Richard A. Shweder, and Gilbert Herdt (Cambridge: Cambridge University Press, 1990), 259–86.

17. Robert W. Wyllie, *Spiritism in Ghana: A Study of New Religious Movements* (Missoula, MT: Scholars Press, 1980), 3.

18. The University of Utah's Institutional Review Board has determined that this study qualifies for an exemption, under 45 CFR 46.101(b), Category 2, from the federal regulations governing human subjects research.

19. Certification obtained from the University of Miami–Miller School of Medicine's Collaborative Institutional Training Initiative, Social/Behavioral Human Research section, in partnership with the Institutional Review Board of the University of Utah.

20. For example, see Juliana Ochs, *Security and Suspicion: An Ethnography of Everyday Life in Israel* (Philadelphia: University of Pennsylvania Press, 2011); and Erica Weiss, *Conscientious Objectors in Israel: Citizenship, Sacrifice, Trials of Fealty* (Philadelphia: University of Pennsylvania Press, 2014).

21. The conversations included in this book were conducted according to the following fieldwork chronology: in India, interviews took place during August–September 2012; in Ghana, during November 2012; and in Cameroon, during May 2014. In Israel, conversations with individuals connected to the same Judaizing movements took place over the course of almost three years, particularly during August 2012, July 2013, and June 2015. The descriptions of each community are current as of August 2016.

22. Ruth Landes, "Comment," *Western Canadian Journal of Anthropology* 3, no. 3 (1973): 44.

23. Bruce Lincoln, *Death, War, and Sacrifice: Studies in Ideology and Practice* (Chicago: University of Chicago Press, 1991), 244.

24. Marla Brettschneider, "African and African Heritage Jews: Western Academic Perspectives," *Sh'ma: A Journal of Jewish Responsibility* (March 2011), http://www.bjpa.org/Publications/downloadFile.cfm?FileID=8426. See also Brettschneider's *The Jewish Phenomenon in Sub-Saharan Africa: The Politics of Contradictory Discourses* (Lewiston, NY: Edwin Mellen, 2015).

25. Brettschneider, "African and African Heritage Jews."

26. Diane Tobin, "Wannabe Demographers?," *Huffington Post*, November 12, 2014, http://www.huffingtonpost.com/diane-tobin/wannabe-demographers_b_6141358.html?.

27. Jan Vansina, *Oral Tradition as History* (Madison: University of Wisconsin Press, 1985), 195.

28. Robert W. Harms, "Bobangi Oral Traditions: Indicators of Changing Perceptions," in *The African Past Speaks: Essays on Oral Tradition and History*, ed. Joseph Calder Miller (Hamden, CT: Archon Press, 1980), 198–99.

29. Robert Jay Lifton, *The Life of the Self* (New York: Basic Books, 1983), 106.

30. The English translation of this community's name is not to be confused with that of the Ghanaian movement discussed in chapter 2, with which it has no affiliation.

31. Zvi Ben-Dor Benite, *The Ten Lost Tribes: A World History* (Oxford: Oxford University Press, 2009), 223.

32. All English translations from the Hebrew Scriptures will follow the translation and verse numbers of the *Jewish Publication Society 1917 Edition*.

33. See Isaiah 11:11; Jeremiah 31:8; and Ezekiel 37:19–24.

34. Tudor Parfitt, *The Lost Tribes of Israel: The History of a Myth* (London: Weiden-feld and Nicolson, 2002), 8.

35. For the background on this mysterious character, see, for example, Max Schloessinger, *The Ritual of Eldad ha-Dani Reconstructed and Edited from Man-uscripts and a Genizah Fragment* (Leipzig: R. Haupt, 1908); David E. Goitein, "Note on Eldad the Danite," *Jewish Quarterly Review* 17, no. 4 (1927): 483; and David J. Wasserstein, "Eldad Ha-Dani," in *Prester John, the Mongols, and the Ten Lost Tribes*, ed. Charles F. Beckingham and Bernard Hamilton (Aldershot, UK: Variorum, 1996), 213–36.

36. For more on the Prester John story in this context, see Edward Ullendorff and Charles F. Beckingham, *The Hebrew Letters of Prester John* (Oxford: Oxford University Press, 1982); and Micha Perry, "The Imaginary War between Prester John and Eldad the Danite and Its Real Implications," *Viator: Medieval and Renaissance Studies* 41, no. 1 (2010): 1–23.

37. I owe this observation to Eric Maroney's *The Other Zions: The Lost Histories of Jewish Nations* (Lanham, MD: Rowman and Littlefield, 2010), 26.

38. Source cited and translated in Vsevolod Slessarev, *Prester John: The Letter and the Legend* (Minneapolis: University of Minnesota Press, 1959), 74.

39. Allen H. Godbey, *The Lost Tribes: A Myth* (Hoboken, NJ: Ktav, 1973), 684.

40. Stuart Kirsch, "Lost Tribes: Indigenous People and the Social Imaginary," *Anthropological Quarterly* 70, no. 2 (1997): 58.

41. William Safire, "Interrupted Exodus," *New York Times*, January 7, 1985.

42. Cited in Louis Rapoport, *The Lost Jews: Last of the Ethiopian Falashas* (New York: Stein and Day, 1980), 194–95.

43. Jacques Faitlovitch, *Notes d'un voyage chez les Falachas* (Paris: Ernest Leroux, 1905).

44. Parfitt, *Black Jews*, 144.

45. Tudor Parfitt, *Operation Moses: The Untold Story of the Secret Exodus of the Falasha Jews from Ethiopia* (New York: Stein and Day, 1985), 55–56.

46. Ibid., 19.

47. See Daniel Summerfield, *From Falashas to Ethiopian Jews: The External Influences for Change c. 1860–1960* (New York: RoutledgeCurzon, 2003), 12–16.

48. Edward Ullendorff, "The 'Death of Moses' in the Literature of the Falashas," *Bulletin of the School of Oriental and African Studies* 24, no. 3 (1961): 420. See also Ullendorff, "Hebraic-Jewish Elements in Abyssinian (Monophysite) Christianity," *Journal of Semitic Studies* 1, no. 3 (1956): 216–56; and Ernst Hammerschmidt, "Jewish Elements in the Cult of the Ethiopian Church," *Journal of Ethiopian Studies* 3, no. 2 (1965): 1–12.

49. Edward Ullendorff, *The Two Zions: Reminiscences of Jerusalem and Ethiopia* (Oxford: Oxford University Press, 1988), 149.

50. Steven Kaplan, "The Invention of Ethiopian Jews: Three Models," *Cahiers d'études africaines* 33, no. 132 (1993): 647. See also Kaplan's *The Beta Israel (Falasha) in Ethiopia: From Earliest Times to the Twentieth Century* (New York: New York University Press, 1992), 13–78.

51. Kaplan, "The Invention of Ethiopian Jews," 647.

52. Daniel Orenstein, "View from the Ivory Tower," *Jerusalem Report* 3, no. 22 (1993): 48.

53. Moran Peled, "Needed: A Dramatic Change of Perception." *Kav haofek* 24 (December 21, 2004): 21. Hebrew. Translation mine.

54. There are thousands of Beta Israel known as *Falash Mura* (converts to Christianity in the two previous centuries) who are still waiting to be brought to Israel. Their eligibility to immigrate has been curtailed due to suspicions regarding their desire to lead fully Jewish lives. In 2013, the Israeli government suspended their immigration indefinitely. For more on their situation, see Michal Shmulovich, "The Last of the Falash Mura?," *Times of Israel*, August 26, 2013, http://www.timesofisrael.com/the-last-of-the-falash-mura/. For information on the quest for recognition by the Jews of Kechene, an apparently related offshoot of the Beta Israel, see Edith Bruder, "The Beit Avraham of Kechene: The Emergence of a New Jewish Community in Ethiopia," in *Beta Israel: The Jews of Ethiopia and Beyond: History, Identity, and Borders*, ed. Emanuela Trevisan Semi and Shalva Weil (Venice: Cafoscarina, 2011), 181–96.

55. See, for example, Yaheli Moran Zelikovich, "Funding of Petah Tikva Schools Refusing Ethiopian Students Cut," *Ynet News*, August 30, 2009, http://www.ynetnews.com/articles/0,7340,L-3769509,00.html; and Gavriel Fiske, "Allegedly Doubting Their Jewishness, Rabbi Won't Wed Ethiopians," *Times of Israel*, September 7, 2014, http://www.timesofisrael.com/petah-tikva-chief-rabbi-reportedly-refuses-ethiopian-marriages/.

56. For more on this subject, see Associated Press, "Israel Putting End to Millennia-Old Tradition of Ethiopian Jewish Priests," *Haaretz*, January 18, 2012, http://www.haaretz.com/jewish-world/israel-putting-end-to-millenia-old-tradition-of-ethiopian-jewish-priests-1.407958.

57. "In those days the house of Judah shall walk with the house of Israel, and they shall come together out of the land of the north to the land that I have given for an inheritance unto your fathers."

58. Hillel Halkin, *Across the Sabbath River: In Search of a Lost Tribe of Israel* (Boston: Houghton Mifflin, 2002).

59. For more on the immigration of the Bnei Menashe and their acculturation process in Israel, see Yulia Egorova, "Redefining the Converted Jewish Self: Race, Religion, and Israel's Bene Menashe," *American Anthropologist* 117, no. 3 (2015): 493–505.

60. Jonas Zianga, "Black Jews in Academic and Institutional Discourse," in *Race, Color, Identity: Rethinking Discourses About "Jews" in the Twenty-First Century*, ed. Efraim Sicher (New York: Berghahn Books, 2013), 184.

61. For more on these and other related subjects, see Walter Arthur McCray, *The Black Presence in the Bible: Discovering the Black and African Identity of Biblical Persons and Nations* (Chicago: Black Light Fellowship, 1990); Knut Holter, *Yahweh in Africa: Essays on Africa and the Old Testament* (New York: Peter Lang, 2000); Cain Hope Felder, *Race, Racism, and the Biblical Narratives* (Minneapolis: Fortress Press, 2002); Rodney Steven Sadler, *Can a Cushite Change His Skin? An Examination of Race, Ethnicity, and Othering in the Hebrew Bible* (New York: T & T Clark, 2005); and Abraham Melamed, *The Image of the Black in Jewish Culture: A History of the Other* (New York: Routledge, 2010), esp. 178–91.

62. Edith R. Sanders, "The Hamitic Hypothesis: Its Origin and Functions in Time Perspective," *Journal of African History* 10, no. 4 (1969): 523. For more on the Hamitic Hypothesis in different national contexts, see Aimable Twagilimana, *The Debris of Ham: Ethnicity, Regionalism, and the 1994 Rwandan Genocide* (Lanham, MD: University Press of America, 2003); Sylvester A. Johnson, *The Myth*

of Ham in Nineteenth-Century American Christianity: Race, Heathens, and the People of God (New York: Palgrave Macmillan, 2004); Robin Law, "The 'Hamitic Hypothesis' in Indigenous West African Historical Thought," *History in Africa* 36 (2009): 293–314; and Tudor Parfitt, "(De)Constructing Black Jews," in *African Zion: Studies in Black Judaism*, ed. Edith Bruder and Tudor Parfitt (Newcastle upon Tyne: Cambridge Scholars, 2012), 12–30.

63. Moses Maimonides, *The Guide for the Perplexed*, ed. and trans. Michael Friedländer (London: Routledge and Kegan Paul, 1956), 384. For an overview of perceptions regarding Ham's descendants in classical Jewish thought, see Aviezer Cohen, "The Curse of Ham in Rabbinic Literature and Its Reference to Blacks and the 'Sons of Cush'" (PhD diss., Bar-Ilan University, 2000) (Hebrew).

64. For the most comprehensive study of the Karaites to date, see Fred Astren's *Karaite Judaism and Historical Understanding* (Columbia: University of South Carolina Press, 2004).

65. Daniel Frank and Leon Nemoy, "Karaites," in *The Encyclopedia of Religion*, 2d ed., ed. Lindsay Jones (Detroit: Macmillan Reference, 2005), 8:5082.

66. Isabel Kershner, "New Generation of Jewish Sect Takes Up Struggle to Protect Place in Modern Israel," *New York Times*, September 4, 2013.

67. For more information on this group, see Robert T. Anderson, *The Keepers: An Introduction to the History and Culture of the Samaritans* (Peabody, MA: Hendrickson, 2002); and Gary N. Knoppers, *Jews and Samaritans: The Origins and History of Their Early Relations* (New York: Oxford University Press, 2013).

68. Andrew Esensten, "Samaritans Make Annual Sacrifice—and Preserve a Way of Life," *Haaretz*, April 24, 2013, http://www.haaretz.com/news/national /samaritans-make-annual-sacrifice-and-preserve-a-way-of-life.premium-1 .517378.

69. See Janet Liebman Jacobs, *Hidden Heritage: The Legacy of the Crypto-Jews* (Berkeley: University of California Press, 2002); Norman Toby Simms, *Masks in the Mirror: Marranism in Jewish Experience* (New York: Peter Lang, 2006); and Miriam Bodian, *Dying in the Law of Moses: Crypto-Jewish Martyrdom in the Iberian World* (Bloomington: Indiana University Press, 2007).

70. The most comprehensive overview of those sources is found in Peter Mark and José da Silva Horta, *The Forgotten Diaspora: Jewish Communities in West Africa and the Making of the Atlantic World* (Cambridge: Cambridge University Press, 2013). See also their article, "Catholics, Jews, and Muslims in Early Seventeenth-Century Guiné," in *Atlantic Diasporas: Jews, Conversos, and Crypto-Jews in the Age of Mercantilism, 1500–1800*, ed. Richard L. Kagan and Philip D. Morgan (Baltimore: Johns Hopkins University Press, 2009), 170–94.

71. Arieh O'Sullivan, "'Gabonese Jews' Prank Prompts Israelis to Offer Help," Associated Press, April 1, 1994, http://www.apnewsarchive .com/1994/-Gabonese-Jews-Prank-Prompts-Israelis-to-Offer-Help/id -62c8e6ade6f41237bfd3cdd02b6b65d4.

72. For more on the Igbo Jews, see William F. S. Miles, *Jews of Nigeria: An Afro-Judaic Odyssey* (Princeton: Markus Wiener, 2012).

73. Chinua Achebe, *Things Fall Apart* (London: Heinemann, 1958).

74. Daniel Lis, "'Ethiopia Shall Soon Stretch Out Her Hands': Ethiopian Jewry and Igbo Identity," *Jewish Culture and History* 11, no. 3 (2009): 28. Other Igbo have

informed me that they trace their lineage to the tribes of Manasseh, Zebulon, or even Judah. See also the monograph by Lis, *Jewish Identity among the Igbo of Nigeria: Israel's "Lost Tribe" and the Question of Belonging in the Jewish State* (Trenton, NJ: Africa World Press, 2015).

75. Remy Ilona, *The Igbos: Jews in Africa?* (Abuja: Mega Press, 2004), 73. See also his more recent *The Igbos and Israel: An Inter-cultural Study of the Largest Jewish Diaspora* (Washington, DC: Street to Street Epic Publications, 2014).

76. On the Lemba, see Tudor Parfitt, *Journey to the Vanished City: The Search for a Lost Tribe of Israel* (New York: St. Martin's Press, 1992); Magdel le Roux, *The Lemba: A Lost Tribe of Israel in Southern Africa* (Pretoria: Unisa Press, 2003); Parfitt and Yulia Egorova, *Genetics, Mass Media, and Identity: A Case Study of the Genetic Research on the Lemba and Bene Israel* (London: Routledge, 2006), esp. 51–88; and Noah Tamarkin, "Religion as Race, Recognition as Democracy: Lemba 'Black Jews' in South Africa," *The Annals of the American Academy of Political and Social Science* 637, no. 1 (2011): 148–64.

77. On this claim, see Tudor Parfitt, *The Lost Ark of the Covenant: The Remarkable Quest for the Legendary Ark* (New York: HarperCollins, 2008).

78. Mark G. Thomas et al., "Origins of Old Testament Priests," *Nature* 394 (1998): 138–40.

79. On the Abayudaya, see James Ross, *Fragile Branches* (New York: Riverhead Trade, 2001), 15–54; and Arye Oded, *Judaism in Africa: The Abayudaya of Uganda: The African Jews of Uganda and Their Contacts with World Jewry* (Jerusalem: Israel-Africa Friendship Association, 2013). Hebrew.

80. Cited in Brad A. Greenberg, "Ugandan Gershom Sizomu Ordained as First Black Sub-Saharan Rabbi," *Jewish Journal*, May 28, 2008, http://www.jewishjournal.com/religion/article/ugandan_gershom_sizomu_ordained_as_first_black_sub_saharan_rabbi.

81. On the Kasuku Jews, see Melanie Lidman, "In Kenya's Highlands, A Jewish Community Struggles for Recognition," *Times of Israel*, March 10, 2015, http://www.timesofisrael.com/in-kenyas-highlands-a-jewish-community-struggles-for-recognition/.

82. On the Zakhor movement, see William F. S. Miles, *Afro-Jewish Encounters: From Timbuktu to the Indian Ocean and Beyond* (Princeton: Markus Wiener, 2013), 3–17.

83. This is in fact a repeat of what Senegal's first independence-era president, Léopold Sédar Senghor, reportedly told former Israeli prime minister Shimon Peres about his family's own Jewish origins. For an account of the exchange, see George E. Lichtblau, "Jewish Roots in Africa," in *Jews in Places You Never Thought Of*, ed. Karen Primack (Hoboken, NJ: Ktav, 1998), 10–11.

84. Cited in Cnaan Liphshiz, "In Senegalese Bush, Bani Israel Tribe Claims Jewish Heritage," *Jewish Telegraphic Agency*, May 23, 2013, http://www.jta.org/2013/05/23/life-religion/in-senegalese-bush-bani-israel-tribe-claims-jewish-heritage.

85. Ibid.

86. For background on the Kemant (sometimes romanized into English as Qemant), see the most comprehensive (albeit outdated) study on that group, Frederick C. Gamst's *The Qemant: A Pagan-Hebraic Peasantry of Ethiopia* (New York: Holt, Rinehart, and Winston, 1969).

87. For an overview of the relevant terminology and taxonomies related to this phenomenon, see Dawid Venter's *Engaging Modernity: Methods and Cases for Studying African Independent Churches in South Africa* (Westport, CT: Praeger, 2004), 13–43.

88. See Nahashon Ndungu, "The Bible in an African Independent Church," in *The Bible in African Christianity*, ed. Hannah W. Kinoti and John M. Waliggo (Nairobi: Acton, 1997), 58–67.

89. Harold W. Turner, *Religious Innovation in Africa: Collected Essays on New Religious Movements* (Boston: G. K. Hall, 1979), 92.

90. Gailyn Van Rheenen, "Indigenous Church and Partnership," in *The Changing Face of World Missions: Engaging Contemporary Issues and Trends*, ed. Michael Pocock, Gailyn Van Rheenen, and Douglas McConnell (Grand Rapids, MI: Baker Academic, 2005), 187.

91. Allan H. Anderson, *African Reformation: African Initiated Christianity in the 20th Century* (Trenton, NJ: Africa World Press, 1995), 220.

92. Kofi A. Opoku, "Changes Within Christianity: The Case of the Musama Disco Christo Church," in *The History of Christianity in West Africa*, ed. Ogbu Kalu (London: Longman, 1980), 309.

93. Ibid., 311.

94. Rosalind Shaw and Charles Steward, "Introduction: Problematizing Syncretism," in *Syncretism/Anti-Syncretism: The Politics of Religious Synthesis*, ed. Rosalind Shaw and Charles Steward (London: Routledge, 1994), 20.

95. Bengt G. M. Sundkler, *Bantu Prophets in South Africa* (New York: Oxford University Press, 1961), 397.

96. For more on this timely subject, see Brian Larkin and Birgit Meyer, "Pentecostalism, Islam, and Culture: New Religious Movements in West Africa," in *Themes in West Africa's History*, ed. Emmanuel Kwaku Akyeampong (Accra, Ghana: Woeli Publication Services, 2005), 283–312.

97. Bengt G. M. Sundkler, *The Christian Ministry in Africa* (Uppsala, Sweden: University of Uppsala Press, 1960), 214. Sundkler further elaborates on this phenomenon elsewhere, explaining, "It has also been pointed out by certain observers . . . that the African pattern of thought is nearer to Hebrew concepts than to Greek ideas. This to some extent explains, or at least indicates, the predilection for the Old Testament, the strength of which sometimes surprises the Western tutor" (pp. 214–15).

98. Godfrey Edward Phillips, *The Old Testament in the World Church, with Special Reference to the Younger Churches* (London: Lutterworth Press, 1942), 9.

99. William D. Reyburn, "The Message of the Old Testament and the African Church," *Practical Anthropology* 7, no. 4 (1960): 152.

100. Ibid.

101. For more on this point, see Jesse N. K. Mugambi, "Religions in East Africa in the Context of Globalization," in *Religions in Eastern Africa Under Globalization*, ed. Jesse N. K. Mugambi and Mary N. Getui (Nairobi: Acton, 2004), 4; and G. C. Oosthuizen, "Hebraic-Judaistic Tenets in the African Independent Churches and Religious Movements in South Africa," in *South African Association of Jewish Studies: Proceedings of the Eleventh Annual Conference, 4–7 September, 1988* (Durban: South African Association of Jewish Studies, 1988), 1–25.

102. See, for instance, Kwesi A. Dickson, "The Old Testament and African Theology," *Ghana Bulletin of Theology* 4, no. 4 (1973): 32–34; and Knut Holter,

Tropical Africa and the Old Testament: A Select and Annotated Bibliography (Oslo: University of Oslo Press, 1996).

103. Magdel le Roux, "Lemba Traditions: An Indispensable Tool for Interpreting the Old Testament in Africa," in *African Zion: Studies in Black Judaism*, ed. Edith Bruder and Tudor Parfitt (Newcastle upon Tyne: Cambridge Scholars, 2012), 175.

104. Phillips, *Old Testament*, 9.

105. Kwesi A. Dickson, *Theology in Africa* (Maryknoll, NY: Orbis Books, 1984), 149–50.

106. Philip Jenkins, *The Next Christendom: The Coming of Global Christianity* (Oxford: Oxford University Press, 2002), 131.

107. Ibid.

108. Nicole Andersen and Scott London, "South Africa's Newest 'Jews': The Moemedi Pentecostal Church and the Construction of Jewish Identity," *Nova Religio: The Journal of Alternative and Emergent Religions* 13, no. 1 (2009): 101.

109. See also the related discussion on "Zionist" and "Israelite" South African churches in Bruder, *Black Jews of Africa*, 173–76.

110. Turner, *Religious Innovation in Africa*, 86.

111. Ibid.

112. Cited in Ella Shohat, "Sephardim in Israel: Zionism from the Standpoint of Its Jewish Victims," in *Dangerous Liaisons: Gender, Nation, and Postcolonial Perspectives*, ed. Anne McClintock, Aamir Mufti, and Ella Shohat (Minneapolis: University of Minnesota Press, 1997), 43.

113. In Deuteronomy 7:4, the prohibition against intermarriage is expressed thus: "For he [i.e., the non-Jewish male spouse] will turn away thy son from following Me, that they may serve other gods; so will the anger of the LORD be kindled against you, and He will destroy thee quickly." No such concern is expressed about the child of a non-Jewish female spouse. See Christine Hayes, "Intermarriage and Impurity in Ancient Jewish Sources," *Harvard Theological Review* 92, no. 1 (1999): 3–36.

114. On this point, see Deuteronomy 21:10–14; Esther 8:17; and Catherine Hezser, *Jewish Slavery in Antiquity* (Oxford: Oxford University Press, 2006), esp. 27–54. With regard to the conversion of slaves owned by Jews, the same policy seems to be true in later eras, as well. For example, regarding the African "servants" of Portuguese or Spanish Jews operating in the area of Senegambia in the seventeenth century, see Jonathan Schorsch, *Jews and Blacks in the Early Modern World* (Cambridge: Cambridge University Press, 2004), 93–94; and Mark and da Silva Horta, *The Forgotten Diaspora*, 71–77.

115. Those who fled Israel after the crumbling of Samaria (as well as those who returned after the Babylonian exile) took non-Jewish women as wives. See Judges 3:5–6: "And the children of Israel dwelt among the Canaanites, the Hittites, and the Amorites, and the Perizzites, and the Hivites, and the Jebusites; and they took their daughters to be their wives, and gave their own daughters to their sons, and served their gods."

116. Shaye J. D. Cohen, *The Beginnings of Jewishness: Boundaries, Varieties, Uncertainties* (Berkeley: University of California Press, 1999), 14.

117. Cited in Yakov M. Rabkin, *A Threat from Within: A Century of Jewish Opposition to Zionism* (New York: Zed Books, 2006), 35.

118. Cited in Dalia Karpel, "Culture Club," *Haaretz Magazine*, October 20, 2006, 8.
119. Richard Goodman, *Genetic Disorders among the Jewish People* (Baltimore: Johns Hopkins University Press, 1979), 29.
120. Alain F. Corcos, *The Myth of the Jewish Race: A Biologist's Point of View* (Bethlehem, PA: Lehigh University Press, 2005), 130.
121. See Parfitt and Egorova, *Genetics, Mass Media, and Identity*; and Ian Vincent McGonigle, "'Jewish Genetics' and the 'Nature' of Israeli Citizenship," *Transversal: Journal of Jewish Studies* 13, no. 2 (2015): 90–102.
122. There is no connection between Kulanu, Inc., the organization profiled here, and Kulanu, the social welfare–focused Israeli political party founded by Moshe Kahlon in 2014.
123. "Welcome to Kulanu, Inc!," Kulanu, accessed April 5, 2015, http://www.kulanu .org/. Worthy of mention with respect to Kulanu's activities is the scholarship conducted on that topic by Nadia Abu El-Haj. Of such activities, Abu El-Haj has written: "In its work in search of Lost Tribes . . . Kulanu joins together the multicultural gesture of Jewish inclusion not just with a missionary fantasy but also with a messianic impulse. . . . Kulanu cooperates with Israelis of the religious-nationalist camp, which has its own investment in Lost Tribes and would-be Jews. Out of that articulation, what is perhaps best described as a postcolonial colonial politics is being forged." From Nadia Abu El-Haj, *The Genealogical Science: The Search for Jewish Origins and the Politics of Epistemology* (Chicago: University of Chicago Press, 2012), 204. Although I disagree with Abu El Haj's characterization of Kulanu as a "missionary" or "messianic" organization based on my extensive contacts with their leadership, I appreciate very much her meticulous academic work on the politics of Jewish multiculturalism and the (perhaps unintended) dynamics of hegemony that are put into play when Jews from the "First World" meet those from the "Third."
124. "Jewish Communities Worldwide," Kulanu, accessed April 5, 2015, http://www .kulanu.org/communities/.
125. Bonita Sussman, e-mail message to author, May 17, 2014.
126. Ibid.
127. "Vision: A Global Jewish People," Be'chol Lashon, accessed April 2, 2015, http:// www.bechollashon.org/about/mission.php.
128. Ibid.
129. Ibid.
130. Gary A. Tobin, *Opening the Gates: How Proactive Conversion Can Revitalize the Jewish Community* (San Francisco: Jossey-Bass, 1999), 11.
131. Ibid., 173.
132. Allan H. Anderson, *To the Ends of the Earth: Pentecostalism and the Transformation of World Christianity* (Oxford: Oxford University Press, 2013), 169.
133. All of these remarks by Rabbi Avichail were communicated to me personally during our interview in Jerusalem, Israel, on July 27, 2013.
134. Yitzhak Baer, *A History of the Jews in Christian Spain* (Philadelphia: Jewish Publication Society of America, 1961), 1:1.
135. Raphael Patai, *Israel between East and West: A Study in Human Relations* (Westport, CT: Greenwood, 1970), 26. For an excellent extension of this argument in the premodern context, see Gabriele Boccaccini, "What Is a Judaism? Perspectives from Second Temple Jewish Studies," in *Religion or Ethnicity? Jewish*

Identities in Evolution, ed. Zvi Gitelman (New Brunswick, NJ: Rutgers University Press, 2009), 24–37.

136. Even the term "Judaism" makes its entry relatively late in this development, appearing for the first time in 2 Maccabees 2:21 and 14:38.

137. Raphael Patai, *The Jewish Mind* (Detroit: Wayne State University Press, 1990), 371.

138. On the parallels between these creeds, See Marc Zvi Brettler, "My Bible: A Jew's Perspective," in *The Bible and the Believer: How to Read the Bible Critically and Religiously*, ed. Marc Zvi Brettler, Peter Enns, and Daniel J. Harrington (Oxford: Oxford University Press, 2012), 21–65.

139. Laurence Rosen, *Bargaining for Reality: The Construction of Social Relations in a Muslim Community* (Chicago: University of Chicago Press, 1984), 7.

140. David Hartman, *A Heart of Many Rooms: Celebrating the Many Voices Within Judaism* (Woodstock, VT: Jewish Lights, 1999), 3.

141. See Mordechai M. Kaplan, *Judaism as a Civilization: Toward a Reconstruction of American Jewish Life* (New York: Schocken Books, 1935).

142. Els van Diggele, *A People Who Live Apart: Jewish Identity and the Future of Israel*, trans. Jeanette K. Ringold (Amherst, NY: Prometheus Books, 2003), 121.

143. For more on Wittgenstein's theory of "family resemblance" in its Jewish context, see Eliezer Ben-Rafael, *Jewish Identities: Fifty Intellectuals Answer Ben Gurion* (Leiden: Brill, 2002), 99–110.

144. See Ludwig Wittgenstein, *Philosophical Investigations*, trans. G. E. M. Anscombe (Oxford: Blackwell, 1953), 65–72.

145. A remark originally given in 1934 at the Lehrhaus in Frankfurt am Main, and reprinted in Martin Buber, *Israel and the World: Essays in a Time of Crisis* (New York: Schocken Books, 1963), 167.

146. Sigmund Freud, "On Being of the B'nai B'rith," *Commentary* 2, no. 3 (1946): 23.

147. Efraim Shmueli, *Seven Jewish Cultures: A Reinterpretation of Jewish History and Thought*, trans. Gila Shmueli (Cambridge: Cambridge University Press, 1990).

148. For more on these ideas, see Benedict Anderson, *Imagined Communities: Reflections on the Origin and Spread of Nationalism* (London: Verso, 1991); and Etienne Balibar and Immanuel Wallerstein, *Race, Nation, Class: Ambiguous Identities*, trans. Chris Turner (New York: Verso, 1991).

149. Shmueli, *Seven Jewish Cultures*, 12.

150. Ibid., 5.

151. Leon Israel Yudkin, *Jewish Writing and Identity in the Twentieth Century* (London: Croom Helm, 1982), 12.

152. Dan Miron, "Modern Hebrew Literature: Zionist Perspectives and Israeli Realities," in *What Is Jewish Literature?*, ed. Hana Wirth-Nesher (Philadelphia: Jewish Publication Society, 1994), 95.

153. Aviv and Shneer, *New Jews*, 175.

CHAPTER 2

1. For background information on Akan history, see Kwaku Effah-Gyamfi, "Some Archaeological Reflections on Akan Traditions of Origin," *West African Journal of Archaeology* 9 (1979): 187–99.

2. Kofi Appiah-Kubi, "Indigenous African Christian Churches: Signs of Authenticity," in *Third World Liberation Theologies: A Reader*, ed. Deane William Ferm (Maryknoll, NY: Orbis Books, 1986), 223.

3. Ibid.

4. Paul A. Silverstein, "Of Rooting and Uprooting: Kabyle Habitus, Domesticity, and Structural Nostalgia," *Ethnography* 5, no. 4 (2004): 554.

5. For the most comprehensive study on this group to date, see John L. Jackson's *Thin Description*. For an overview of their relationship to Ghana, see Martina Könighofer, *The New Ship of Zion: Dynamic Diaspora Dimensions of the African Hebrew Israelites of Jerusalem* (Berlin: LIT Verlag, 2008), 56–64. On the interaction between "white" Jews and Jews of color in the modern American multicultural context, see Janice W. Fernheimer, *Stepping into Zion: Hatzaad Harishon, Black Jews, and the Remaking of Jewish Identity* (Tuscaloosa: University of Alabama Press, 2014).

6. Institute for Cultural Diplomacy, "The African Hebrew Development Agency," accessed January 23, 2015, http://www.culturaldiplomacy.org/experienceafrica /index.php?en_diaspora_ahi_projects_ahda.

7. In 2011, Israel reopened its embassy in Ghana after thirty-eight years of closure.

8. Harold W. Turner, *Living Tribal Religions* (London: Ward Lock Educational, 1971).

9. Ibid., 5.

10. White House, Office of the Press Secretary, "Remarks by the President to the Ghanaian Parliament," July 11, 2009, http://www.whitehouse.gov/the-press -office/remarks-president-ghanaian-parliament.

11. According to Ghana Embassy, "Population," accessed November 4, 2014, http://www.ghanaembassy.org/index.php?page=population.

12. *Globe*, "A Muslim Can Be President—Kufuor," GhanaWeb, September 20, 2011, http://www.ghanaweb.com/GhanaHomePage/NewsArchive/artikel.php ?ID=219384.

13. Willie F. Page, "Sefwi," in *Encyclopedia of African History and Culture*, vol. 3, *From Conquest to Colonization (1500 to 1850)* (New York: Facts on File, 2001), 238.

14. For suppositions regarding Sefwi provenance, see Diagram Group, "Sefwi," in *Encyclopedia of African Peoples* (New York: Facts on File, 2000), 183; H. P. Holtsbaum, "Sefwi and Its Peoples," *Gold Coast Review* 1 (1925): 76–94; and Eva Meyerowitz, *Akan Traditions of Origin* (London: Faber and Faber, 1952), 124.

15. For general information on Ashanti history and society, see Osei Kwafwo, *Outline of Asante History* (Wiamoase-Ashanti, Ghana: O. Kwadwo Enterprise, 1994); Merrick Posnansky, "Archaeology and the Origins of the Akan Society in Ghana," in *Problems in Economic and Social Archaeology*, ed. G. de G. Sieveking, I. H. Longworth, and K. E. Wilson (London: Duckworth, 1976), 49–59; again, Posnansky, "The Search for Asante Origins: Archaeological Evidence," in *The Golden Stool: Studies of the Asante Center and Periphery*, ed. Enid Schildkrout (New York: Anthropological Papers of the American Museum of Natural History, 1987), 14–22; and Peter Sarpong, "Some Myths of the Origins from Ashanti (Ghana)," in *Naissance du monde et de l'homme* (Rome: Gregorian University Press, 1969), 195–99.

16. Kwame Yeboah Daaku, "A History of the Sefwi: A Survey of Oral Evidence," *Research Review* 7, no. 3 (1971): 32.

17. Ibid.

18. Eva Meyerowitz, *The Early History of the Akan States* (London: Red Candle Press, 1974), 116.

19. Rachel Naylor, *Ghana* (Oxford: Oxfam, 2000), 74. On the introduction of the *ntoro* cult and the move toward matrilocal marriage practices, see K. A. Busia, "The Ashanti," in *African Worlds: Studies in the Cosmological Ideas and Social Values of African Peoples*, ed. Daryll Forde (Hamburg: LIT Verlag, 1999), 196; and Eva Meyerowitz, *The Akan of Ghana: Their Ancient Beliefs* (London: Faber and Faber, 1958), 99.

20. Robert Sutherland Rattray, *Religion and Art in Ashanti* (Kumasi, Ghana: Basel Mission Book Depot, 1954), 140.

21. Ibid., 141.

22. Thomas Edward Bowdich, *An Essay on the Superstitions, Customs and Arts Common to the Ancient Egyptians, Abyssinians, and Ashantees* (Paris: J. Smith, 1821).

23. Joseph John Williams, *Hebrewisms of West Africa: From the Nile to Niger with the Jews* (London: Allen and Unwin, 1930), 3.

24. Ibid., 72.

25. I owe this observation to Busia's "The Ashanti," 196.

26. Ibid., 319–20.

27. Lawrence Green, *Old Africa's Last Secrets* (London: Putnam, 1961), 177.

28. Ibid.

29. On the possible migrations of Saharan Jews into these areas, see the following general titles: S. D. Goitein, "R. Isaac b. Ibrahim al-Tu'ati (ca. 1235): The Most Ancient Reference to Jews in the Touat," *Revue des études juives* 140, nos. 1–2 (1981): 193–210; and Jacob Oliel, *Les juifs au sahara: Le touat au moyen âge* (Paris: CNRS, 1994).

30. Charles Monteil, "Les 'Ghâna': Des géographes arabes et des européens," *Hespéris* 38, nos. 3–4 (1951): 287–88. Concerning tales of Jewish blacksmiths in the region, see Edith Bruder's explanation in *Black Jews of Africa*, 149–51, especially with regard to the oral histories about Wagadu, legendary founder of Ghana and supposed descendant of King Solomon.

31. See Peter Mark and José da Silva Horta, *The Forgotten Diaspora*, as well as their "Catholics, Jews, and Muslims in Early Seventeenth-Century Guiné," 170–94.

32. I owe this observation to Tudor Parfitt, who discusses it in his *Black Jews*, 115. The original citation, which Thomas McCaskie traces to the papers of Asantehene Osei Agyeman Prempeh II, dated January 11, 1946, and stored in the archive at Manhyia Palace, Kumasi, appears in Thomas McCaskie, "Asante Origins, Egypt, and the Near East: An Idea and Its History," in *Recasting the Past: History Writing and Political Work in Modern Africa*, ed. Derek Peterson and Giacomo Macola (Athens: Ohio University Press, 2009), 137.

33. Parfitt, *Black Jews*, 115.

34. Ibid., 116.

35. Thomas McCaskie, "Inventing Asante," in *Self-Assertion and Brokerage: Early Cultural Nationalism in West Africa*, ed. Paulo Fernando de Moraes Farias and Karin Barber (Birmingham, UK: Centre of West African Studies, University of Birmingham, 1990), 63.

36. Interview with Omanhene of Anhwiaso, Nana Kofi Adjai, recorded in 1932 by District Commissioner M. M. Miln and listed in Appendix 1b of Kwame Yeboah Daaku, *Oral Traditions of Sefwi*, vol. 1 (Legon: Institute of African Studies, University of Ghana, 1974), n.p.

37. Stefano Boni, e-mail message to author, December 27, 2012.

38. Meyerowitz, *Akan of Ghana*, 21. Also see her *Akan Traditions of Origin*, 124, for suppositions that most Akans are descended from Saharan Libyan Berbers.

39. As recounted in H. Kullas and G. A. Ayer, *What the Elders of Ashanti Say* (Kumasi, Ghana: Kumasi University Press, 1967), 1.

40. Abu 'Ubayd al-Bakri, "The Book of Routes and Realms," in *Corpus of Early Arabic Sources for West African History*, ed. N. Levtzion and J. E. F. Hopkins (Cambridge: Cambridge University Press, 1981), 79–80. For general information on the Islamic presence in premodern Ghana, see also Ivor Wilks, *The Northern Factor in Ashanti History* (Legon: Institute of African Studies, University of Ghana, 1961).

41. Jones Darkwa Amanor, "Pentecostalism in Ghana: An African Reformation," *Cyberjournal for Pentecostal-Charismatic Research*, April 13, 2004, http://www.pctii.org/cyberj/cyberj13/amanor.html.

42. These figures are according to Jon Miller, *Missionary Zeal and Institutional Control: Organizational Contradictions in the Basel Mission on the Gold Coast, 1828–1917* (Grand Rapids, MI: William B. Eerdmans, 2003), 27. For general background on the topic, see Seth Quartey, *Missionary Practices on the Gold Coast, 1832–1895: Discourse, Gaze, and Gender in the Basel Mission in Pre-colonial West Africa* (London: Cambria Press, 2007).

43. Remark attributed to S. K. Odamtten. Cited in George Bob-Milliar and Gloria Bob-Milliar, "Christianity in the Ghanaian State in the Past Fifty Years," GhanaWeb, February 28, 2007, http://www.ghanaweb.com/GhanaHomePage/features/artikel.php?ID=119921.

44. For more on the introduction of schools in Sefwi areas, see Penelope Roberts, "The Village Schoolteacher in Ghana," in *The Changing Social Structure of Ghana*, ed. J. Goody (London: International African Institute, 1972), 245–60.

45. According to Penelope Roberts, "Whose School? Conflicts over School Management in Sefwi Wiawso, Ghana," *Anthropology and Education Quarterly* 13, no. 3 (1982): 268–78, esp. 269.

46. For further details on this early stage of interaction, see John S. Pobee, *The Anglican Story in Ghana: From Mission Beginnings to Province of Ghana* (Accra, Ghana: African Books Collective, 2009), 167.

47. As reported by Penelope Roberts, "The Court Records of Sefwi Wiawso, Western Region, Ghana," *History in Africa* 12 (1985): 380.

48. Pobee, *Anglican Story in Ghana*, 167.

49. Government of Ghana, "Western Region," accessed January 26, 2015, http://www.ghana.gov.gh/index.php/about-ghana/regions/western.

50. "Sefwi Wiawso District," City Population Index, accessed January 30, 2015, http://www.citypopulation.de/php/ghana-admin.php?adm2id=1012.

51. Busia, "Ashanti," 209. On such syncretism, see Patrick Nkrumah, "The Interaction between Christianity and Ashanti Religion" (PhD diss., Drew University, 1992).

52. Kwesi A. Dickson, "Continuity and Discontinuity between the Old Testament and African Life and Thought," in *African Theology en Route: Papers from the*

Pan-African Conference of Third World Theologians, December 17–23, 1977, Accra, Ghana, ed. Kofi Appiah-Kubi and Sergio Torres (Maryknoll, NY: Orbis Books, 1979), 98.

53. Homi Bhabha, *Location of Culture*, 122–29.
54. Cited in Jessica Romer, "Religious Assimilation: The Ideological Foundations of a Ghanaian Jewish Community" (undergraduate thesis, University of Colorado–Boulder, 2005), 13.
55. Cited in Florence Gbolu, "Shabbat in Ghana: Young Journalist Seeks out African Jewish Community," Kulanu, 2004, http://www.kulanu.org/ghana/Gbolu.php.
56. The chronology of this particular incident varies depending on the source consulted. For alternate perspectives, see the article of Daniel Baiden, "The Ghanaian Village that Wants to Be Jewish," in *Jews in Places You Never Thought Of*, ed. Karen Primack (Hoboken, NJ: Ktav, 1998), 269.
57. Ibid., 267.
58. Ibid.
59. Ibid.
60. Cited in Romer, "Religious Assimilation," 29.
61. Cited in Gbolu, "Shabbat in Ghana."
62. Ibid.
63. Cited in Romer, "Religious Assimilation," 18.
64. For a description of one such student's time in Ghana, see Michael Ramberg, "Jewish Learning Takes a Village," *Kulanu Newsletter* 14, no. 3 (2007): 1, 10; and Wendy Univer, "Across the Globe, Eager Students Have Something to Teach," *Reconstructionist Rabbinical College Annual Report*, 2008, 10–15.
65. Nili Salem, "The Secret of Sefwi Wiawso" (undergraduate thesis, University of California–Santa Barbara, 2005), 122–23.
66. Cited in Ramberg, "Jewish Learning."
67. Ibid.
68. Cited in Romer, "Religious Assimilation," 22.
69. Cited in ibid., 21.
70. Cited in ibid.
71. Cited in ibid.
72. Cited in ibid., 17.
73. Vanessa L. Ochs, "What Makes a Jewish Home Jewish?," Material History of American Religion Project, accessed July 3, 2014, http://www.materialreligion.org/journal/jewish.html.
74. Jono David, "House of Israel, Ghana: Day 3 (of 5), 'Meshuggah for Mezuzah,'" Jewish Africa: A Cultural and Historical Photographic Survey, February 27, 2014, http://www.jewishphotolibrary.wordpress.com/2014/02/27/house-of-israel-ghana-day-3-of-5-meshuggah-for-mezuzah/.
75. Ronald H. Isaacs, *Becoming Jewish: A Handbook for Conversion* (New York: Rabbinical Assembly, 1993).
76. Ibid.
77. Eric Silver, "Yitzhak Shamir: Member of the Stern Gang Who Became a Hawkish Prime Minister of Israel," *The Independent*, July 2, 2012, http://www.independent.co.uk/news/obituaries/yitzhak-shamir-member-of-the-stern-gang-who-became-a-hawkish-prime-minister-of-israel-7902674.html.
78. Stefano Boni, "History and Ideology of an Akan Centre: The Cosmological Topography of Wiawso," *History and Anthropology* 18, no. 1 (2007): 45.

79. For more on this Akan restriction and its connection with childbirth taboos, see Dickson, *Theology in Africa*, 154. For comparative studies on menstrual taboos in Ghana, see Ofosu Adutwum, "The Suspected Adulteress: Ancient Israelite and Traditional Akan Treatment," *Expository Times* 104, no. 2 (1992): 38–42; Kofi Agyekum, "Menstruation as a Verbal Taboo among the Akan of Ghana," *Journal of Anthropological Research* 58, no. 3 (2002): 367–87; and Christine Oppong, "Notes on Cultural Aspects of Menstruation in Ghana," *Research Review* 9, no. 2 (1973): 33–38.

80. Elizabeth Amoah, "The Woman Who Decided to Break the Rules," in *New Eyes for Reading: Biblical and Theological Reflections by Women from the Third World*, ed. John S. Pobee and Barbel Van Wartenberg-Potter (Geneva: World Council of Churches, 1986), 3.

81. Ibid.

82. Cited in Romer, "Religious Assimilation," 25.

83. Ibid., 26.

84. I. Gordon, "Ehud, the Fat Man, and the Power of Praise!," Jesus Plus Nothing, accessed January 2, 2015, http://www.jesusplusnothing.com/studies/online /judges6.htm.

85. Marcus Borg, *Speaking Christian: Why Christian Words Have Lost Their Meaning and Power—And How They Can Be Restored* (New York: HarperCollins, 2011), 115.

86. Brent Nongbri, *Before Religion: A History of a Modern Concept* (New Haven: Yale University Press, 2013), 24.

87. A particularly lucid explanation of this influence may be found in Suzanne M. Spencer-Wood, "The Formation of Ethnic-American Identities: Jewish Communities in Boston," in *Historical Archaeology: Back from the Edge*, ed. Pedro Paulo A. Funari, Martin Hall, and Siân Jones (New York: Routledge, 2013), 284–307.

88. For more on the Ewe, see Jakob Spieth and W. K. Amoaku, *The Ewe People: A Study of the Ewe People in German Togo* (Accra: Sub-Saharan, 2011).

89. Seba Damani, "Distorting Truth: Ewe History?," November 16, 2013, http:// www.sebadamani.com/blog/distorting-truth-ewe-history.

90. Justice Sarpong, "Are Ewes Ghanaian Jews? Don't Bet on It," August 13, 2011, http://www.ghanaweb.com/GhanaHomePage/features/artikel.php?ID=216176.

91. Ibid.

92. For an example of an early colonial opinion regarding the cultural similarities between Gas and Jews, see Carl Christian Reindorf, *History of the Gold Coast and Asante*, 3d ed. (Accra: Ghana University Press, 2007), esp. 56. For a more general early view on Ga provenance, see M. Bruce Myers, "The Origin of the Gas," *Journal of the African Society* 27 (1927–1928): 69–76, 167–73.

93. Most of the critical studies on the Ga, including those listed in these references, are somewhat outdated. I should mention that I look forward to the upcoming work of Daniel Lis on this important topic.

94. Joseph Nii Abekar Mensah, *Traditions and Customs of Gadangmes of Ghana: Descendants of Authentic Biblical Hebrew Israelites* (Houston: Strategic Book Publishing, 2013).

95. Ibid., 1.

96. Joseph Nii Abekar Mensah, "Gadangme Origins," Gadangme Heritage and Cultural Foundation, accessed February 1, 2015, http://www.gadangme.weebly .com/ga-dangme-origins.html.

97. Ibid.
98. Gadangme Nikasemo Asafo, "Lecture 1: A People Blessed," accessed May 5, 2014, http://www.gadangmenikasemoasafo.wordpress.com/the-king-taki-tawiah-memorial-lectures/lecture-i-a-people-blessed/.
99. Ibid.
100. Ibid.
101. For sources on this supposed correlation, see Ebenezer Allotey-Pappoe, "The Homowo Festival: The Harvest Festival of the Ga People," *Ghana Bulletin of Theology* 1, no. 7 (1959): 1; and Charles Amah, *Ga Homowo and Other Ga-Adangme Festivals* (Accra: Sedco, 1982). One dissenting voice from such claims is that of Emmanuel Isaac Kpakpo Addo, who points out that, in his experience, nothing in the pre-Christian Gadangme oral history supports such origins. For more on this, see his *Worldview, Way of Life, and Worship: The Continuing Encounter between the Christian Faith and Ga Religion and Culture* (Zoetermeer, Netherlands: Boekencentrum Academic, 2009), esp. 29.
102. Hubert Nii Abbey, *Homowo in Ghana* (Accra: Studio Brian Communications, 2010), 5.
103. Ibid.
104. Mensah, "Gadangme Origins."
105. Mensah, *Traditions and Customs*, 151.
106. Abbey, *Homowo in Ghana*, 7.
107. Marion Kilson, *Dancing with the Gods: Aspects of Ga Ritual* (Lanham, MD: University Press of America, 2013), 92.
108. I have not been able to find a "Semitic" parallel to the so-called "outdooring" ceremony, although the basic supposition according to which a child's name will carry great significance in life (for instance, see 1 Sam. 25:25) is indeed part of Jewish cultural heritage.
109. David K. Henderson-Quartey, *The Ga of Ghana: The History and Culture of a West African People* (London: David K. Henderson-Quartey, 2002), 62.
110. Mensah, *Traditions and Customs*, 50.
111. See ibid., 53.
112. Kofi Appiah-Kubi, "Indigenous African Christian Churches," 225.
113. For an overview of these and other independent churches in Ghana, see José Antunes da Silva, "African Independent Churches: Origin and Development," *Anthropos* 88, nos. 4–6 (1993): 393–402. For more on the national recognition of a Saturday Sabbath, see Kofi Owusu-Mensah, *Saturday God and Adventism in Ghana* (Oxford: Peter Lang International Academic, 1993).
114. Deji Ayegboyin and S. Ademola Ishola, "African Indigenous Churches: An Historical Perspective," Institute for Religious Research, 1997, accessed October 20, 2013, http://www.irr.org/african-indigenous-churches-chapter-fourteen.
115. Michael Herzfeld, *Cultural Intimacy: Social Poetics in the Nation-State* (New York: Routledge, 1997), 109.
116. Israel Gerber, *The Heritage Seekers* (New York: Jonathan David, 1977), 187.
117. I refer here to the English translation of the title of Fanon's *Les damnés de la terre* (Paris: Éditions Maspero, 1961).
118. See Osepetetreku Kwame Osei, *The Ancient Egyptians Are Here* (Kumasi, Ghana: Vytall, 2001).
119. McCaskie, "Asante Origins," 143.
120. Ibid., 141.

CHAPTER 3

1. I would like to acknowledge here that my use of the term "Internet Jews" has been inspired by the work of William F. S. Miles, who employs it to describe the development of Jewish identity among the Igbo of Nigeria, which "coincide[d] with the computerization and global wiring of Nigeria" (*Jews of Nigeria*, xvi). Similar discussions on the influence of the Internet in the construction of (Nigerian) Jewish identities can be found in Bruder, *Black Jews of Africa*, 147–48; and Lis, *Jewish Identity among the Igbo*, 134–35.
2. Heidi A. Campbell, "Understanding the Relationship between Religion Online and Offline in a Networked Society," *Journal of the American Academy of Religion* 80, no. 1 (2012): 85. See also Manuel Castells, *The Rise of the Network Society*, vol. 1, 2d ed. (Chichester, West Sussex: Wiley-Blackwell, 2009), and Jan A. G. M. van Dijk, *The Network Society: Social Aspects of New Media* (Thousand Oaks, CA: Sage, 1999). For Jewish iterations of "networked religion," see Campbell's "Introduction: Studying Jewish Engagement with Digital Media and Culture," in *Digital Judaism: Jewish Negotiations with Digital Media and Culture*, ed. Heidi A. Campbell (New York: Routledge, 2015), 1–15. For a useful comparison between the Cameroonian Jewish movement's Internet activities and online Christian initiatives in Africa, see J. Kwabena Asamoah-Gyadu, "'We Are on the Internet': Contemporary Pentecostalism in Africa and the New Culture of Online Religion," in *New Media and Religious Transformation in Africa*, ed. Rosalind I. J. Hackett and Benjamin F. Soares (Bloomington: Indiana University Press, 2015), 157–170.
3. Stephen Ellis and Gerrie ter Haar, *Worlds of Power: Religious Thought and Political Practice in Africa* (New York: Oxford University Press, 2004), 1.
4. Byang H. Kato, *Theological Pitfalls in Africa* (Kisumu, Kenya: Evangelical, 1975), 50.
5. See "Beth Yeshourun: The Cameroon Jewish Community," http://beth-yeshurun.agilityhoster.com/index.php; "Beth Yeshourun: La Communauté Juive du Cameroun," http://bethyeshourun.org/nous_connaitre.php. Both accessed February 5, 2015.
6. "Du Christianisme au Judaïsme: nos raisons," Beth Yeshourun, accessed February 5, 2015, http://bethyeshourun.org/chabbath.php#.
7. "Conversion au Judaïsme," Beth Yeshourun, accessed February 5, 2015, http://beth-yeshouroun.mywebcommunity.org/conversion.php.
8. *Encyclopedia Britannica*, s.v. "Cameroon," accessed July 10, 2014, http://www.britannica.com/EBchecked/topic/90925/Cameroon/55097/Plant-and-animal-life#toc55099.
9. Ibid.
10. Pew Research Center, "Overview: Pentecostalism in Africa," October 5, 2006, http://www.pewforum.org/2006/10/05/overview-pentecostalism-in-africa/.
11. On this point, see Mervyn David Waldegrave Jeffreys, "An Extinct Jewish Colony (Victoria, Cameroon)," *Jewish Affairs* (1954): 47–48.
12. For more on the system of *dosage*, see Victor T. Le Vine, *Politics in Francophone Africa* (Boulder, CO: Lynne Rienner, 2007), 215–18.
13. Tatah H. Mbuy, *Where Do We Stand? An Examination of Some Problems Affecting Christianity in Modern Cameroon* (Ashing-Kom, Cameroon: St. Bede's College, 1987), 11.

14. Kenneth D. Kaunda, *Letter to My Children* (London: Longman, 1973), 17.

15. Fran Markovitz, "Blood, Soul, Race, and Suffering: Full-Bodied Ethnography and Expressions of Jewish Belonging," in *Race, Color, Identity: Rethinking Discourses About "Jews" in the Twenty-First Century*, ed. Efraim Sicher (New York: Berghahn Books, 2013), 263.

16. Ibid.

17. The issue of the comparative evil of this or that colonial (or neocolonial) system is obviously far too complex to treat here. An excellent overview of the debates and scholarship on this topic may be found in William F. S. Miles, *Scars of Partition: Postcolonial Legacies in French and British Borderlands* (Lincoln: University of Nebraska Press, 2014), 1–20.

18. Cited in Diadie Ba, "Africans Still Seething over Sarkozy Speech," Reuters, September 5, 2007, http://www.uk.reuters.com/article/2007/09/05/uk-africa-sarkozy-idUKL0513034620070905.

19. On the major doctrines of Messianic Judaism, see Dan Cohn-Sherbok, *Messianic Judaism* (New York: Continuum, 2000); and David J. Rudolph and Joel Willitts, *Introduction to Messianic Judaism: Its Ecclesial Context and Biblical Foundations* (Grand Rapids, MI: Zondervan, 2013).

20. Accessed February 4, 2015, http://www.torahbox.com.

21. "La charte Akadem," Akadem, accessed December 10, 2014, http://www.akadem.org/charte/.

22. Cited in Antoine Glaser, *Africafrance: Quand les dirigeants africains deviennent les maîtres du jeu* (Paris: Fayard, 2014), 127.

23. Judy Manelis, "What's Happening in Africa: Cameroon, Kenya, Ghana, Uganda, Zimbabwe (August 2013)," Kulanu, accessed September 2, 2014, http://www.kulanu.org/abayudaya/progressinafrica.php.

24. Bonita Sussman, e-mail message to author, May 13, 2014.

25. Manelis, "What's Happening in Africa."

26. Ibid.

27. Shema Yisrael Torah Network, "Welcome to the Pirchei Shoshanim College Recommended Program," accessed January 19, 2015, http://www.shemayisrael.com/edu/.

28. Cited in Manelis, "What's Happening in Africa."

29. "Bienvenu sur le site web de la communauté juive Beth Yeshourun du Cameroun," Beth Yeshourun, accessed July 2, 2014, http://beth-yeshouroun.mywebcommunity.org/.

30. The presence of Seventh-day Adventists in Cameroon dates to approximately 1930. Although there are no reliable figures concerning the present number of Seventh-day Adventist churches in Cameroon, adherents of this denomination likely number in the hundreds of thousands. See Gary Land, *The A to Z of the Seventh-Day Adventists* (Lanham, MD: Scarecrow Press, 2009), 53. Other religious communities with similar Adventist-like concerns (forbidding certain impure foods, mandating circumcision, menstrual taboos, etc.), such as Sabbaterians, maintain a strong presence in the country, although their precise numbers are also unverifiable.

31. Menachem Kuchar, "My Visit to Cameroon: A Very Jewish Experience," *Menachem's Writings* (blog), accessed July 20, 2014, http://menachemkuchar.com/Writings/235-My-Cameroon-Visit-to-the-Jews.htm.

32. Vittorio Lanternari, *The Religions of the Oppressed: A Study of Modern Messianic Cults*, trans. Lisa Sergio (New York: Alfred A. Knopf, 1963), 36.
33. Dieudonné Toukam, *Histoire et anthropologie du peuple bamiléké* (Paris: L'Harmattan, 2010), 242.
34. Cited in "Cameroon," Shavei Israel, accessed April 23, 2014, http://www.shavei.org/category/communities/other_communities/africa/cameroon/?lang=en.
35. Cited in Doreen Wachman, "The Mystery of the Ten Lost Tribes: The Jews of Cameroon," Haruth Communications, accessed July 15, 2014, http://www.haruth.com/jw/JewsCameroon.htm.
36. Ibid.
37. Cited in Gaspard Ngono, "Saa Kameni: L'alphabet moderne est une imitation de l'alphabet hébraïque antique donc camerounaise," Mboa Guide, August 4, 2013, http://www.guide.mboa.info/histoire-des-peuples/fr/connaitre/actualite/2625,saa-kameni-lalphabet-moderne-est-une-imitation-de-lalphabet-hebraique-antique-donc-camerounais-.html.
38. See Yaphet Kotto, *The Royalty: A Spiritual Awakening* (N.p.: Cauldwell/Bissell, 1997). Although much of the book discusses his supposed Jewish roots, see esp. 360–511.
39. Cited in Hap Erstein, "Jewish-American Prince: Actor Yaphet Kotto—The Bar Mitzvahed Heir to Cameroon Aims for the 'Fences,'" *Washington Times*, May 10, 1990.
40. Edith Bruder (*Black Jews: Les juifs noirs*, 216–23) has written about this issue of Bassa hereditary heritage briefly, as has Serge Etele, who concludes, "We will probably never know if they [i.e., the Bassa] represent a real link to the ancient Israelites." Serge Etele, "Are There Lost Jewish Tribes in Cameroon?" Kulanu, 2015, http://cyan.olm.net/~kulanu/cameroon/losttribesincameroon.php.
41. On the Beti practice of circumcision, see P. Mviena, *Univers culturel et religieux du peuple béti* (Yaoundé, Cameroon: Imprimerie St. Paul, 1970), 119–21.
42. One of the few written versions of this origin story can be found in Engelbert Fouda Etoundi, *La tradition béti et la pratique de ses rites* (Yaoundé, Cameroon: Éditions Sopecam, 2012), 13–14.
43. For this singular narrative, see Jean-Marie Aubame, *Les béti du Gabon et d'ailleurs*, with Fidèle-Pierre Nze-Nguema and Henry Panhuys, vol. 1 (Paris: L'Harmattan, 2002), 97–118.
44. On the Christianization of the Beti, see Alexandre Nana, *Anthropologie béti et sens chrétien de l'homme* (Paris: L'Harmattan, 2010), 30–41; and Isidore Tabi, *Les rites béti au Christ: Essai de pastorale liturgique sur quelques rites de nos ancêtres* (Yaoundé, Cameroon: Imprimerie St. Paul, 1991), 8–10.
45. Estimates of the Bassa population range wildly, and I have been unable to find any reliable, recent sources to corroborate this figure.
46. This oral tradition has been recounted to me by Bassa elders. Versions that are very close to this one are available for perusal on numerous websites and online cultural heritage fora. For written sources focusing on supposed Jewish heritage, see Pierre Sende, *La route du sel: Chez les bassa du Cameroun* (Paris: L'Harmattan, 2014), 13–18; Jean Marcel Eugène Wognou, *Les basaa du Cameroun: Monographie historique d'après la tradition orale* (Niamey, Niger: Organisation de l'unité africaine, 1985), 24; and Eugène Wonyu, *L'histoire des basaa du Cameroun de l'Égypte des Pharaons à nos jours* (Paris: UNESCO, 1972).

47. See Sigmund Freud, *Moses and Monotheism*, trans. Katherine Jones (New York: Vintage Books, 1967).
48. For more on Bassa resistance, see Martin-René Atangana, *The End of French Rule in Cameroon* (Lanham, MD: University Press of America, 2010), 57–62.
49. A full explanation of this concept can be found in Mark Dike DeLancey, Rebecca Neh Mbuh, and Mark W. DeLancey, *Historical Dictionary of the Republic of Cameroon* (Metuchen, NJ: Scarecrow Press, 1990), 63–64.
50. Deane W. Ferm, *Third World Liberation Theologies: An Introductory Survey* (Maryknoll, NY: Orbis Books, 1987), 59.
51. Cited in Claire Robertson, "Violence and Tribes: Beyond Politics in Kenya," *Origins: Current Events in Historical Perspective* 1, no. 7 (2008), http://www .origins.osu.edu/article/beyond-tribes-violence-and-politics-kenya/page/0/1.
52. Cited in Armand Alain Mbili, *D'une église missionnaire à une église africaine nationale: L'observatoire du grand séminaire d'Otélé, 1949–1968* (Paris: L'Harmattan, 2009), 96–97.
53. Kato, *Theological Pitfalls in Africa*, 50.
54. Albert de Surgy, *L'église du christianisme céleste: Un exemple d'église prophétique au Bénin* (Paris: Karthala, 2001), 60.
55. Christine Henry, *Force des anges: Rites, hiérarchie et divination dans le Christianisme Céleste* (Turnhout, Belgium: Brepols, 2008), 263.
56. M. L. Daneel, *Quest for Belonging: Introduction to a Study of African Independent Churches* (Gweru, Zimbabwe: Mambo Press, 1987), 241–42.
57. For the reasons that Gentiles have traditionally been considered exempt from following Mosaic Law, see Romans 8:1 and Acts 15:1–11.
58. Amy-Jill Levine and Marc Zvi Brettler, *The Jewish Annotated New Testament: New Revised Standard Version Bible Translation* (Oxford: Oxford University Press, 2011).
59. Daniel Boyarin, *The Jewish Gospels: The Story of the Jewish Christ* (New York: New Press, 2012), 157.
60. John S. Mbiti, "The Role of the Jewish Bible in African Independent Churches," *International Review of Missions* 93, no. 369 (2004): 221.
61. Séverin Cécile Abega, "Prologue: Le Cameroun et la religion traditionelle," in *Histoire du christianisme au Cameroun: Des origines à nos jours*, ed. Jean-Paul Messina and Jaap van Slageren (Paris: Karthala, 2005), 20.
62. Henry, *Force des anges*, 262.
63. Matthew Eric Engelke, *A Problem of Presence: Beyond Scripture in an African Church* (Berkeley: University of California Press, 2007), 64.
64. Éloi Messi Metogo, "Introduction: African Christianities," in *African Christianities*, ed. Éloi Messi Metogo (London: SCM Press, 2006), 7.

CHAPTER 4

1. The most comprehensive surveys of conventional Indian Jewish communities include Thomas A. Timberg, *Jews in India* (New York: Advent Books, 1986); Orpa Slapak, *The Jews of India: A Story of Three Communities* (Jerusalem: Israel Museum Press, 1995); and Nathan Katz, *Who Are the Jews of India?* (Berkeley: University of California Press, 2000). Yulia Egorova's *Jews and India:*

Perceptions and Image (London: Routledge, 2006) not only presents detailed histories of each community, but also provides the historical context for the image of the Jew in the Indian imagination. For an overview of Jewish Pakistan, see Yoel Moses Reuben, *The Jews of Pakistan: A Forgotten Heritage* (Mumbai: Bene Israel Heritage Museum and Genealogical Research Centre, 2010).

2. See, for example, Myer Samra, "The Tribe of Manasseh: 'Judaism' in the Hills of Manipur and Mizoram," *Man in India* 71, no. 1 (1991): 183–202; again, Samra, "Judaism in Manipur and Mizoram: A By-product of Christian Mission," *Australian Journal of Jewish Studies* 6, no. 1 (1992): 7–22; and Shalva Weil, "Lost Israelites from the Indo-Burmese Borderlands: Re-traditionalisation and Conversion among the Shinlung or Bene Menasseh," *Anthropologist* 6, no. 3 (2004): 219–33.

3. The most relevant works by Egorova and Perwez are "Old Memories, New Histories"; "Telugu Jews"; and *Jews of Andhra Pradesh*.

4. Differences between my perspectives on the Bene Ephraim and those of Egorova and Perwez may be attributed to several factors. First, my time with the community was spent almost entirely in the vicinity of Shmuel Yacobi's headquarters in Vijayawada and Machilipatnam, while Egorova and Perwez concentrated their time on the ground in Sadok Yacobi's community in Kothareddypalem. Second, my experience of the movement, from the time of my fieldwork and since, has been with Shmuel at the head of all the community's leadership tasks, whereas the experience of Egorova and Perwez included the period in which Sadok still played a role in most activities. Third, our perspectives differ somewhat due to disciplinary variables. For instance, the ethnographic work of Egorova and Perwez tends to focus on quotidian "performances" of Jewishness in social, political, and historical (South) Indian contexts, while mine leans more toward discursive examinations of oral history, rhetorical practice, and creative multimedia, especially in the realm of textually articulated ideologies.

5. For general information on the Madiga, see Tulja Ram Singh, *The Madiga: A Study in Social Structure and Change* (Lucknow, India: Ethnographic and Folk Culture Society, 1969); and K. Rajasekhara Reddy, "The Madigas: A Scheduled Caste Population of Andhra Pradesh," *Man and Life: Journal of the Institute of Social Research and Applied Anthropology, Calcutta* 33, no. 1–2 (2007): 81–88.

6. See David Mosse, "The Catholic Church and Dalit Christian Activism in Contemporary Tamil Nadu," in *Margins of Faith: Dalit and Tribal Christianity in India*, ed. Rowena Robinson and Joseph Marianus Kujur (Thousand Oaks, CA: Sage, 2010), 250–51.

7. For background on the Christianization of the Dravidian Scheduled Castes, see Chandra Mallampalli, *Christians and Public Life in Colonial South India, 1863–1937: Contending with Marginality* (New York: RoutledgeCurzon, 2004). For specific information on the Christianization of the Telugu, see G. A. Oddie, "Christian Conversion in the Telugu Country, 1860–1900: A Case Study of One Protestant Movement in the Godavery-Krishna Delta," *Indian Economic and Social History Review* 12, no. 1 (1975): 61–79. See also the historiographic analysis of the phenomenon by James Elisha Taneti in his *History of the Telugu Christians: A Bibliography* (Lanham, MD: Scarecrow Press, 2011), 1–15.

8. Jason L. Francisco, "'Discovering' the Telugu Jews of India," in *Jews in Places You Never Thought Of*, ed. Karen Primack (Hoboken, NJ: Ktav, 1998), 256.

9. Egorova and Perwez, *Jews of Andhra Pradesh*, 15.

10. According to the 2001 census (which contains the latest reliable demographic figures on Andhra Pradesh's lower castes), Madiga constitute 49.2 percent of the Scheduled Caste population in Andhra Pradesh—over six million people. Government of India, Ministry of Home Affairs, "Andhra Pradesh Data Highlights: The Scheduled Castes," accessed August 19, 2015, http://censusindia.gov .in/Tables_Published/SCST/dh_sc_andhra.pdf.

11. According to the same census, Mala (who figure slightly higher than Madiga in social status) constitute 41.6 percent of the Scheduled Castes in Andhra Pradesh, which brings their numbers to over five million people. Ibid. For general information on the Mala, see K. Rathnaiah, *Social Change among Malas: An Ex-untouchable Caste in South India* (New Delhi: Discovery, 1991). For relations between the Mala and Madiga, see P. Pratap Kumar, "Andhra Pradesh: Economic and Social Relations," in *The Modern Anthropology of India: Ethnography, Themes and Theory*, ed. Peter Berger and Frank Heidemann (New York: Routledge, 2013), 15–17; and B. Sunil Vara Kumar, *Dynamics of Power Sharing between Mala and Madiga in Church* (Delhi: ISPCK, 2010), esp. 27–72. On the development of the concept of Sanskritisation, see A. M. Shah, "Sanskritisation Revisited," *Sociological Bulletin* 54, no. 2 (2005): 238–49; and Mysore Narasimhachar Srinivas, *Caste in Modern India: And Other Essays* (New York: Asia Publishing House, 1962), 42–62. See also Egorova's perspective on Sanskritisation among the Bene Ephraim in her *Jews and India*, 123–25. For the Islamic equivalent of this concept, frequently dubbed "genealogical sophistication," see Fallou Ngom, "Murid Ajami Sources of Knowledge: The Myth and the Reality," in *From Dust to Digital: Ten Years of the Endangered Archives Programme*, ed. Maja Kominko (Cambridge: Open Book, 2015), 348. Finally it is worthy of mention that during my fieldwork in India, I encountered at least half a dozen Bene Ephraim community members who hail from the Mala caste. This is a notable increase from the previous reports of only one Mala (Egorova and Perwez, *Jews of Andhra Pradesh*, 159) among the other Bene Ephraim congregants of Madiga parentage.

12. See Egorova and Perwez, *Jews of Andhra Pradesh*, 132–39, for more on Yehoshua Yacobi.

13. Shmuel Yacobi, "Eretz Ephraim Pictures—Educate, Work, and Achieve Peace," Writers-Network, accessed August 4, 2015, http://www.writers-network.com /index.cgi?m=1&do=profile&who=21560.

14. Ibid.

15. Ibid.

16. Shmuel Yacobi, "Writer and His Background," Booksie, accessed July 7, 2015, http://www.booksie.com/shmuel_yacobi.

17. Shmuel Yacobi, "The Religious Myth of the Lost Tribes of Israel," *The Lost Tribes of Israel* (blog), June 4, 2011, http://shmuelyacobimssraju.blogspot.com /2011/06/religious-myth-of-lost-tribes-of-israel.html.

18. Debarshi Dasgupta, "Come as You Are, David," *Outlook*, July 15, 2013, http:// www.outlookindia.com/article/come-as-you-are-david/286668.

19. World Bank, "India Overview," accessed May 13, 2014, http://www.worldbank .org/en/country/india/overview; Associated Press, "India Census Says 70 Percent Live in Villages, Most Are Poor," *New York Times*, July 3, 2015, http://www .nytimes.com/aponline/2015/07/03/world/asia/ap-as-india-rural-poverty.html.

20. This is, of course, a gross generalization, but a common one nonetheless. See, for instance, Dean Nelson, "Guide Launched 'To Help Overcome Fear of

India's Corrupt Police,'" *The Telegraph*, August 30, 2011, http://www.telegraph .co.uk/news/worldnews/asia/india/8731260/Guide-launched-to-help-overcome -fear-of-Indias-corrupt-police.html.

21. World Bank, Poverty Reduction and Economic Management Network, "The State of the Poor: Where Are the Poor and Where Are They Poorest?," accessed August 10, 2015, http://www.worldbank.org/content/dam/Worldbank /document/State_of_the_poor_paper_April17.pdf.

22. *The Hindu*, "India Can Become Economically Developed by 2020: Kalam," April 29, 2011, http://www.thehindu.com/business/Economy/india-can -become-economically-developed-by-2020-kalam/article1821445.ece.

23. Government of India, Ministry of Home Affairs, "Religion," accessed August 20, 2015, http://censusindia.gov.in/Census_And_You/religion.aspx.

24. Ibid.

25. Fritz Blackwell, *India: A Global Studies Handbook* (Santa Barbara, CA: ABC-CLIO, 2004), 102.

26. Government of India, Ministry of Information and Broadcasting, *Jawaharlal Nehru's Speeches*, vol. 3, *September 1953–August 1957* (Delhi: Publications Division, Ministry of Information and Broadcasting, 1950), 36–37.

27. See Sumit Ganguly, *Hindu Nationalism and the Foreign Policy of India's Bharatiya Janata Party*, Transatlantic Academy Paper Series, 2014–15, vol. 2 (Washington, DC: Transatlantic Academy, 2015), 1–15.

28. According to the constitutional amendment on the religious orders of Scheduled Castes (enacted in 1990), only Hindu, Buddhist, or Sikh religious affiliations are possible for those belonging to disadvantaged groups.

29. Government of India, Ministry of Home Affairs, "Scheduled Castes and Scheduled Tribes," accessed July 30, 2015, http://censusindia.gov.in/Census_And _You/scheduled_castes_and_sceduled_tribes.aspx; Subodh Ghildiyal, "SCs/STs Form Half of India's Poor: Survey," *Times of India*, April 12, 2011, http://www .timesofindia.indiatimes.com/india/SCs/STs-form-half-of-Indias-poor-Survey /articleshow/7953487.cms.

30. Subodh Ghildiyal, "SCs/STs Form Half of India's Poor."

31. On the religious origins of the caste system, see, for example, Marut Lama, *Classifying the Universe: The Ancient Indian Varna System and the Origins of Caste* (Oxford: Oxford University Press, 1994); and Hira Singh, *Recasting Caste: From the Sacred to the Profane* (New Delhi: Sage, 2014).

32. V. B. Krishnaiah Chetty, *Scheduled Castes and Development Programmes in India* (Allahabad, India: Vohra, 1991), 35.

33. Herbert Hope Risley, *The People of India* (Calcutta: Thacker, Spink, 1915), 5.

34. Ibid.

35. Cited in *Young India*, January 21, 1926, 30.

36. On this topic, see Gail Omvedt, *Buddhism in India: Challenging Brahmanism and Caste* (Thousand Oaks, CA: Sage, 2003). See also Egorova and Perwez, *Jews of Andhra Pradesh*, 171–72, for a discussion on Ambedkar and the comparative conversion strategies of Dalits.

37. Cited in Deepak M. Wankhede, *Geographical Thought of Dr. B. R. Ambedkar* (Delhi: Gautam Book Centre, 2009), 164.

38. Ankur Barua, *Debating "Conversion" in Hinduism and Christianity* (New York: Routledge, 2015), 42.

39. Rowena Robinson and Joseph Marianus Kujur, introduction to *Margins of Faith: Dalit and Tribal Christianity in India*, ed. Rowena Robinson and Joseph Marianus Kujur (Thousand Oaks, CA: Sage, 2010), 5.

40. On the subject of caste differentiation among Muslims in India, see Syed Ali, "Collective and Elective Ethnicity: Caste among Urban Muslims in India," *Sociological Forum* 17, no. 4 (2002): 593–620; and the case study authored by Mattison Mines, "Social Stratification among Muslim Tamils in Tamil Nadu, South India," in *Caste and Social Stratification among Muslims in India*, ed. Imtiaz Ahmad (New Delhi: Manohar, 1978), 159–69.

41. Katz, *Who Are the Jews of India?*, 3.

42. Nathan Katz and Ellen S. Goldberg, *Kashrut, Caste, and Kabbalah: The Religious Life of the Jews of Cochin* (New Delhi: Manohar, 2007), 15.

43. For an overview of such theories, see Abraham Benhur, *The Jewish Background of Indian People: A Historical, Archaeological, Anthropological, and Etymological Study of the Lost Tribes* (Calcutta: Jeevanist Books, 2011); Holger Kersten, *Jesus Lived in India: His Unknown Life Before and After the Crucifixion* (Rockport, MA: Element, 1994), esp. 40–55 and 219–32; and Levi, *The Aquarian Gospel of Jesus the Christ: The Philosophic and Practical Basis of the Religion of the Aquarian Age of the World* (Los Angeles: DeVorss, 1964), esp. 39–60.

44. Shalva Weil, "The Heritage and Legacy of the Jews of India," in *India's Jewish Heritage: Ritual, Art, and Life-Cycle*, ed. Shalva Weil (Mumbai: Marg, 2002), 9.

45. Ibid.

46. Ibid., 10. There are less reliable accounts attesting to such a presence (in Cochin) dating to the second century CE, which are found in the apocryphal compilation of the "Acts of Thomas." For more on these legends, see Nathan Katz and Ellen S. Goldberg, *The Last Jews of Cochin: Jewish Identity in Hindu India* (Columbia: University of South Carolina Press, 1993), 8–13.

47. For specifics, see Parfitt, *Thirteenth Gate*, 37.

48. For more on the Jews of Cochin, see Katz, *Who Are the Jews of India?*, 9–89; and Katz and Goldberg, *Kashrut, Caste, and Kabbalah*.

49. On this "discovery," see Parfitt, *Thirteenth Gate*, 38. For more on the Bene Israel, see Shirley Berry Isenberg, "The Bene Israel," in *The Jews of India: A Story of Three Communities*, ed. Orpa Slapak (Jerusalem: Israel Museum, 1995), 17–23; and Katz, *Who Are the Jews of India?*, 90–125.

50. Estimate according to Ruchama Weiss and Levi Brackman, "India's Young Jews Eye Israel," *Ynet News*, June 20, 2015, http://www.ynetnews.com/articles/0,7340,L-4670233,00.html.

51. Ibid.

52. Jael Miriam Silliman, *Jewish Portraits, Indian Frames: Women's Narratives from a Diaspora of Hope* (Hanover, NH: University Press of New England, 2001), 18. For information on the Baghdadi Jews, see Katz, *Who Are the Jews of India?*, 126–60.

53. I take these qualifiers from Yulia Egorova, "Jewish Themes in the Press of Independent India," in *Jews, Muslims, and Mass Media: Mediating the "Other,"* ed. Yulia Egorova and Tudor Parfitt (London: RoutledgeCurzon, 2007), 91.

54. David Cohen, "No Country Has More Friends of Israel Than . . . India?," *Daily Caller*, August 18, 2014, http://dailycaller.com/2014/08/18/no-country-has-more-friends-of-israel-than-india/.

55. For more on these attacks, see James Glanz, Sebastian Rotella, and David E. Sanger, "In 2008 Mumbai Attacks, Piles of Spy Data, but an Uncompleted Puzzle," *New York Times*, December 21, 2014, http://www.nytimes.com/2014/12 /22/world/asia/in-2008-mumbai-attacks-piles-of-spy-data-but-an-uncompleted -puzzle.html?_r=0.

56. On the relationship between Sharon Galsulkar and the Bene Ephraim, see the film *Next Year in Bombay*, directed by Jonas Parienté and Mathias Mangin (Tel-Aviv: J.M.T. Films, 2011), DVD; and Egorova and Perwez, *Jews of Andhra Pradesh*, 106–7. On the similarities between the Children of Manasseh and Bene Ephraim movements, see Egorova and Perwez, *Jews of Andhra Pradesh*, 74–75.

57. Yacobi, "Religious Myth."

58. Cited in Dasgupta, "Come as You Are, David."

59. I did not have access to this typescript, *The History of Telugu Jewish Community of A. P. India*, as it was apparently lost before the time of my fieldwork in India.

60. Shmuel Yacobi, *The Cultural Hermeneutics: An Introduction to the Cultural Trans-lations of the Hebrew Bible among the Ancient Nations of the Thalmulic Telugu Empire of India* (Vijayawada, India: Hebrew Open University, 2002). (Note: in Shmuel's writings, the term "Thalmulic" is equated with the term "Talmudic.")

61. Ibid., 133.

62. This idea has much in common with (for instance) the theory propagated by George Moore, in *The Lost Tribes and the Saxons of the East and of the West, with New Views of Buddhism, and Translations of Rock-Records in India* (London: Longman, Green, Longman, and Roberts, 1861), 143–60.

63. For background on the characters of Manu and Harishchandra, see John Dow-son, *A Classical Dictionary of Hindu Mythology and Religion, Geography, History, and Literature* (London: Routledge and K. Paul, 1961), 199–201 and 118–19, respectively. For more on Draupadi, see Tripurari Chakravarti, "Main Women Characters in the Mahabharata," in *Great Women of India*, ed. Swami Madhava-nanda and Ramesh C. Majumdar (Mayavati: Advaita Ashram, 1963), 169–81.

64. Egorova and Perwez, *Jews of Andhra Pradesh*, 11.

65. The portions of the Cavilah as they appear in this section were recounted to me in English by Shmuel.

66. The most comprehensive account of the golem legend is Moshe Idel's *Golem: Jewish Magical and Mystical Traditions on the Artificial Anthropoid* (Albany: State University of New York Press, 1990).

67. For more on the origins and symbolism of the *Shekhinah*, see Raphael Patai, *The Hebrew Goddess*, 3d ed. (Detroit: Wayne State University Press, 1990), esp. 96–135.

68. Shmuel Yacobi, "Three-Tier Human Lives," *Three-Tier Human Lives* (blog), December 23, 2012, http://www.threetierhumanlives.blogspot.com/2012/12 /three-tier-human-lives-we-humans-have.html.

69. See Santosha Bharatiya, *Dalit and Minority Empowerment* (New Delhi: Rajkamal Prakashan, 2008), 52; and Raj Kumar, *Encyclopaedia of Untouchables Ancient, Medieval, and Modern* (Delhi: Kalpaz, 2008), 399.

70. A detailed summary of and examples buttressing this theory can be found in Yacobi, *Cultural Hermeneutics*, 295–374. Similar arguments on such lin-guistic connections have been posited in the past, most notably by Madan Mohan Shukla. For more on this topic, see Shukla's "Hebrews and Vedic

Aryans," *Vishveshvaranand Indological Journal* 14, no. 1 (1976): 41–47; and his "The Hebrews Belong to a Branch of Vedic Aryans," *Journal of the Oriental Institute* (University of Baroda) 28, no. 3–4 (1979): 44–57.

71. See P. K. Mohanty, *Encyclopedia of Scheduled Tribes in India* (Delhi: Isha Books, 2006), 75.

72. Dianne E. Jenett, "Menstruating Women/Menstruating Goddesses: Sites of Sacred Power in India," in *Menstruation: A Cultural History*, ed. Andrew Shail and Gillian Howie (New York: Palgrave Macmillian, 2005), 176. For more on the rituals connected to menstruation in South India, see Sarah Caldwell, *Oh Terrifying Mother: Sexuality, Violence, and Worship of the Goddess Kali* (New York: Oxford University Press, 1999), 115–22.

73. For instance: "The Aryans had their strong Brahminical hierarchy, while the priests of the Dravidians were self-created, respected according to their skill in magic and sorcery. The Aryans burned their dead; their widows were not allowed to re-marry; they abhorred the eating of flesh and the spilling of blood. The Dravidians, on the other hand, buried their dead; their widows re-married; they ate flesh of all kinds, and no ceremony could take place without the excessive use of strong drink and the spilling of blood." Emma Rauschenbusch-Clough, *While Sewing Sandals; Or, Tales of a Telugu Pariah Tribe* (London: Hodder and Stoughton, 1899), 11.

74. See also Egorova and Perwez, *Jews of Andhra Pradesh*, 73.

75. Despite Shmuel's claims that the Bene Ephraim do not lend credence to the ideas of miracles or divine healing, several visitors to the community have commented on this very tendency. For instance, see the account of Francisco, "'Discovering' the Telugu Jews of India," 259.

76. From the community's perspective, the most important such visit to occur thus far was that of Rabbi Eliyahu Avichail of Amishav, in 1994.

77. Other persons associated with Kulanu have visited since that time, but no visit has been so high-profile. For a detailed account of the relationship between Kulanu and the Bene Ephraim, see Egorova and Perwez, *Jews of Andhra Pradesh*, 97–113.

78. Ibid., 109.

79. For more on the debate surrounding formal conversion, see the account in ibid., 71–72 and 120.

80. Ibid., 142–67.

81. Michael Shelomo Bar-Ron, *Guide for the Noahide* (Springdale, AR: Lightcatcher Books, 2009), 3.

82. Shmuel Yacobi, "World Peace at Last!," *World Peace Through Hebrew Culture* (blog), December 22, 2012, http://www.worldpeacethroughhebrewculture .blogspot.com/2012/12/world-peace-at-last-majority-humans.html.

83. Noahide World Center, "Our Center," January 9, 2011, http://www .noahideworldcenter.org/wp_en/category/about/.

84. Interaction with members of this group took place during a return trip to India in December 2013.

85. Shmuel Yacobi, "Hebrew Cultural Family Counseling Center," *Hebrew Cultural Family Counseling Center* (blog), December 21, 2012, http://www .hebrewculturalfamilycounselingcenter.blogspot.com/2012/12/hebrew-cultural -family-counseling.html.

86. Ibid.
87. Shahid Perwez, e-mail message to author, July 18, 2010.
88. Shmuel Yacobi, "John Milton at Pandemonium," accessed October 6, 2011, http://www.poetrypoem.com/cgi-bin/index.pl?poemnumber=1098240&sitename=shmuelyacobi&poemoffset=0&displaypoem=t&item=poetry.
89. Ibid.
90. Shmuel Yacobi, "The Prince of Whales," accessed October 2, 2012, http://www.storymania.com/cgibin/sm2/smreadtitle.cgi?action=display&file=novels/YacobiS-ThePrinceOfWhales.htm.
91. Shmuel Yacobi, *Hebrew and Telugu Menorah Songs* (Vijayawada, India: Eretz Ephraim Productions, 2011).
92. See, for instance, Shmuel Yacobi, "Tel-English Songs from South India," YouTube video, 4:12, posted by shmuelyacobi, February 17, 2011, https://www.youtube.com/watch?v=WiOf_7eTSOs.
93. Shmuel Yacobi, "Tel-English Songs from South India," YouTube video, 5:26, posted by shmuelyacobi, February 16, 2011, https://www.youtube.com/watch?v=jdTxY9C6Nbo.
94. Shmuel Yacobi, "Hebrew Menorah Songs from South India," YouTube video, 4:05, posted by shmuelyacobi, February 7, 2011, https://www.youtube.com/watch?v=ZgoEyyn2oP8; and Shmuel Yacobi, "Hebrew Menorah Songs from South India," YouTube video, 5:02, posted by shmuelyacobi, February 7, 2011, https://www.youtube.com/watch?v=4i6FEvaapGo.
95. Shmuel Yacobi, "Tel-English Songs from South India," YouTube video, 3:17, posted by shmuelyacobi, February 16, 2011, https://www.youtube.com/watch?v=a-diuPbeG8I; and Yacobi, "Tel-English Songs from South India," YouTube video, 4:12.
96. Shmuel Yacobi, "Tel-English Songs from South India," YouTube video, 2:08, posted by shmuelyacobi, February 17, 2011, https://www.youtube.com/watch?v=QoR8bxSlPU8.
97. Yacobi, "Tel-English Songs from South India," YouTube video, 4:12.
98. The only difference between the singer's words and the biblical text is the pronominal suffix attached to the proper noun, "Shulamite" (*shulamiti* in Hebrew).
99. Shmuel Yacobi, "Hebrew Menorah Songs from South India," YouTube video, 4:22, posted by shmuelyacobi, February 16, 2011, https://www.youtube.com/watch?v=1Nd2qxwf8as.
100. Shmuel Yacobi, "Hebrew Menorah Songs from South India," YouTube video, 7:14, posted by shmuelyacobi, February 16, 2011, https://www.youtube.com/watch?v=gaFwnyLRgQs.
101. Shmuel Yacobi, "Hebrew Menorah Songs from South India," YouTube video, 4:05.
102. Shmuel Yacobi, "Eretz Ephraim Pictures and World Peace Promotion," *World Peace* (blog), May 22, 2011, http://internationalprotestantpope.blogspot.com/.
103. Ibid.
104. The full verse is as follows: "Is Ephraim a darling son unto Me? Is he a child that is dandled? For as often as I speak of him, I do earnestly remember him still; therefore My heart yearneth for him, I will surely have compassion upon him, saith the LORD."

105. Tudor Parfitt, "DNA, Indian Jews, Manipuris, and the Telugu Speaking Community," Kulanu, 2002, http://www.kulanu.org/india/dnamarker.php. See the similar comment by Parfitt in his article "Tribal Jews" in *Indo-Judaic Studies in the Twenty-First Century: A View from the Margin*, ed. Nathan Katz et al. (New York: Palgrave Macmillan, 2007), 190.

106. Shmuel Yacobi, "The Andhra Pradesh Bene Ephraim Community," *Bene Ephraim Community* (blog), September 12, 2012, http://www .thebeneephraimcommunity.blogspot.com/2012/09/the-andhra-pradesh-bene -ephraim.html.

107. The film in question is *Next Year in Bombay*, directed by Jonas Parienté and Mathias Mangin. The CD is by Irene Orleansky, *Music of Israelites and Jews of Africa and Asia* (Moscow: Music Brothers Records, 2014).

108. Shmuel Yacobi, "Eretz Ephraim," Bnei Ephraim Community, accessed August 2, 2015, http://www.bneiephraimcommunity.com/eretz_ephraim.html.

109. Ibid.

CHAPTER 5

1. Timothy C. Tennent, *Theology in the Context of World Christianity: How the Global Church Is Influencing the Way We Think About and Discuss Theology* (Grand Rapids, MI: Zondervan, 2007), 2.

2. Joane Nagel, "False Faces: Ethnic Identity, Authenticity, and Fraud in Native American Discourse and Politics," in *Identity and Social Change*, ed. J. E. Davis (New Brunswick, NJ: Transaction, 2000), 83.

3. See Jeremy Stolow, "Salvation by Electricity," in *Religion: Beyond a Concept*, ed. Hent de Vries (New York: Fordham University Press, 2007), 668–86.

4. Cited in Sam Kestenbaum, "Black Jewish Congregations Get Their Own Prayer Book, After Nearly a Century," *Tablet*, September 9, 2014, http://www .tabletmag.com/jewish-life-and-religion/183821/black-jewish-siddur.

5. See "Ugandan Jews Get Official Recognition from Jewish Agency," Jewish Telegraphic Agency, April 12, 2016, http://www.jta.org/2016/04/12/news -opinion/israel-middle-east/ugandan-jews-get-official-recognition-from-jewish -agency.

6. Yisrael Yeshayahu, "A Visit to Eritrea and Abyssinia," *Gesher* 4 (1958): 56. Hebrew. Translation mine.

7. Dan Sperber, *Explaining Culture: A Naturalistic Approach* (Oxford: Blackwell, 1996), 25.

8. Peter Berger, "Secularism in Retreat," *The National Interest* 46 (1996): 3.

9. For example, see "Who Are Britain's Jihadists?," *BBC*, September 8, 2015, http://www.bbc.com/news/uk-32026985.

10. Jeffrey Haynes, *Religious Transnational Actors and Soft Power* (Burlington: Ashgate, 2012), 6.

11. On the conversions to Islam of these two leaders, see "Bokassa, Jean-Bedel" and "Bongo Ondimba, Omar," in *Dictionary of African Biography*, vol. 1, ed. Emmanuel Kwaku Akyeampong and Henry Louis Gates Jr. (Oxford: Oxford University Press, 2012), 480 and 489, respectively.

12. On the community in Madagascar, see William F. S. Miles, "The Malagasy Secret," *Jerusalem Report*, September 3, 2015, http://www.jpost.com/Jerusalem-Report/The-Malagasy-secret-415164; Sam Kestenbaum, "'Joining Fabric of World Jewish Community,' 100 Convert on African Island of Madagascar," *Forward*, May 24, 2016, http://forward.com/news/341106/joining-fabric-of-world-jewish-community-100-convert-on-african-island-of-m; Adam Eliyahu Berkowitz, "Mysterious Madagascar Community Practicing Jewish Rituals Officially Enters Covenant of Abraham," *Breaking Israel News*, May 30, 2016, http://www.breakingisraelnews.com/68765/100-members-of-lost-jewish-community-of-madagascar-enter-covenant-of-abraham-05-16; and Deborah Josefson, "In Remote Madagascar, a New Community Chooses to Be Jewish," Jewish Telegraphic Agency, June 5, 2016, http://www.jta.org/2016/06/05/news-opinion/world/in-remote-madagascar-a-new-community-chooses-to-be-jewish.

13. On these perceptions of Israelite provenance, see Edith Bruder, *Black Jews of Africa*, 124–32, 178–84; and again, Bruder, "The Descendants of David in Madagascar: Crypto-Judaism in Twentieth-Century Africa," in *Race, Color, Identity: Rethinking Discourses About "Jews" in the Twenty-First Century*, ed. Efraim Sicher (New York: Berghahn Books, 2013), 196–214.

Abbey, Hubert Nii. *Homowo in Ghana*. Accra: Studio Brian Communications, 2010.

Abega, Séverin Cécile. "Prologue: Le Cameroun et la religion traditionelle." In *Histoire du christianisme au Cameroun: Des origines à nos jours*, edited by Jean-Paul Messina and Jaap van Slageren, 15–21. Paris: Karthala, 2005.

Abu El-Haj, Nadia. *The Genealogical Science: The Search for Jewish Origins and the Politics of Epistemology*. Chicago: University of Chicago Press, 2012.

Achebe, Chinua. *Things Fall Apart*. London: Heinemann, 1958.

Addo, Emmanuel Isaac Kpakpo. *Worldview, Way of Life, and Worship: The Continuing Encounter between the Christian Faith and Ga Religion and Culture*. Zoetermeer, Netherlands: Boekencentrum Academic, 2009.

Adutwum, Ofosu. "The Suspected Adulteress: Ancient Israelite and Traditional Akan Treatment." *Expository Times* 104, no. 2 (1992): 38–42.

Agyekum, Kofi. "Menstruation as a Verbal Taboo among the Akan of Ghana." *Journal of Anthropological Research* 58, no. 3 (2002): 367–87.

Ahmad, Aijaz. *In Theory: Classes, Nations, Literatures*. New York: Verso, 1992.

Akyeampong, Emmanuel Kwaku, and Henry Louis Gates Jr., eds. *Dictionary of African Biography*. Vol. 1. Oxford: Oxford University Press, 2012.

Al-Bakri, Abu 'Ubayd. "The Book of Routes and Realms." In *Corpus of Early Arabic Sources for West African History*, edited by N. Levtzion and J. E. F. Hopkins, 79–80. Cambridge: Cambridge University Press, 1981.

Ali, Syed. "Collective and Elective Ethnicity: Caste among Urban Muslims in India." *Sociological Forum* 17, no. 4 (2002): 593–620.

Allotey-Pappoe, Ebenezer. "The Homowo Festival: The Harvest Festival of the Ga People." *Ghana Bulletin of Theology* 1, no. 7 (1959): 1–3.

Amah, Charles. *Ga Homowo and Other Ga-Adangme Festivals*. Accra, Ghana: Sedco, 1982.

Amanor, Jones Darkwa. "Pentecostalism in Ghana: An African Reformation." *Cyberjournal for Pentecostal-Charismatic Research*, April 13, 2004. http://www.pctii.org/cyberj/cyberj13/amanor.html.

Amoah, Elizabeth. "The Woman Who Decided to Break the Rules." In *New Eyes for Reading: Biblical and Theological Reflections by Women from the Third World*, edited by John S. Pobee and Barbel Van Wartenberg-Potter, 3–4. Geneva: World Council of Churches, 1986.

Andersen, Nicole, and Scott London. "South Africa's Newest 'Jews': The Moemedi Pentecostal Church and the Construction of Jewish Identity." *Nova Religio: The Journal of Alternative and Emergent Religions* 13, no. 1 (2009): 92–105.

Anderson, Allan H. *African Reformation: African Initiated Christianity in the 20th Century.* Trenton, NJ: Africa World Press, 1995.
———. *To the Ends of the Earth: Pentecostalism and the Transformation of World Christianity.* Oxford: Oxford University Press, 2013.
Anderson, Benedict. *Imagined Communities: Reflections on the Origin and Spread of Nationalism.* London: Verso, 1991.
Anderson, Robert T. *The Keepers: An Introduction to the History and Culture of the Samaritans.* Peabody, MA: Hendrickson, 2002.
Appiah-Kubi, Kofi. "Indigenous African Christian Churches: Signs of Authenticity." In *Third World Liberation Theologies: A Reader,* edited by Deane William Ferm, 222–30. Maryknoll, NY: Orbis Books, 1986.
Asafo, Nikasemo. "Lecture 1: A People Blessed." Accessed May 5, 2014. http://www.gadangmenikasemoasafo.wordpress.com/the-king-taki-tawiah-memorial-lectures/lecture-i-a-people-blessed/.
Asamoah-Gyadu, J. Kwabena. "'We Are on the Internet': Contemporary Pentecostalism in Africa and the New Culture of Online Religion." In *New Media and Religious Transformation in Africa,* edited by Rosalind I. J. Hackett and Benjamin F. Soares, 157–70. Bloomington: Indiana University Press, 2015.
Astren, Fred. *Karaite Judaism and Historical Understanding.* Columbia: University of South Carolina Press, 2004.
Atangana, Martin-René. *The End of French Rule in Cameroon.* Lanham, MD: University Press of America, 2010.
Aubame, Jean-Marie. *Les béti du Gabon et d'ailleurs.* With Fidèle-Pierre Nze-Nguema and Henry Panhuys. Vol. 1. Paris: L'Harmattan, 2002.
Aviv, Caryn, and David Shneer. *New Jews: The End of the Jewish Diaspora.* New York: New York University Press, 2005.
Ayegboyin, Deji, and S. Ademola Ishola. "African Indigenous Churches: An Historical Perspective." Institute for Religious Research, 1997. http://www.irr.org/african-indigenous-churches-chapter-fourteen.
Ba, Diadie. "Africans Still Seething over Sarkozy Speech." Reuters, September 5, 2007. http://www.uk.reuters.com/article/2007/09/05/uk-africa-sarkozy-idUKL0513034620070905.
Baer, Yitzhak. *A History of the Jews in Christian Spain.* Vol. 1. Philadelphia: Jewish Publication Society of America, 1961.
Baiden, Daniel. "The Ghanaian Village that Wants to Be Jewish." In *Jews in Places You Never Thought Of,* edited by Karen Primack, 264–70. Hoboken, NJ: Ktav, 1998.
Balibar, Etienne, and Immanuel Wallerstein. *Race, Nation, Class: Ambiguous Identities.* Translated by Chris Turner. New York: Verso, 1991.
Bar-Ron, Michael Shelomo. *Guide for the Noahide.* Springdale, AR: Lightcatcher Books, 2009.
Barua, Ankur. *Debating "Conversion" in Hinduism and Christianity.* New York: Routledge, 2015.
Benhur, Abraham. *The Jewish Background of Indian People: A Historical, Archaeological, Anthropological, and Etymological Study of the Lost Tribes.* Calcutta: Jeevanist Books, 2011.
Benite, Zvi Ben-Dor. *The Ten Lost Tribes: A World History.* Oxford: Oxford University Press, 2009.

Ben-Rafael, Eliezer. *Jewish Identities: Fifty Intellectuals Answer Ben Gurion*. Leiden: Brill, 2002.

Berger, Peter. "Secularism in Retreat." *The National Interest* 46 (Winter 1996): 3–13.

Berkowitz, Adam Eliyahu. "Mysterious Madagascar Community Practicing Jewish Rituals Officially Enters Covenant of Abraham." *Breaking Israel News*. May 30, 2016. http://www.breakingisraelnews.com/68765/100-members-of-lost-jewish-community-of-madagascar-enter-covenant-of-abraham-05-16.

Bhabha, Homi. *The Location of Culture*. London: Routledge, 1994.

Bharatiya, Santosha. *Dalit and Minority Empowerment*. New Delhi: Rajkamal Prakashan, 2008.

"Bienvenu sur le site web de la communauté juive Beth Yeshourun du Cameroun." Beth Yeshourun. Accessed July 2, 2014. http://beth-yeshouroun.mywebcommunity.org/.

Blackwell, Fritz. *India: A Global Studies Handbook*. Santa Barbara, CA: ABC-CLIO, 2004.

Bob-Milliar, George, and Gloria Bob-Milliar. "Christianity in the Ghanaian State in the Past Fifty Years." GhanaWeb, February 28, 2007. http://www.ghanaweb.com/GhanaHomePage/features/artikel.php?ID=119921.

Boccaccini, Gabriele. "What Is a Judaism? Perspectives from Second Temple Jewish Studies." In *Religion or Ethnicity? Jewish Identities in Evolution*, edited by Zvi Gitelman, 24–37. New Brunswick, NJ: Rutgers University Press, 2009.

Bodian, Miriam. *Dying in the Law of Moses: Crypto-Jewish Martyrdom in the Iberian World*. Bloomington: Indiana University Press, 2007.

Boni, Stefano. "History and Ideology of an Akan Centre: The Cosmological Topography of Wiawso." *History and Anthropology* 18, no. 1 (2007): 25–50.

Borg, Marcus. *Speaking Christian: Why Christian Words Have Lost Their Meaning and Power—And How They Can Be Restored*. New York: HarperCollins, 2011.

Bowdich, Thomas Edward. *An Essay on the Superstitions, Customs and Arts Common to the Ancient Egyptians, Abyssinians, and Ashantees*. Paris: J. Smith, 1821.

Boyarin, Daniel. *The Jewish Gospels: The Story of the Jewish Christ*. New York: New Press, 2012.

Brettler, Marc Zvi. "My Bible: A Jew's Perspective." In *The Bible and the Believer: How to Read the Bible Critically and Religiously*, edited by Marc Zvi Brettler, Peter Enns, and Daniel J. Harrington, 21–65. Oxford: Oxford University Press, 2012.

Brettschneider, Marla. "African and African Heritage Jews: Western Academic Perspectives." *Sh'ma: A Journal of Jewish Responsibility*, March 2011. http://www.bjpa.org/Publications/downloadFile.cfm?FileID=8426.

———. *The Jewish Phenomenon in Sub-Saharan Africa: The Politics of Contradictory Discourses*. Lewiston, NY: Edwin Mellen, 2015.

Bruder, Edith. "The Beit Avraham of Kechene: The Emergence of a New Jewish Community in Ethiopia." In *Beta Israel: The Jews of Ethiopia and Beyond: History, Identity, and Borders*, edited by Emanuela Trevisan Semi and Shalva Weil, 181–96. Venice: Cafoscarina, 2011.

———. *The Black Jews of Africa: History, Religion, Identity*. Oxford: Oxford University Press, 2008.

———. *Black Jews: Les juifs noirs d'Afrique et le mythe des tribus perdues*. Paris: Albin Michel, 2014.

————. "The Descendants of David in Madagascar: Crypto-Judaism in Twentieth-Century Africa." In *Race, Color, Identity: Rethinking Discourses About "Jews" in the Twenty-First Century*, edited by Efraim Sicher, 196–214. New York: Berghahn Books, 2013.

Buber, Martin. *Israel and the World: Essays in a Time of Crisis.* New York: Schocken Books, 1963.

Busia, K. A. "The Ashanti." In *African Worlds: Studies in the Cosmological Ideas and Social Values of African Peoples*, edited by Daryll Forde, 190–209. Hamburg: LIT Verlag, 1999.

Caldwell, Sarah. *Oh Terrifying Mother: Sexuality, Violence, and Worship of the Goddess Kali.* New York: Oxford University Press, 1999.

"Cameroon." Shavei Israel. Accessed April 23, 2014. http://www.shavei.org/category /communities/other_communities/africa/cameroon/?lang=en.

Campbell, Heidi A. "Introduction: Studying Jewish Engagement with Digital Media and Culture." In *Digital Judaism: Jewish Negotiations with Digital Media and Culture*, edited by Heidi A. Campbell, 1–15. New York: Routledge, 2015.

————. "Understanding the Relationship between Religion Online and Offline in a Networked Society." *Journal of the American Academy of Religion* 80, no. 1 (2012): 64–93.

Castells, Manuel. *The Rise of the Network Society.* Vol. 1. 2d ed. Chichester, West Sussex: Wiley-Blackwell, 2009.

Chakravarti, Tripurari. "Main Women Characters in the Mahabharata." In *Great Women of India*, edited by Swami Madhavananda and Ramesh C. Majumdar, 169–81. Mayavati, India: Advaita Ashram, 1963.

"La charte Akadem." Akadem. Accessed December 10, 2014. http://www.akadem.org /charte/.

Cohen, Aviezer. "The Curse of Ham in Rabbinic Literature and Its Reference to Blacks and the 'Sons of Cush.'" PhD diss., Bar-Ilan University, 2000. (Hebrew)

Cohen, David. "No Country Has More Friends of Israel Than . . . India?" *Daily Caller*, August 18, 2014. http://dailycaller.com/2014/08/18/no-country-has-more-friends -of-israel-than-india/.

Cohen, Shaye J. D. *The Beginnings of Jewishness: Boundaries, Varieties, Uncertainties.* Berkeley: University of California Press, 1999.

Cohn-Sherbok, Dan. *Messianic Judaism.* New York: Continuum, 2000.

"Conversion au Judaïsme." Beth Yeshourun. Accessed February 5, 2015. http://beth -yeshouroun.mywebcommunity.org/conversion.php.

Corcos, Alain F. *The Myth of the Jewish Race: A Biologist's Point of View.* Bethlehem, PA: Lehigh University Press, 2005.

Daaku, Kwame Yeboah. "A History of the Sefwi: A Survey of Oral Evidence." *Research Review* 7, no. 3 (1971): 32–47.

————. *Oral Traditions of Sefwi.* 2 vols. Legon: Institute of African Studies, University of Ghana, 1974.

Damani, Seba. "Distorting Truth: Ewe History?" November 16, 2013. http://www .sebadamani.com/blog/distorting-truth-ewe-history.

Daneel, M. L. *Quest for Belonging: Introduction to a Study of African Independent Churches.* Gweru, Zimbabwe: Mambo Press, 1987.

Dasgupta, Debarshi. "Come as You Are, David." *Outlook*, July 15, 2013. http://www .outlookindia.com/article/come-as-you-are-david/286668.

Da Silva, José Antunes. "African Independent Churches: Origin and Development." *Anthropos* 88, nos. 4–6 (1993): 393–402.

David, Jono. "House of Israel, Ghana: Day 3 (of 5), 'Meshuggah for Mezuzah.'" Jewish Africa: A Cultural and Historical Photographic Survey, February 27, 2014. http://www.jewishphotolibrary.wordpress.com/2014/02/27/house-of-israel-ghana-day-3-of-5-meshuggah-for-mezuzah/.

DeLancey, Mark Dike, Rebecca Neh Mbuh, and Mark W. DeLancey. *Historical Dictionary of the Republic of Cameroon.* Metuchen, NJ: Scarecrow Press, 1990.

De Surgy, Albert. *L'Église du christianisme céleste: Un exemple d'église prophétique au Bénin.* Paris: Karthala, 2001.

Diagram Group. "Sefwi." In *Encyclopedia of African Peoples.* New York: Facts on File, 2000.

Dickson, Kwesi A. "Continuity and Discontinuity between the Old Testament and African Life and Thought." In *African Theology en Route: Papers from the Pan-African Conference of Third World Theologians, December 17–23, 1977, Accra, Ghana,* edited by Kofi Appiah-Kubi and Sergio Torres, 95–108. Maryknoll, NY: Orbis Books, 1979.

———. "The Old Testament and African Theology." *Ghana Bulletin of Theology* 4, no. 4 (1973): 31–41.

———. *Theology in Africa.* Maryknoll, NY: Orbis Books, 1984.

Dowson, John. *A Classical Dictionary of Hindu Mythology and Religion, Geography, History, and Literature.* London: Routledge and K. Paul, 1961.

"Du Christianisme au Judaïsme: nos raisons." Beth Yeshourun. Accessed February 5, 2015. http://bethyeshourun.org/chabbath.php#.

Effah-Gyamfi, Kwaku. "Some Archaeological Reflections on Akan Traditions of Origin." *West African Journal of Archaeology* 9 (1979): 187–99.

Egorova, Yulia. "Jewish Themes in the Press of Independent India." In *Jews, Muslims, and Mass Media: Mediating the "Other,"* edited by Yulia Egorova and Tudor Parfitt, 93–106. London: RoutledgeCurzon, 2007.

———. *Jews and India: Perceptions and Image.* London: Routledge, 2006.

———. "Redefining the Converted Jewish Self: Race, Religion, and Israel's Bene Menashe." *American Anthropologist* 117, no. 3 (2015): 493–505.

Egorova, Yulia, and Shahid Perwez. *The Jews of Andhra Pradesh: Contesting Caste and Religion in South India.* Oxford: Oxford University Press, 2013.

———. "Old Memories, New Histories: (Re)discovering the Past of Jewish Dalits." *History and Anthropology* 23, no. 1 (2012): 1–15.

———. "Telugu Jews: Are the Dalits of Coastal Andhra Going Caste-Awry?" *South Asianist* 1, no. 1 (2012): 7–16.

Ellis, Stephen, and Gerrie ter Haar. *Worlds of Power: Religious Thought and Political Practice in Africa.* New York: Oxford University Press, 2004.

Engelke, Matthew Eric. *A Problem of Presence: Beyond Scripture in an African Church.* Berkeley: University of California Press, 2007.

Etele, Serge. "Are There Lost Jewish Tribes in Cameroon?" Kulanu, 2015. http://cyan.olm.net/~kulanu/cameroon/losttribesincameroon.php.

Faitlovitch, Jacques. *Notes d'un voyage chez les Falachas.* Paris: Ernest Leroux, 1905.

Fanon, Frantz. *Black Skin, White Masks.* Translated by Richard Philcox. New York: Grove Press, 2008.

———. *Les damnés de la terre.* Paris: Éditions Maspero, 1961.

————. *The Wretched of the Earth*. Translated by Richard Philcox. New York: Grove Press, 2004.

Felder, Cain Hope. *Race, Racism, and the Biblical Narratives*. Minneapolis: Fortress Press, 2002.

Ferm, Deane W. *Third World Liberation Theologies: An Introductory Survey*. Maryknoll, NY: Orbis Books, 1987.

Fernheimer, Janice W. *Stepping into Zion: Hatzaad Harishon, Black Jews, and the Remaking of Jewish Identity*. Tuscaloosa: University of Alabama Press, 2014.

Fouda Etoundi, Engelbert. *La tradition béti et la pratique de ses rites*. Yaoundé, Cameroon: Éditions Sopecam, 2012.

Francisco, Jason L. "'Discovering' the Telugu Jews of India." In *Jews in Places You Never Thought Of*, edited by Karen Primack, 253–62. Hoboken, NJ: Ktav, 1998.

Frank, Daniel, and Leon Nemoy. "Karaites." In *The Encyclopedia of Religion*, 2d ed., edited by Lindsay Jones. Vol. 8. Detroit: Macmillan Reference, 2005.

Freud, Sigmund. *Moses and Monotheism*. Translated by Katherine Jones. New York: Vintage Books, 1967.

————. "On Being of the B'nai B'rith." *Commentary* 2, no. 3 (1946): 23.

Gadangme Nikasemo Asafo. "Lecture 1: A People Blessed." Accessed May 5, 2014. http://www.gadangmenikasemoasafo.wordpress.com/the-king-taki-tawiah -memorial-lectures/lecture-i-a-people-blessed/.

Gamst, Frederick C. *The Qemant: A Pagan-Hebraic Peasantry of Ethiopia*. New York: Holt, Rinehart, and Winston, 1969.

Ganguly, Sumit. *Hindu Nationalism and the Foreign Policy of India's Bharatiya Janata Party*. Transatlantic Academy Paper Series, 2014–15, vol. 2. Washington, DC: Transatlantic Academy, 2015.

Gbolu, Florence. "Shabbat in Ghana: Young Journalist Seeks out African Jewish Community." Kulanu, 2004. http://www.kulanu.org/ghana/Gbolu.php.

Gerber, Israel. *The Heritage Seekers*. New York: Jonathan David, 1977.

Ghana Embassy. "Population." Accessed November 4, 2014. http://www .ghanaembassy.org/index.php?page=population.

Ghildiyal, Subodh. "SCs/STs Form Half of India's Poor: Survey." *Times of India*, April 12, 2011. http://www.timesofindia.indiatimes.com/india/SCs/STs-form-half -of-Indias-poor-Survey/articleshow/7953487.cms.

Glanz, James, Sebastian Rotella, and David E. Sanger. "In 2008 Mumbai Attacks, Piles of Spy Data, but an Uncompleted Puzzle." *New York Times*, December 21, 2014. http://www.nytimes.com/2014/12/22/world/asia/in-2008-mumbai-attacks -piles-of-spy-data-but-an-uncompleted-puzzle.html?_r=0.

Glaser, Antoine. *Africafrance: Quand les dirigeants africains deviennent les maîtres du jeu*. Paris: Fayard, 2014.

Globe. "A Muslim Can Be President—Kufuor." GhanaWeb, September 20, 2011. http:// www.ghanaweb.com/GhanaHomePage/NewsArchive/artikel.php?ID=219384.

Godbey, Allen H. *The Lost Tribes: A Myth*. Hoboken, NJ: Ktav, 1973.

Goitein, David E. "Note on Eldad the Danite." *Jewish Quarterly Review* 17, no. 4 (1927): 483.

Goitein, S. D. "R. Isaac b. Ibrahim al-Tu'ati (ca. 1235): The Most Ancient Reference to Jews in the Touat." *Revue des études juives* 140, nos. 1–2 (1981): 193–210.

Goodman, Richard. *Genetic Disorders among the Jewish People*. Baltimore: Johns Hopkins University Press, 1979.

Goodnow, J. J. "The Socialization of Cognition: What's Involved?" In *Cultural Psychology: Essays on Comparative Human Development*, edited by James W. Stigler, Richard A. Shweder, and Gilbert Herdt, 259–86. Cambridge: Cambridge University Press, 1990.

Gordon, I. "Ehud, the Fat Man, and the Power of Praise!" Jesus Plus Nothing. Accessed January 2, 2015. http://www.jesusplusnothing.com/studies/online/judges6.htm.

Government of Ghana. "Western Region." Accessed January 26, 2015. http://www.ghana.gov.gh/index.php/about-ghana/regions/western.

Government of India, Ministry of Home Affairs. "Andhra Pradesh Data Highlights: The Scheduled Castes." Accessed August 19, 2015. http://www.censusindia.gov.in/Tables_Published/SCST/dh_sc_andhra.pdf.

———. "Religion." Accessed August 20, 2015. http://www.censusindia.gov.in/Census_And_You/religion.aspx.

———. "Scheduled Castes and Scheduled Tribes." Accessed July 30, 2015. http://www.censusindia.gov.in/Census_And_You/scheduled_castes_and_sceduled_tribes.aspx.

Government of India, Ministry of Information and Broadcasting. *Jawaharlal Nehru's Speeches*. Vol. 3, *September 1953–August 1957*. Delhi: Publications Division, Ministry of Information and Broadcasting, 1950.

Green, Lawrence. *Old Africa's Last Secrets*. London: Putnam, 1961.

Greenberg, Brad A. "Ugandan Gershom Sizomu Ordained as First Black Sub-Saharan Rabbi." *Jewish Journal*, May 28, 2008. http://www.jewishjournal.com/religion/article/ugandan_gershom_sizomu_ordained_as_first_black_sub_saharan_rabbi.

Halkin, Hillel. *Across the Sabbath River: In Search of a Lost Tribe of Israel*. Boston: Houghton Mifflin, 2002.

Hammerschmidt, Ernst. "Jewish Elements in the Cult of the Ethiopian Church." *Journal of Ethiopian Studies* 3, no. 2 (1965): 1–12.

Harms, Robert W. "Bobangi Oral Traditions: Indicators of Changing Perceptions." In *The African Past Speaks: Essays on Oral Tradition and History*, edited by Joseph Calder Miller, 178–200. Hamden, CT: Archon Press, 1980.

Hartman, David. *A Heart of Many Rooms: Celebrating the Many Voices within Judaism*. Woodstock, VT: Jewish Lights, 1999.

Hayes, Christine. "Intermarriage and Impurity in Ancient Jewish Sources." *Harvard Theological Review* 92, no. 1 (1999): 3–36.

Haynes, Jeffrey. *Religious Transnational Actors and Soft Power*. Burlington: Ashgate, 2012.

Henderson-Quartey, David K. *The Ga of Ghana: The History and Culture of a West African People*. London: David K. Henderson-Quartey, 2002.

Henry, Christine. *Force des anges: Rites, hiérarchie et divination dans le Christianisme Céleste*. Turnhout, Belgium: Brepols, 2008.

Herzfeld, Michael. *Cultural Intimacy: Social Poetics in the Nation-State*. New York: Routledge, 1997.

Hezser, Catherine. *Jewish Slavery in Antiquity*. Oxford: Oxford University Press, 2006.

The Hindu. "India Can Become Economically Developed by 2020: Kalam." April 29, 2011. http://www.thehindu.com/business/Economy/india-can-become-economically-developed-by-2020-kalam/article1821445.ece.

Holter, Knut. *Tropical Africa and the Old Testament: A Select and Annotated Bibliography*. Oslo: University of Oslo Press, 1996.

————. *Yahweh in Africa: Essays on Africa and the Old Testament.* New York: Peter Lang, 2000.

Holtsbaum, H. P. "Sefwi and Its Peoples." *Gold Coast Review* 1 (1925): 76–94.

Hopper, Paul. *Understanding Cultural Globalization.* Cambridge: Polity Press, 2007.

Idel, Moshe. *Golem: Jewish Magical and Mystical Traditions on the Artificial Anthropoid.* Albany: State University of New York Press, 1990.

Ilona, Remy. *The Igbos and Israel: An Inter-cultural Study of the Largest Jewish Diaspora.* Washington, DC: Street to Street Epic Publications, 2014.

————. *The Igbos: Jews in Africa?* Abuja: Mega Press, 2004.

Institute for Cultural Diplomacy. "The African Hebrew Development Agency." Accessed January 23, 2015. http://www.culturaldiplomacy.org/experienceafrica /index.php?en_diaspora_ahi_projects_ahda.

Isaacs, Ronald H. *Becoming Jewish: A Handbook for Conversion.* New York: Rabbinical Assembly, 1993.

Isenberg, Shirley Berry. "The Bene Israel." In *The Jews of India: A Story of Three Communities,* edited by Orpa Slapak, 17–26. Jerusalem: Israel Museum, 1995.

Jackson, John L. *Thin Description: Ethnography and the African Hebrew Israelites of Jerusalem.* Cambridge: Harvard University Press, 2013.

Jacobs, Janet Liebman. *Hidden Heritage: The Legacy of the Crypto-Jews.* Berkeley: University of California Press, 2002.

Jeffreys, Mervyn David Waldegrave. "An Extinct Jewish Colony (Victoria, Cameroon)." *Jewish Affairs* (1954): 47–48.

Jenett, Dianne E. "Menstruating Women/Menstruating Goddesses: Sites of Sacred Power in India." In *Menstruation: A Cultural History,* edited by Andrew Shail and Gillian Howie, 176–87. New York: Palgrave Macmillian, 2005.

Jenkins, Philip. *The Next Christendom: The Coming of Global Christianity.* Oxford: Oxford University Press, 2002.

"Jewish Communities Worldwide." Kulanu. Accessed April 5, 2015. http://www .kulanu.org/communities/.

Johnson, Sylvester A. *The Myth of Ham in Nineteenth-Century American Christianity: Race, Heathens, and the People of God.* New York: Palgrave Macmillan, 2004.

Josefson, Deborah. "In Remote Madagascar, a New Community Chooses to Be Jewish." Jewish Telegraphic Agency. June 5, 2016. http://www.jta.org/2016/06/05 /news-opinion/world/in-remote-madagascar-a-new-community-chooses-to-be -jewish.

Kaplan, Mordechai M. *Judaism as a Civilization: Toward a Reconstruction of American Jewish Life.* New York: Schocken Books, 1935.

Kaplan, Steven. *The Beta Israel (Falasha) in Ethiopia: From Earliest Times to the Twentieth Century.* New York: New York University Press, 1992.

————. "The Invention of Ethiopian Jews: Three Models." *Cahiers d'études africaines* 33, no. 132 (1993): 645–58.

Kato, Byang H. *Theological Pitfalls in Africa.* Kisumu, Kenya: Evangelical, 1975.

Katz, Nathan. *Who Are the Jews of India?* Berkeley: University of California Press, 2000.

Katz, Nathan, and Ellen S. Goldberg. *Kashrut, Caste, and Kabbalah: The Religious Life of the Jews of Cochin.* New Delhi: Manohar, 2007.

————. *The Last Jews of Cochin: Jewish Identity in Hindu India.* Columbia: University of South Carolina Press, 1993.

Kaunda, Kenneth D. *Letter to My Children.* London: Longman, 1973.

Kershner, Isabel. "New Generation of Jewish Sect Takes Up Struggle to Protect Place in Modern Israel." *New York Times*, September 4, 2013.

Kersten, Holger. *Jesus Lived in India: His Unknown Life Before and After the Crucifixion.* Rockport, MA: Element, 1994.

Kestenbaum, Sam. "Black Jewish Congregations Get Their Own Prayer Book, After Nearly a Century." *Tablet*, September 9, 2014. http://www.tabletmag.com/jewish-life-and-religion/183821/black-jewish-siddur.

Kilson, Marion. *Dancing with the Gods: Aspects of Ga Ritual.* Lanham, MD: University Press of America, 2013.

Kirsch, Stuart. "Lost Tribes: Indigenous People and the Social Imaginary." *Anthropological Quarterly* 70, no. 2 (1997): 58–67.

Knoppers, Gary N. *Jews and Samaritans: The Origins and History of Their Early Relations.* New York: Oxford University Press, 2013.

Könighofer, Martina. *The New Ship of Zion: Dynamic Diaspora Dimensions of the African Hebrew Israelites of Jerusalem.* Berlin: LIT Verlag, 2008.

Kotto, Yaphet. *The Royalty: A Spiritual Awakening.* N.p.: Cauldwell/Bissell, 1997.

Krishnaiah Chetty, V. B. *Scheduled Castes and Development Programmes in India.* Allahabad, India: Vohra, 1991.

Kuchar, Menachem. "My Visit to Cameroon: A Very Jewish Experience." *Menachem's Writings* (blog). Accessed July 20, 2014. http://menachemkuchar.com/Writings/235-My-Cameroon-Visit-to-the-Jews.htm.

Kullas, H., and G. A. Ayer. *What the Elders of Ashanti Say.* Kumasi, Ghana: Kumasi University Press, 1967.

Kumar, P. Pratap. "Andhra Pradesh: Economic and Social Relations." In *The Modern Anthropology of India: Ethnography, Themes, and Theory*, edited by Peter Berger and Frank Heidemann, 12–28. New York: Routledge, 2013.

Kumar, Raj. *Encyclopaedia of Untouchables Ancient, Medieval, and Modern.* Delhi: Kalpaz, 2008.

Kwafwo, Osei. *Outline of Asante History.* Wiamoase-Ashanti, Ghana: O. Kwadwo Enterprise, 1994.

Lama, Marut. *Classifying the Universe: The Ancient Indian Varna System and the Origins of Caste.* Oxford: Oxford University Press, 1994.

Land, Gary. *The A to Z of the Seventh-Day Adventists.* Lanham, MD: Scarecrow Press, 2009.

Landes, Ruth. "Comment." *Western Canadian Journal of Anthropology* 3, no. 3 (1973): 44–46.

Lanternari, Vittorio. *The Religions of the Oppressed: A Study of Modern Messianic Cults.* Translated by Lisa Sergio. New York: Alfred A. Knopf, 1963.

Larkin, Brian, and Birgit Meyer. "Pentecostalism, Islam, and Culture: New Religious Movements in West Africa." In *Themes in West Africa's History*, edited by Emmanuel Kwaku Akyeampong, 283–312. Accra, Ghana: Woeli Publication Services, 2005.

Law, Robin. "The 'Hamitic Hypothesis' in Indigenous West African Historical Thought." *History in Africa* 36, no. 1 (2009): 293–314.

Le Roux, Magdel. *The Lemba: A Lost Tribe of Israel in Southern Africa.* Pretoria: Unisa Press, 2003.

———. "Lemba Traditions: An Indispensable Tool for Interpreting the Old Testament in Africa." In *African Zion: Studies in Black Judaism*, edited by Edith Bruder and Tudor Parfitt, 175–90. Newcastle upon Tyne: Cambridge Scholars, 2012.

Levi. *The Aquarian Gospel of Jesus the Christ: The Philosophic and Practical Basis of the Religion of the Aquarian Age of the World*. Los Angeles: DeVorss, 1964.

Levi, Janice. "The House of Israel: Judaism in Ghana." In *African Zion: Studies in Black Judaism*, edited by Edith Bruder and Tudor Parfitt, 117–35. Newcastle upon Tyne: Cambridge Scholars, 2012.

Levine, Amy-Jill, and Marc Zvi Brettler. *The Jewish Annotated New Testament: New Revised Standard Version Bible Translation*. Oxford: Oxford University Press, 2011.

Le Vine, Victor T. *Politics in Francophone Africa*. Boulder, CO: Lynne Rienner, 2007.

Lichtblau, George E. "Jewish Roots in Africa." In *Jews in Places You Never Thought Of*, edited by Karen Primack, 8–13. Hoboken, NJ: Ktav, 1998.

Liebman, Charles. "Jewish Identity in Transition: Transformation or Attenuation?" In *New Jewish Identities*, edited by Zvi Gitelman, Barry Kosmin, and Andras Kovacs, 341–49. Budapest: Central European University Press, 2003.

Lifton, Robert Jay. *The Life of the Self*. New York: Basic Books, 1983.

Lincoln, Bruce. *Death, War, and Sacrifice: Studies in Ideology and Practice*. Chicago: University of Chicago Press, 1991.

Liphshiz, Cnaan. "In Senegalese Bush, Bani Israel Tribe Claims Jewish Heritage." Jewish Telegraphic Agency, May 23, 2013. http://www.jta.org/2013/05/23/life -religion/in-senegalese-bush-bani-israel-tribe-claims-jewish-heritage.

Lis, Daniel. "'Ethiopia Shall Soon Stretch Out Her Hands': Ethiopian Jewry and Igbo Identity." *Jewish Culture and History* 11, no. 3 (2009): 21–38.

———. *Jewish Identity among the Igbo of Nigeria: Israel's "Lost Tribe" and the Question of Belonging in the Jewish State*. Trenton, NJ: Africa World Press, 2015.

Maimonides, Moses. *The Guide for the Perplexed*. Edited and translated by Michael Friedländer. London: Routledge and Kegan Paul, 1956.

Mallampalli, Chandra. *Christians and Public Life in Colonial South India, 1863–1937: Contending with Marginality*. New York: RoutledgeCurzon, 2004.

Manelis, Judy. "What's Happening in Africa: Cameroon, Kenya, Ghana, Uganda, Zimbabwe (August 2013)." Kulanu. Accessed September 2, 2014. http://www .kulanu.org/abayudaya/progressinafrica.php.

Margolis, Max Leopold, ed. *The Holy Scriptures According to the Masoretic Text*. Philadelphia: Jewish Publication Society of America, 1917.

Mark, Peter, and José da Silva Horta. "Catholics, Jews, and Muslims in Early Seventeenth-Century Guiné." In *Atlantic Diasporas: Jews, Conversos, and Crypto- Jews in the Age of Mercantilism, 1500–1800*, edited by Richard L. Kagan and Philip D. Morgan, 170–94. Baltimore: Johns Hopkins University Press, 2009.

———. *The Forgotten Diaspora: Jewish Communities in West Africa and the Making of the Atlantic World*. Cambridge: Cambridge University Press, 2013.

Markovitz, Fran. "Blood, Soul, Race, and Suffering: Full-Bodied Ethnography and Expressions of Jewish Belonging." In *Race, Color, Identity: Rethinking Discourses About "Jews" in the Twenty-First Century*, edited by Efraim Sicher, 261–80. New York: Berghahn Books, 2013.

Maroney, Eric. *The Other Zions: The Lost Histories of Jewish Nations*. Lanham, MD: Rowman and Littlefield, 2010.

Mbili, Armand Alain. *D'une église missionnaire à une église africaine nationale: L'obser- vatoire du grand séminaire d'Otélé, 1949–1968*. Paris: L'Harmattan, 2009.

Mbiti, John S. *African Religions and Philosophy*. 2d ed. Oxford: Heinemann, 1990.

———. "The Role of the Jewish Bible in African Independent Churches." *International Review of Missions* 93, no. 369 (2004): 219–37.

Mbuy, Tatah H. *Where Do We Stand? An Examination of Some Problems Affecting Christianity in Modern Cameroon*. Ashing-Kom, Cameroon: St. Bede's College, 1987.

McCaskie, Thomas. "Asante Origins, Egypt, and the Near East: An Idea and Its History." In *Recasting the Past: History Writing and Political Work in Modern Africa*, edited by Derek Peterson and Giacomo Macola, 125–48. Athens: Ohio University Press, 2009.

———. "Inventing Asante." In *Self-Assertion and Brokerage: Early Cultural Nationalism in West Africa*, edited by Paulo Fernando de Moraes Farias and Karin Barber, 55–67. Birmingham, UK: Centre of West African Studies, University of Birmingham, 1990.

McCray, Walter Arthur. *The Black Presence in the Bible: Discovering the Black and African Identity of Biblical Persons and Nations*. Chicago: Black Light Fellowship, 1990.

McGonigle, Ian Vincent. "'Jewish Genetics' and the 'Nature' of Israeli Citizenship." *Transversal: Journal of Jewish Studies* 13, no. 2 (2015): 90–102.

Melamed, Abraham. *The Image of the Black in Jewish Culture: A History of the Other*. New York: Routledge, 2010.

Memmi, Albert. *The Colonizer and the Colonized*. Translated by Howard Greenfeld. New York: Orion Press, 1965.

Mensah, Joseph Nii Abekar. "Gadangme Origins." Gadangme Heritage and Cultural Foundation. Accessed February 1, 2015. http://www.gadangme.weebly.com/ga-dangme-origins.html.

———. *Traditions and Customs of Gadangmes of Ghana: Descendants of Authentic Biblical Hebrew Israelites*. Houston: Strategic Book Publishing, 2013.

Metogo, Éloi Messi. "Introduction: African Christianities." In *African Christianities*, edited by Éloi Messi Metogo, 7–21. London: SCM Press, 2006.

Meyerowitz, Eva. *The Akan of Ghana: Their Ancient Beliefs*. London: Faber and Faber, 1958.

———. *Akan Traditions of Origin*. London: Faber and Faber, 1952.

———. *The Early History of the Akan States*. London: Red Candle Press, 1974.

Miles, William F. S. *Afro-Jewish Encounters: From Timbuktu to the Indian Ocean and Beyond*. Princeton: Markus Wiener, 2013.

———. *Jews of Nigeria: An Afro-Judaic Odyssey*. Princeton: Markus Wiener, 2012.

———. "The Malagasy Secret." *Jerusalem Report*. September 3, 2015. http://www.jpost.com/Jerusalem-Report/The-Malagasy-secret-415164.

———. *Scars of Partition: Postcolonial Legacies in French and British Borderlands*. Lincoln: University of Nebraska Press, 2014.

Miller, Jon. *Missionary Zeal and Institutional Control: Organizational Contradictions in the Basel Mission on the Gold Coast, 1828–1917*. Grand Rapids, MI: William B. Eerdmans, 2003.

Mines, Mattison. "Social Stratification among Muslim Tamils in Tamil Nadu, South India." In *Caste and Social Stratification among Muslims in India*, edited by Imtiaz Ahmad, 159–69. New Delhi: Manohar, 1978.

Miron, Dan. "Modern Hebrew Literature: Zionist Perspectives and Israeli Realities." In *What Is Jewish Literature?*, edited by Hana Wirth-Nesher, 95–115. Philadelphia: Jewish Publication Society, 1994.

Mohanty, P. K. *Encyclopedia of Scheduled Tribes in India*. Delhi: Isha Books, 2006.

Monteil, Charles. "Les 'Ghâna': Des géographes arabes et des européens." *Hespéris* 38, nos. 3–4 (1951): 287–88.

Moore, George. *The Lost Tribes and the Saxons of the East and of the West, with New Views of Buddhism, and Translations of Rock-Records in India*. London: Longman, Green, Longman, and Roberts, 1861.

Mosse, David. "The Catholic Church and Dalit Christian Activism in Contemporary Tamil Nadu." In *Margins of Faith: Dalit and Tribal Christianity in India*, edited by Rowena Robinson and Joseph Marianus Kujur, 235–62. Thousand Oaks, CA: Sage, 2010.

Mudimbe, Valentin Y. *The Invention of Africa: Gnosis, Philosophy, and the Order of Knowledge*. Bloomington: Indiana University Press, 1985.

Mugambi, Jesse N. K. "Religions in East Africa in the Context of Globalization." In *Religions in Eastern Africa under Globalization*, edited by Jesse N. K. Mugambi and Mary N. Getui, 1–11. Nairobi: Acton, 2004.

Mviena, P. *Univers culturel et religieux du peuple béti*. Yaoundé, Cameroon: Imprimerie St. Paul, 1970.

Myers, M. Bruce. "The Origin of the Gas." *Journal of the African Society* 27 (1927–1928): 69–76, 167–73.

Nagel, Joane. "False Faces: Ethnic Identity, Authenticity, and Fraud in Native American Discourse and Politics." In *Identity and Social Change*, edited by J. E. Davis, 81–108. New Brunswick, NJ: Transaction, 2000.

Nana, Alexandre. *Anthropologie béti et sens chrétien de l'homme*. Paris: L'Harmattan, 2010.

Naylor, Rachel. *Ghana*. Oxford: Oxfam, 2000.

Ndungu, Nahashon. "The Bible in an African Independent Church." In *The Bible in African Christianity*, edited by Hannah W. Kinoti and John M. Waliggo, 58–67. Nairobi: Acton, 1997.

Next Year in Bombay. Directed by Jonas Parienté and Mathias Mangin. Tel-Aviv: J.M.T. Films, 2011. DVD.

Ngom, Fallou. "Murid Ajami Sources of Knowledge: The Myth and the Reality." In *From Dust to Digital: Ten Years of the Endangered Archives Programme*, edited by Maja Kominko, 331–76. Cambridge: Open Book, 2015.

Ngono, Gaspard. "Saa Kameni: L'alphabet moderne est une imitation de l'alphabet hébraïque antique donc camerounaise." Mboa Guide, August 4, 2013. http://www .guide.mboa.info/histoire-des-peuples/fr/connaitre/actualite/2625,saa-kameni -lalphabet-moderne-est-une-imitation-de-lalphabet-hebraique-antique-donc -camerounais-.html.

Nkrumah, Patrick. "The Interaction between Christianity and Ashanti Religion." PhD diss., Drew University, 1992.

Noahide World Center. "Our Center." January 9, 2011. http://www.noahideworldcenter .org/wp_en/category/about/.

Nongbri, Brent. *Before Religion: A History of a Modern Concept*. New Haven: Yale University Press, 2013.

Ochs, Juliana. *Security and Suspicion: An Ethnography of Everyday Life in Israel*. Philadelphia: University of Pennsylvania Press, 2011.

Ochs, Vanessa L. "What Makes a Jewish Home Jewish?" Material History of American Religion Project. Accessed July 3, 2014. http://www.materialreligion.org /journal/jewish.html.

Oddie, G. A. "Christian Conversion in the Telugu Country, 1860–1900: A Case Study of One Protestant Movement in the Godavery-Krishna Delta." *Indian Economic and Social History Review* 12, no. 1 (1975): 61–79.

Oded, Arye. *Judaism in Africa: The Abayudaya of Uganda: The African Jews of Uganda and Their Contacts with World Jewry.* Jerusalem: Israel-Africa Friendship Association, 2013. (Hebrew)

Oliel, Jacob. *Les juifs au sahara: Le touat au moyen âge.* Paris: CNRS, 1994.

Omvedt, Gail. *Buddhism in India: Challenging Brahmanism and Caste.* Thousand Oaks, CA: Sage, 2003.

Oosthuizen, G. C. "Hebraic-Judaistic Tenets in the African Independent Churches and Religious Movements in South Africa." In *South African Association of Jewish Studies: Proceedings of the Eleventh Annual Conference, 4–7 September, 1988,* 1–25. Durban: South African Association of Jewish Studies, 1988.

Opoku, Kofi A. "Changes Within Christianity: The Case of the Musama Disco Christo Church." In *The History of Christianity in West Africa,* edited by Ogbu Kalu, 38–58. London: Longman, 1980.

Oppong, Christine. "Notes on Cultural Aspects of Menstruation in Ghana." *Research Review* 9, no. 2 (1973): 33–38.

Orenstein, Daniel. "View from the Ivory Tower." *Jerusalem Report* 3, no. 22 (1993): 47–48.

Orleansky, Irene. *Music of Israelites and Jews of Africa and Asia.* Moscow: Music Brothers Records, 2014. Compact disc.

Osei, Osepetetreku Kwame. *The Ancient Egyptians Are Here.* Kumasi, Ghana: Vytall, 2001.

O'Sullivan, Arieh. "'Gabonese Jews' Prank Prompts Israelis to Offer Help." Associated Press, April 1, 1994. http://www.apnewsarchive.com/1994/-Gabonese-Jews -Prank-Prompts-Israelis-to-Offer-Help/id-62c8e6ade6f41237bfd3cdd02b6b65d4.

Owusu-Mensah, Kofi. *Saturday God and Adventism in Ghana.* Oxford: Peter Lang International Academic, 1993.

Page, Willie F. "Sefwi." In *Encyclopedia of African History and Culture.* Vol. 3, *From Conquest to Colonization (1500 to 1850).* New York: Facts on File, 2001.

Parfitt, Tudor. *Black Jews in Africa and the Americas.* Cambridge: Harvard University Press, 2013.

———. "(De)Constructing Black Jews." In *African Zion: Studies in Black Judaism,* edited by Edith Bruder and Tudor Parfitt, 12–30. Newcastle upon Tyne: Cambridge Scholars, 2012.

———. "DNA, Indian Jews, Manipuris, and the Telugu Speaking Community." Kulanu, 2002. Accessed June 14, 2013. http://www.kulanu.org/india/dnamarker .php.

———. "Hebrew in Colonial Discourse." *Journal of Modern Jewish Studies* 2, no. 2 (2003): 159–73.

———. *Journey to the Vanished City: The Search for a Lost Tribe of Israel.* New York: St. Martin's Press, 1992.

———. "Judaising Movements and Colonial Discourse." In *Judaising Movements: Studies in the Margins of Judaism in Modern Times,* edited by Tudor Parfitt and Emanuela Trevisan Semi, 1–16. New York: RoutledgeCurzon, 2002.

———. *The Lost Ark of the Covenant: The Remarkable Quest for the Legendary Ark.* New York: HarperCollins, 2008.

————. *The Lost Tribes of Israel: The History of a Myth*. London: Weidenfeld and Nicolson, 2002.

————. *Operation Moses: The Untold Story of the Secret Exodus of the Falasha Jews from
Ethiopia*. New York: Stein and Day, 1985.

————. *The Thirteenth Gate: Travels among the Lost Tribes of Israel*. Bethesda, MD:
Adler and Adler, 1987.

————. "Tribal Jews." In *Indo-Judaic Studies in the Twenty-First Century: A View from
the Margin*, edited by Nathan Katz et al., 181–96. New York: Palgrave Macmillan,
2007.

Parfitt, Tudor, and Yulia Egorova. *Genetics, Mass Media, and Identity: A Case Study of
the Genetic Research on the Lemba and Bene Israel*. London: Routledge, 2006.

Patai, Raphael. *The Hebrew Goddess*. 3d ed. Detroit: Wayne State University Press,
1990.

————. *Israel between East and West: A Study in Human Relations*. Westport, CT:
Greenwood, 1970.

————. *The Jewish Mind*. Detroit: Wayne State University Press, 1990.

Peled, Moran. "Needed: A Dramatic Change of Perception." *Kav haofek* 24 (December 21, 2004): 3. (Hebrew)

Perry, Micha. "The Imaginary War between Prester John and Eldad the Danite and Its
Real Implications." *Viator: Medieval and Renaissance Studies* 41, no. 1 (2010): 1–23.

Pew Forum on Religion and Public Life. *Global Christianity: A Report on the Size and
Distribution of the World's Christian Population*. Washington, DC: Pew Research
Center, 2011.

Pew Research Center. "Overview: Pentecostalism in Africa." October 5, 2006. http://
www.pewforum.org/2006/10/05/overview-pentecostalism-in-africa/.

Phillips, Godfrey Edward. *The Old Testament in the World Church, with Special Reference to Younger Churches*. London: Lutterworth Press, 1942.

Pobee, John S. *The Anglican Story in Ghana: From Mission Beginnings to Province of
Ghana*. Accra, Ghana: African Books Collective, 2009.

Posnansky, Merrick. "Archaeology and the Origins of the Akan Society in Ghana."
In *Problems in Economic and Social Archaeology*, edited by G. de G. Sieveking,
I. H. Longworth, and K. E. Wilson, 49–59. London: Duckworth, 1976.

————. "The Search for Asante Origins: Archaeological Evidence." In *The Golden
Stool: Studies of the Asante Center and Periphery*, edited by Enid Schildkrout, 14–22.
New York: Anthropological Papers of the American Museum of Natural History,
1987.

Quartey, Seth. *Missionary Practices on the Gold Coast, 1832–1895: Discourse, Gaze, and
Gender in the Basel Mission in Pre-colonial West Africa*. London: Cambria Press,
2007.

Rabkin, Yakov M. *A Threat from Within: A Century of Jewish Opposition to Zionism*.
New York: Zed Books, 2006.

Rajasekhara Reddy, K. "The Madigas: A Scheduled Caste Population of Andhra
Pradesh." *Man and Life: Journal of the Institute of Social Research and Applied
Anthropology, Calcutta* 33, no. 1–2 (2007): 81–88.

Ramberg, Michael. "Jewish Learning Takes a Village." *Kulanu Newsletter* 14, no. 3
(2007): 1, 10.

Rapoport, Louis. *The Lost Jews: Last of the Ethiopian Falashas*. New York: Stein and
Day, 1980.

Rathnaiah, K. *Social Change among Malas: An Ex-untouchable Caste in South India.* New Delhi: Discovery, 1991.

Rattray, Robert Sutherland. *Religion and Art in Ashanti.* Kumasi, Ghana: Basel Mission Book Depot, 1954.

Rauschenbusch-Clough, Emma. *While Sewing Sandals; or, Tales of a Telugu Pariah Tribe.* London: Hodder and Stoughton, 1899.

Reindorf, Carl Christian. *History of the Gold Coast and Asante.* 3d ed. Accra: Ghana University Press, 2007.

Reuben, Yoel Moses. *The Jews of Pakistan: A Forgotten Heritage.* Mumbai: Bene Israel Heritage Museum and Genealogical Research Centre, 2010.

Reyburn, William D. "The Message of the Old Testament and the African Church." *Practical Anthropology* 7, no. 4 (1960): 152–56.

Risley, Herbert Hope. *The People of India.* Calcutta: Thacker, Spink, 1915.

Roberts, Penelope. "The Court Records of Sefwi Wiawso, Western Region, Ghana." *History in Africa* 12 (1985): 379–83.

———. "The Village Schoolteacher in Ghana." In *The Changing Social Structure of Ghana*, edited by J. Goody, 245–60. London: International African Institute, 1972.

———. "Whose School? Conflicts over School Management in Sefwi Wiawso, Ghana." *Anthropology and Education Quarterly* 13, no. 3 (1982): 268–78.

Robertson, Claire. "Violence and Tribes: Beyond Politics in Kenya." *Origins: Current Events in Historical Perspective* 1, no. 7 (2008). http://www.origins.osu.edu/article/beyond-tribes-violence-and-politics-kenya/page/0/1.

Robinson, Rowena, and Joseph Marianus Kujur. Introduction to *Margins of Faith: Dalit and Tribal Christianity in India*, edited by Rowena Robinson and Joseph Marianus Kujur, 1–28. Thousand Oaks, CA: Sage, 2010.

Romer, Jessica. "Religious Assimilation: The Ideological Foundations of a Ghanaian Jewish Community." Undergraduate thesis, University of Colorado–Boulder, 2005.

Rosen, Laurence. *Bargaining for Reality: The Construction of Social Relations in a Muslim Community.* Chicago: University of Chicago Press, 1984.

Ross, James. *Fragile Branches.* New York: Riverhead Trade, 2001.

Rudolph, David J., and Joel Willitts. *Introduction to Messianic Judaism: Its Ecclesial Context and Biblical Foundations.* Grand Rapids, MI: Zondervan, 2013.

Sadler, Rodney Steven. *Can a Cushite Change His Skin? An Examination of Race, Ethnicity, and Othering in the Hebrew Bible.* New York: T & T Clark, 2005.

Salem, Nili. "The Secret of Sefwi Wiawso." Undergraduate thesis, University of California–Santa Barbara, 2005.

Samra, Myer. "Judaism in Manipur and Mizoram: A By-product of Christian Mission." *Australian Journal of Jewish Studies* 6, no. 1 (1992): 7–22.

———. "The Tribe of Manasseh: 'Judaism' in the Hills of Manipur and Mizoram." *Man in India* 71, no. 1 (1991): 183–202.

Sanders, Edith R. "The Hamitic Hypothesis: Its Origin and Functions in Time Perspective." *Journal of African History* 10, no. 4 (1969): 521–32.

Sarpong, Justice. "Are Ewes Ghanaian Jews? Don't Bet on It." GhanaWeb, August 13, 2011. http://www.ghanaweb.com/GhanaHomePage/features/artikel.php?ID=216176.

Sarpong, Peter. "Some Myths of the Origins from Ashanti (Ghana)." In *Naissance du monde et de l'homme*, 195–99. Rome: Gregorian University Press, 1969.

Schloessinger, Max. *The Ritual of Eldad ha-Dani Reconstructed and Edited from Manuscripts and a Genizah Fragment.* Leipzig: R. Haupt, 1908.

Schorsch, Jonathan. *Jews and Blacks in the Early Modern World.* Cambridge: Cambridge University Press, 2004.

"Sefwi Wiawso District." City Population Index. Accessed January 30, 2015. http://www.citypopulation.de/php/ghana-admin.php?adm2id=1012.

Sende, Pierre. *La route du sel: Chez les bassa du Cameroun.* Paris: L'Harmattan, 2014.

Shah, A. M. "Sanskritisation Revisited." *Sociological Bulletin* 54, no. 2 (2005): 238–49.

Shaw, Rosalind, and Charles Steward. "Introduction: Problematizing Syncretism." In *Syncretism/Anti-Syncretism: The Politics of Religious Synthesis*, edited by Rosalind Shaw and Charles Steward, 1–26. London: Routledge, 1994.

Shema Yisrael Torah Network. "Welcome to the Pirchei Shoshanim College Recommended Program." Accessed January 19, 2015. http://www.shemayisrael.com/edu/.

Shiraev, Eric, and David A. Levy. *Cross-cultural Psychology: Critical Thinking and Contemporary Applications.* Boston: Pearson/Allyn and Bacon, 2007.

Shmueli, Ephraim. *Seven Jewish Cultures: A Reinterpretation of Jewish History and Thought.* Translated by Gila Shmueli. Cambridge: Cambridge University Press, 1990.

Shohat, Ella. "Sephardim in Israel: Zionism from the Standpoint of Its Jewish Victims." In *Dangerous Liaisons: Gender, Nation, and Postcolonial Perspectives*, edited by Anne McClintock, Aamir Mufti, and Ella Shohat, 39–68. Minneapolis: University of Minnesota Press, 1997.

———. *Taboo Memories, Diasporic Voices.* Durham, NC: Duke University Press, 2006.

Shukla, Madan Mohan. "Hebrews and Vedic Aryans." *Vishveshvaranand Indological Journal* 14, no. 1 (1976): 41–47.

———. "The Hebrews Belong to a Branch of Vedic Aryans." *Journal of the Oriental Institute* (University of Baroda) 28, nos. 3–4 (1979): 44–57.

Silliman, Jael Miriam. *Jewish Portraits, Indian Frames: Women's Narratives from a Diaspora of Hope.* Hanover, NH: University Press of New England, 2001.

Silver, Eric. "Yitzhak Shamir: Member of the Stern Gang Who Became a Hawkish Prime Minister of Israel." *The Independent*, July 2, 2012. http://www.independent.co.uk/news/obituaries/yitzhak-shamir-member-of-the-stern-gang-who-became-a-hawkish-prime-minister-of-israel-7902674.html.

Silverstein, Paul A. "Of Rooting and Uprooting: Kabyle Habitus, Domesticity, and Structural Nostalgia." *Ethnography* 5, no. 4 (2004): 553–78.

Simms, Norman Toby. *Masks in the Mirror: Marranism in Jewish Experience.* New York: Peter Lang, 2006.

Singh, Hira. *Recasting Caste: From the Sacred to the Profane.* New Delhi: Sage, 2014.

Singh, Tulja Ram. *The Madiga: A Study in Social Structure and Change.* Lucknow, India: Ethnographic and Folk Culture Society, 1969.

Slapak, Orpa. *The Jews of India: A Story of Three Communities.* Jerusalem: Israel Museum Press, 1995.

Slessarev, Vsevolod. *Prester John: The Letter and the Legend.* Minneapolis: University of Minnesota Press, 1959.

Spencer-Wood, Suzanne M. "The Formation of Ethnic-American Identities: Jewish Communities in Boston." In *Historical Archaeology: Back from the Edge*, edited by

Pedro Paulo A. Funari, Martin Hall, and Siân Jones, 284–307. New York: Routledge, 2013.

Sperber, Dan. *Explaining Culture: A Naturalistic Approach.* Oxford: Blackwell, 1996.

Spieth, Jakob, and W. K. Amoaku. *The Ewe People: A Study of the Ewe People in German Togo.* Accra, Ghana: Sub-Saharan, 2011.

Spivak, Gayatri. *A Critique of Postcolonial Reason: Toward a History of the Vanishing
Present.* Cambridge: Harvard University Press, 1999.

Srinivas, Mysore Narasimhachar. *Caste in Modern India: And Other Essays.* New York:
Asia Publishing House, 1962.

Stolow, Jeremy. "Salvation by Electricity." In *Religion: Beyond a Concept,* edited by
Hent de Vries, 668–86. New York: Fordham University Press, 2007.

Summerfield, Daniel. *From Falashas to Ethiopian Jews: The External Influences for
Change, c. 1860–1960.* New York: RoutledgeCurzon, 2003.

Sundkler, Bengt G. M. *Bantu Prophets in South Africa.* New York: Oxford University
Press, 1961.

———. *The Christian Ministry in Africa.* Uppsala, Sweden: University of Uppsala
Press, 1960.

Sunil Vara Kumar, B. *Dynamics of Power Sharing between Mala and Madiga in Church.*
Delhi: ISPCK, 2010.

Tabi, Isidore. *Les rites béti au Christ: Essai de pastorale liturgique sur quelques rites de nos
ancêtres.* Yaoundé, Cameroon: Imprimerie St. Paul, 1991.

Tamarkin, Noah. "Religion as Race, Recognition as Democracy: Lemba 'Black Jews'
in South Africa." *The Annals of the American Academy of Political and Social Science*
637, no. 1 (2011): 148–64.

Taneti, James Elisha. *History of the Telugu Christians: A Bibliography.* Lanham, MD:
Scarecrow Press, 2011.

Tennent, Timothy C. *Theology in the Context of World Christianity: How the Global
Church Is Influencing the Way We Think About and Discuss Theology.* Grand Rapids, MI: Zondervan, 2007.

Thomas, Mark G., et al. "Origins of Old Testament Priests." *Nature* 394 (July 9,
1998): 138–40.

Timberg, Thomas A. *Jews in India.* New York: Advent Books, 1986.

Tobin, Diane. "Wannabe Demographers?" *Huffington Post,* November 12, 2014. http://
www.huffingtonpost.com/diane-tobin/wannabe-demographers_b_6141358.html?.

Tobin, Gary A. *Opening the Gates: How Proactive Conversion Can Revitalize the Jewish
Community.* San Francisco: Jossey-Bass, 1999.

Toukam, Dieudonné. *Histoire et anthropologie du peuple bamiléké.* Paris: L'Harmattan,
2010.

Turner, Harold W. *Living Tribal Religions.* London: Ward Lock Educational, 1971.

———. *Religious Innovation in Africa: Collected Essays on New Religious Movements.*
Boston: G. K. Hall, 1979.

Twagilimana, Aimable. *The Debris of Ham: Ethnicity, Regionalism, and the 1994 Rwandan Genocide.* Lanham, MD: University Press of America, 2003.

"Ugandan Jews Get Official Recognition from Jewish Agency." *Jewish Telegraphic
Agency.* April 12, 2016. http://www.jta.org/2016/04/12/news-opinion/israel
-middle-east/ugandan-jews-get-official-recognition-from-jewish-agency.

Ullendorff, Edward. "The 'Death of Moses' in the Literature of the Falashas." *Bulletin
of the School of Oriental and African Studies* 24, no. 3 (1961): 419–43.

———. "Hebraic-Jewish Elements in Abyssinian (Monophysite) Christianity." *Journal of Semitic Studies* 1, no. 3 (1956): 216–56.

———. *The Two Zions: Reminiscences of Jerusalem and Ethiopia.* Oxford: Oxford University Press, 1988.

Ullendorff, Edward, and Charles F. Beckingham. *The Hebrew Letters of Prester John.* Oxford: Oxford University Press, 1982.

Univer, Wendy. "Across the Globe, Eager Students Have Something to Teach." *Reconstructionist Rabbinical College Annual Report,* 2008, 10–15.

van Diggele, Els. *A People Who Live Apart: Jewish Identity and the Future of Israel.* Translated by Jeanette K. Ringold. Amherst, NY: Prometheus Books, 2003.

Van Dijk, Jan A. G. M. *The Network Society: Social Aspects of New Media.* Thousand Oaks, CA: Sage, 1999.

Van Rheenen, Gailyn. "Indigenous Church and Partnership." In *The Changing Face of World Missions: Engaging Contemporary Issues and Trends,* edited by Michael Pocock, Gailyn Van Rheenen, and Douglas McConnell, 179–205. Grand Rapids, MI: Baker Academic, 2005.

Vansina, Jan. *Oral Tradition as History.* Madison: University of Wisconsin Press, 1985.

Venter, Dawid. *Engaging Modernity: Methods and Cases for Studying African Independent Churches in South Africa.* Westport, CT: Praeger, 2004.

"Vision: A Global Jewish People." Be'chol Lashon. Accessed April 2, 2015. http://www.bechollashon.org/about/mission.php.

Wachman, Doreen. "The Mystery of the Ten Lost Tribes: The Jews of Cameroon." Haruth Communications. Accessed July 15, 2014. http://www.haruth.com/jw/JewsCameroon.htm.

Wankhede, Deepak M. *Geographical Thought of Dr. B. R. Ambedkar.* Delhi: Gautam Book Centre, 2009.

Wasserstein, David J. "Eldad Ha-Dani." In *Prester John, the Mongols, and the Ten Lost Tribes,* edited by Charles F. Beckingham and Bernard Hamilton, 213–36. Aldershot, UK: Variorum, 1996.

Weil, Shalva. "The Heritage and Legacy of the Jews of India." In *India's Jewish Heritage: Ritual, Art, and Life-Cycle,* edited by Shalva Weil, 9–21. Mumbai: Marg, 2002.

———. "Lost Israelites from the Indo-Burmese Borderlands: Re-traditionalisation and Conversion among the Shinlung or Bene Menasseh." *Anthropologist* 6, no. 3 (2004): 219–33.

Weiss, Erica. *Conscientious Objectors in Israel: Citizenship, Sacrifice, Trials of Fealty.* Philadelphia: University of Pennsylvania Press, 2014.

Weiss, Ruchama, and Levi Brackman. "India's Young Jews Eye Israel." *Ynet News,* June 20, 2015. http://www.ynetnews.com/articles/0,7340,L-4670233,00.html.

"Welcome to Kulanu, Inc!" Kulanu. Accessed April 5, 2015. http://www.kulanu.org/.

White House, Office of the Press Secretary. "Remarks by the President to the Ghanaian Parliament." July 11, 2009. http://www.whitehouse.gov/the-press-office/remarks-president-ghanaian-parliament.

"Who Are Britain's Jihadists?" *BBC,* September 8, 2015. http://www.bbc.com/news/uk-32026985.

Wilks, Ivor. *The Northern Factor in Ashanti History.* Legon: Institute of African Studies, University of Ghana, 1961.

Williams, Joseph John. *Hebrewisms of West Africa: From the Nile to Niger with the Jews.* London: Allen and Unwin, 1930.

Wittgenstein, Ludwig. *Philosophical Investigations*. Translated by G. E. M. Anscombe. Oxford: Blackwell, 1953.

Wognou, Jean Marcel Eugène. *Les basaa du Cameroun: Monographie historique d'après la tradition orale*. Niamey, Niger: Organisation de l'unité africaine, 1985.

Wonyu, Eugène. *L'histoire des basaa du Cameroun de l'Égypte des Pharaons à nos jours*. Paris: UNESCO, 1972.

World Bank. "India Overview." Accessed May 13, 2014. http://www.worldbank.org/en /country/india/overview.

World Bank, Poverty Reduction and Economic Management Network. "The State of the Poor: Where Are the Poor and Where Are They Poorest?" Accessed August 10, 2015. http://www.worldbank.org/content/dam/Worldbank/document /State_of_the_poor_paper_April17.pdf.

Wyllie, Robert W. *Spiritism in Ghana: A Study of New Religious Movements*. Missoula, MT: Scholars Press, 1980.

Yacobi, Shmuel. "The Andhra Pradesh Bene Ephraim Community." *Bene Ephraim Community* (blog), September 12, 2012. http://www.thebeneephraimcommunity .blogspot.com/2012/09/the-andhra-pradesh-bene-ephraim.html.

———. *The Cultural Hermeneutics: An Introduction to the Cultural Translations of the Hebrew Bible among the Ancient Nations of the Thalmulic Telugu Empire of India*. Vijayawada, India: Hebrew Open University, 2002.

———. "Eretz Ephraim." Bnei Ephraim Community. Accessed August 2, 2015. http:// www.bneiephraimcommunity.com/eretz_ephraim.html.

———. "Eretz Ephraim Pictures—Educate, Work, and Achieve Peace." Writers-Network. Accessed August 4, 2015. http://www.writers-network.com/index.cgi?m =1&do=profile&who=21560.

———. "Eretz Ephraim Pictures and World Peace Promotion." *World Peace* (blog), May 22, 2011. http://internationalprotestantpope.blogspot.com/.

———. "Hebrew Cultural Family Counseling Center." *Hebrew Cultural Family Counseling Center* (blog), December 21, 2012. http://www .hebrewculturalfamilycounselingcenter.blogspot.com/2012/12/hebrew-cultural -family-counseling.html.

———. "Hebrew Menorah Songs from South India." YouTube video, 4:05. Posted by shmuelyacobi, February 7, 2011. https://www.youtube.com/watch?v= ZgoEyyn2oP8.

———. "Hebrew Menorah Songs from South India." YouTube video, 4:22. Posted by shmuelyacobi, February 16, 2011. https://www.youtube.com/watch?v= 1Nd2qxwf8as.

———. "Hebrew Menorah Songs from South India." YouTube video, 5:02. Posted by shmuelyacobi, February 7, 2011. https://www.youtube.com/watch?v= 4i6FEvaapGo.

———. "Hebrew Menorah Songs from South India." YouTube video, 7:14. Posted by shmuelyacobi, February 16, 2011. https://www.youtube.com/watch?v= gaFwnyLRgQs.

———. *Hebrew and Telugu Menorah Songs*. Vijayawada, India: Eretz Ephraim Productions, 2011.

———. "John Milton at Pandemonium." Accessed October 6, 2011. http://www .poetrypoem.com/cgi-bin/index.pl?poemnumber=1098240&sitename= shmuelyacobi&poemoffset=0&displaypoem=t&item=poetry.

———. "The Prince of Whales." Accessed October 2, 2012. http://www.storymania
.com/cgibin/sm2/smreadtitle.cgi?action=display&file=novels/YacobiS
-ThePrinceOfWhales.htm.

———. "The Religious Myth of the Lost Tribes of Israel." *The Lost Tribes of Israel*
(blog), June 4, 2011. http://www.shmuelyacobimssraju.blogspot.com/2011/06
/religious-myth-of-lost-tribes-of-israel.html.

———. "Tel-English Songs from South India." YouTube video, 2:08. Posted
by shmuelyacobi, February 17, 2011. https://www.youtube.com/watch?v=
QoR8bxSlPU8.

———. "Tel-English Songs from South India." YouTube video, 3:17. Posted
by shmuelyacobi, February 16, 2011. https://www.youtube.com/watch?v=a
-diuPbeG8I.

———. "Tel-English Songs from South India." YouTube video, 4:12. Posted by
shmuelyacobi, February 17, 2011. https://www.youtube.com/watch?v=WiOf
_7eTSOs.

———. "Tel-English Songs from South India." YouTube video, 5:26. Posted
by shmuelyacobi, February 16, 2011. https://www.youtube.com/watch?v=
jdTxY9C6Nbo.

———. "Three-Tier Human Lives." *Three-Tier Human Lives* (blog), December 23,
2012. http://www.threetierhumanlives.blogspot.com/2012/12/three-tier-human
-lives-we-humans-have.html.

———. "World Peace at Last!" *World Peace Through Hebrew Culture* (blog), December 22, 2012. http://www.worldpeacethroughhebrewculture.blogspot.com/2012
/12/world-peace-at-last-majority-humans.html.

———. "Writer and His Background." Booksie. Accessed July 7, 2015. http://www
.booksie.com/shmuel_yacobi.

Yeshayahu, Yisrael. "A Visit to Eritrea and Abyssinia." *Gesher* 4 (1958): 56–65.
(Hebrew)

Yudkin, Leon Israel. *Jewish Writing and Identity in the Twentieth Century*. London:
Croom Helm, 1982.

Zelikovich, Yaheli Moran. "Funding of Petah Tikva Schools Refusing Ethiopian Students Cut." *Ynet News*, August 30, 2009. http://www.ynetnews.com/articles/0
,7340,L-3769509,00.html.

Zianga, Jonas. "Black Jews in Academic and Institutional Discourse." In *Race, Color,
Identity: Rethinking Discourses About "Jews" in the Twenty-First Century*, edited by
Efraim Sicher, 182–95. New York: Berghahn Books, 2013.

Numbers in *italics* indicate maps

Abayudaya community, *xviii*, 31–32, 45, 90, 140, 225
Across the Sabbath River: In Search of a Lost Tribe of Israel (Halkin), 24
African groups: Abayudaya community, 31–32, 45, 90, 140, 225; Igbo people, 30–32, 105, 147; Jewish communities in, 29–30; Lemba, 30–32, 105, 111; other ethnicities, 32. *See also* Judaizing communities
African Independent Churches, 34–35, 37–38, 131, 164, 168
afterlife concept, 198, 199
Ahenkorah, David, 56–58, 75, 83–84, 89
Ahowi, Nana, 74, 80, 85–86
Akan peoples, 55–57, 63, 89
Akan subgroups, 63, 65, 66, 102
American Jews, 20, 191, 219
Ancient Egyptians Are Here, The (Osei), 115
Andagme group, 103
An Essay on the Superstitions, Customs, and Arts Common to the Ancient Egyptians, Abyssinians, and Ashantees (Bowdich), 64
animal sacrifices, 28, 36, 73, 114, 222
anticolonial movement, 114, 159, 161
anti-Semitism, 107, 133–34, 182, 187, 223
Aowin rule, 62, 63
Apocrypha, 98
April Fool's Day radio prank, 29–30
Ark of the Covenant, 111–12, 114
Armah, Alex, 89–90, 96, 99
Aryans, 96, 193, 194, 201, 259n73
Ashanti region, 62–64, 66–67, 69, 80, 89
Ashkenazi community, 19, 38–39, 225

Baganda community. *See* Abayudaya community
Baghdadi Jews, 189
Baiden, Daniel, 76, 78
Bamileke people, 155
Bantu groups, 154, 158
Bassa group, 157–65, 168, 252n40, 252n46
Be'chol Lashon organization, 44, 45, 90
Beit Israel Judaizing community, *xviii*, 15
Beit Talmidim Judaizing community, *xviii*, 228
beliefs and customs: African ethnicities, 32; Ashanti region, 64; Bene Ephraim movement, 199–211; Beth Yeshourun community, 142–43; conclusion about, 222–23; Ethiopian Jews, 21; Gadangme people, 106, 109; House of Israel community, 93–94; Sefwi Wiaswo community, 64–65, 73
Bene Ephraim community: agrarian-style, 209–11; becoming members of, 202–3; beliefs and customs, 199–211; circumcision issues, 200; comparison with other groups, 172–73; congregants pool for, 208; future of, 221; genealogical trope, 173, 174; Hebrew Open University Center and, 175–76; Hebrew Scriptures and, 201, 210; heritage narratives, 190; introduction to, 171–72; Israelis' visits to, 205–6; location of, *xviii*, 170; manner of responses by, 203–4; marriage issues in, 202; menstrual seclusion and, 200–201; modern India and,

Hutu militias, 132

Iberian Jews, 28–29
idol worship, 74, 197
Igbo people, 30–32, 105, 147; location of
    Judaizing movement, *xviii*
immigration and immigrants: Ashke-
    nazi, 38; of Children of Manasseh,
    24; to Israel, 19, 23, 39, 42, 91–92,
    147–49; Sephardic, 38–39
independent churches, 34, 37, 113–14,
    163, 223
India: caste system, 184–86; introduc-
    tion to, 182–83; as a Jewish cornu-
    copia, 187–90; religious diversity in,
    183–84. *See also* Children of Ephraim
    movement
intermarriage, prohibition against, 41,
    241n113, 241n115
"Internet Jews," 117, 181, 250n1
interviewees: author's experiences with,
    87–88; initiating contact with, 10;
    open interaction and trust with, 8;
    oral consent through, 9; Serge Etele,
    120–25, 134–35; Shmuel Yacobi,
    174–82
Islam: impact of, 68; introduction to, 35,
    40
Israel: criticisms of life in, 148; immi-
    gration to, 19, 23, 39, 42, 91–92,
    147–49; negligible knowledge about,
    204–5; position on new communi-
    ties, 225–26; "sister state" to, 174,
    220; true remnants of, 47; views on,
    144–45
Israeli Citizenship, 42, 174, 206
Israeli-Palestinian conflict, 145–46

Jewish Annotated New Testament (Levine
    and Brettler), 165
Jewish Community of Madagascar, *xviii*,
    228–31
Jewish denominations, 43, 65, 218
"Jewish" diseases, 43
Jewish Gospels, The (Boyarin), 165
Jewish groups: American, 30; contacts
    with, 201, 206; House of Israel
    community and, 82; mainstream,

15, 78; nonpartisan, 44; overseas,
    39, 82, 200, 201. *See also* Judaizing
    communities
Jewish identity, 2, 6, 28, 52–53
Jewish infrastructure, 49, 92, 123, 125,
    206
Jewish law: conversion issues and, 41,
    42, 88, 126; Ethiopian Jews and, 21;
    food taboos and, 136; prayer prac-
    tices and, 77–78
Jewishness: of Cameroonian commu-
    nities, 120–26; claims of, 30–31, 48;
    continuum of, 50–51; as a culture,
    153–54; defining, 48–54; Ga society
    and, 110; genealogical trope and, 16;
    Hebrew Scriptures and, 52; hereditary
    signifiers issue, 47; historical phases
    of, 52; introduction to, 1–6; investiga-
    tion of, 49–50; perceptions, 49; racial
    supposition and, 43; recognition of,
    47–48; what constitutes, 12, 13
Jewish organizations, 44, 46–47, 78,
    206–7, 226
Jewish seminary, 31, 32, 174
Jewish values, 151, 227
Jewish War, The (Josephus), 17
Jews: of color, 26, 39, 44; connections
    with, 86–87; of Ethiopia, 18–24,
    79–80, 105, 147, 148; "family resem-
    blance" theory of, 51–52; famous,
    48–49; of Iberian Peninsula,
    28–29; of India, 187–90, 253–54n1;
    self-defining, 2, 47, 60, 65, 129;
    self-identifying, 29–30, 49, 72, 188;
    slaves of, 41, 241n114
Judaism: Cavilah teachings and, 191–99;
    conversion issues, 88, 139, 149–51,
    218; globalized, 227; integration
    into, 21; introduction to, 2–3; Juda-
    izing communities and, 13; Karaites
    sect and, 26–28; as a logical religion,
    179–80; matrilineal descent and,
    27, 40, 125; New Testament and, 85,
    136; normative, 21, 26–28, 71–72,
    82, 201, 229; notion of miracles
    in, 178–79; Orthodox, 24, 25, 150,
    195, 231; perceptions about, 85–87;
    for potential congregants, 122–25;